ONE WORLD

BY E. ALYN MITCHNER
AND R. JOANNE TUFFS

REIDMORE BOOKS INC.
EDMONTON, CANADA

© 1989 Reidmore Books Inc.

All rights reserved. No part of this book covered by the copyrights hereon may be reproduced or used in any form or by any means without the prior written consent of the publisher, except for brief passages quoted by reviewers. Reproducing passages from this book by any means, including mimeographic, photocopying, recording, or by any information storage and retrieval system, is an infringement of copyright law.

Canadian Cataloguing in Publication Data

Mitchner, E. Alyn, 1937-
   One world

   Includes index.
   ISBN 0-919091-62-8

   1. Anthropo-geography. 2. Human ecology. I. Tuffs, R. Joanne, 1944- II. Title. GF41.M52   1988   304.2   C88-091419-X

Printed and Bound in Canada

CONTENTS

A MESSAGE FROM THE AUTHORS v
A Note On Numbers vi
On Doubling vi

MINI-ATLAS
MA- 2	World States and Geography
MA- 4	The Nation State System
MA- 5	The Nuclear Age
MA- 6	A Comparison of World Incomes
MA- 7	Socio-Economic Indicators
MA- 8	World Population (1)
MA- 9	World Population (2)
MA-10	Energy and Oil Production and Consumption
MA-11	Migration and Refugees
MA-12	The Urban Magnet
MA-14	World Pollution and Desertification
MA-15	Standard of Living Chart
MA-16	World Food Consumption and Famine Locations

1. INTRODUCTION 1
   Humans and the Environment 1
   The Structure of the Book 2
   People 3
   Urbanization 4
   Food 5
   Energy 5
   Industrialization 5
   Global Co-Operation 6
   Conclusion 6

2. PLANET EARTH 9
   Energy from the Sun 11
   The Atmosphere 12
   The Hydrosphere 13
   The Restless Oceans 13
   Our Fragile Reserves 15
   The Lithosphere 17
   Conclusion 19
   Questions 20
   Activities 21

3. INTERRELATED HUMAN ENVIRONMENTS 23
   International Co-Operation 25
   Supranationalism 28
   Transnationals 31
   Conclusion 34
   Questions 35
   Activities 35

4. THE HUMAN EXPERIENCE 37
   Hunter Folk 38
   The Beginnings of Agriculture 40
   The First Cities 41
   Resources and Trade 42
   The Growth of Empires 42
   The Feudal Age 43
   European Globalism 44
   The Industrial Revolution 45
   Social Changes 46
   Transportation and Communication 47
   The Twentieth Century 47
   Human Rights 48
   Conclusion 50
   Questions 50
   Activities 51

5. HUMAN RESOURCES 53
   The Global Population Perspective 54
   Lifestyle in Underdeveloped Countries 56
   Population Management 58
   Case Study: Progress in China 61
   Conclusion 62
   Questions 62
   Activities 63

6. URBAN CULTURE 65
   Global Urbanization 66
   Urbanization in Underdeveloped Regions 68
   Urban Problems 70
   Case Study: The Tokyo-Tama New Town Experiment 72
   Conclusion 72
   Questions 73
   Activities 73

ONE

WORLD

7. **FOOD AND AGRICULTURAL RESOURCES** 75
   World Food Consumption 75
   Global Food Supplies 77
   Global Land Use 78
   Agriculture in Underdeveloped Nations 80
   Case Study: Kenya—An Agricultural Success 82
   "Agribusiness" 84
   Agricultural Possibilities 84
   Conclusion 86
   Questions 87
   Activities 87

8. **ENERGY AND DEVELOPMENT** 89
   The Ultimate Resource 89
   World Energy Development 89
   The End in Sight? 91
   Case Study: Brazilian Alcohol Energy 93
   Nuclear Energy's Power and Perils 95
   Alternative Sources 96
   The Value of Conservation 97
   The Greenhouse Effect 98
   Case Study: Thermal Garbage 100
   Conclusion 101
   Questions 102
   Activities 103

9. **INDUSTRY AND LIVING STANDARDS** 105
   The Industrial Development Gap 105
   The History of Industrial Development 106
   The Costs of Industrialization 108
   Case Study: South Korea's Economic "Miracle" 110
   The Latin American Experience 112
   The History of Development 113
   Reversing the Trend 115
   Conclusion 116
   Questions 116
   Activities 117

10. **INTERNATIONAL CO-OPERATION** 119
    Law of the Sea 120
    Case Study: The Antarctic 122
    Foreign Assistance 124
    Perspective on Aid 127
    Perspective One 127
    Perspective Two 128
    Conclusion 128
    Questions 129
    Activities 129

11. **TOMORROW** 131
    Wasteful Humanity 132
    Nuclear Winter 134
    Managing Our Future 135
    Life Off Earth 136
    Conclusion 138

GLOSSARY 140

INDEX 142

CREDITS 147

A MESSAGE FROM THE AUTHORS

WE LIVE IN A global environment. The realities of the earth's natural forces, in combination with human-made influences, establish the limits of our lifestyle. Dependent on the **biosphere** for life support, we are sustained by the air, water, and soil around us. As such, we are an integral part of nature.

All living things are unable to survive without the biosphere. Human societies, however, have adapted nature to their own unique needs. The development of a variety of cultures has resulted from human settlement around the globe. These groups of people make use of the planet's resources in order to improve their lifestyle. With time, each group develops unique characteristics which are identified in cultural and spiritual mores. This diversity of cultures now demands that we become more tolerant of each other's needs and desires. We live in an interrelated world; one which links humans, society, and nature. Therefore, disparity in standard of living between societies is a matter of global concern. What happens in one part of our world ultimately affects the entire earth.

This book explores the relationship between humans and their environment. This dynamic relationship yields a particular standard of living and quality of life. It is apparent that human activity is governed in part by cultural and religious traditions. Economic development also serves to modify the way we live. In an effort to create a better standard of living through material wealth and industrial development, humans have had a negative impact on the fragile natural systems that support life on earth. Polluted oceans, a damaged ozone layer, the **greenhouse effect**, and overpopulation are just a few of the critical problems generated by human beings.

Human activities have also affected human-made environments. Political decisions determine whether nations will act in co-operation with each other or will instead come into conflict. Economic decisions determine the kind and amount of energy consumption of the nation and the extent of industrial development. Thus, many of the global problems such as hunger, overcrowding, and inadequate social services are more the result of decision-making by national leaders than of scarcity in nature. Nature can sustain a far larger population at a comfortable standard of living if the planet's natural resources are properly managed.

This book will not give you the solutions to these and other problems. In fact, you will find that the book raises more questions than it answers. Global issues of poverty, overpopulation, deteriorating environment, and depleting resources are all complex problems. The aim of the book is to inform you about the present condition of humans and their world, and to make you aware of the urgency of addressing global issues.

The book opens with a mini-atlas that is provided to emphasize the diversity of culture, and the disparity in quality of life and standard of living among the world's peoples. Chapter 1 examines the interdependence between the environment and living species. Chapter 2 includes an analysis of the delicate interdependent components that make up our planet—our air, water, and land. Chapter 3 looks at the man-made nation state system and the emergence of transnational associations. Chapter 4 outlines the historical relationships between humans, industrial development, and the standard of living. Chapter 5 deals with the structure of human cultural environments, population densities, and with the preciousness of human resources.

The next five chapters look at some of the important factors that affect our standard of living and quality of life. These factors are urbanization, food production, energy resources, industrialization, and the effects of the "consumer society." Promising beginnings of international co-operation in meeting these problems and the growing idea of global stewardship are examined in chapter 10. The book ends by outlining four possible scenarios for our world's future, weighing the consequences of each for the earth and all life on it.

Note on Glossary: You will notice that certain words and phrases are highlighted in boldface type the first time they appear in the book. You will find explanations of these words and phrases in the Glossary on page 140.

ONE
WORLD

A NOTE ON NUMBERS

Please note that the figures used in this book are only approximations. We do not have any way of counting all the people on the earth or of finding out exactly how much of a given resource we have left. Even in the most developed countries, census-takers miss large numbers of people who do not want to be counted. Canadians are happy if they get within 2 to 3 per cent of the real population numbers. Many other nations do not even bother to count.

However, these figures are based on the best available data. If all are in error by the same amount, the relationship is reasonable and useful. In the end some inaccuracy doesn't really matter because the figures are so large that virtually any error does not make a great difference. For example, if the number of people the earth can sustain is around 11 billion, what do another 500 000 really matter? If we are expected to reach the 11 billion mark in the next century does it matter if we do so in the year 2050 or 2075?

What is important is the relationship between the amount of resources available for use and the rate at which they are being used up. If the rate of consumption is steady, that is one thing. But if the rate is in itself increasing, that is a very different matter. The rate of consumption is of particular concern for non-renewable resources such as conventional fuels where the demand is doubling every decade. When they are fully depleted we must have ready alternative materials or man-made synthetics to take their place.

ON DOUBLING

When we talk of the number of people or things *doubling* every 20 years, what does this actually mean? It does not mean much at the first doubling. The last two doublings, however, are more serious, using up 75 per cent of the total.

For example, we may seem to have unlimited resources. But if we are using them up at a rate that doubles every 10 years, it would take only about 266 years to exhaust them. This assumes we have not yet used up 1 per cent of our resources, when we have in fact used up more than that. Environmentalists suggest that we might approach the last doubling for some of our natural resources by the middle of the next century.

The following explains the doubling process. The king of an ancient kingdom faced an impossible crisis. The king promised his wizard that he could have anything he wanted in the world if he could solve the dilemma. The wizard asked for payment in coins: one coin on the first day of the month, two coins on the second, four coins on the third, eight coins on the fourth, and so on until the end of the month. The king readily agreed. But he was not thinking of the amount of money in the last doubling on the last day. How much money was paid on the last day? When we talk of doubling in the text remember that it is the last two doublings that really count.

MINI-ATLAS

MINI-ATLAS

MA- 2	World States and Geography
MA- 4	The Nation State System
MA- 5	The Nuclear Age
MA- 6	A Comparison of World Incomes
MA- 7	Socio-Economic Indicators
MA- 8	World Population (1)
MA- 9	World Population (2)
MA-10	Energy and Oil Production and Consumption
MA-11	Migration and Refugees
MA-12	The Urban Magnet
MA-14	World Pollution and Desertification
MA-15	Standard of Living Chart
MA-16	World Food Consumption and Famine Locations

ONE

WORLD

WORLD STATES AND GEOGRAPHY

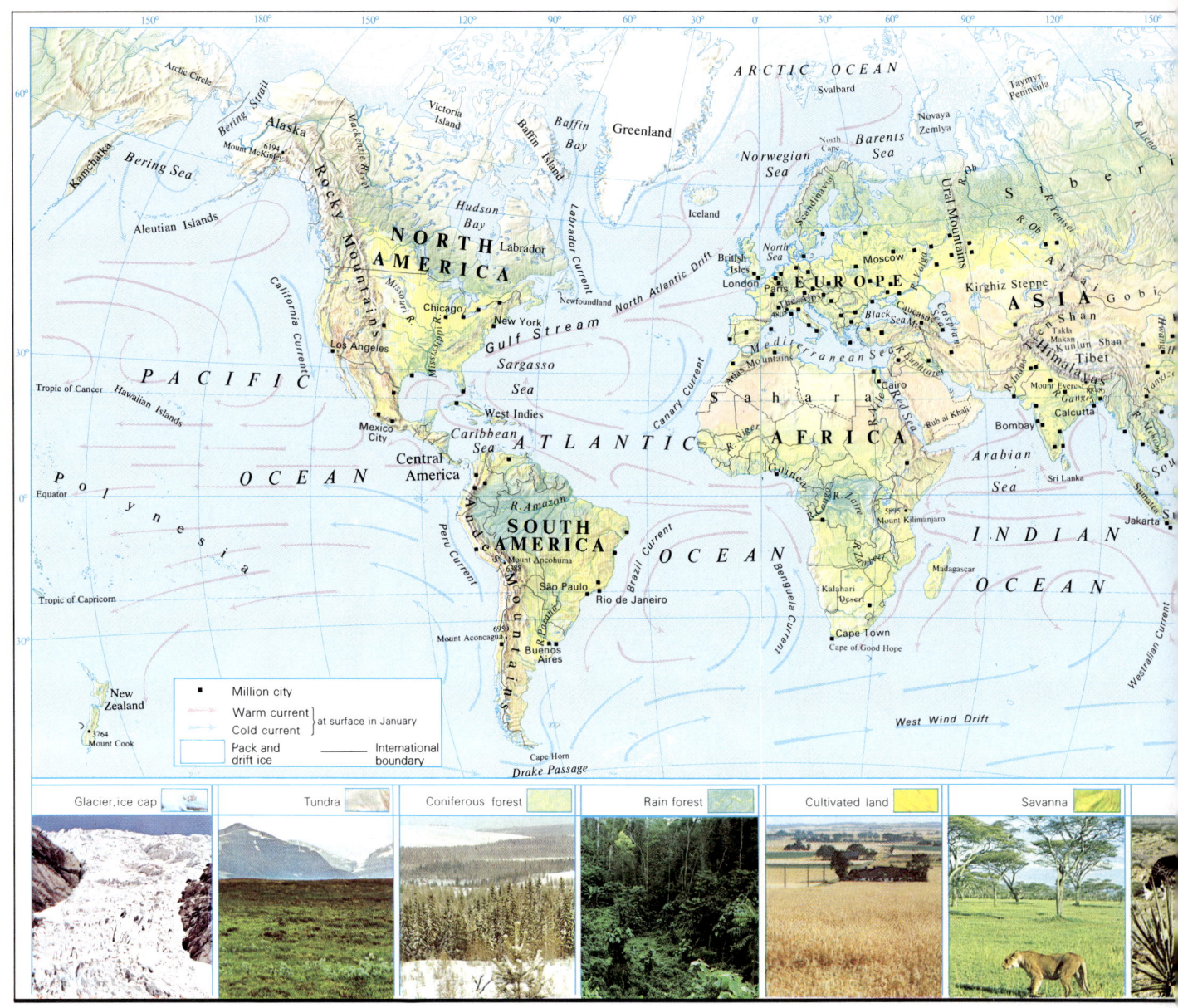

Nearly 6 billion people live on the land surface of the earth. The manner in which they make use of the natural resources of the planet helps to determine their standard of living and quality of life. The haphazard way in which these resources are scattered over the globe results in disparities in wealth between nations. Separated by geographic barriers, the different societies have created a variety of diverse lifestyles and cultures.

Not all of the land surfaces are suitable for human use. Land which lies at high latitudes or under desert conditions is largely unfit for settlement. Fully a quarter of the land is composed of mountains and highlands. Forests and woodlands cover another third while land fit only for pasture and grazing amounts to over another quarter. Just over 11 per

MINI-ATLAS

2

MINI-ATLAS

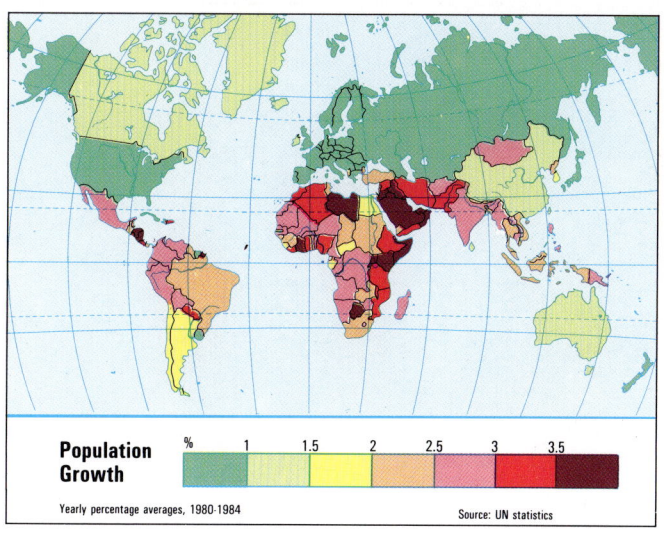

Population Growth
% 1 1.5 2 2.5 3 3.5
Yearly percentage averages, 1980-1984   Source: UN statistics

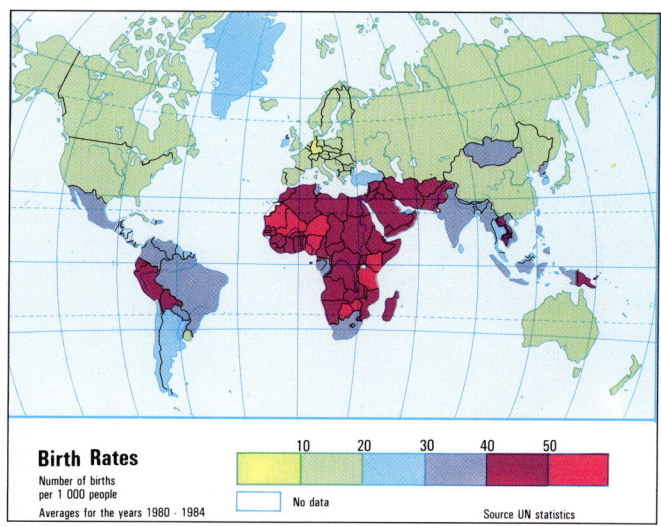

Birth Rates
Number of births per 1 000 people
Averages for the years 1980 - 1984
10 20 30 40 50
No data   Source UN statistics

cent of the land surface is deemed suitable for the growing of cereal crops for food production.

QUESTIONS

1. Name five countries which have significant proportions of cultivated land.
2. Identify two regions dominated by rain forests.
3. Name 10 cities with over a million people. In what part of the world do most of these cities lie?
4. Identify three large desert areas.
5. What affect do mountains, ice caps, and deserts have on human habitation?

ONE

WORLD

THE NATION STATE SYSTEM

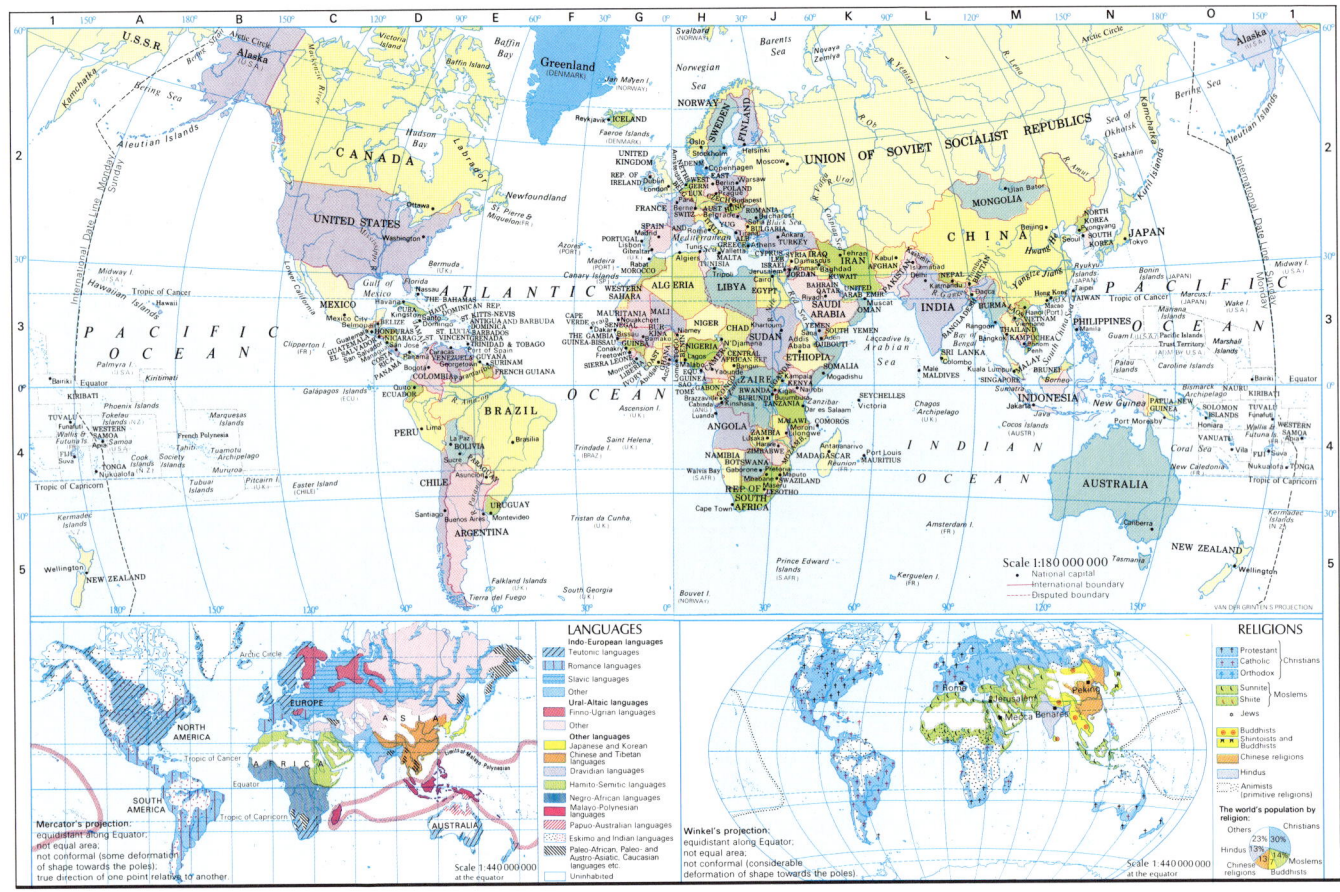

Through conflict and negotiation humans have divided the world into nearly 170 nation states of varying sizes and power. National boundaries cut across geographic regions and cultural groups, separating peoples of the same language and fostering a diversity of global cultures. The smallest 36 nations have populations of under 1 million people while China contains a fifth of the world's population.

No single nation, not even the two superpowers of the USA and the USSR, is strong enough in its own right to guarantee the military and economic security of its people. Alliances by like-minded nations for purposes of mutual interest have resulted in growing interrelatedness amongst the nation states.

The nation state system is designed for tension and conflict and not for co-operation. Nationalism is encouraged by political leaders who often divert attention from problems at home by becoming involved in matters outside their own countries' boundaries. Ultranationalist movements leave no room for compromise or negotiation but demand victory as the only solution to international problems.

The United Nations organization is the only supranational political organization that has close to universal membership. From its Secretariat in New York, it directs co-operative efforts to maintain world peace and advance the material well-being of all the world's people through a variety of military, economic, social, scientific, health, and cultural agencies.

MINI-ATLAS

4

THE NUCLEAR AGE

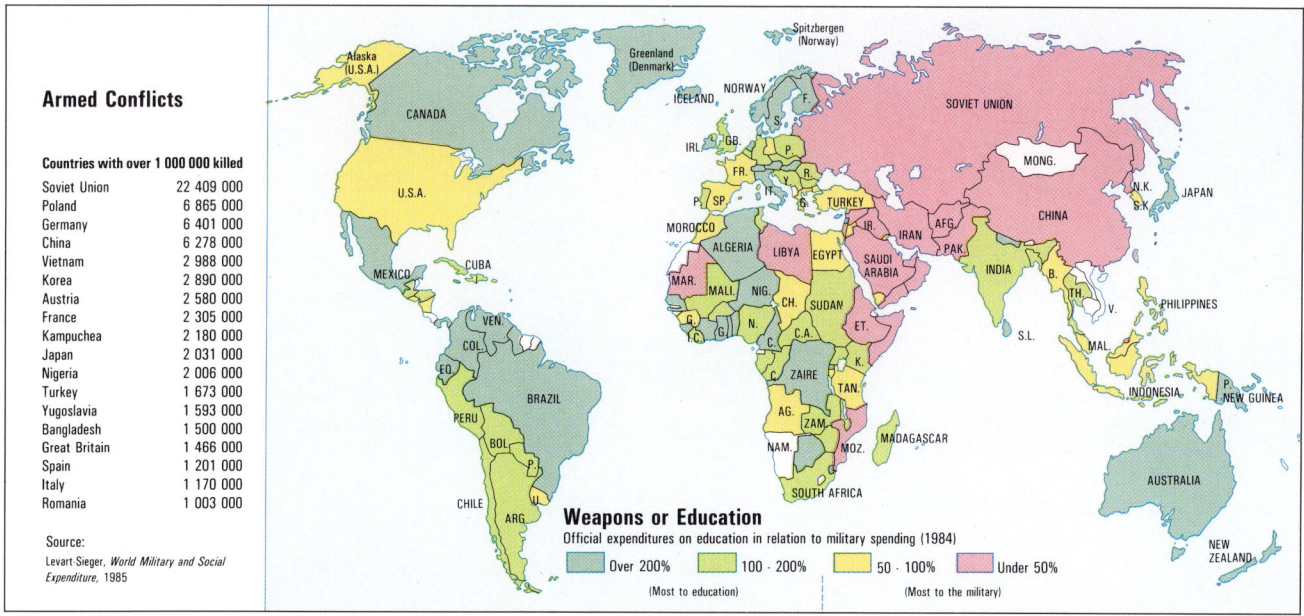

Armed Conflicts

Countries with over 1 000 000 killed

Soviet Union	22 409 000
Poland	6 865 000
Germany	6 401 000
China	6 278 000
Vietnam	2 988 000
Korea	2 890 000
Austria	2 580 000
France	2 305 000
Kampuchea	2 180 000
Japan	2 031 000
Nigeria	2 006 000
Turkey	1 673 000
Yugoslavia	1 593 000
Bangladesh	1 500 000
Great Britain	1 466 000
Spain	1 201 000
Italy	1 170 000
Romania	1 003 000

Source: Levart-Sieger, *World Military and Social Expenditure*, 1985

Weapons or Education
Official expenditures on education in relation to military spending (1984)

- Over 200% (Most to education)
- 100 - 200%
- 50 - 100%
- Under 50% (Most to the military)

In 1945, the USA was the only nation that had nuclear weapons. Since then, a number of states including Great Britain, France, the USSR, and the People's Republic of China have deployed thermonuclear weapons along their borders. Other, smaller nations may also have designed nuclear weapons to make up for their lack of conventional forces. Nuclear devices placed in intercontinental missiles can strike anywhere in the world. The number of these missiles is so great that their use in war would kill every living thing on earth several times over. At present they are used as a deterrent. The superpowers have agreed not to place nuclear weapons in outer space, on the seabeds, or in the Antarctic or other nuclear free zones. Should a nuclear war break out, the smoke from burning forests, cities, and energy reserves would blanket the earth, touching off a sudden drop in temperatures to well below freezing—an event described as nuclear winter.

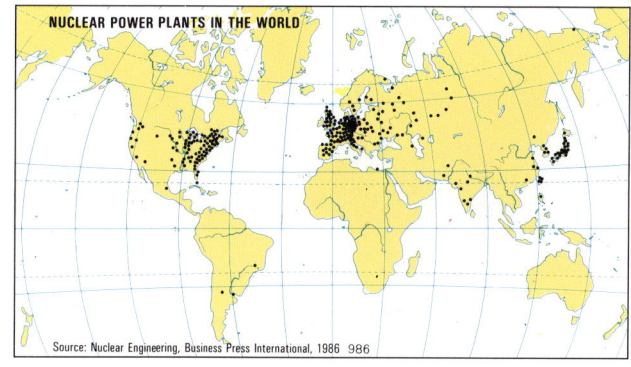

QUESTIONS

1. Identify the countries which possess nuclear weapons.
2. Should nuclear proliferation be stopped? What guidelines should be used in determining how the possession of weapons might be limited?

ONE

WORLD

A COMPARISON OF WORLD INCOMES

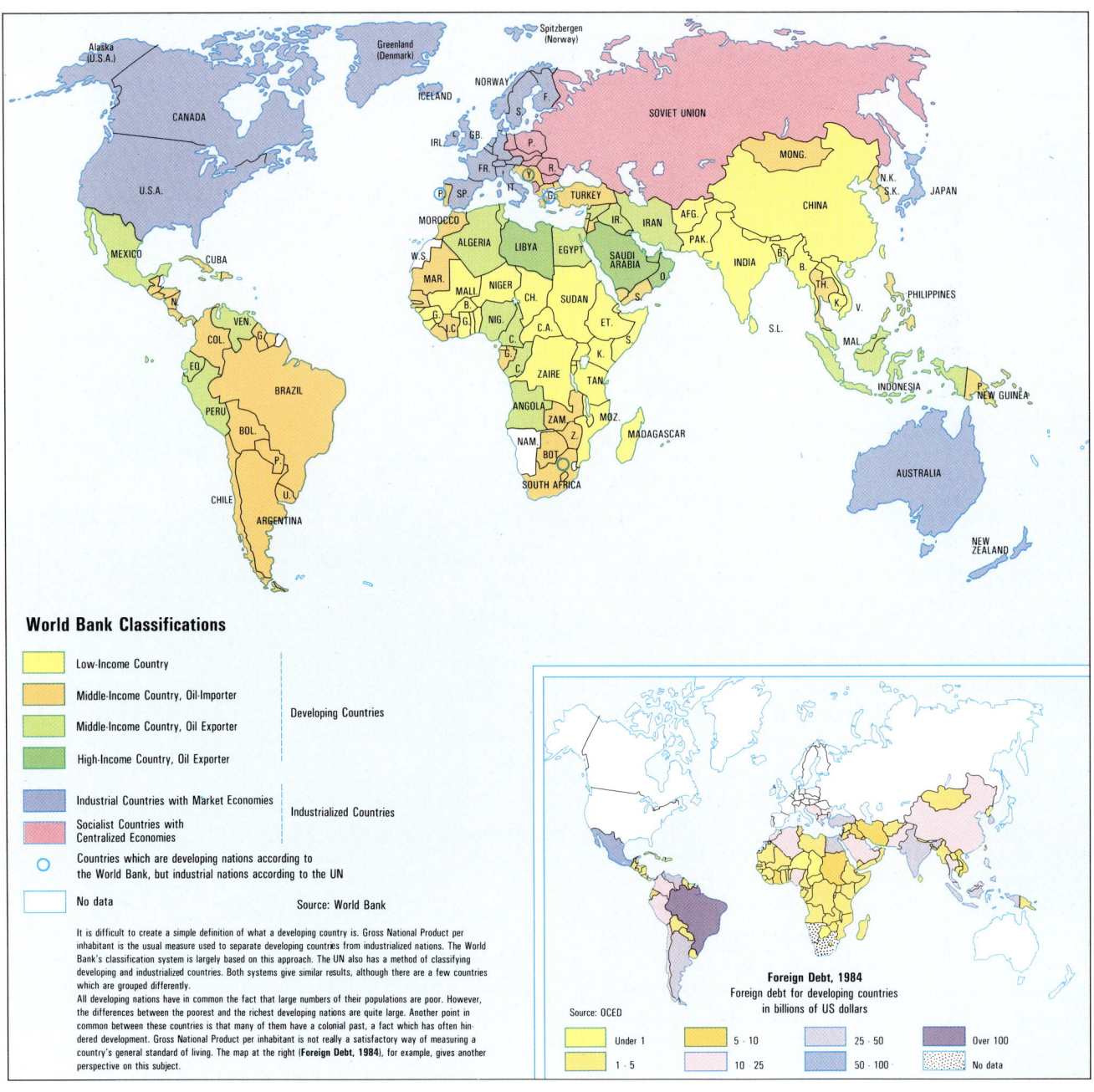

The disparity between the rich and poor nations of the world is widening daily. Because most industrial nations reside in the northern hemisphere, the world appears to be divided upon north-south lines.

Beset by insurmountable problems of overcrowding, urban growth, insufficient food supplies, and stagnant economies, the poor nations have little hope of closing the gap. They depend increasingly on a transfer of resources from the rich nations in order to maintain minimum living standards.

MINI-ATLAS
6

SOCIO-ECONOMIC INDICATORS

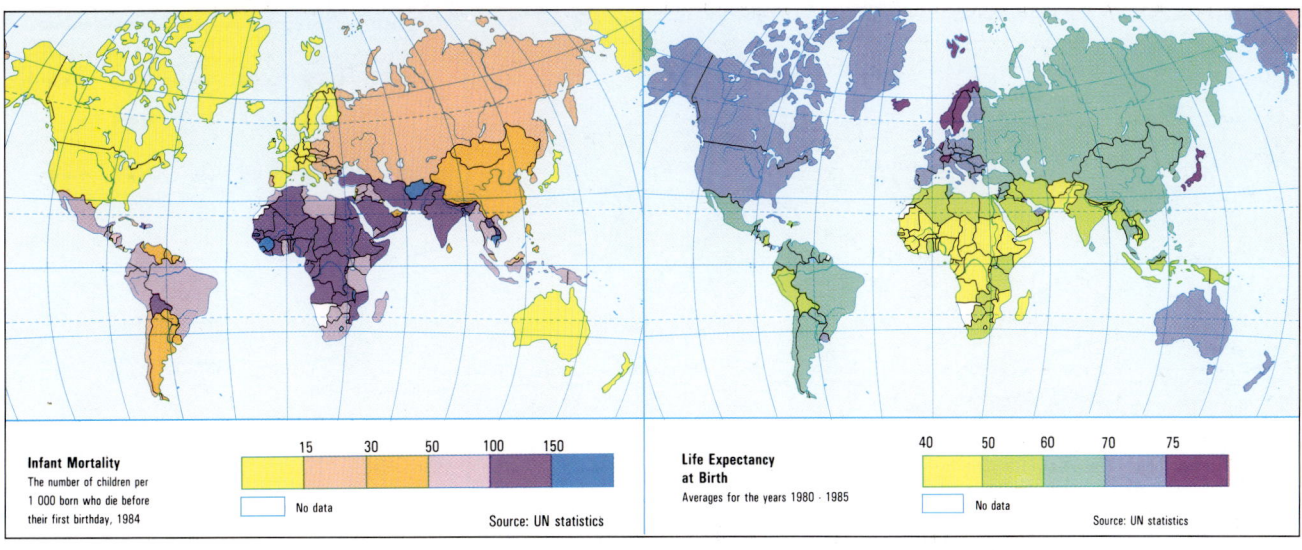

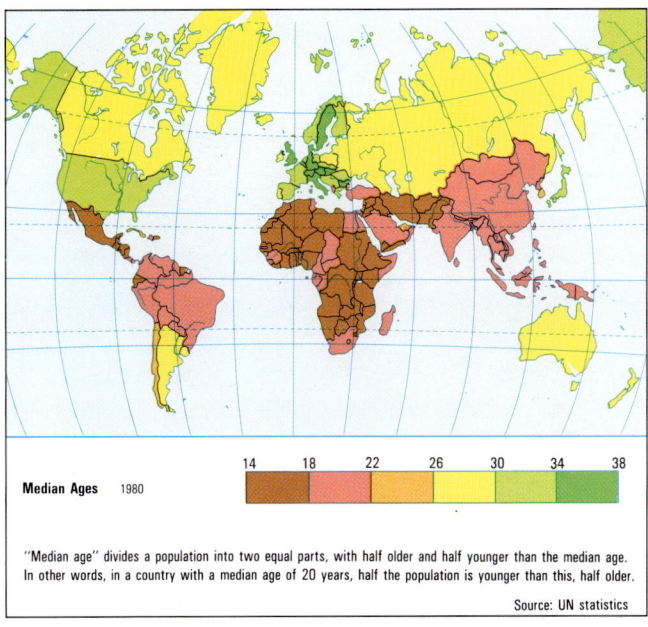

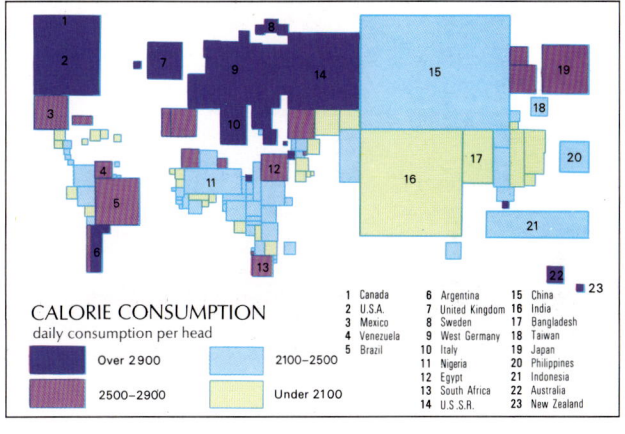

The socio-economic ranking of nations depends on a number of measurable factors relating to the relative material well-being of society. The Standard of Living Chart, on Mini-Atlas page 15, gives some of the commonly accepted indicators of the human condition in several of the world's nations. Higher per capita incomes, longer lifespans, and a larger caloric intake characterize the lifestyles of the wealthier and more developed nations. The figures used in the chart are averages based on submissions from national governments and reflect an official view. One should also keep in mind that even in the richest country there are many poor, just as in the poorest country there will be an economic elite. Information of this type is extremely useful in designing programs aimed at reducing global disparity.

MINI-ATLAS

ONE

WORLD

WORLD POPULATION (1)

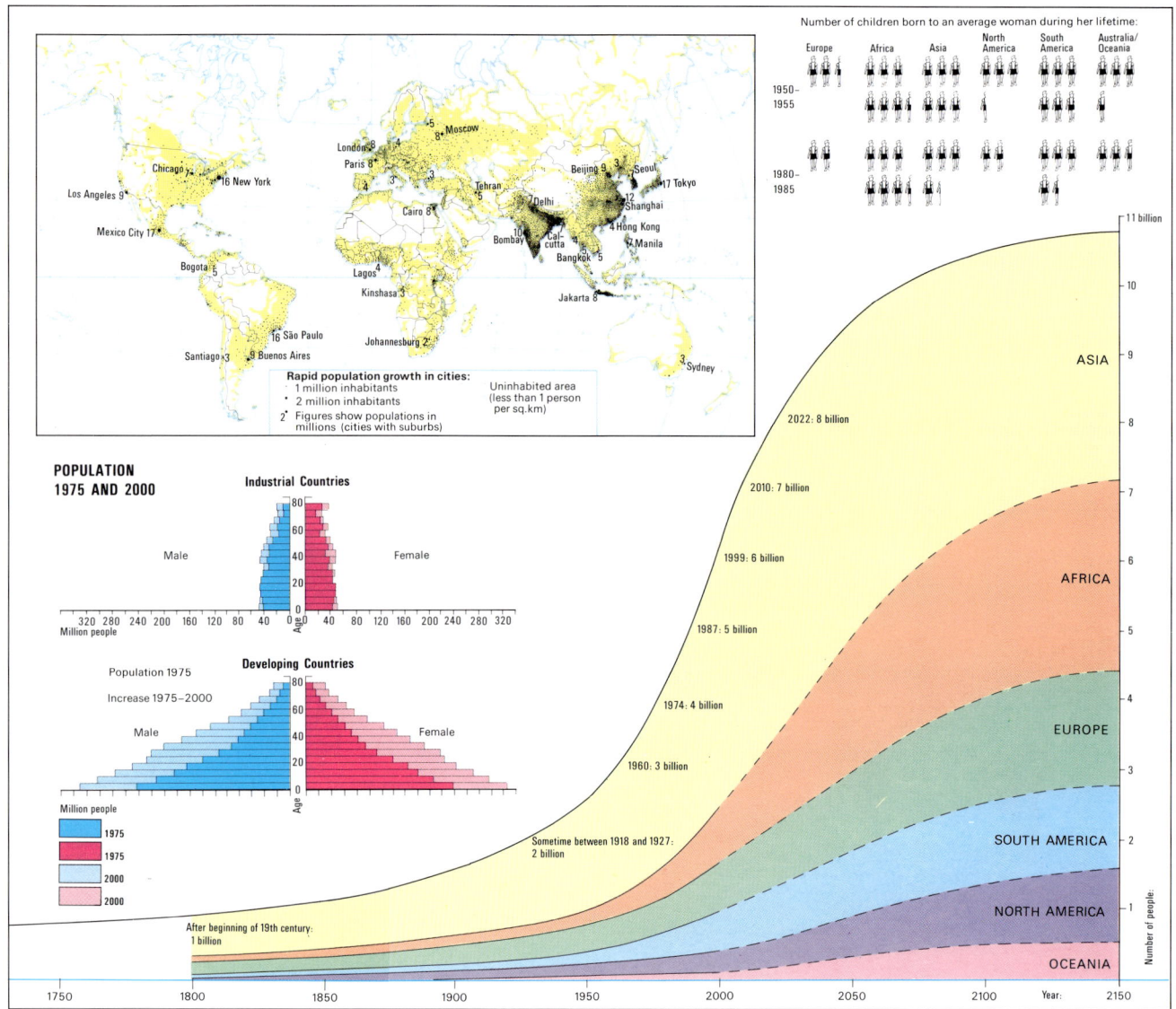

The earth's 6 billion people are not evenly distributed over the planet's land surface. Instead they tend to congregate in large cities, in warmer climates close to adequate food and water reserves. Their escalating growth has become an urgent matter of international concern due to the demands the larger, future generations will make on limited global resources. What level of standard of living will the biosphere be able to provide for them?

By the year AD 2000, it is estimated that 4 billion people will live in non-industrialized, underdeveloped countries that even now cannot provide an adequate standard of living for their peoples. Malnutrition, poverty, inadequate housing, and slum conditions characterize their situation. These same nations have high birth rates and will have to absorb 94 per cent of the world's growth of population.

MINI-ATLAS

8

WORLD POPULATION (2)

Urban and Rural Populations, 1950 - 2025

Mexico City 1900 - 2000

In 1980, Mexico City was the third-largest city in the world – only Tokyo and New York City were larger. According to UN estimates, by the year 2000, Mexico's capital will take over first place, with a population of over 26 million people.

In 1981, the twin cities of Lima/Callao had a population of 4.6 million people. Of these citizens, 32% lived in so-called *barrios*. These communities spring up when poor people simply take over or are given an area where they build simple shanties of cheap material. These "shanty towns" are common elements of urban growth in many developing countries.

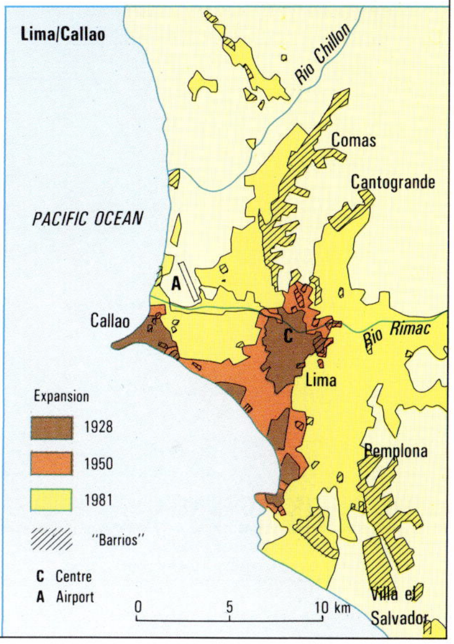

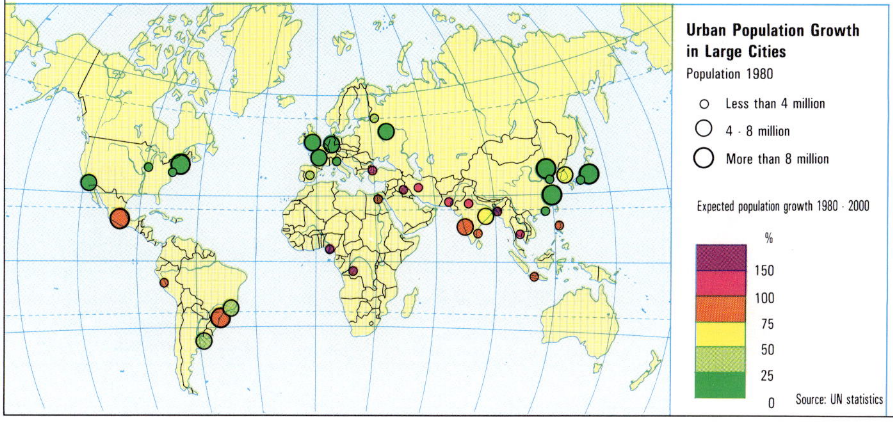

The technique of graphic distortion was used to draw the adjacent map which compares the population of nations schematically, while preserving the geographic relationship between nations. At a glance, one can readily pick out the relative size of national populations. Do you find this map easier to read than the ones on the previous pages? What are the reasons for your answer?

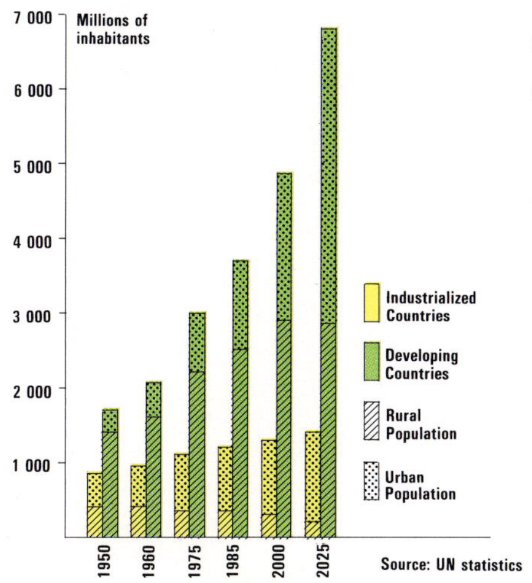

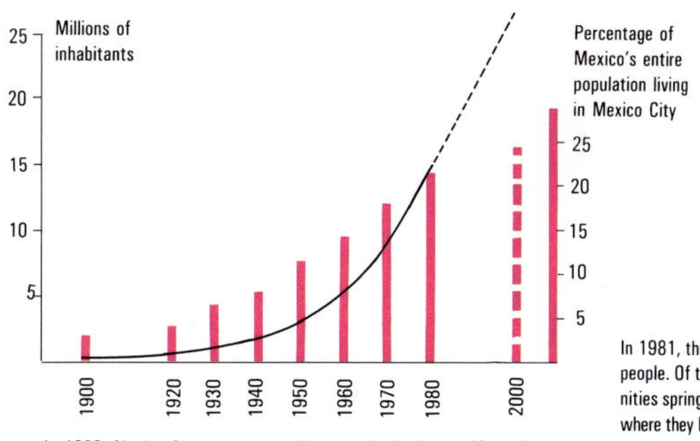

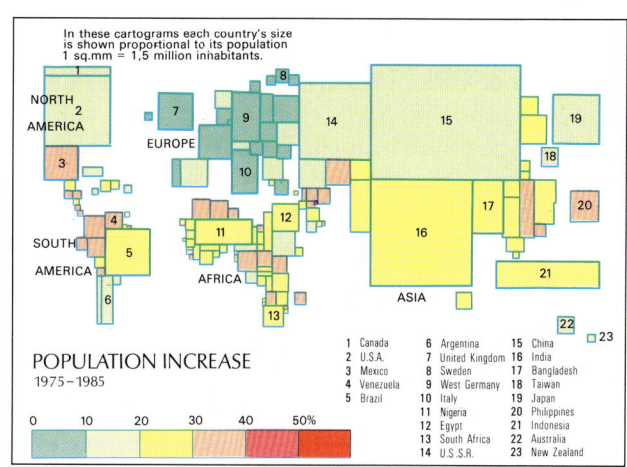

QUESTIONS

1. From the population block map, identify the five most populated countries.
2. Name three areas with the most number of large cities?

ONE

WORLD

ENERGY AND OIL PRODUCTION AND CONSUMPTION

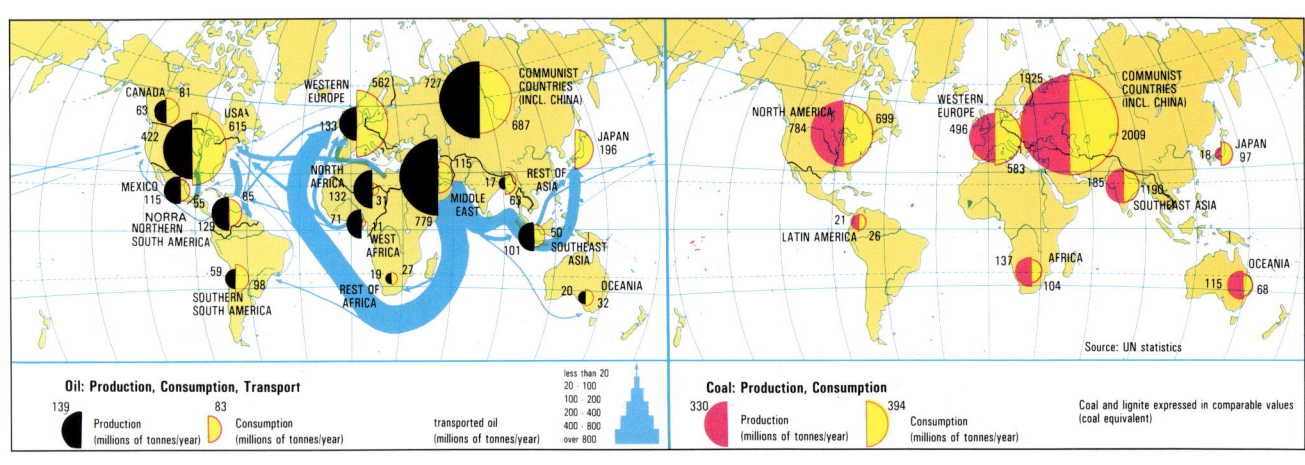

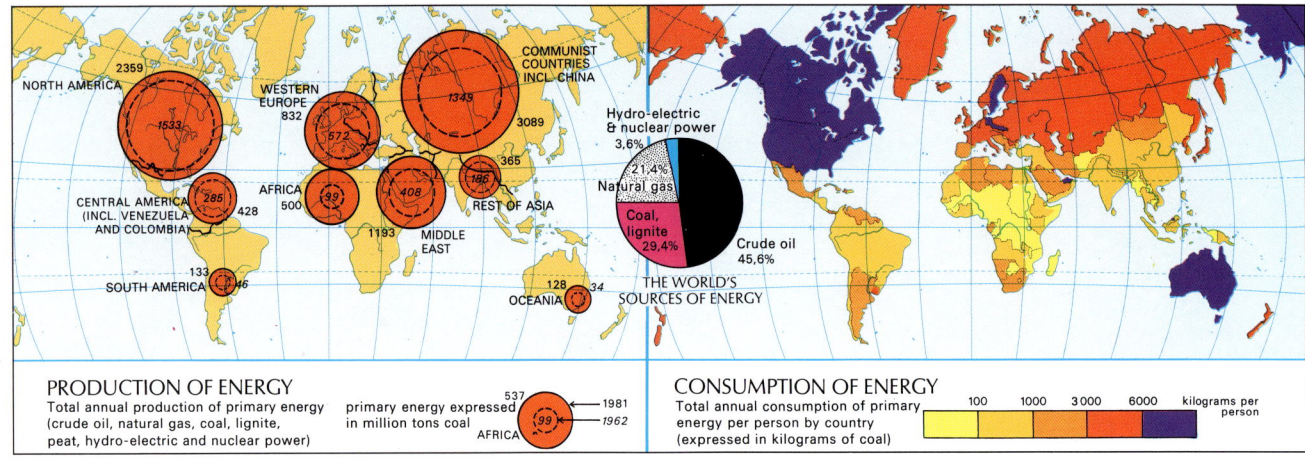

A global network of supertankers, transcontinental pipelines, and unit trains carry a continuous supply of oil and gasoline from the fields to the developed regions. Oil was used as a political weapon by the OPEC countries in the decade after 1973. Saudi Arabia is the largest oil exporter in the world and the most influential in establishing prices. The reaction of the developed world to the major OPEC price increases was to turn to strategies of self-sufficiency. The North Sea oil and gas fields have eased the pressure on Western Europe. Brazil has turned to ethanol produced from sugar cane to fuel its trucks and cars, while other importers have turned increasingly to nuclear power. So critical are energy supplies in the modern world that any threat to disrupt them leads to conflict.

QUESTIONS

1. What are the three largest oil producing areas?
2. Where are the three largest coal consuming areas?
3. Identify the areas of the world which consume the most energy.

MINI-ATLAS
10

MIGRATION AND REFUGEES

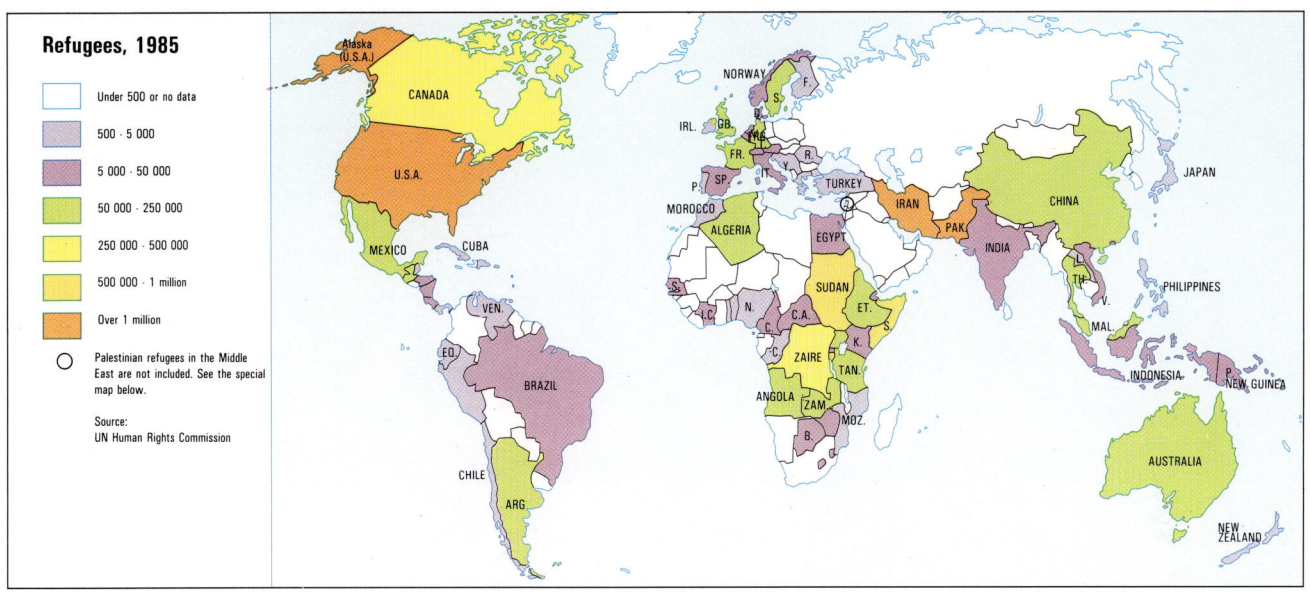

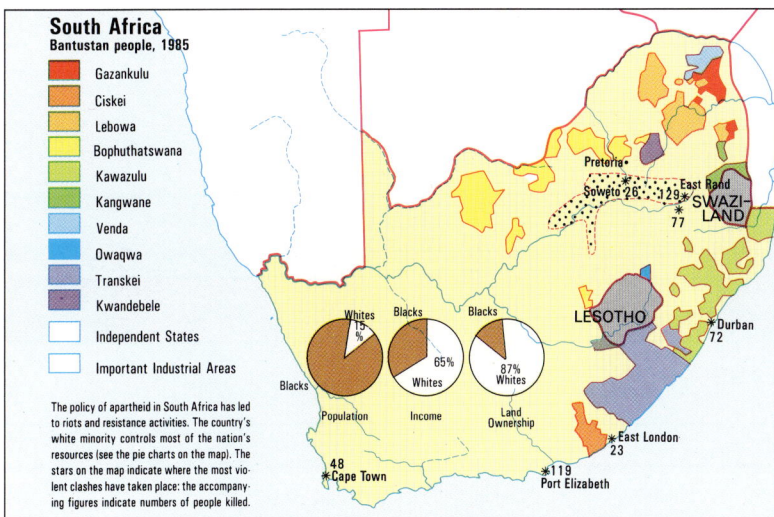

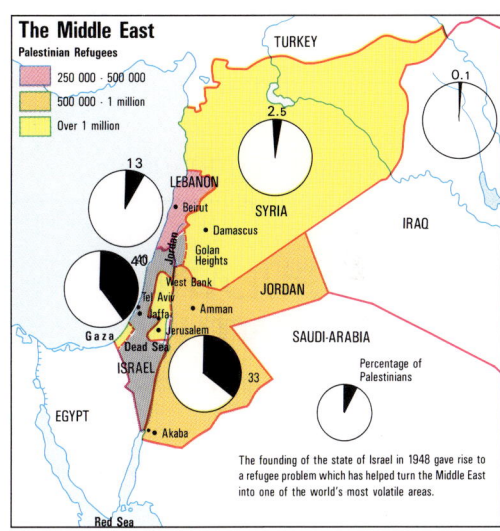

Workers tend to migrate from rural to urban areas and from less developed nations to those which have growing economies. Most countries limit the number of entrants in order to protect their own citizens. Hence, unless a particular trade or profession is short of labour, it is sometimes very difficult to enter a new country. Conflict around the world has resulted in the displacement of significant numbers of people. South-east Asia, southern Africa, the Middle East, and Central America have been hotbeds of unrest for the last two to three decades. Refugees from these areas are finding it increasingly difficult to find a new home. As a result, desperate individuals have sometimes been drawn into costly and dangerous schemes designed to circumvent regular entry into a country. The recent incidents involving the Tamils who were being channelled through West Germany to Canada are a case in point. Should countries like Canada restrict the entry of political refugees?

MINI-ATLAS
11

ONE WORLD

THE URBAN MAGNET

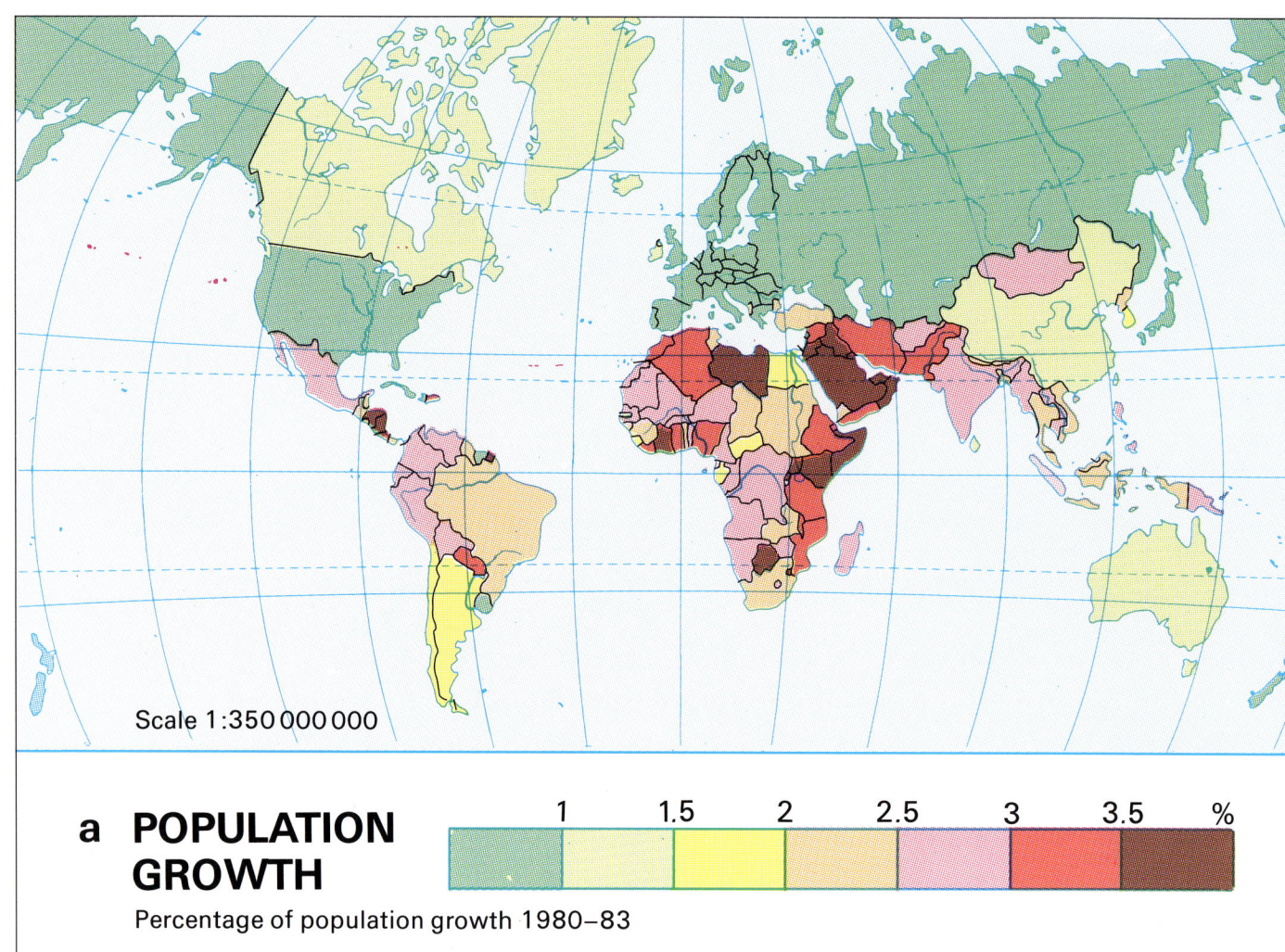

a POPULATION GROWTH
Percentage of population growth 1980–83

World populations display a disturbing global pattern of rural to urban migration. Escalating urban growth places extreme pressures on regional governments to provide adequate standards of living in the way of food, housing, health, and sanitation. How does a city cope with the addition of thousands of newcomers every month? Imagine the resources needed to keep them at minimum living standards.

The migration of rural residents to the cities has produced congested human habitations undreamed of 50 years ago. The modern megapolis provides the basic needs of an international culture plus much more in the way of attractive entertainment and a hustle of human activity. Cities act as magnets, drawing to them tens of thousands on an annual basis. The pressures placed on local governments to pro-

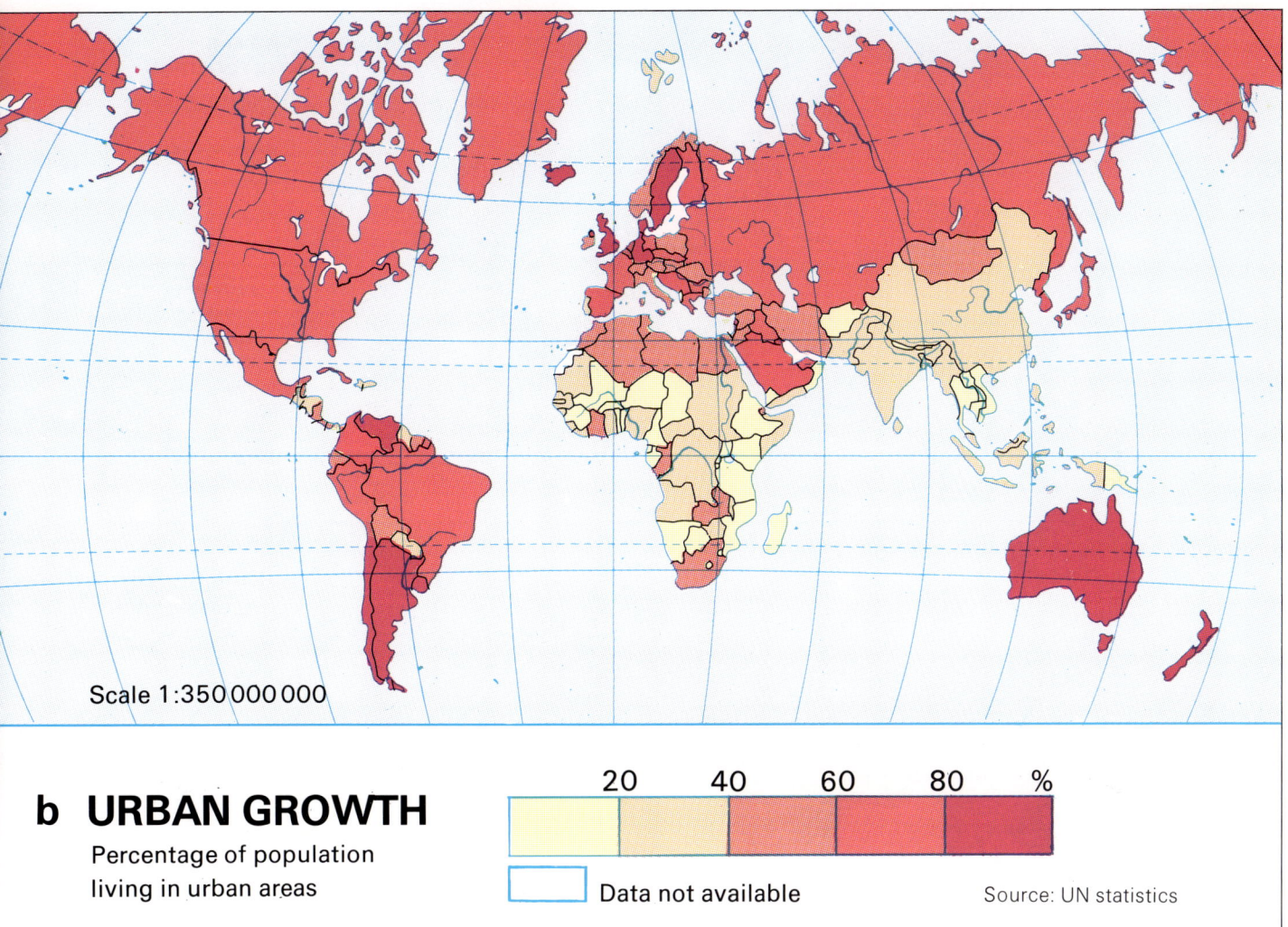

b URBAN GROWTH
Percentage of population living in urban areas

Scale 1:350 000 000

Source: UN statistics

vide for the migrants have become unacceptably high. Some cities have moved to decentralize some of their millions of inhabitants into self-contained outlying mini-cities. Within the cities, a similarity of lifestyle is developing from the presence of tourists, transnational corporate interests, and global media facilities. The result for part of the population is the adoption of a materialist Western culture. For those not part of the international jet set, the city holds only the hope that the condition of their lifestyle can be improved should some form of employment be found.

ONE

WORLD

WORLD POLLUTION AND DESERTIFICATION

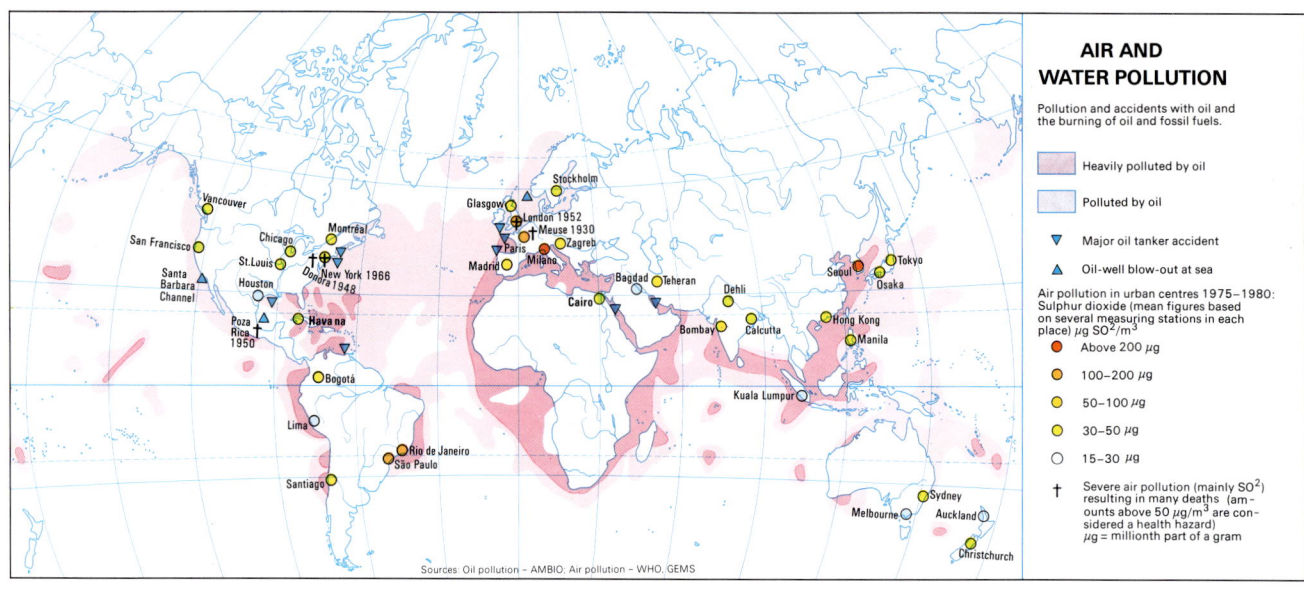

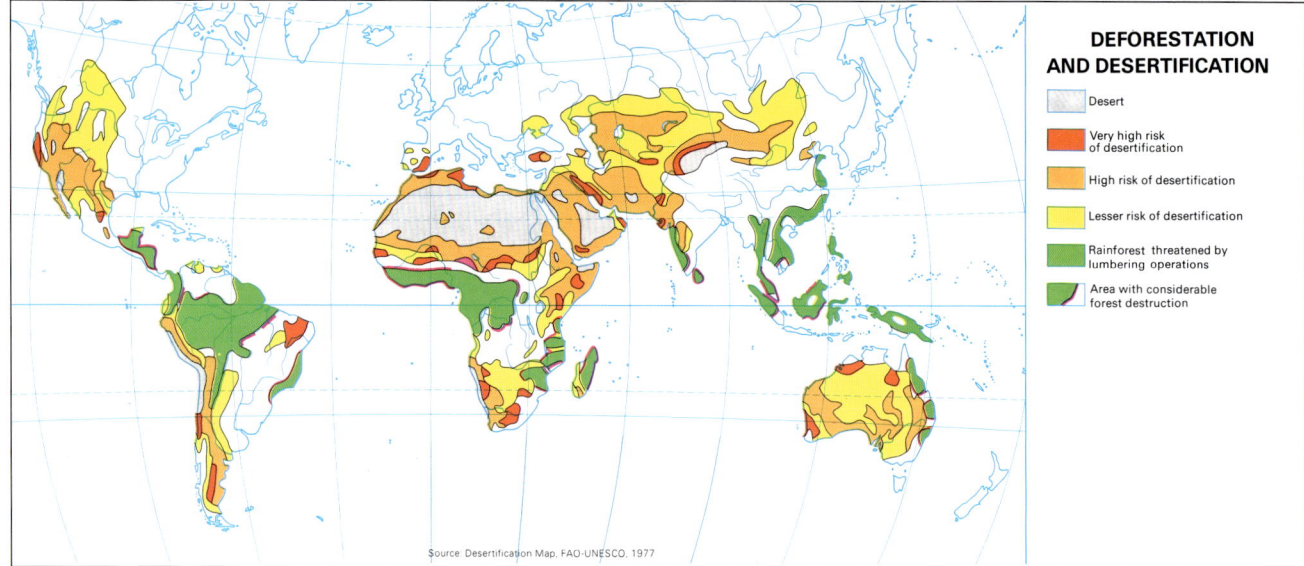

Man's assault on the environment has resulted in a crisis which demands immediate action. Depletion of resources, destruction of our land base, and pollution of air, land, and water can all be directly linked to the industrial process. Sewage is dumped directly into the oceans; fertilizers and chemicals seep into our groundwater; toxic wastes from industrial activity are pumped into the air. Plant and animal life are destroyed. Human beings suffer a variety of diseases. Industrialized nations are attempting to solve the problem with pollution control devices and emission controls. However, solving pollution problems is very expensive. Nations which are just now industrializing do not have enough money to safeguard the environment. Should there be some type of global control established to deal with industrial pollution?

MINI-ATLAS

14

STANDARD OF LIVING CHART

	Population (millions) 1985	Population (millions) 2000	Area (thousands of square kilometres)	GNP per capita Dollars 1985	Life expectancy at birth (yrs.) 1985 male	Life expectancy at birth (yrs.) 1985 female	Daily calorie supply/ capita 1985
Low-income economies	2439	3177	32 547	270	60	61	2339
Ethiopia	42	65	1 222	110	43	47	1681
Bangladesh	101	141	144	150	50	51	1899
Central African Rep.	3	4	623	260	47	50	2050
India	765	996	3 288	270	57	56	2189
Kenya	20	36	583	290	52	56	2151
Tanzania	22	37	945	290	50	54	2335
China	1040	1274	9 561	310	68	72	2602
Haiti	6	8	28	310	53	56	1855
Ghana	13	20	239	380	51	55	1747
Pakistan	96	146	804	380	52	50	2159
Sri Lanka	16	20	66	380	68	72	2385
Zambia	7	11	753	390	50	54	2137
Afghanistan	—	—	648	—	—	—	—
Chad	5	7	1 284	—	43	46	1504
Kampuchea (Cambodia)	—	—	181	—	—	—	—
Middle-income economies	1242	1663	38 071	1290	60	64	2731
Bolivia	6	9	1 099	470	51	54	2146
Egypt, Arab Rep.	49	67	1 001	610	59	63	3263
Zimbabwe	8	13	391	680	55	59	2054
Nicaragua	3	5	130	770	57	61	2425
Nigeria	100	163	924	800	48	52	2038
Thailand	52	66	514	800	62	66	2462
Peru	19	25	1 285	1010	57	60	2171
Turkey	50	67	781	1080	62	67	3167
Colombia	28	37	1 139	1320	63	67	2574
Chile	12	15	757	1430	67	74	2602
Syrian Arab Rep.	11	17	185	1570	62	65	2947
Upper middle-income	567	716	21 981	1850	64	69	2987
Brazil	136	178	8 512	1640	62	67	2633
Hungary	11	11	93	1950	67	74	3482
Portugal	10	11	92	1970	71	77	3161
Malaysia	16	21	330	2000	66	70	2684
South Africa	32	45	1 221	2010	53	57	2979
Poland	37	41	313	2050	67	76	3280
Yugoslavia	23	25	256	2070	69	75	3602
Mexico	79	110	1 973	2080	64	69	3177
Argentina	31	37	2 767	2130	67	74	3221
Korea, Rep. of	41	49	98	2150	65	72	2841
Algeria	22	34	2 382	2550	59	63	2677
Venezuela	17	24	912	3 080	66	73	2583
Israel	4	5	21	4 990	73	77	3060
Hong Kong	5	6	1	6 230	73	79	2698
Oman	1	2	300	6 730	52	55	—
Singapore	3	3	1	7 420	70	75	2771
High-income oil exporters	18	31	4 012	9 800	61	65	3265
Libya	4	7	1 760	7 170	59	62	3612
Saudi Arabia	12	20	2 150	8 850	60	64	3128
Kuwait	2	3	18	14 480	69	74	3138
United Arab Emirates	1	2	84	19 270	68	73	3625
Industrial market economies	737	781	30 935	11 810	73	79	3417
Spain	39	42	505	4 290	74	80	3358
Ireland	4	4	70	4 850	71	76	3831
Italy	57	58	301	6 520	74	79	3538
New Zealand	3	4	269	7 010	71	77	3386
Belgium	10	10	31	8 280	72	78	3679
United Kingdom	57	57	245	8 460	72	77	3131
Austria	8	8	84	9 120	70	77	3514
Netherlands	14	15	41	9 290	73	80	3343
France	55	59	547	9 540	75	81	3359
Australia	16	18	7 687	10 843	75	80	3389
Finland	5	5	337	10 890	72	79	3026
Germany, Fed. Rep.	61	59	249	10 940	72	78	3474
Denmark	5	5	43	11 200	72	78	3547
Japan	121	129	372	11 300	75	80	2856
Sweden	8	8	450	11 890	74	80	3097
Canada	25	28	9 976	13 680	72	80	3432
Norway	4	4	324	14 370	74	80	3239
Switzerland	6	7	41	16 370	73	80	3432
United States	239	262	9 363	16 690	72	80	3663

* Figures on the Soviet Union are not available.

The standard of living of a people can in part be gauged by measurable demographic and economic indicators. Although wealth is not evenly distributed in a population, a population's income is an indication of where it stands in relation to the other 168 countries in the world. The per capita gross national product (GNP) is a comparison of the total goods and services produced in a year divided by the total population—man, woman, and child. Current and predicted population size and density, and age groupings also characterize a society. A nation's geographic size likely indicates if a society has enough land and mineral resources for a good life. Life expectancy and the daily calorie intake are indicators of the health of the population, the health services available, and the abundance of food supplies. The larger the figures, the higher the standard of living. Although these are rough estimates, based on official reporting, these figures are used to rank nations according to their average lifestyle.

ONE

WORLD

WORLD FOOD CONSUMPTION AND FAMINE LOCATIONS

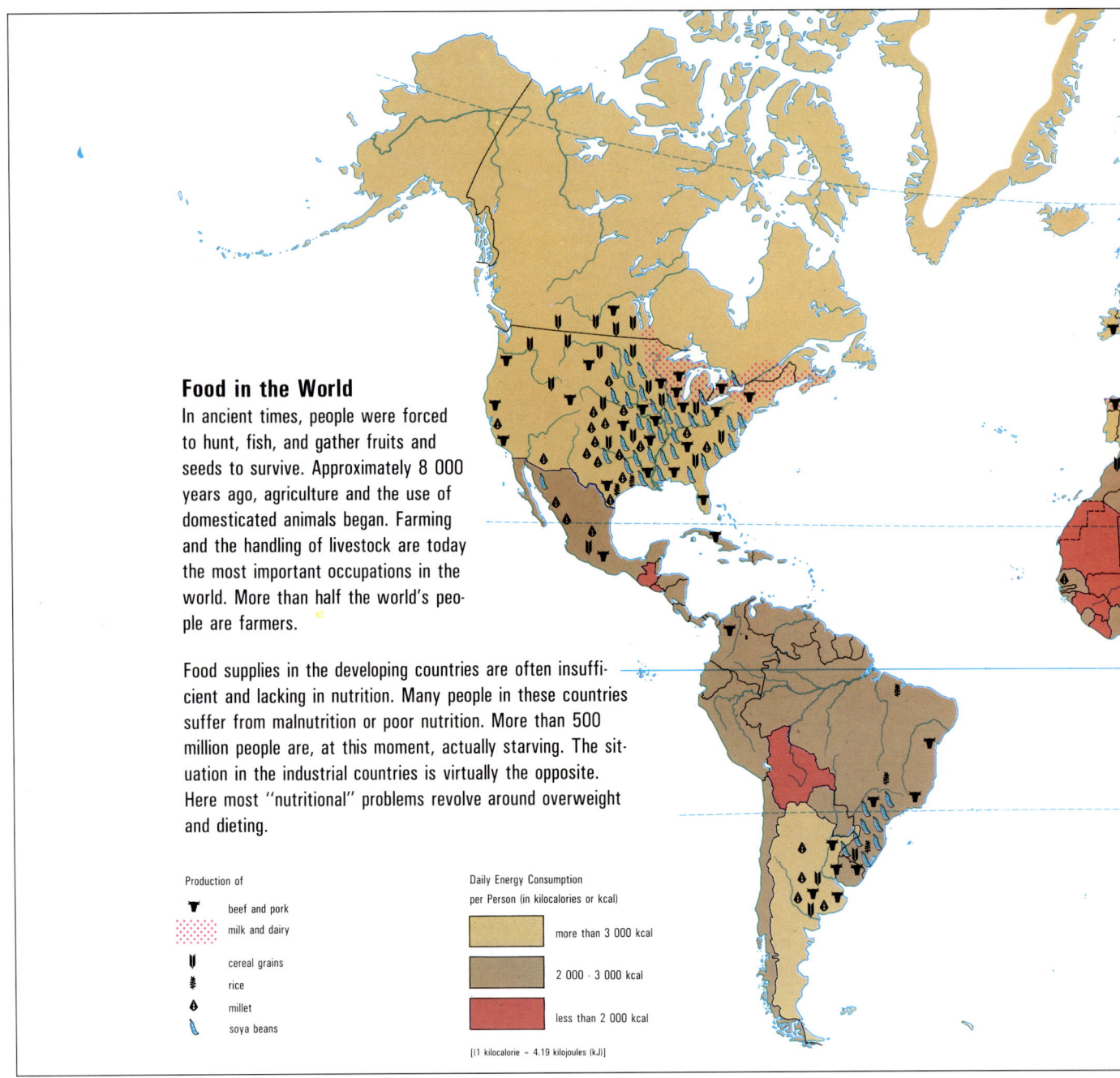

Food in the World

In ancient times, people were forced to hunt, fish, and gather fruits and seeds to survive. Approximately 8 000 years ago, agriculture and the use of domesticated animals began. Farming and the handling of livestock are today the most important occupations in the world. More than half the world's people are farmers.

Food supplies in the developing countries are often insufficient and lacking in nutrition. Many people in these countries suffer from malnutrition or poor nutrition. More than 500 million people are, at this moment, actually starving. The situation in the industrial countries is virtually the opposite. Here most "nutritional" problems revolve around overweight and dieting.

Production of
- beef and pork
- milk and dairy
- cereal grains
- rice
- millet
- soya beans

Daily Energy Consumption per Person (in kilocalories or kcal)
- more than 3 000 kcal
- 2 000 - 3 000 kcal
- less than 2 000 kcal

[(1 kilocalorie = 4.19 kilojoules (kJ)]

There are significant differences in food availability around the world. Some of this inequality is due to a lack of sufficient arable land. Sometimes the inequity results from the manner in which arable land is used. For example, many underdeveloped countries devote much of their land to the production of cash crops. The foreign currency earned by this practice is essential for the development process. Some-

MINI-ATLAS

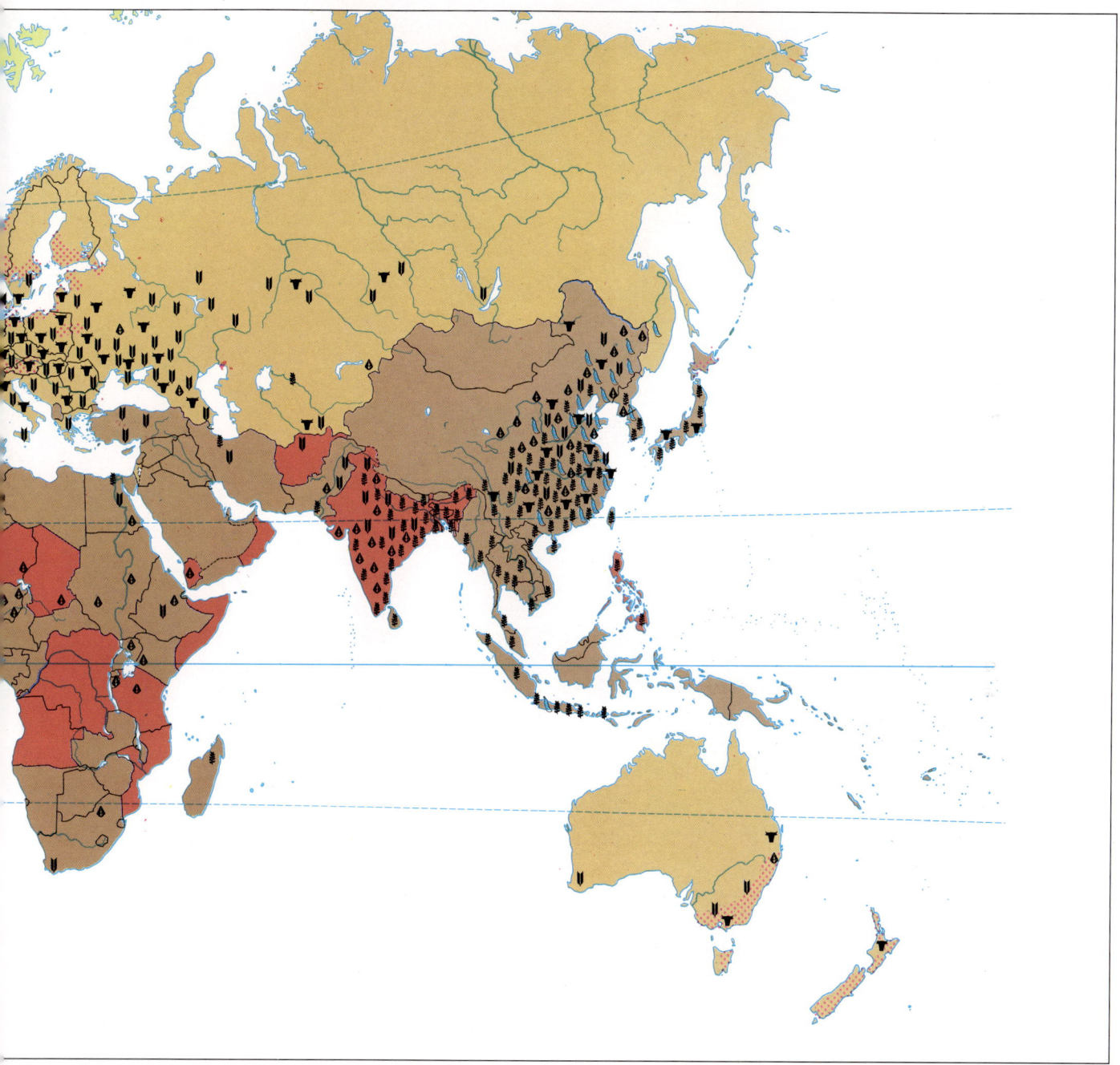

times environmental disasters interfere with food production, as in the case of drought in Ethiopia or flooding in Bangladesh. There are many causes of food shortages, but poverty appears to be a major contributor to the unavailability of basic nutrition. An inability to buy food results in widespread hunger in many areas of the world.

INTRODUCTION   1

EARTH, THE LIVING PLANET, sustains a variety of plants and animals in a complex, interwoven system. On this planet, energy and nutrients come from the sun, water, air, and land, all of which give energy and food to a vast array of living things. Undisturbed, these systems could support life forever through nature's built-in renewal mechanism. Humans are part of this system. However, they strain earth's natural limits. In trying to improve their quality of life and enhance their standard of living, they have launched an assault on the planet's resources from which earth may not recover. Only recently have we become aware of the fragility of the physical environment and the danger posed to it by human activity.

The physical environment imposes limits on our quality of life. There are other limitations too. National leaders make political, economic, military, and social decisions based on their interpretation of their societies' values and desires. These decisions are made with the intention of maintaining and perhaps enhancing a particular style of living. Sometimes nations have gone to war in order to secure more land or to obtain the resources needed to sustain their own peculiar lifestyle. Within the nation state, people find themselves drawn into a complex network of political, economic, military, and social relationships. These relationships reveal significant differences in status and well-being amongst the world's people. Tensions arising from both the diversity of cultures and global disparity can lead to conflict or to co-operation. The development of thermo-nuclear devices and the perfection of chemical and bacteriological weapons suggests the urgency of the need to find peaceful solutions.

Standard of living and quality of life are products of both the physical environment and the human-made cultural environment.

HUMANS AND THE ENVIRONMENT

The first major human impact on the physical environment was the discovery of agriculture. Permanent settlements meant that land was used for crop production. Houses and other buildings were constructed. People began to control the environment. Their control increased during the industrial revolution with the introduction of machines. Technology, it seemed, would make humans rulers of the globe. At first this was not a concern. With the growth of the world's population to 5 billion, the interdependence of people from all parts of the globe has placed a strain on the earth's natural bounty. Since the eighteenth century, people have made nature pay dearly for their attempts to enhance their lifestyle. For example, people have used resources in vast quantities with little or no regard

ONE
WORLD

The world's population is so large that it places strain on the earth's natural bounty. At times, people in Bangladesh have been dependent on foreign aid to provide them with food. The world is becoming increasingly interdependent.

for the future. In addition, our industries pollute the environment, poisoning our food and other life support systems.

There is growing concern about the environmental consequences of many human activities. We now realize that global **eco-systems** are in jeopardy. A critical mix of gases provides our life supporting atmosphere. The human impact on the environment has disrupted this critical environment. Stable, livable temperatures, insulation from the sun's harmful rays, and the availability of water vapour from plant life are all at risk because of growing industrial activity. Can we act now to preserve the delicate balance of interdependent systems which give us life? Is it too late? What factors must we consider in determining our future? What factors are critical to our standard of living?

Cultural environments result from human interaction as people strive to build an identity which is controlled by traditional practices. Cultural environments are built within the framework of a particular geographical location. This human-made environment is under continuous tension as nations strive to improve their standard of living. Industrial development is seen as the solution to material wealth. Competition for energy and raw materials was and will continue to be a source of friction and war. The interrelated nature of political, economic, and military systems leads as often to conflict as to co-operation. How can every nation develop a high standard of living in a world where natural resources are running out? Can the world sustain continued ic development? If not, what must people do without? Who is to blame for the disparity we find amongst humans who live on the same planet but in different places?

Global interdependence means that changes to the environment in one part of the world affect the world as a whole.

Global interdependence has resulted from economic growth and development. Changes to the environment in one part of the world affect the earth as a whole. This is the true meaning of global interdependence. Environmental limits, global imbalances of resources, and conflicting cultural interests challenge people's attempts to improve their quality of life. We have a global responsibility. We need to understand the world situation, look at alternative futures, and examine means of change. The economic and social needs of our global community demand that we consider ourselves citizens of the world.

THE STRUCTURE OF THE BOOK

This book explores the relationship between humans and their physical and cultural environments. A mini-atlas opens the book to provide a visual picture of the wide diversity of nation states. The mini-atlas shows the growing disparity of lifestyles

Chapter 1
INTRODUCTION

between the wealthy developed people and the underdeveloped poor. In order to understand these relationships it is first necessary to look at the planet's natural life supporting systems and how they function in relation to humans and to each other. Chapter 2 examines the natural forces of the biosphere. The fragile balance of the physical environment is underlined.

Chapter 3 looks at interrelated human environments, exploring the political and economic organization of the world. Chapter 4 focuses on the major changes in human history—the agricultural and industrial revolutions—and how these two revolutions have led to many environmental problems we face today. Chapters 5 to 10 explore six major factors that determine the quality of life in a world characterized by global interdependence. These are outlined below.

1. **People.** Large numbers of people place pressure on our natural resources. As our numbers grow, our individual share of resources may lessen.
2. **Urbanization.** Huge concentrations of people must be fed, housed, transported, and provided with urban services. This exerts tremendous pressure on the environment.
3. **Food.** The planet can only feed a finite number of people. If we run short of food who will do without? How does hunger affect a people? What decisions have led to starvation?
4. **Energy.** Energy drives our industries and gives us our material well-being. However, we must look at alternative sources of energy. We are rapidly depleting available non-renewable energy sources.
5. **Industrialization.** Industrial development improves our lifestyle at a direct cost to the environment.
6. **Global Co-Operation.** Problems within the human-made cultural environment can be solved through the co-operation of the earth's diverse societies. Examples of this are the redistribution of resources through aid and the agreements on the Antarctic and the Law of the Sea.

Chapter 11 lays out four possible scenarios for our future. What will happen largely depends on you. Some of the key issues discussed in *One World* are summarized in the following pages.

PEOPLE

One of the most urgent global problems is the relationship of human numbers to the availability of resources. Five billion people now live on the earth and this number will increase by about 83 million per year.

Humans live in a world of disparity. Less than 25 per cent of the world's population lives in industrial nations, yet these nations use more than 75 per cent of the earth's resources. These developed nations have food choices, sophisticated material goods, modern housing and transportation, and access to many leisure activities. In contrast, 75 per cent of the world's people live in underdeveloped regions.

Underdeveloped areas have not yet industrialized and they lack most of the goods which developed nations take for granted. One billion of these people live in abject poverty without adequate housing. These people subsist on a diet lacking both calories and nutrients. Many millions die at an early age. While the population is declining in developed

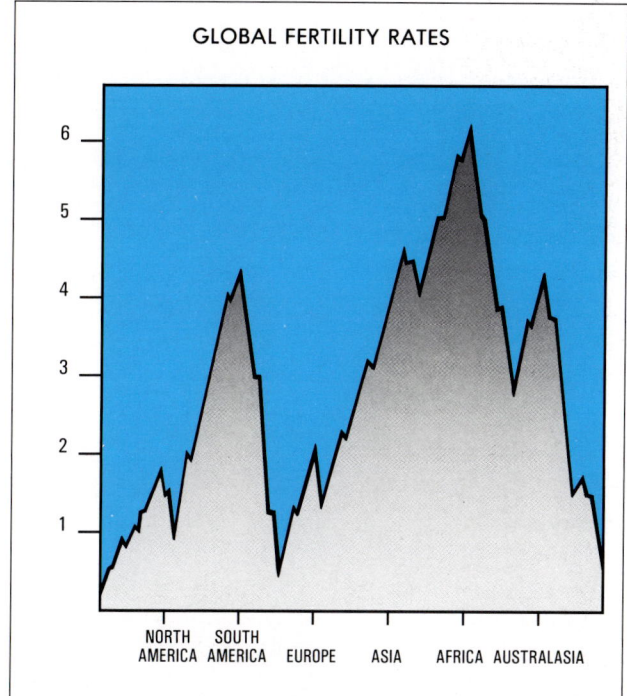

This graph shows global fertility rates (the average number of children born per woman over her lifetime). While the population is declining in developed nations, it is increasing in underdeveloped nations.

ONE

WORLD

regions, it is increasing in the underdeveloped areas. What does this mean to the relative standard of living between the two worlds? Can the quality of life be improved in the face of large population increases? Can the world support increasing numbers of people at a decent standard of living?

URBANIZATION

Industrialization led to the creation of large cities in the developed areas, and now urbanization is taking place in underdeveloped regions as well. When the population swells people leave rural areas hoping for a better life. A global urban culture is emerging;

Urbanization is one of the major factors affecting quality of life. A global urban culture is emerging as more and more of the world's people choose to live in cities.

Chapter 1
INTRODUCTION

by the twenty-first century more than one-half of the world will live in cities. Such high density puts great pressure on the environment. Society must choose how it will house, feed, and transport large concentrations of people. Will there be work for these new city dwellers? Can we provide education, health care, and recreation facilities? The mega-city of tomorrow will challenge humanity's creativity. Can we meet the demands of increased numbers in this new environment?

FOOD

One of our basic needs is food. Global food production keeps increasing faster than global population. Yet 730 million people do not get enough to eat every day. Distribution of food is uneven because poor people cannot *afford* food. In addition, farmland in many underdeveloped regions is now in cash-crop production. These cash crops can earn the money needed for foreign imports, such as energy, but local traditional farmers are driven onto marginal land. Cash cropping has degraded the land—erosion, desertification, and deforestation are now serious problems.

Industrial nations have mechanized agriculture. One result of this new kind of farming is that chemicals and pesticides have poisoned our **groundwater** and food. New farming techniques are now being tested to try to preserve our food supply. Will this be enough? Can we develop other food sources to adequately feed humankind? Are we willing to explore new methods of sharing the earth's resources?

ENERGY

Energy is needed for industrial development. There could be an endless supply of energy in the world. However, humans have relied on easily accessible **fossil fuels**. We have now run down these nonrenewable resources to dangerously low levels. Another serious problem is that the uncontrolled use of fossil fuels has resulted in high levels of pollution. This damage to the environment threatens life support systems. Danger signs include the warming of the earth's atmosphere because of the greenhouse effect and thermal heat waste, the pollution of water and soil from **acid rain**, and the destruction of the earth's forests.

Are there other sources of energy? Nuclear energy is controversial because, although clean, it is still quite inefficient, and the disposal of radioactive waste poses tremendous problems. Perhaps solar energy is the answer. Can we harness the power of the sun effectively and economically? Until we harness other sources of energy we may have to conserve our current energy sources. How can we limit energy demands and still sustain economic growth?

INDUSTRIALIZATION

Industrialization is perhaps the greatest boon to our standard of living. People in industrial nations live much more comfortably than people in underdeveloped countries. Industrialization has shortened working hours, improved diets, made more material goods available, and enabled more people to enjoy their leisure. As resources in industrial countries run out, these nations look elsewhere for the raw materials for industry. By contrast, underdeveloped nations struggle to feed increasing numbers of people. Industrialization is costly, and many

Along with industrialization comes an improved standard of living. Industrial workers assist in the growth of their country's economy.

ONE WORLD

countries are deeply in debt because of their attempts to build industrial plants. There are also other barriers to industrialization. Traditional societies sometimes find it hard to adapt to an industrial culture. Development projects aimed at producing goods to enhance the quality of life have had mixed results which are often the result of political, religious, social, and military interference.

Whenever it takes place, industrialization directly threatens our **biosphere**. Precious resources are consumed and industrial wastes pollute our environment. Thus, our desire for ever-higher standards of living threatens our very lives. Can we use our remarkable technology without destroying the environment? Is industrialization of the entire globe advisable or even possible?

GLOBAL CO-OPERATION

The problems humans have created in their physical and cultural environments are global in nature. What happens to one part of the total environment affects all the other parts. The solution to these problems can only be reached by co-operation among the world's peoples and their national leaders. The interdependence of the environmental systems dictates a joint approach so that future generations might enjoy the earth's bounty. Years of warfare have destroyed large quantities of both human and physical resources. It now seems that an international crisis is coming as we scramble for a share of the resources which remain.

Will nations go to war to maintain their standard of living? Can we co-operate in solving our mutual problems without destroying the environment? Do we have alternatives? Foreign aid to industrialize the underdeveloped world, sharing resources in the Antarctic, and controlling the oceans' wealth are only some of the issues we must deal with globally.

CONCLUSION

Humans have survived by adapting to and controlling their natural environment. In the process, we have developed technology to better our condition. Unfortunately, as a result of the uncontrolled use of natural resources, our very life support systems are in jeopardy. We are using up our natural resources

The solutions to the world's problems are arrived at by co-operation or by conflict. Through conflict, much of the earth's human and physical resources have been destroyed.

and polluting our environment, ultimately threatening our very lives. The earth will continue to exist without us, but we cannot exist without the vital elements of the biosphere. Can we sustain economic growth and development without damaging our supply of natural resources? Will the scarcity of resources lead to conflict or co-operation amongst societies? How will we deal with this challenge?

The first step is to find out as much as possible about the environment and our impact on it. Once we begin to understand our role on the earth, we can begin to search for practical ways to secure a future for the biosphere and its living species. Physical and cultural solutions to global threats to ourselves

Chapter 1
INTRODUCTION

Solutions to our global problems are possible. We must co-operate with one another to learn about these threats and to devise methods of solving them.

and the environment are possible. We must act together to find them. To continue as we are invites disaster. Our response as individuals may well determine the fate of the earth.

2

PLANET EARTH

The quality of life is increasingly affected by environmental issues of an interdependent global concern.

WARMED BY THE RADIATION from a nearby star, the planet earth is, as far as we know, the only planet in our universe capable of sustaining life. Only earth has the precise conditions that make life possible. Of these the most important is the presence of large amounts of surface water and an atmosphere that sustains respiration. On the planet's surface, some 5 million species of animals and plants live. All life on earth exists within a thin layer called the biosphere. The biosphere includes the atmosphere (air), hydrosphere (water), and lithosphere (land). Within the biosphere natural forces maintain the correct mixtures of gases, solids, and liquids necessary for life. Anything that interferes with the forces of the biosphere places, to some extent, all life at risk. If we destroy our biosphere, we have nowhere else to go.

Life is fragile and requires precise conditions. To our knowledge only the planet earth has the conditions suitable for life.

Humans have overcome some of nature's apparent limits by constructing artificial environments. However, for the most part, we remain overwhelmingly dependent on the natural environment. But care must be taken if the planet is to remain habitable. In the past, relatively small numbers of humans have had little impact on the biosphere. Today an increasing global population has placed new strains on those natural forces that create and sustain life to a point where what happens to one affects them all. Earth can exist without humans but humans cannot exist without the earth.

The direct link between increased human activity and the state of the biosphere is a matter of growing concern. Air pollution attacks the atmosphere and affects global weather patterns. Toxic wastes make soil and water resources unusable. The oceans have the food potential to sustain a far larger world population than now exists, but they have become a sewer for human and industrial wastes. Constant demands for more consumer goods and higher standards of living have put a heavy burden on chemical and mineral resources. Many of these non-renewable resources are being used far faster than they can be replaced.

Whether the planet stays habitable or not will depend on several factors, including population growth and global lifestyles. To preserve the future we need to learn as much as we can about the natural forces that sustain life and what these forces can tolerate. We must begin to better understand the

ONE WORLD

physical limits to growth if we are to avoid crossing the threshold into extinction.

Humans are part of the biosphere. Our activities have a direct affect on natural life support systems.

Earth-sensing satellites help scientists to unravel some of the mysteries of earth's natural forces. Scientists now know that natural forces once thought to be separate systems are in fact all part of a complex global whole. What happens to one system has a direct affect on all the others. Scientists have only begun to study the affect of humans

As far as we know, earth is the only planet in the universe that is able to support life. Pictured here is a whirlpool galaxy in deep space. Earth is but one planet in one galaxy.

Chapter 2

PLANET EARTH

on the biosphere and its systems. It is likely that the biosphere can support many more people at a high standard of living if the planet's resources are managed wisely. But first we must learn more about the natural forces that sustain life: the sun, and the biosphere and its constituent parts—the atmosphere, hydrosphere, and lithosphere.

Scientists use pictures taken from space in order to assess the weather patterns on earth. For the first time humans are able to achieve a global perspective.

EARTH-SENSING SATELLITES

Earth-sensing satellites use false colour imagery to gather data about the biosphere. Fed into sophisticated computers, this information is used by scientists to create predictive models for the future. Gathering a database on current conditions is the first step in attempting to understand how the planet's life support systems work, and in discovering what they will tolerate.

ENERGY FROM THE SUN

The earth moves at millions of kilometres an hour towards an unknown destination. Our planet is linked to the sun, which holds it captive and decides its fate. Its radiation energizes the world's life support systems. Solar energy powers the oceans and atmosphere. The food we eat is solar energy converted through photosynthesis. The fuels we use are stored sunlight. Without **solar radiation**, the earth's liquids would freeze and its gases would puddle on the frozen ground. The cooling of a solar eclipse or the chill of a cloudy day remind us of what would happen without the sun.

Our nearest star, the sun, acts as an energy pump. Solar flares, like the one shown in this photograph, change the amount of energy the sun gives off.

Only a small portion of the total solar radiation reaches the earth. Cloud cover reflects some back into space. Water vapour and carbon dioxide absorb some into the atmosphere. Much of that radiation which reaches us reflects back into space when it strikes the earth's surface. Different ground cover reflects different amounts of radiation. Ice and snow reflect the most and forested regions the least. This uneven reflection causes the atmosphere to move, and mixes the gases we need for life. Some of the radiation absorbed by the earth goes back into space as heat waves. These heat waves cannot go through cloud cover or smog, and are thus often trapped close to the surface. They raise temperatures in what is called a greenhouse effect. Generally, the radiation absorbed by the earth each day must be balanced by a similar amount of radiation sent back into space. One can guess what would happen if this balance were upset.

ONE WORLD

Changes in the amount of solar radiation govern the earth's natural forces. From 150 million kilometres away, the sun seems a steady and constant source of heat and light. The sun's rays, however, are not uniform. There are huge storms on and below its surface. Solar flares and sunspots vary in the amount of energy given off. This affects the amount of energy received by the earth and disrupts the planet's natural forces. Droughts and monsoons have now been linked to unusual solar activity. More threatening is the 40 per cent increase in lethal gamma rays and ultraviolet rays which reach the earth during heavy sunspot activity.

Thus, life on earth is tied to the relationship between the sun and our planet. Other planets are cold and barren. Only earth has the conditions to support abundant life. Our star, the sun, provides the energy we need to exist.

THE ATMOSPHERE

The atmosphere is the thin layer of gases that surrounds the earth. It protects life from dangerous radiation, changes solar rays into energy, and contains the right mix of gases for life. Almost all of the atmosphere lies within 29 kilometres of the earth's surface. The remaining 1 per cent extends to a distance of 10 000 kilometres into space. This ocean of gases and water vapour weighs 5000 million tonnes and presses down upon us at 101.3 kilopascals, balancing the outward pressure of our body fluids.

High above the earth the **ozone layer** shields against dangerous high energy solar rays. Ozone, unfortunately, is vulnerable to a number of things made by people. Nitrous oxides from jet engine exhausts, freons used in refrigerants, and **chloroflourocarbons** used in propellants can stop the formation of ozone. These gases have no toxic effect on humans. However, in the stratosphere they react with ultraviolet rays and impede the production of ozone. They could reduce or destroy this vital shield which protects life from deadly rays.

At lower levels, winds and currents made by the uneven heating of the earth's surface maintain a constant mix of gases. Without this mixing, the gases would become concentrated in dangerous amounts. A mixture of 76 per cent nitrogen and 21 per cent oxygen is optimal for life. Nitrogen prevents the oxygen from bursting into flame. If there were more oxygen, the entire planet would become a raging inferno. The remainder of the air is composed of many other gases. These include argon, an inactive gas, and very small amounts of carbon dioxide. Increased carbon dioxide levels would mean painful suffocation.

Carbon dioxide helps change solar energy into sugars and starches. Plants inhale it and break it down into the carbon atoms that are the building blocks of life. Excess oxygen is sent into the air. Animals inhale the oxygen and exhale carbon dioxide, which in turn is used by plants. This natural cycle is now upset by human activity. Since the industrial revolution began, some 230 billion tonnes of human-made carbon dioxide have gone into the air. Water vapour and accelerating plant and forest growth absorb much of it. Despite this, carbon dioxide levels have increased by as much as 17 per cent. This figure could double by the turn of the century.

Other industrial waste gases, such as dioxides of sulfur and nitrogen, have also changed the composition of the atmosphere. These waste gases trap heat waves close to the ground, raising temperatures. A 4 to 5 degree Celsius rise in global temperatures would be a planetary disaster. The polar ice caps would melt, the oceans would rise, and

---

A HOLE IN THE OZONE

Chlorofluorocarbons (CFCs) and other synthetic chlorinated chemicals contribute enormously to the growing "hole" in the ozone layer over Antarctica. The present level of ozone depletion over Canada is about 10 per cent. A 1 per cent decrease in ozone means a 2 per cent increase in harmful ultra-violet rays from the sun, and a potential 4 per cent increase in skin cancer among humans.

CFCs have been banned in aerosol deodorants, anti-perspirants, and hairsprays, but are still used in other aerosols, such as insecticides, spray-on shoe polish, household cleaning agents, car care products, and artificial whipped cream. CFCs are also found in refrigerators, air conditioners, foam production, and certain solvents.

Chapter 2

PLANET EARTH

Pictured here is a Sudbury, Ontario plant. The effluent coming out of the stack contains sulfuric acid. The acid in the effluent will fall back to contaminate the earth with acid rain.

coastal cities would be flooded. These gases also mix with water vapour in the air and fall back to earth as acid rain. Acid rain damages the landscape and destroys fresh water lakes, as well as harming many plants and animals.

Any change to the atmosphere is cause for concern. Until recently, humans did not trigger most climatic changes. However, people are now changing the atmosphere in significant ways. Humans have almost totally re-shaped the planet's cover through the construction of enormous cities and the expansion of farmlands and pastures. This has changed the way in which land surfaces reflect and absorb solar energy, and has dramatically altered the pattern of air currents. The effect of all this on global weather and climate gives cause for increasing concern.

THE HYDROSPHERE

The hydrosphere is made up of all the bodies of water on earth. Oceans cover most of the world's surface. The Pacific Ocean alone is greater in area than all the planet's landmass above sea level. The interplay between the oceans' surfaces and the atmosphere determines our climate and influences our environment. The oceans and seas are also the source of vast quantities of food and the millions of tonnes of fresh water humans need daily.

THE RESTLESS OCEANS

We most often think of oceans as stable, even though their surfaces are stirred by currents and winds. But the world's waters are far from quiet. They are restless and teeming with life. They conceal currents and whirling gyres, as well as upwellings and downflows that are as spectacular as any storm in the atmosphere. With the help of satellites, scientists are only now beginning to understand the ocean deeps.

Seen from above, the oceans appear alive with streams and gyres. The gulf stream in the North Atlantic shimmers like a river as it meanders towards Europe. It carries 5000 times the amount of water as the total volume of the Mississippi River. It can travel as far as 161 kilometres a day as it sweeps into the Atlantic through the straits of Florida. The gulf stream has no banks, yet does not mix with the water around it. Bluer than the water that confines it to its path, its edges are marked by enormous schools of fish.

The stream breaks into two parts in the northeastern Atlantic. One part goes on to influence the climate of Iceland. The other part turns and heads down to the coast of Africa before turning in on itself. It is a vast gyre, or wheel, some 2092 kilometres round. A single revolution takes years. A similar stream in the Pacific is called the black current because of its deep indigo or dark violet-blue colour. It sweeps warm waters from the tropics against the shores of Japan and back to the coast of California. Each of these streams and gyres eventually breaks up against the continental shores, splitting into many smaller eddies and currents.

The oceans are also mixed vertically. If they were stagnant, the bottom layers would quickly fill with

13

ONE
WORLD

This oceanic waterspout demonstrates the bond between sea and air. Ocean water that evaporates into the air falls to the surface again as fresh water or snow. Tornadoes that form over water are called waterspouts.

the decay of dead sea animals. Without deep currents to stir the waters, noxious fumes would kill all the creatures living on the bottom. The earth's heat would warm the animal and plant decay until it was much hotter and lighter than the water above it. The unstable ocean would then turn over, bringing the whole mess to the surface, poisoning the atmosphere.

Fortunately, the deeps are restless. Water is forever sinking from the surface to the bottom and rising again. Water cooled at the poles is denser and heavier than water elsewhere, and sinks. It then forces the water at the bottom to rise in great upwellings along distant shorelines. On the oceans' bottoms the water advances in a thousand-year journey towards the equator. It does this in horizontal layers that tend not to mix with other layers except along the ocean rims. Each layer has a slightly different salinity and temperature.

When the horizontal currents reach the continental shelves, they rise, carrying rich nutrients to the surface. Sunlight acts on these nutrients and stimulates the growth of small sea plants called plankton. The plankton blossom in cool waters and they are in turn eaten by tiny fish: an entire food chain springs to life.

A DANGEROUS CLIMATIC PHENOMENON

El Niño is a climatic phenomenon located mainly along the coast of Peru. In most years the fishing off the coast is good. Trade winds blow steadily across the Pacific, pushing the surface waters westwards towards Japan. The winds heap up the water on the western side of the ocean. But when the trade winds die down or reverse themselves, the water piled up off Asia sloshes back across the Pacific, forming a ceiling of hot water about 9 degrees Celsius above normal and some 137 metres thick. This seals in the cooler bottom waters and prevents upwelling. Plankton are killed and the food chain is interrupted, with disastrous effects on the fishing industry. The water grows hot and still. The fish stocks disappear as feverish water spreads out a quarter of the way around the world, covering half of the Pacific Ocean.

At the same time, the hot surface water heats the air above it, keeping the winds from reasserting themselves and causing a major disruption to the atmosphere. This creates a chain reaction that affects the climate around the world, leading to unusual storms and droughts. In 1983, it caused torrential rains in Ecuador and Peru, drowning deserts in 4.5 metres of water. Huge storms raged along the North American coastlines. Typhoons struck in the Pacific and El Niño probably contributed to the terrible droughts in South Africa, Indonesia, and Australia.

Chapter 2

PLANET EARTH

Drought renders vast areas of land uninhabitable. These woven grain-storage huts have been abandoned because of the effects of El Niño.

OUR FRAGILE RESERVES

Oceans are also the source of the world's fresh water reserves. A trillion tonnes of liquid evaporate each day from the planet's surface. Taken into the atmosphere as water vapour, this vapour falls to the surface as rain or snow. Most falls directly back into the oceans but enough falls over land to moisten the soil and fill lakes and streams before returning to its source.

Humans use only 1 per cent of the earth's total fresh water reserves. There are enough fresh water stocks in the ice caps and glaciers to sustain far larger human demands. But the uneven distribution of rainfall has resulted in large desert regions. To remedy this, humans have built extensive water storage and water transfer systems. The nearly 1000 dams that are built each year add to the controlled reserves, to the extent that humanity now manages about 30 per cent of the world's run-off groundwater. Engineers totally regulate some rivers. These rivers fill the needs of the people living along their banks, but create problems of sedimentation, soil salinization, and increase the likelihood of earthquakes. The Netherlands' diking system and the construction of the Aswan dam are examples of humanity's ingenuity in bending nature to its needs.

Humans affect water quality and quantity in many ways. Changes to river and stream basins interfere with the natural hydrological cycle. The need to increase food production has led to the use of chemical fertilizers and pesticides. These now

The Aswan Dam on the Nile River, in Egypt, stores enough water to irrigate almost 3 million hectares of farmland. The hydroelectric capacity of the dam is 10 billion kilowatts per hour.

find their way into our water supplies. Around 500 million tonnes of dissolved salts are carried into the oceans each year. Human and industrial wastes have already poisoned some coastal waters, inland lakes, and rivers. Because many of these chemicals are synthetic, nature cannot break them down. They stay intact over the years, and when eaten by fish, can be transmitted into the food chain where they often prove toxic to animal life.

We do not know how much abuse the oceans can sustain before they are damaged beyond repair. The oceans' resources, including fish, are fragile. However, oceans are renewable, and can maintain a larger population if properly managed.

The dumping of industrial waste into the Fraser Estuary in British Columbia has a negative impact on the composition of the water.

THE LITHOSPHERE

The lithosphere is made up of all the land on the planet. The human impact on the planet's land surface is greater than on any other part of the biosphere. There are few human activities that do not change the natural landscape in some way, from the creation of new land formations for housing, to activities associated with business, industry, and leisure pursuits. In many regions of the world there are no natural habitats left. By changing the landscape, humans set in motion unexpected chains of events.

The ability to change the natural environment is one of the major characteristics of humans. The need to modify the resources of the lithosphere is brought about because of the uneven and disparate nature of the planet's natural resources of soil and minerals. To a great extent one's standard of living and materal wealth depend on one's location on the earth's surface. Those cultures that are rich and powerful owe their position to the fact that they contain within their borders the world's industrial heartlands. For the many other nations who are not so blessed, life is much simpler and much poorer.

There is not as much soil on the planet as we might think. It is the thinnest and most vulnerable of the globe's life support systems. It provides the chemicals and minerals our bodies need for life; in fact, all forms of life require nutrients from the soil. Yet in places the soil is only a few centimetres thick. In many areas, such as mountainous and desert regions, it is non-existent. Soil is far more precious to our future than the rarest diamonds and jewels.

Geography and location determine the disparity between human societies.

Demands for more food, as well as minerals for the creation of manufactured goods, have sped up changes to the lithosphere. Most easily accessible land that can produce food is now under cultivation. Additional land is added to the total through drainage and irrigation, or through the process of deliberate deforestation. This has caused increased erosion of forest soils. Cultivation breaks open the top soil, making it vulnerable to wind erosion. Some areas of the globe are feeling the effect of

ONE

WORLD

Mechanized harvesting is a way of life in industrialized countries.

the loss of fertile soil, a loss which totals more than 25 million tonnes a year. A loss of 2.5 centimetres of topsoil can reduce crop yields by as much as 6 per cent. Short-term gains from wasteful farming practices are exhausting a basic resource.

Humans have changed the planet's soil to increase short-term crop yields. Fertilizers and herbicides are routinely tilled into the farmlands, while pesticides are sprayed over crops and pastures. Some of the additives dissolve in water and end up polluting lakes and rivers. Nitrate, phosphate, and potash fertilizers produce short-term gains, but cause disastrous soil exhaustion in the long run.

Besides depleting the soil, we have placed heavy demands on the earth's mineral and chemical deposits. These resources take geological ages to form and store. Their rate of replacement is very slow. Most metals, apart from iron and aluminum, have only a fraction of their reserves left. Yet their exploitation continues. Humans move around 3000 million tonnes of rock and dirt every year to extract minerals needed by industry. We will probably double this massive output by the turn of the century.

Mineral exploitation is also a fact of industrialization. This picture shows iron ore mining in Newfoundland. Note the devastation to the lands surrounding the mining activity.

As surface minerals have been depleted, industry has looked underground. New processes of refining and smelting were invented to extract the last gram of metal from base ores. By-products of the refining processes often pollute the atmosphere. Lead, mercury, and sulfur and nitrous oxides are damaging pollutants, as are automobile exhaust and carbon dioxide from burning fossil fuels. These are the side effects of the human demand for more industrial products.

Industrial peoples maintain a high standard of living at great cost to the environment. Using up resources to sustain material wealth cannot go on forever. The industrial nations want to replace dwindling conventional mineral supplies by mining the ocean floors. Rich deposits of magnesium, nickle, copper, and cobalt have been located on the world's seabeds. Industrial nations are already developing ways to extract them, driven by a concern that they not be left without crucial, but increasingly scarce, strategic minerals.

Technological progress, industrial and economic growth, and development place critical strains on the biosphere.

The immediate, or at least short-term, answer to scarcity is to replace natural minerals with synthetics. The use of synthetics has increased a hundredfold in the last decade. Over 150 chemicals are now produced in annual amounts greater than 45 million kilograms. Another 70 000 are in use. A thousand new ones are added every year. They are usually not toxic in themselves, but as wastes they tend to concentrate as sediments in lakes and rivers. From there they can enter the food chain in dangerous amounts as concentrates in chemical structures which nature is unable to break down. PCBs, known cancer-causing agents, are now found in all species. They remain in the fatty tissues of the body for long periods of time. The most life-threatening of all these materials, though, are the wastes from nuclear power installations. Nuclear waste is highly radioactive, and will remain so for thousands of years.

The continued exploitation of the earth's crust for minerals and construction materials should be a matter of widespread concern. In 300 years we have used up treasures that took millions of years to create. We are consuming them faster than they can be replaced. It took, for example, 600 million years to form the conventional oil that we will likely use up in just two centuries.

The earth's natural resources could support a far larger population at a higher average standard of living. Different approaches to using resources will have to be used to reach this goal.

Oil is one of the most demanded resources on earth. How long will supplies last?

CONCLUSION

The only viable life we know exists within a thin layer on the surface of the earth called the biosphere. The biosphere is the only place in the universe that has the correct conditions for life. It is made up of the atmosphere, hydrosphere, and lithosphere. All these are interconnected. What affects one system affects them all. Humans are part of the biosphere and as part of the system what we do affects all the other parts. We cannot exist apart from other forms of plant and animal life.

Human activity endangers the biosphere in many ways. Humans interfere with the natural processes by taking energy and matter from nature and converting them for domestic and industrial use. This is done to improve their standard of living and quality of life. We are using the earth's resources at an alarming rate, and inevitably they must give out. As a result of demands for higher standards of living, new substances are being added to the planet's air, water, and land. Synthetic compounds enter the natural cycles and food chains, where they are a hazard to life and a stress on the environment. Rapid population growth and the hectic pace of technical development mean that the effect of future changes to the environment will be even greater. We can better manage and modify the rate of change. It may be more difficult to change the frequency of human impact. This will require political and social action, involving controlled management of the earth's natural forces.

Much human activity endangers the biosphere, but with changes in human activity, like bottle recycling, humans can help to save the biosphere.

QUESTIONS

1. Describe the composition of the biosphere.
2. How is life maintained in the biosphere?
3. Describe four effects of human activities which threaten the make-up of the biosphere and, ultimately, life on earth.
4. What is the relationship between the biosphere and life on the planet?
5. Describe how solar energy is transformed into heat and food.
6. How does unusual solar activity affect the earth?
7. How does the composition of the atmosphere support life?
8. What is the ozone layer? What can be done to help preserve the ozone layer? Can it be replaced?
9. How do humans affect the atmosphere? What are the likely results of this activity?
10. What natural processes keep the ocean waters in motion? Why must both air and water be kept in motion?
11. Describe how the surface temperature of the oceans affects global climate and weather. Is this the same relationship as between land cover and atmosphere?
12. What natural processes change brine into fresh water?
13. Why are major cities sited on rivers, lake shores, and coastlines? List the many uses that humans make of water.
14. Explain how humans affect both the quality and quantity of water supplies.
15. Is the earth in danger of running out of water? Explain your answer.
16. How does the lithosphere support life?
17. Describe the ways people have changed the surface of the lithosphere to increase farmland for food production. What are the dangers in these processes?
18. Shortages in natural energy and mineral supplies have resulted in the creation of synthetics. These substitutes pose special dangers to the environment. What are these dangers? How can they be overcome?

19. How does changing the landscape affect climate and weather patterns?
20. What approaches to using resources should be taken to improve living standards for the world's peoples?

ACTIVITIES

1. **Scrapbook Assignment:**
   Collect newspaper and magazine articles and pictures on current environmental issues. Consider all parts of the biosphere, i.e., articles on air, land, and water. Write a brief summary for each part of the environment and predict solutions for the problems mentioned.

2. **Research Report:**
   Write a research report on one of the following topics:
   a) the ozone layer
   b) the greenhouse effect
   c) El Niño
   d) La Niña
   e) air pollution
   f) water pollution
   g) mineral depletion
   h) PCBs

   In your report, define your topic clearly, explain the current state of this topic, and evaluate future effects. Suggest possible actions for the reversal of any negative effects.

3. **Display:**
   Prepare a bulletin board display illustrating the interrelated nature of our life support systems. Draw diagrams illustrating the hydrosphere, atmosphere, and lithosphere, and show how they are connected cyclically in the production of water, gases, and nutrients.

4. **Chart:**
   Make a chart of the vitamins and minerals humans need in their diet. Where do humans get these essentials? In what form are they ingested?

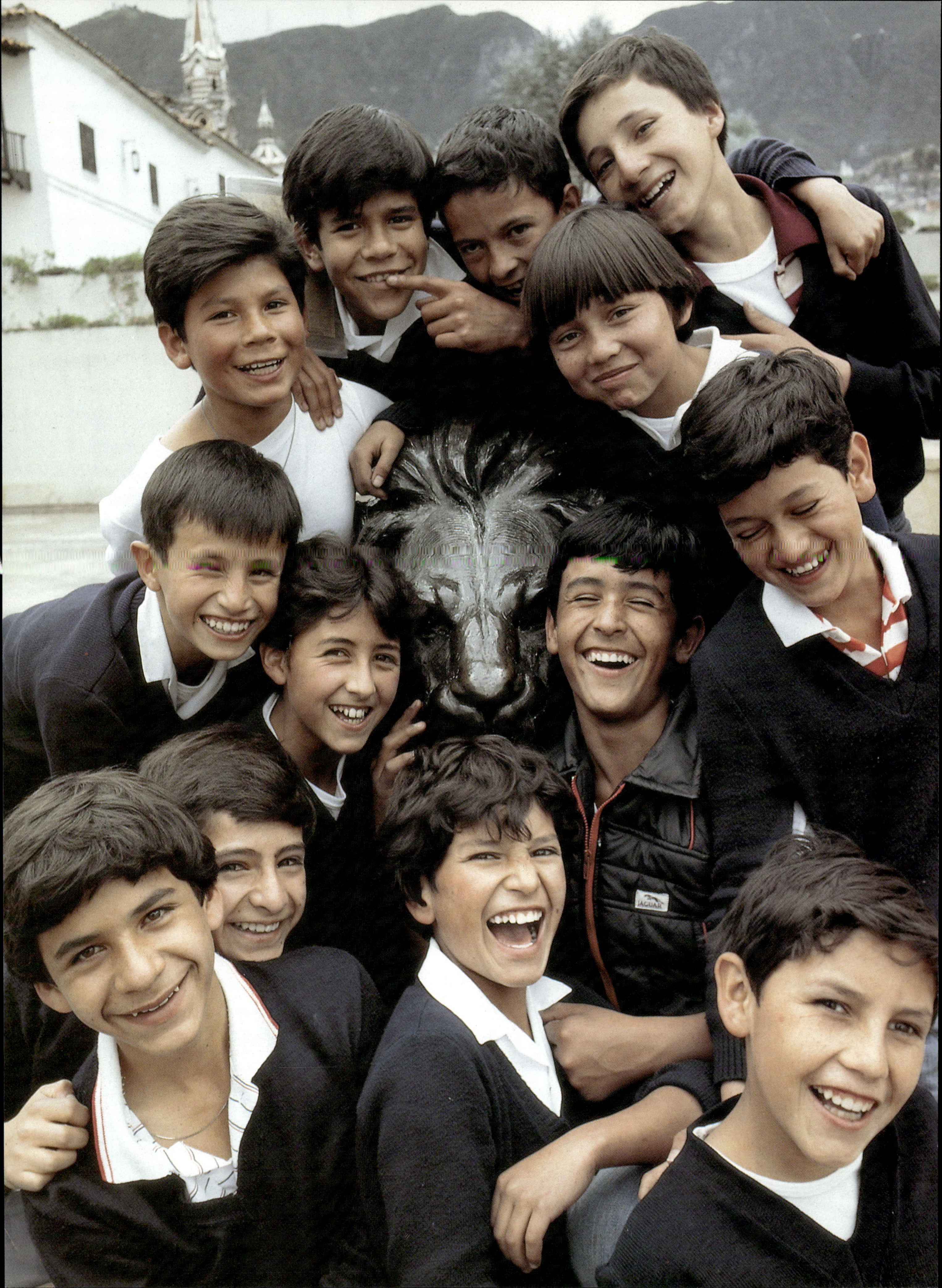
JAGUAR

3
INTERRELATED HUMAN ENVIRONMENTS

HUMANS ARE ACTIVELY organizing their world into a growing number of transnational associations. National governments, business corporations, academics, professionals, entertainers, and athletes have quite suddenly taken up the challenge of international participation. Multiple networks now connect societies in both the public and private spheres. Political, military, business, and professional leaders have taken on a cosmopolitan outlook in which they display their power through world-wide financial and economic control.

Advances in technology have broken down the barriers of space and time. Travel between continents is only a matter of hours, while communications between parts of the world are for the most part instantaneous. In the past, development strategies had to take into account how to get people and goods from one point to another. Today transportation of humans, raw materials, and finished goods, in any quantity at any time, is taken for granted. So great are the numbers of people traveling that sophisticated service industries have been developed to cater to their every need. Cities that want to be part of the emerging global culture must have acceptable airport facilities, and limosine service to modern hotels and eating establishments. These facilities are suprisingly like those found at home or in the last city visited. If the international elite demand steak sandwiches, wine, cable television, and high-tech communications, that is what they will get. The demands of travel for business or pleasure have created a transnational urban culture that recognizes no boundaries.

Today business is carried out on a global scale. Advances in technology allow people to meet on an international basis more often than was possible in the past.

ONE
WORLD

The intermingling of political and business leaders has had a positive effect. Leaders more often see things in a global setting, rather than the narrow limits of their own nation state. International co-operation is coming to be viewed as a matter of routine policy. World leaders are beginning to co-operate in the search for solutions to pressing world issues such as foreign aid, the use of natural resources, and environmental pollution controls. These matters are discussed in chapter 10.

CULTURAL BELIEFS

Isolated by geographic barriers and in possession of varying amounts of population, land, and raw materials, humans have developed a diversity of cultures. These are characterized by different languages, spiritual beliefs, and lifestyles, and an in-grown suspicion of outsiders. In the presence of strangers whom they deem alien to their way of life, they tend to be defensive. This attitude often leads to war.

Humans have chopped up the land surface of the globe into over 160 nations. In doing so they have artificially divided the human race into separate nationalities. Any atlas shows the wide variety of shapes and sizes given these units. The 36 smallest nations have populations of less than 1 million. Yet their leaders maintain they should have a voice equal to that of nations whose populations are in the hundreds of millions. Each nation jealously guards boundaries marking the extent of its territory. Some boundaries coincide with geographical barriers, such as mountain ranges, deserts, or rivers. Other boundaries are the result of war or negotiation. Yet all seem to enclose a separate nationality. This is hardly ever the case. France and Japan are two of the few truly national states. The rest have boundaries that either force different cultures to live together or divide and separate peoples. As in Nazi Germany, some states have tried to get rid of minorities within their borders through brutal massacres. The slaughters in Cambodia, the massacres in Uganda, and genocide in Ethiopia come to mind. Yet each government insists on the absolute right to manage its people without any outside interference. Problems of a global nature or processes of co-operation and negotiation are not part of their world view.

Less powerful nations fight amongst themselves, often at the behest of the superpowers. This guerilla soldier fights in Angola.

Although the less powerful nations suffer interference and invasion from time to time, the superpowers such as the USA and the USSR do not. Powerful nations are a law unto themselves and they have the military, industrial, and economic strength to prove it. Successful international action needs the agreement of the superpowers because without it failure is almost certain.

Humans have divided the globe into territorial units called nation states. Each state claims the right to complete sovereignty within its borders.

The world's political make-up appears stable and permanent. In reality, it is under constant pressure to change as each state seeks to extend its influence.

Chapter 3
INTERRELATED HUMAN ENVIRONMENTS

A CLASH OF WORLDS

When advanced, industrial cultures meet non-industrial societies, the latter usually emerge as losers. Aboriginal peoples around the world find themselves in a difficult struggle to maintain traditional cultures and lifestyles in the face of determined inroads from powerful, often foreign forces.

Nowhere is this more in evidence than in the vast interior of Brazil. There, in a constant search for new mineral and forest wealth, outsiders have forced the South American country's native peoples ever-deeper into their traditional homelands, and in some cases have literally wiped out entire nations.

The Kayapo people, who live along the Xingu River in the eastern section of the Amazon Basin, are under constant attack from gold-hungry outsiders. Skirmishes have left both Kayapo and non-Indians dead and maimed. Once-pristine rivers are polluted beyond all safe use, wild game killed off or driven away. The Brazilian government's National Indian Foundation (FUNAI) attempts to serve as a buffer between the two worlds, with little success.

For the Kayapo who have survived, the future looks cloudy. Old ceremonies and dances are now observed by participants lugging cheap tape decks. Magnificent parrot-feather headdresses are augmented by gaudy synthetic neckties. As one North American anthropologist put it, "Tape recorders and clubs, aluminum cookware and thatched roofs—the Kayapo of Gorotire find themselves torn between old ways and new."

In a world slowly awakening to the realities of a fragile and damaged global environment, the struggles of peoples like Brazil's Kayapo to find a new path into the future, yet retain sensitive links to their physical surroundings, may serve as a model for societies everywhere.

Most often scarce resources or overcrowding cause these pressures. Large parts of Africa and Asia were not even independent until after World War II. Scores of new countries then formed out of the break-up of the old empires to give us the world's present political make-up. Decolonization brought political independence to most of the world's people. At the same time they took on the responsibilities of nationhood. They immediately wanted to become powerful and industrial but were sensitive to any outside influence that might replace their former masters. Tragically many of them were ill-equipped to manage their newly gained independence. Left without the ability to administer their governments, manage their resources or develop their industries, their condition rapidly deteriorated. For many of them, more often than not, civil war, economic collapse, and internal racial conflict have marked the brief period since independence.

INTERNATIONAL CO-OPERATION

The human-made international state system is designed for conflict and does not usually operate through co-operation. Tension and war are characteristic of international relations. Victory generally goes to the state with the most military and economic power. The power of a state depends on many things, including its population, food, mineral, and energy supplies, strategic location, and military capabilities. Some smaller states have developed nuclear weapons to overcome their deficiencies.

People within a nation look to the state to guarantee their security and well-being. Given a choice, they always act in their own interests and view outsiders as a threat. They and their governments are not attuned to co-operation. Yet this is exactly what is needed to solve the problems of a global nature such as human rights, the use of the planet's natural resources, and the danger human activity places on the environment.

The boundaries of the nation states are in a state of flux. They are changed by international agreement or by force.

Today's world map is the result of hundreds of years of negotiation and warfare. War between states has been common. However, modern nuclear, chemical, and biological weapons pose a threat to the biosphere as well as to the combatants. Unleashed, they could destroy the planet through radiation or by destroying food chains or the other life support systems. The world's peoples must ensure that their leaders do not resort to these weapons. Knowing from past experience that war is the great consumer of human and physical resources, there is a growing movement to choose co-operation and negotiation instead of conflict. This trend can be seen in the growing number of

ONE WORLD

regional alliances, both military and economic, and in a demonstrated popular support for co-existence. But will the nations use co-operation or will they use force to achieve their goals?

Differences over the treatment of the defeated enemies at the end of World War II, and different perspectives on the function of the state and its treatment of its peoples led to a major confrontation between the USA and the USSR. Known as the Cold War, because no shooting occurred, the two superpowers forged strong military and economic alliances with other nations such as the North Atlantic Treaty Organization and the Warsaw Pact. Unwilling to co-operate, they perfected a variety of nuclear, chemical, and biological weapons for their arsenals. Although never brought into use, these dangerous weapons helped to maintain an uneasy balance of power between the rival blocs. The readiness with which military commanders were prepared to use them during the Cuban Missile Crisis of 1962 brought a sobering reality to the world's political leaders. Since then there has been a noticeable lessening of tension and a greater willingness to co-operate. The ability of world leaders to co-operate is essential to the solution of the critical problems of a global nature that we face today.

The forces of nationalism, a devotion to one's country, make co-operation between states difficult. Political leaders do not hesitate to rouse public opinion in response to any perceived threat to

These UN soldiers are trained to maintain peace by use of military force.

Chapter 3

INTERRELATED HUMAN ENVIRONMENTS

the homeland. By effectively using staged media events, they can easily turn healthy national feelings into a frenzy of hatred for their neighbours. Apart from the risk of war, which many leaders are prepared to take, this has the advantage of explaining failures at home in terms of evil outside interference. Properly channeled, the crusading hysteria of the mob can be used to wage lengthy war, or to at least solidify the power of the regime. The extremes of supernationalism make peaceful international relations impossible.

The next major international crisis could well be over environmental issues. Industrial and non-industrial nations competing for the earth's dwindling supply of resources could cause conflict. The

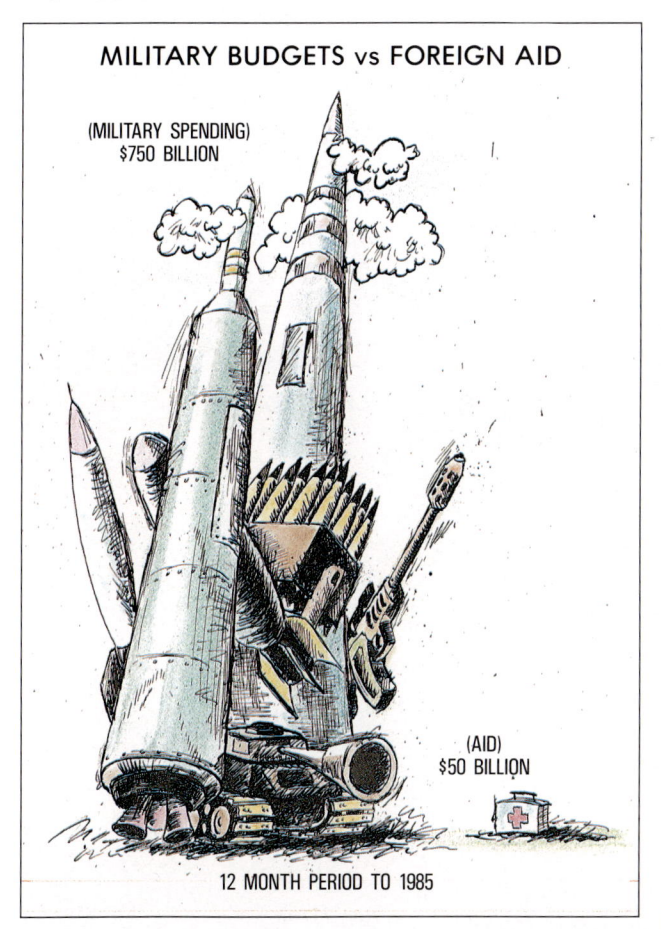

MILITARY BUDGETS vs FOREIGN AID

(MILITARY SPENDING) $750 BILLION

(AID) $50 BILLION

12 MONTH PERIOD TO 1985

Developed countries spend 30 times more on their military budgets than they do on foreign aid. The equivalent of just one year's world military spending could run the entire United Nations system for 200 years.

developed nations have grown rich and powerful but in doing so they have strained the earth's ability to support life. Their industrial plants and the uncontrolled exploitation of non-renewable resources will eventually cause irreversible damage.

Public pressure might be able to force governments to agree to co-operate before it is too late. Until now people have simply adapted to worsening conditions and tolerated poverty, slum conditions, smog, and chemically treated food and water. But there is a limit to what humans can withstand. Will the powerful nations be willing to co-operate with others in order to improve the environment?

Extreme nationalism makes international co-operation improbable.

The global environmental crisis that faces us is more complex, more dangerous, and more costly than any of the major wars of the century. The global problems of food supplies, energy shortages, air and water pollution, and population growth are all international in scope. Even reversing the damage already done will take a great combined effort. No matter what action is taken, it will get a fierce reaction from the underdeveloped world. Most of the pollution, poor resource management, and growing population are in the non-industrial world, where frantic efforts are being made to catch up. The underdeveloped nations will not willingly give up their plans to industrialize in the interests of cleaner air. They want to industrialize first and then turn to environmental matters. Nor are they concerned about proper management of scarce soils when large numbers of their people are starving. Once everyone is fed they might turn to measures that would improve the environment. For now, they want a greater share of the world's industry to improve the standard of living for their own people, regardless of cost.

There are many facets to the problem of environmental damage. No one agrees about who is causing the greenhouse effect, the depletion of the ozone layer, or any of the other threats to the biosphere, let alone who should clean it up. Who would volunteer to reduce his or her standard of living to lessen environmental damage? What would you be willing to give up?

ONE WORLD

It will take a concentrated international effort to set things right. Some governments have begun to at least officially recognize that environmental damage is being done. After long negotiations, Canada and the USA have agreed to try to eliminate acid rain. Western European governments record air and water pollution. Environmental agencies monitor the biosphere and publicize their findings. Few, especially industry, take their reports seriously, but at least they are published. The UN has convened international conferences to alert the public to the problem. But talk is not action. Action means great cost. Yet something must be done before it is too late.

SUPRANATIONALISM

During the twentieth century a number of supranational organizations were founded. A number of states agreed to act together towards common goals.

> **THE WORLD COMMISSION ON ENVIRONMENT**
>
> *In 1983, the UN created the World Commission on Environment and Development. Led by Gro Harlem Brundtland, the prime minister of Norway, the commission's mandate was to propose new and practical ways to deal with the interrelated issues of development and the environment, to strengthen international co-operation on the environment, and to increase understanding of these issues and promote action by individuals, businesses, voluntary organizations, institutes, and governments. The "Brundtland Report" was published in 1987 and since then has gone back to the UN's member states for approval. In Canada, the report led to the creation of the National Task Force on the Environment, an association of environment ministers, senior executives from industry, environmentalists, and academics. The report has also spurred a number of major international conferences on the environment, such as the World Conference on the Changing Atmosphere, held in Toronto in 1988.*

Alex Chisholm (left to right) talks to Norweigen Prime Minister Gro Harlem Brundtland while Canadian Prime Minister Brian Mulroney and Minister of the Environment Tom McMillan look on during a break at the Changing Atmosphere conference in Toronto, June 1988.

Chapter 3

INTERRELATED HUMAN ENVIRONMENTS

Modern international co-operation between states dates from the League of Nations after World War I. The victors were sickened by the cost in human lives and the massive physical destruction. They founded the League as an expression of their desire to seek peace through the strategy of collective security. The concept was that all the nations were to promote peace and international stability through joint efforts. Altogether, 63 nations took part in the organization, although the total membership at any one time was not that large. Germany joined the League in 1926 and the USSR in 1934. Germany and Japan withdrew in 1933 followed by a number of other countries. The League expelled the USSR in 1939 because it invaded Finland. The USA was never a member. The League identified several areas of international concern. For example, the League set up advisory commissions on narcotics, refugees, and world health. The League created the Permanent Court of International Justice and the International Labour Organization. The concept that some difficulties were common to humankind and could be dealt with internationally outside the recognized state system was daring for its time.

Extreme nationalism, raised to fever pitch during the war by the media, doomed the League to failure. It never received the public support needed to survive. No nation would surrender its sovereignty to a supranational organization. The mood was not right for international co-operation. In addition, today's fading distinction between domestic and foreign affairs was not present then. The UN replaced the League organization at the end of World War II.

The aims of the UN were broader in scope than those of the League. Like the League, the UN was to maintain world peace and stability. In addition, it was to promote international social and economic

World peace is often maintained by show of military force.

co-operation and a universal respect for human rights. Over 80 per cent of the UN budget is for improving the standard of living of the underdeveloped world. By removing hunger and poverty as causes of instability, the UN hopes also to remove some of the causes of war. Using global agencies, like the World Health Organization (WHO), the Food and Agriculture Organization (FAO), and the United Nations Educational, Scientific, and Cultural Organization (UNESCO), it has removed some of the world's suffering. These agencies are funded by UN members, but report directly to the organization.

No organization is more aware of the global inequalities of wealth and resources than the UN. It has always sought to equalize the sharing of the world's natural resources between the developed and underdeveloped nations. Technical aid and training, development loans, famine and health relief aid, and the transfer of appropriate technology are ways the UN has promoted economic growth in the developing world.

Conflicting national interests must give way to co-operation in an increasingly interdependent world.

The UN has also helped to maintain world peace by military force. It has no army of its own. However, it relies on troops from member states to take military action when called upon. The first UN military action in the Korean War from 1950 to 1953 was a limited success. This was followed in 1956 by the astounding success in Egypt. Since that time the UN has been involved in a number of police actions. The major advantage of UN action is that no superpower is involved. Keeping the superpowers at bay greatly reduces world tensions. The UN is able to do this because the superpowers agree not to become involved.

The international military co-operation of UN peace-keeping operations has contributed to world stability. Ensuring that major powers do not become involved in regional disputes, the UN forces reduce the chance of a confrontation leading to a general war. National military units under a supranational command are only one solution to local conflicts. The superpowers appear to have accepted the process as a legitimate international activity.

The UN was not the only supranational political organization founded after the world wars. Several multi-nation alliances formed to increase the total strength and power of each member. Groups of nations banded together to form military alliances such as the North Atlantic Treaty Organization (NATO), the North American Air Defence Command, and the Warsaw Pact. Many countries co-operated in the Marshall Plan for the reconstructing of war-torn Europe, the European Common Market, Comecon (economic association of communist states), and the Organization of American States which was revived. At the same time,

---

CONFLICT IN ZAIRE

The crisis in the Belgian Congo (Zaire), after independence in 1960, showed the danger of superpower involvement in local wars. Zaire is a large landlocked country in central Africa. At the time of the Belgium withdrawal, only 14 of its 14 million people held university degrees. Europeans held all government and economic positions. Five days after independence the army mutinied and began indiscriminately killing civilians. President Kasavubu first appealed to the USA and then the UN for aid in restoring order. The superpowers and some of the large transnational corporations destroyed the stability of the newly independent nation, hoping to control the mineral-rich province of Katanga. Tensions increased, so that a major war over scarce mineral resources became possible. It was important to defuse the situation.

A combined UN force drawn from 34 nations entered Zaire in the second week of its independence. They were mainly from neighbouring African states, although Canadian forces gave communications and administrative support. The UN troops did not engage in battle. Instead, they separated the fighting factions and protected life and property. Total political collapse took place in Zaire between September 1960 and August 1961. The UN forces then found themselves fighting European-financed mercenary armies. Secretary-General Dag Hammarskjold died when his plane crashed en route to a meeting with rival factions. When the Katangese kept breaking the cease-fire, the UN forces deported all mercenaries and other foreigners in the country. The conflict did not end until 1963. After UN forces withdrew in 1964, the UN provided some technical assistance programs and other development aid to the region. UN agencies still serve some of the basic needs of the people to this day.

Chapter 3

INTERRELATED HUMAN ENVIRONMENTS

Transnational corporations link the world's businesses together and employ people in both developed and underdeveloped nations.

churches, universities and schools, corporations, and individuals sponsored thousands of new non-governmental organizations (NGOs). All aimed to provide aid to other nations and peoples. Their international activities help to cement the interrelated nature of the world's peoples.

TRANSNATIONALS

Transnational corporations are visible signs of the growing interrelatedness between the world's economies. They are linking the world's business into an integrated global economy controlled by a handful of economic giants. The idea of businesses investing in another country is not new, but the scope of today's operations raise multinationalism to new levels. Almost every large firm in the developed world has at least one international subsidiary. These provide a source of employment, low cost production, raw materials, and markets for finished goods. The concentration of global wealth in the hands of the larger transnationals is often translated into political affairs. American transnationals budgeted well over $100 million in 1984 in order to influence local governments.

ONE WORLD

FORD'S TRANSNATIONAL INVOLVEMENT

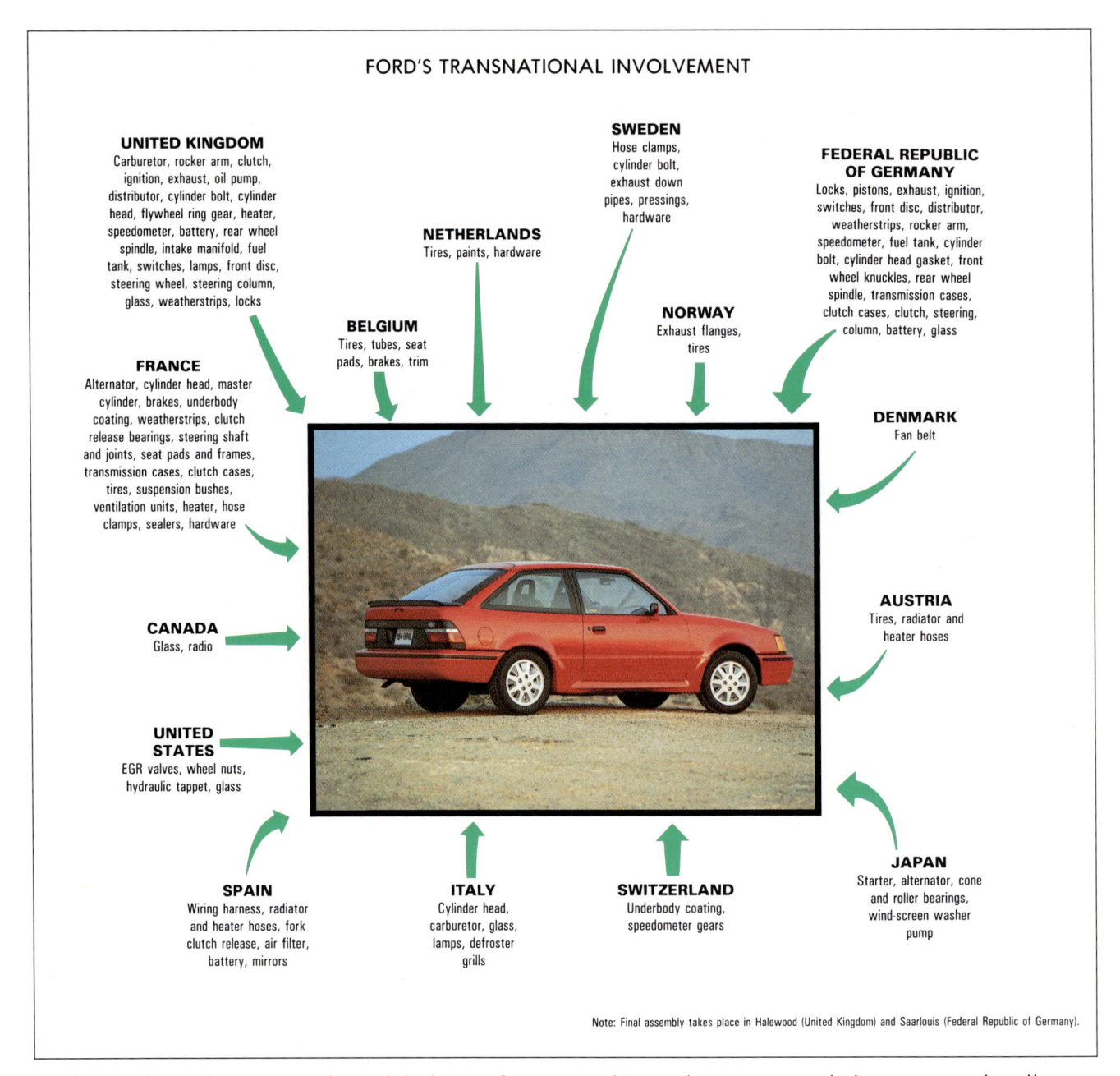

UNITED KINGDOM
Carburetor, rocker arm, clutch, ignition, exhaust, oil pump, distributor, cylinder bolt, cylinder head, flywheel ring gear, heater, speedometer, battery, rear wheel spindle, intake manifold, fuel tank, switches, lamps, front disc, steering wheel, steering column, glass, weatherstrips, locks

SWEDEN
Hose clamps, cylinder bolt, exhaust down pipes, pressings, hardware

FEDERAL REPUBLIC OF GERMANY
Locks, pistons, exhaust, ignition, switches, front disc, distributor, weatherstrips, rocker arm, speedometer, fuel tank, cylinder bolt, cylinder head gasket, front wheel knuckles, rear wheel spindle, transmission cases, clutch cases, clutch, steering column, battery, glass

NETHERLANDS
Tires, paints, hardware

BELGIUM
Tires, tubes, seat pads, brakes, trim

NORWAY
Exhaust flanges, tires

FRANCE
Alternator, cylinder head, master cylinder, brakes, underbody coating, weatherstrips, clutch release bearings, steering shaft and joints, seat pads and frames, transmission cases, clutch cases, tires, suspension bushes, ventilation units, heater, hose clamps, sealers, hardware

DENMARK
Fan belt

CANADA
Glass, radio

AUSTRIA
Tires, radiator and heater hoses

UNITED STATES
EGR valves, wheel nuts, hydraulic tappet, glass

JAPAN
Starter, alternator, cone and roller bearings, wind-screen washer pump

SPAIN
Wiring harness, radiator and heater hoses, fork clutch release, air filter, battery, mirrors

ITALY
Cylinder head, carburetor, glass, lamps, defroster grills

SWITZERLAND
Underbody coating, speedometer gears

Note: Final assembly takes place in Halewood (United Kingdom) and Saarlouis (Federal Republic of Germany).

Modern industrialization involves global manufacturing. This Ford Escort network diagram graphically portrays the transnational involvement of Ford's operation.

The larger transnationals such as General Motors and Sony have enough economic power and influence that they can dictate policies that affect the well-being of most people in the free world. Their profits and budgets are larger than all but the largest nation state. The number of their employees far outstrips most government bureaucracies. With some degree of legitimacy, transnationals are viewed by host nations as a threat to their own power. The very fact that they could pull out their operations and relocate plants and jobs elsewhere is enough to make government agencies pause to take notice.

Chapter 3
INTERRELATED HUMAN ENVIRONMENTS

> **TRANSNATIONAL CORPORATIONS**
>
> *There are those who believe that transnational corporations have ushered in a genuine world economy —what some experts have called the "global shopping centre."*
>
> *These experts argue that the global corporation is the first institution in human history dedicated to central planning on a world scale. They point out that these companies measure their successes and their failures, not by the profits or losses of a single national subsidiary, but by the growth in global profits, and global market share increase or decrease.*
>
> *Supporters of the transnational corporations point out that, under the threat of nuclear annihilation and an ecological crisis that hang over all air-breathing creatures, the logic of global planning has become irresistible. These people, usually from the developed world where virtually all transnational corporations are ultimately based, point out that in a world whose planetary resources may well not last forever, efficiency is worthy of reverence. For them, notions of nationhood and nationalism are completely outdated. As the chairman of the board of IBM once asserted, "the boundaries that separate one nation from another are no more real than the equator."*

Transnationals have been the vehicle by which a flow of finances and knowledge has been transferred from the developed to the underdeveloped world. Investment has created industrial production. Management and technical education programs have introduced millions of managers and workers to the mysteries of manufacture. The location of production and assembly plants has led to the development of new cities and transportation facilities along with the amenities of a modern urban culture. Health services, schools, better housing, and a general increase in the standard of living for those involved are all part of the scene. Other benefits include access to world markets through the parent company, the development of a local management group, and access to the latest research technology. In return, the host country is expected to establish a climate favourable to the transnational by way of low cost labour, raw materials, or energy reserves. Both parent and subsidiary are supposed to benefit.

Too often the subsidiary is left captive to the policy of the parent company. American-owned subsidiaries in Canada were forbidden to sell merchant ships or diesel locomotives to Cuba after the Castro revolution. The American government threatened to charge the parent company with trading with the enemy if the deal went through. Canada had also to rethink negotiated wheat sales to the Republic of China lest they damage trade relations with the USA. Transnationals are often used as instruments of foreign policy in deciding who can trade and who cannot.

Difficulties over possession and ownership of the Suez Canal in the early 1950s led to President Nasser of Egypt nationalizing the canal and expelling all foreigners from its operations. Compensation was given the transnationals involved for the building and maintenance of the canal over the years. In the case of the Mid-East's oil refinery nationalizations, no compensation was given the transnationals. The efforts of IT&T to subvert the Allende government in Chile, and many other examples, point out the reality that most transnationals have their own foreign policy.

Global urban culture is influenced by the presence of transnational corporations.

ONE WORLD

> **ECONOMIC IMPERIALISM**
>
> *The threat of economic imperialism to local authorities is not imaginary. By the turn of the century the transnationals will control more than three-quarters of the world's production. Who is to say this is a bad thing? Transnationals have managed to operate their world-wide networks without resorting to a major war. This is a far better record than national governments'. Since 1970 they have grown at a rate faster than national governments and have created a global system of production and distribution. Exxon, General Motors, Ford, Texaco, CitiCorp, IBM, BankAmerica, General Electric, Datsun, Sony, and Dawoo are each more wealthy and powerful than all but the most advanced nations.*

This oil tanker is part of a global transnational system.

The danger to the world economy of the power of transnationals was best illustrated during the OPEC oil crisis of the 1970s. Although referred to as a cartel, the OPEC organization does not have universal membership of all oil producing states. However, the largest volume of energy supplies for the western European nations came from OPEC sources. This made them vulnerable to the price of oil supplies on the world market. After the Yom Kippur War of 1973, the OPEC nations began a rapid escalation of oil prices from $3 a barrel to an eventual high of $34 a barrel. In addition to the increase in revenues, the move was made to force consuming countries to take a more pro-Arab stance in the disputes between Israel and its Arab neighbours. Western nations such as England, France, and Spain responded with a softening of their support for Israel, calling for that nation to retreat to the pre-1967 border. The USA began arms shipments to Saudi Arabia. Since then all the affected nations have sought to secure energy reserves against further OPEC action. Western Europe developed its own supplies from the North Sea, making England an oil exporter for the first time. After stockpiling several month's worth of supplies in underground caverns and in its own exhausted oil and gas fields, the USA returned to a more independent foreign policy.

The threat of a global cartel gaining control of vital resources and holding the world hostage is not a pleasant prospect. Attempts by individuals to gain control of the world's silver supplies were unsuccessful. But what would happen should a group of nations secure control of global food supplies through stock market manipulation? The interrelatedness of the world's economies is such that major anomalies of this nature could cause a major stock market crash, and would not be tolerated.

CONCLUSION

The nation state system is more likely to lead to conflict than to co-operation. Scarcity of resources and overcrowding are current concerns which cause pressures on national governments. Internationalism is being promoted, however, by individuals in a wide range of human activities. Supranational organizations like the UN, NATO, and the Warsaw Pact are now supplemented by non-governmental organizations. Recently the World Commission on Environment and Development demonstrated global co-operation in an effort to address the environmental crisis.

Transnationals seem to be the most striking illustration of global interrelatedness. They channel

Chapter 3
INTERRELATED HUMAN ENVIRONMENTS

A visible military presence in many countries attests to the concern nations have for their own welfare.

resources, technology, knowledge, and human energy into a global network. They wield tremendous power, and as such, must temper this power with some degree of concern for global welfare. Will they?

QUESTIONS

1. Describe the political organization of the world.
2. What pressures are placed on nation states?
3. Explain how nations arising from decolonization have dealt with independence.
4. Explain why industrialization has affected the Kayapo people of Brazil.
5. Explain how the international state system promotes conflict rather than co-operation.
6. Explain how environmental issues could lead to conflict between nation states.
7. What government action is now being taken to address environmental concerns?
8. How does the UN differ in scope and organization from the League of Nations?
9. How does the UN promote economic growth in the underdeveloped world?
10. Explain how the UN peace keeping operations contribute to world stability.
11. Explain three characteristics of transnational corporations.
12. How can transnational corporations influence government?
13. Name four benefits of transnationals to the underdeveloped world.
14. Explain how transnationals can threaten world governments.

ACTIVITIES

1. **Research Report:**
   Write a report about the effect of industrial society on the lifestyle of either Canada's native Indian people or the Inuit. Consider how family life, eating habits, livelihood, and other aspects of traditional lifestyle are affected.

2. **Citizen Action:**
   Structure a group which is committed to creating an awareness of problems in our environment and to the necessity of global co-operation in solving the problems. What specific action could you take?

3. **Collage:**
   Make a poster collage illustrating both the advantages and the disadvantages which come to an underdeveloped country as a result of transnationals.

4. **Role Play:**
   Set up groups of students to emulate the leaders of oil-rich nations and underdeveloped nations which must import oil. Each leader could have an advisory board. The oil-rich nation is attempting to influence the policy of the underdeveloped nation by threatening to withhold oil. What methods will each side use to get what it wants? Remember the global consequences of any action that is taken.

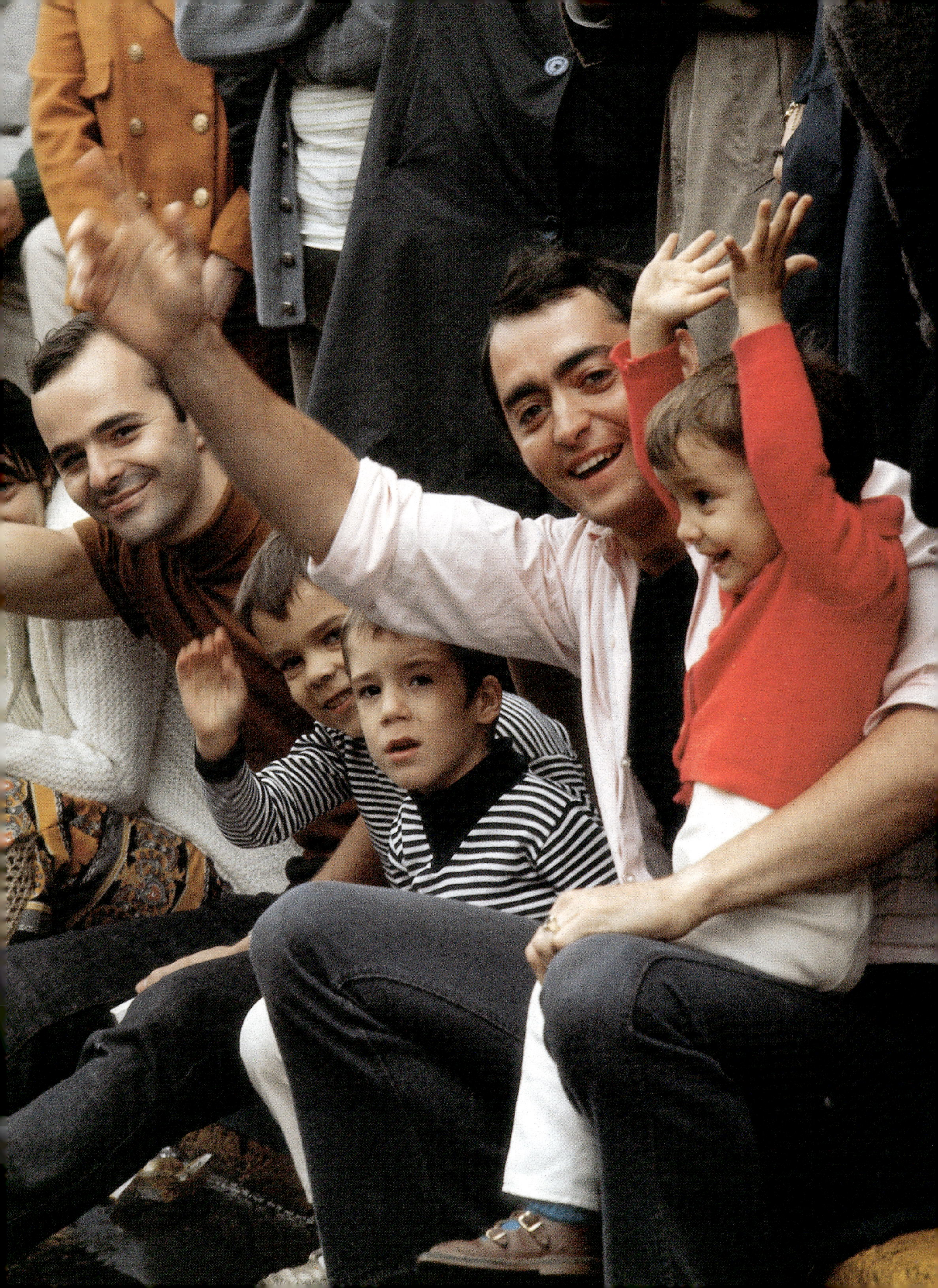

4
THE HUMAN EXPERIENCE

Humans are able to gather, interpret, and store information. They can understand relationships between themselves and nature and they can communicate. Being able to invent tools and machines has enabled them to impose their own cultural environment on nature.

HUMANS HAVE BEEN changing their natural environment for millions of years. Because they can invent tools and make machines they are able to break the bonds of nature and better their lifestyle. Through technology they can control nature and adapt to new habitats. Depending on the availability of natural resources, different societies developed different lifestyles based on their own needs. The diversity of cultures and standards of living we have today bears testimony to the ingenuity of the human spirit—needless to say each culture views the world from a different perspective. People have undergone two major cultural changes. The first was the discovery of agriculture. This led to permanent settlements and the creation of villages and cities. The second was the industrial revolution of the eighteenth and nineteenth centuries. The industrial revolution substituted machine for animal labour and led to modern urban society. Rapid increases in population and dramatic changes in culture and technology were part of both transformations.

There have been two major changes to the human condition. Agriculture led to the development of cities. Industrialization created a working class and the prospect of material plenty for large numbers of people.

In the time that humans have lived on earth they have grown in number from a few hundred thousand to over 5 billion. At first they had neither the numbers nor the skills to have much of an impact on their environment. As hunter folk they consumed mostly renewable resources. Today, however, their numbers are so great that any human activity has a direct effect on the environment. Our ability to manufacture tools and machines makes us dominant and gives us the power to control and sometimes damage our natural environment. We are just beginning to understand the impact of human activity on our natural world.

Technology adapts science to industrial processes. Technology increases humanity's control over nature and raises the standard of living.

ONE
WORLD

The human population is so great today that any human activity impacts on the environment. And yet, these ancient statues, monuments to human achievement, can last for thousands of years. It is ironic that other testimonials to human technology, like pollution, can actually inadvertently damage these statues.

At first the pace of discovery was uneven. There were long periods between important inventions. In the last few decades, however, the rate of change has sped up to the extent that it is now almost continuous. Most of the discoveries that give us our high standard of living have taken place in the last 30 years. But each change has its price in the depletion of natural resources. The scale of human activity now threatens the earth's natural resources and strains the planet's life support systems.

HUNTER FOLK

Humans are fragile despite being very adaptable. It is remarkable that they survived when other animal and plant species became extinct. Humans are inferior to other animals in many ways. Yet they survived at least three ice ages of about a million years each when many other species did not. They have lived through all of the natural disasters and have prospered. This was in part due to their diet, a flexible mixture of berries, cereals, and meats. Another great advantage was being able to walk upright. This gave them greater mobility and also freed their hands for gathering and defence. These advantages meant that humans were able to survive by moving their habitat to a new area and find alternative food sources as circumstances dictated.

Some cultures preserve their dead as mummies in order that the body may be prepared to be reunited with the soul in the afterlife.

Chapter 4

THE HUMAN EXPERIENCE

Humans would still not have survived if not for the advantage of a complex brain. Their brains allowed them to reason and to find ways of overcoming difficulties. By reasoning, people are able to respond to a situation and then choose the best action. We do not have to react instinctively as do other animals. We can think and, more importantly, we *know* that we are thinking. We can gather

In the vast lands of Africa, early humans learned to survive by adapting to their environment.

information and pass it on to others through language. Information and experience can be stored as knowledge. Humanity's ability to pass on knowledge is one of its greatest advantages. Knowledge and reasoning have placed us far beyond the other species.

People invented tools that would compensate for what their bodies lacked in strength. The making and use of tools, starting about 2.5 million years ago, were major steps in humanity's cultural development. Human needs could be thus met more efficiently, their surroundings better controlled with tools, and time made available for other things. As tools became more complex, people could control more of their natural environment. By the end of the last ice age, humans had many highly refined tools, such as bi-faced axes and knives, clothing, pottery, canoes, spears, and bows and arrows. These made life easier and improved the overall standard of living. This in turn led to population increases. Most of the processes and tools developed long ago are still in common use today.

Fire was another great discovery. The use of fire, from about half a million years ago, meant that people could live on the very fringes of the retreating ice sheets. Using fire to warm caves meant that people could truly begin to control their environment. People also used fire as a weapon to frighten predators or to stampede entire herds over cliffs during communal hunts. Food which had accidentally fallen into the fire tasted better and soon became the way to prepare raw meat and grain. The tips of animal bones and antlers hardened in the fire made better and stronger weapons. Fire greatly improved humankind's way of life.

For most of history humanity has hunted. People were parasites on the herds that shared their habitat. Generally, there were many animals close by for food. Until the climatic changes of 12 000 years ago there was little reason to change this way of life. After people had hunted to extinction the herds of giant mammoths and mastodons, they began to hunt waterfowl and smaller animals in the wetlands created by the melting ice. This new food began to disappear when the wetlands started to dry up. By the time climate had changed again, becoming similar to that of today, humans again needed to find new sources of food. About 10 000 BC, some of them began to settle along rivers and on deltas. There, on land well suited to the purpose, they began to domesticate animals. They soon came to depend more on sheep and goats than wild animals for their food, although they still hunted. Then, in many places at the same time, agriculture became a way of life.

THE BEGINNINGS OF AGRICULTURE

Agriculture was one of the two most important discoveries in history. It created a new form of civilization and made possible all the political, economic, and social institutions that we have today. It ended the hunter society that had existed for millions of years. Farming replaced all the technology of the hunt. As people began to produce their own food, society changed totally. The decision to farm began the most decisive revolution in history.

This Mbuti pygmy gardener carries bananas on his back the way others would have at the time of the discovery of agriculture.

Chapter 4

THE HUMAN EXPERIENCE

Agriculture deliberately modifies nature to establish a regular food supply. It is based on harvesting cereal crops and domesticating animals. It requires a settled population and thus cannot be undertaken by hunters who move continually. Farming led directly to the setting up of villages and cities as centres of trade and defence. It totally changed the way people lived.

Agriculture, as far as we know, started around 8000 BC at Jericho on the west bank of the Jordan River. Jericho had wheat, barley, sheep, and goats. Wild grasses and cereals on the hills around Jericho cross-pollinated and produced rye and oats. These bread grains had heavy seeds that did not fly away in the wind but dropped to the ground where they sprouted year after year. Jericho is one of the oldest cities we have discovered to date.

JERICHO

There is no doubt that humans used the wells at Jericho long before the city itself was built. The walls, which enclosed a 4 hectare plot which eventually provided a home for about 3000 people, are what remains of the first Jericho. Some small houses and a large tower, probably used to store surplus grain, are among the earliest examples of humanity-as-builder. People may have used larger houses within the city for public or religious purposes. Joshua led the tribes of Israel to lay seige to Jericho in 1200 BC. The city was important because it was the entrance to the fertile coastal plains, the fabled "land of milk and honey."

Surprisingly, cross-pollination did not have the same results in the other continents. Maize became widespread in America. In China rice became the staple crop. Vegetables and lentils dominated in India. Today there are 28 different kinds of nutritious cereal crops. However, only a few of these are in widespread use. By 5000 BC, people regularly used many plant and animal products, including milk and cheese. The agricultural revolution made possible one of the larger increases in population. By the seventeenth century the world's population was over 550 million and most of the cities were becoming vastly overcrowded.

THE FIRST CITIES

The city led to new societal relationships and responsibilities. City people had a different perspective on life based on their different lifestyle and higher standard of living. City people did not have to produce their own food and could engage in other activities. Property determined wealth and social standing. The powers and relationships of rulers, priests, soldiers, and other urban classes to each other evolved. Arts, sports, and entertainment developed in response to a need in urban people to express their creativity outside of the routine of work and to fill leisure time.

Scarcity of resources can lead to war and territorial expansion.

This ancient building is a reminder of the wealth and power of an early empire.

ONE
WORLD

Apart from its role as a storehouse and centre for trade, defence was one important function of the city. Bands of hunters pillaged the cattle and grain of rich villages. A new warrior class protected city walls against attack. The successful defence of the local region depended on the city being able to wage war. War was a human invention. Its purpose was to protect or seize scarce resources needed for survival. It was the ultimate consumer of people and materials, and soldiering became one of humanity's oldest professions. The size and number of defence positions around the first cities show that war between them was quite common.

Thus, agriculture led to the creation of cities. The cities changed the social relationships and responsibilities between humans. They also acted as storehouses and centres of trade and defence. The siege of the fortified city of Troy on the Aegean coast was one of the earliest wars recorded.

RESOURCES AND TRADE

One of the disadvantages of the city was a shortage of easily accessed basic resources. The world's natural resources are unevenly scattered over the continents. Mobile hunter folk could go to the resources. Urban dwellers could not. Those living in cities seldom had enough food, water, and mineral supplies close by. They relied on trade to make good the differences. Land and sea routes were developed to carry goods between cities and between other empires. By 500 BC, land routes linked the Mediterranean empires with those of Parthia, India, and China.

Water became valuable as cities grew in size and numbers. Fresh water is needed for life but it too is unevenly distributed around the world. In Sumeria, a system of deep underground wells tapped the water table 91 metres below the surface. These *qanats* are still in use today. But the most impressive engineering works were the Roman aquaducts. These carried millions of litres of water daily to the imperial cities from sources dozens of kilometres away. The amount and availability of fresh water determined the size and location of settlements.

Minerals and metals for making weapons and tools were also often in short local supply. Metal weapons had a sharp and hard cutting edge. Copper, bronze, and iron: each in turn gave its name to the period in history when it was predominant. When the surface ores, such as malachite, were used up, other supplies had to be found through mining. Iron was particularly valuable for swords and spears because it was both hard and flexible. The secret lay in banding the layers at high temperatures followed by rapid quenching (plunging into liquid to cool). The ability to slice through bronze shields with their iron weapons gave the Hittites temporary mastery of the eastern Mediterranean. Many roads were built to link the mines and forges of the hills to the urban centres.

This ancient aquaduct in Segovia, Spain, is a legacy to early Roman technology.

THE GROWTH OF EMPIRES

A number of cities banded together to form the first empire in the fertile and populous region of the Tigris and Euphrates rivers. Parallel developments in India and Asia are just now being studied and may predate this. The high cost of imperial administration and defence could only be met by constantly conquering new territories. War was the way to get

Chapter 4

THE HUMAN EXPERIENCE

Early Athens was at the centre of ancient Greek civilization.

additional food and mineral resources. Failure to exploit captured human and physical resources always led to decline. The decay of the agricultural base or a series of military defeats almost always led to an empire's destruction.

Nearly all the early European empires centred around the Mediterranean. There, food supplies were large enough to support significant non-farming populations. The Egyptian empire and the Greek and Roman empires that followed left great architectural monuments to their wealth and power. The pyramids, the lighthouse at Alexandria, the Parthenon, and the Colliseum in Rome that could seat 100 000 were marvels of their day. By AD 100, Rome, with its 1 million people, was the capital of the largest empire of its time. A permanent force of 35 legions kept the barbarians away from its boundaries for a thousand years. The *Pax Romana* was an outstanding example of human economic, political, military, and social organization.

But it too would outrun its agricultural base. Rome continued to expand until the year AD 212. In that year the Emperor Hadrian began to establish permanent frontiers. Within two centuries the geographic barriers of mountains, deserts, and rivers were breeched. The empire came to a sudden end.

THE FEUDAL AGE

The folk wanderings of the fifth and sixth centuries were another cause of the destruction of the Roman empire. The nomadic peoples of the Gobi Desert began to leave their traditional habitat for more attractive surroundings. They came away with what they could carry on their horses or in their carts. Attilla the Hun led the largest incursion into the West, bringing his people into Spain around AD 450. Their marauding set western civilization back by centuries and cut off the land link with India and Asia.

ONE WORLD

In place of the *Pax Romana*, a self-sufficient feudal system was created to meet local needs. Its produce sustained Europe's population for the next 10 centuries. However, it could never support more than 10 per cent of the population in a non-food producing role. During this time new inventions, such as gunpowder, paper, and mathematics, were introduced in India and China. They were not brought into Europe until the fourteenth century.

During this long period of time, people began to substitute mechanical power for manual labour in water-powered mills. Cistercian monks began to convert the energy of streams to rotary motion. From the eighth century on, water mills began to flourish. Mills had a variety of purposes, such as grinding grains, crushing sugar cane or poppy seeds, and grinding ore. The Doomsday Record of 1080 noted 5624 mills in England. That was an average of one for every fifty households. In the seventeenth century, France had 8000 flour mills, 1500 industrial mills, and 500 iron mills. Some of these were hooked together to generate as much as 120 horsepower.

The feudal system was shaken to its foundation by the Black Death in 1343. The Great Pestilence was to last until 1352, and then recur from time to time. The last major outbreak was in Marseilles in 1720, when over half of the city's population died. The plague is a toxic form of bacteria carried by fleas and spread by rats. Europe lost 20 million of its 100 million people during the first appearance. This was a disaster for an economic system based on human labour. The resultant critical shortage of labour led to the surviving workers abandoning the fields for work in urban centres. They brought with them an impetus for change.

EUROPEAN GLOBALISM

The expansion of Europe overseas, which began about 1500, was one of the most important modern developments. Daring Portuguese and Spanish sailors began to throw back or expand the ocean frontiers of Europe. They sailed on long voyages in search of the rich cities of India and Asia. Those who returned brought back fabulous cargoes of spices, teas, silks, and precious metals. Their success started a frenzied period of exploration. Hundreds of European ships swept the oceans in search of treasure and, in the process, established the first worldwide trading networks.

Europeans built fortress-cities as they expanded their empires.

Within a few generations Europeans had visited all the parts of the world accessible by sea. They colonized new lands, conquered older and more populous civilizations, and built empires that stretched around the globe. The Europeans occupied North America, Australia, New Zealand, and South Africa, and created ruling classes in Central and South America. They carved out large empires in India, Africa, and Asia, and imposed their will on China and, to a lesser extent, Japan. The wealth and resources of the other peoples of the globe seemed to be there for the taking. The riches of the planet began to flow into Europe.

By the nineteenth century, European overseas empires dominated the world. No one was strong enough to withstand them. Their colonies were new markets for manufactured goods and provided seemingly unlimited raw materials. The wealth that flowed back into Europe stimulated European economies as never before. In return, Europeans introduced their customs, technology, and languages to the rest of the world. European culture brought about far-reaching changes in their colonies. In 1790, Europe was on the verge of an even greater change. The social, political, and cultural upheavals of the industrial revolution would dwarf anything that had gone before.

THE INDUSTRIAL REVOLUTION

England was the first nation to make widespread use of mechanical power in manufacturing. This led to great increases in productive capacity and wealth. With the use of steam power in the textile industry, the British became the world's only industrial people for over 100 years beginning in the 1760s. Germany, France, and the United States became serious rivals only at the end of the nineteenth century. Just before World War I, these few nations owned or controlled most of the world's industries and more than half its wealth.

Using steam and electric power resulted in a spectacular output of goods. Industry seemed able to provide abundantly for all. The new technologies of the factory and the assembly line led to an explosion of mass-produced goods. These changes eventually led to major improvements in the standard of living. Industrialization also provided the military power that allowed the industrial states to dominate the rest of the world.

The mining of coal and other minerals helped to fuel the industrial revolution. New mining technologies have greatly increased the pace of global mineral extraction.

But the industrial revolution was more than just a change in production methods. Its effects brought about the second major change of the human condition: the replacement of human and animal power by faster and more efficient machines affected all of society.

SOCIAL CHANGES

The British experienced the political, economic, and social dislocations of industrialization first. Millions of people looking for work flooded into the unprepared cities. They thronged into the older cities and the new manufacturing towns of Birmingham, Manchester, Glasgow, and Newcastle, whose factories were on the edge of the coalfields. There they found inadequate housing and few jobs. They gathered in increasing numbers in crowded, disease-ridden slums. Society underwent a major social and political re-organization.

Urbanization destroyed the centuries-old traditions and relationships of rural society. Urban people were without the security of the village. Wage-earners had to learn a new way of life. They had to use the unfamiliar skills of specialized production methods. Workers learned to arrive at work at a set time and labour long hours tending impersonal machinery.

The entire rhythm of life was different. There was no time off as there had been between planting and harvesting. They now toiled every day to increase the output of goods. They could not provide their own food and clothing. They became dependent on others for their daily needs. They lived in large numbers in squalid tenements, hoping to earn enough money to survive. It did not seem that industrialization was of any benefit to them. This was especially true as changes in technology had also triggered an even larger surge in population growth, making each person's share of goods that much smaller.

The first solution was to move the excess population out of the cities. In the nineteenth century, the unwanted went to the "vacant" lands overseas. In one of the most remarkable mass migrations in history, between 10 and 15 million Europeans left the continent. North America received most of them, the arrival of the newcomers forming a colourful chapter in the development of the Canadian and American West. They worked the farmlands and supplied the mother country when natural resources at home ran out. The European settlers seized the opportunities their new surroundings provided with an almost religious frenzy. Wherever they went, they carried with them their European heritage. This outward migration continued until the 1890s, when European nations began keeping their populations in preparation for war.

Those who stayed home sought to better their condition through demonstrations and revolution. The power of the urban mob was first seen during the French Revolution in 1789. Later European urban uprisings triggered the political and social revolutions of 1832 and 1848, which governments ruthlessly suppressed. But the workers' demands for a

Some of the millions of Europeans who left their homelands to try their luck in the New World.

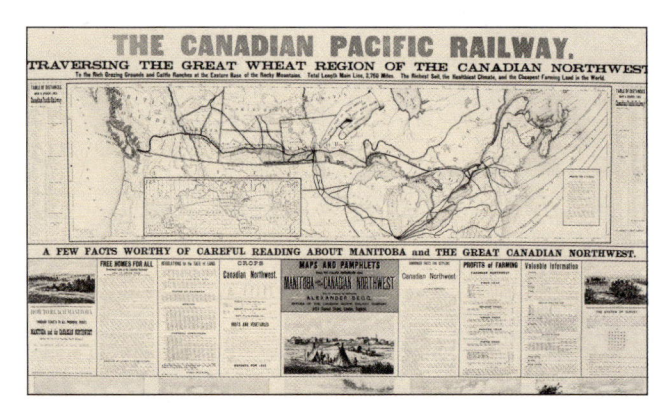

The CPR was one of the railway lines that opened up the Canadian West for millions of settlers.

better life did not stop. Tensions between the other classes and the workers heightened as the working class grew. One of the key issues of the nineteenth and twentieth centuries was and remains the relationship between workers and the rest of society.

TRANSPORTATION AND COMMUNICATION

Startling changes in transportation and communication accompanied the industrial revolution. Complex inland canal systems in England and then continental Europe carried bulk cargoes from place to place. The Suez and Panama canals shortened the sea lanes between Europe and Asia in both distance and time. But the invention of the railway was the most far-reaching change.

The railway age began with the Rainhills trials in 1829. In that year, a steam boiler outpulled a team of horses. Like the discovery of fire, the use of steam-powered engines expanded the area of human activities on earth. Until the railways, most people lived along the coastlines or beside rivers and inland lakes. People thought in terms of sea and water transport. But railways made it possible to exploit the interior of continents. By the turn of the century, transcontinental railroads thrust inland to claim the wealth of the hinterlands. The Canadian Pacific, the TransSiberian, and a network of continental lines in the United States were essential elements in the race to acquire new agricultural and mineral resources.

Settlers and miners went by the millions to work the newly opened lands. The Canadian West became a farming region of 30 million hectares providing food for a Europe that could no longer feed itself.

Railways, steam ships, and the telegraph and undersea cables that went with them began to bind the world under European rule. By 1890, Britain had built the All Red Route of imperial transportation. It was possible to travel around the world and never leave British rule.

THE TWENTIETH CENTURY

In the first half of the twentieth century world power centred in Europe. Between 1870 and 1945, the military and economic strength of Europe's industrial powers enabled them to dominate the globe. Every part of the world fell within their sphere of influence. They gained access to the natural resources of the non-industrialized countries. They set up global networks of trade and commerce, linking raw materials to factories and markets. Europe's vast colonial holdings supported the highest standard of living in history. Europeans would not accept governments that could not increase their standard of living. They wanted world-power status regardless of the cost. In fact the non-industrialized world paid a price for European prosperity.

Industrialization divides the world into developed and underdeveloped categories. Rich by accident of location, the developed countries depend on the underdeveloped nations for raw materials and energy supplies. This dependency causes the interrelated nature of human societies.

The gap between industrial and non-industrial peoples widened as the Europeans increasingly dominated. Envy of foreign things began to turn to resentment in the underdeveloped world. People began to wonder why they could not develop their own resources for their own benefit. Their resentment spurred anti-imperial independence movements after the two world wars.

Between 1947 and 1962, most former colonies gained their freedom. Few were ready for so rapid and complete an end to European rule. They were poor, overpopulated, and under-industrialized. Many of the former colonies found they could not meet their citizens' demands for consumer goods and modern lifestyles. This often led to political turmoil.

Standard of living relates directly to the degree of industrial development.

The European dominance of the world ended in 1945 because of losses in the world wars. The human and physical costs of these two tragedies were appalling. What it had cost eventually overshadowed victories on the battlefield. The huge military and economic forces used to achieve a final victory affected everyone on earth. When the wars were over, the old order came to an end.

New global systems came into an existence in which the superpowers were no longer European.

ONE WORLD

The USA and the USSR emerged as the dominant powers after World War II. Their industrial and scientific power, used for military purposes, created new weapons of mass destruction. These could destroy the human race if unleashed. We now have the ability to destroy all life on earth. The question is, will we do so?

The USA came out of World War II as the most powerful of the undamaged economic powers. At that time, the Americans decided to create a new economic order based on reconstruction and free trade. The American Marshall Plan was designed to rebuild Western Europe. The Americans also financed the world's recovery with reconstruction loans to other war-torn regions. The success of their policy created the economic "miracles" of West Germany and Japan. These were new centres of economic power by 1970.

A space shuttle on the launch pad. The USA is a world leader in space exploration as well as in "Star Wars" technology.

"CHIMES OF FREEDOM"

Eighty-five thousand fans, most clad in t-shirts and jeans, screamed at the top of their lungs as Bruce Springsteen and the E-Street Band ripped into the opening chord of **Born in the USA**.

THE DATE: *September 1988.*
THE PLACE: *The Mepstadion, Budapest, Hungary.*

Beginning with a performance at London's Wembley Stadium on September 2, performers such as Springsteen, Sting, Peter Gabriel, Tracy Chapman, and Youssou N'Dour took their rock 'n roll extravaganza to 15 countries, including Canada, the USA, Costa Rica, Japan, India, Ivory Coast, Zimbabwe, and Brazil.

But this tour, dubbed HUMAN RIGHTS NOW!, was much more than a simple, albeit massive, rock roadshow. Organized to celebrate the fortieth anniversary of the Universal Declaration of Human Rights—a document drawn up and adopted by the United Nations on December 10, 1948—organizers referred to HUMAN RIGHTS NOW! as the most elaborate rock event, as well as the biggest human rights event, in history.

Sponsored by the human rights organization Amnesty International, over a million fans saw the concerts, and millions more received, if indirectly, the central message of the **Declaration**—*that every citizen of the world should be treated with dignity and respect. HUMAN RIGHTS NOW! demonstrated that music had become a powerful medium, not only for international entertainment, but perhaps for international justice and change as well.*

HUMAN RIGHTS

The latter half of the twentieth century is witnessing the unprecedented gathering of a growing human population into urban areas. More than half of the world's population will live in congested cityscapes by the end of the century. The large numbers of people living in close quarters in a world becoming more interrelated has given rise to public debate on the relationship between the individual and society. What basic rights are essential to the dignity of the human being? In an unequal world, is equality of human beings possible? Setting aside the apparent physical differences, should all people have an equal claim to social

Chapter 4

THE HUMAN EXPERIENCE

Human rights movements make statements and attract publicity through marches and concerts. In 1963, these Americans marched for civil rights.

justice, useful employment, natural resources, and the material wealth of the society in which they live? If so, how is the redistribution of material wealth and resources to be accomplished? Who is to see that political and social equality becomes a reality? These are some of the questions that motivate the mass public demonstrations in support of human rights movements around the world.

Eloquently inspired by the leadership of Dr. Martin Luther King in the 1960s, the position of the black minority in the United States has significantly improved. Since then efforts to improve the lot of women, the world's children, political prisoners, refugees, and the physically impaired have all had their champions. And, although there is much to do, they have all met with some success, particularly in the developed world and in the cities of the global urban culture where more cosmopolitan mores prevail over traditional roles. Accepted as a more equal part of society, women are now involved in all of the political, military, economic, and cultural environments of the developed societies. Only a decade ago this was not the case. They have brought with them a different perspective which is emerging as a new strength in the ongoing process of improving the quality of life.

The quest for social equality and, more importantly, the acceptance of the idea that all humans regardless of sex, race, language, or country of origin are valuable and have something to offer to the human condition is just beginning. The Canadian Charter of Rights, the United Nation's Declaration on the Rights of Man, and the Helsinki Agreements are important statements of belief. In the undeveloped world, especially in the more traditional societies, human rights are more often breeched than honoured. Women and children are still cast in traditional roles and, for the main, are regarded as second class citizens, if not the property of male-dominated families. Within other nations, minorities are viewed as threatening to the majority, and political action is taken against them. Current practises by some states to rid themselves of the unwanted have resulted in tragic massacres amounting to genocide.

Through the use of the media and mass public demonstrations, human rights leaders are attempting to set things right. In an interdependent world where whatever happens to a single human being has some effect on us all, any progress in securing justice and dignity for the individual is welcome.

The twentieth century has been a period of startling inventions and discoveries. Mass education in the industrial nations has meant significant advances in every field. Medicine has conquered many of the world's diseases. Biochemists seek ways to replace parts of the human body. Fibre optics and the micro-chip radically alter the way information flows. And now we are conquering space. Today we exist in a revolutionary era of continuous change. How the human race adapts to the flood of new discoveries is up to you.

The rate of change is speeding up. The numbers of ways changes are taking effect are also increasing.

CONCLUSION

Humans dominate other species because they can gather information and reason. Inventing tools and machines means a greater control of natural forces and a higher standard of living. After each major discovery the total population increased.

Two major revolutions led to a total change in human lifestyle. The agricultural revolution created cities and an urban culture. The industrial revolution matched machine power to mass production. The industrial nations reached into the non-industrial world to gain control over the planet's natural resources when there were shortages at home.

By the twentieth century, the industrial European powers controlled most of the globe. Undeveloped colonies supplied the raw materials for the industries of the home nations. They did so until they achieved independence after the world wars. Since then, they have tried to raise the standards of living of their own people. After the wars the industrial nations dominated again. They widened the gap between themselves and the others. Many of the industrial nations now plan to explore other planets.

A family gathers around their home computer.

QUESTIONS

1. In what ways do humans control nature?
2. Describe how fire changed human society and lifestyles.
3. What changes does a surplus food supply bring about in a society?
4. Why do we need to trade?
5. Why did humans make war? What makes a warrior class possible? Of what value is a warrior class to a country?
6. How did cities change personal relationships?
7. What problems have arisen from the surge in population growth after major inventions?
8. Why did the classical empires of Rome and Greece end?
9. How did the Black Death affect European society?
10. In what ways did powered machines in factories change production?
11. How did Europe handle its surplus population in the nineteenth century? Why is this method not used today?

12. Why did industrialization not affect all nations equally?
13. How have the two major wars during this century affected human and physical resources?
14. What changes came about in the lifestyle of the colonial peoples after independence?
15. Explain what progress has been made in the area of human rights.
16. What is the basis for the rapid expansion of knowledge during the last half century?
17. The twentieth century has been called the age of materialism. Explain this concept.
18. Identify characteristics of materialism in your own lifestyle.
19. How do humans react to continuous change?

ACTIVITIES

1. **Diary:**
   Assume the role of a teenager living in any one period of history such as the Middle Ages, the age of exploration, the railway age, or during the world wars. Read enough of the history of the age to understand what life might be like. In your diary, detail your activities for a week. Be specific. Where do you live? What do you eat? Do you work? Do you go to school? What do you do in your leisure time? Be accurate but imaginative.

2. **Time Line:**
   Draw a time line showing the important discoveries from the age of the hunter folk to the present.

3. **Research Report or Picture Display:**
   Compare and contrast the life of an average family in a North American town with that of an average family in a village in India, South America, or Thailand. You may do this in words or pictures. Consider access to food and water, clothing, housing, education, work opportunities, health facilities, transportation, sport and other leisure time activities, entertainment, access to radio, tv, and newspapers, and pace of life.

4. **Debate:**
   Structure a debate on the following issue:
   Resolved that
   "The world's natural resources should be equally shared among its people."

5. **Panel Discussion:**
   Establish a panel of four people to discuss the following issue: "Industrial development should stop in order to conserve scarce resources." Two people could represent the viewpoint of the industrial world and two people could represent the viewpoint of the underdeveloped world. Choose a moderator to control the discussion. Questions could be addressed to the panel from the general group.

SIMINTI PRIMARY SCHOOL kadi
FIKA LOCAL GOVT. EDUCATION DEPARTMENT POTISKUM
NO ROOM FOR LAZINESS
PRINTED BY D.Y. AHMED K.G.

5

HUMAN RESOURCES

OF ALL THE EARTH'S RESOURCES, human beings are the most precious. Humans draw on the earth's resources to improve their quality of life. However, as the populations grow, resources are depleted and environmental conditions change. We must develop human potential in harmony with the environment. This, in turn, will allow us in the future to live life with dignity.

> *Human beings are the ultimate resource, but there is a limit to the numbers the earth can sustain. All human activity draws on finite environmental support systems.*

The human population will be more than 6 billion by the turn of the century. It is growing at a rate of 25 people every 10 seconds or more than 150 000 per week. If population growth stabilizes, the total will be 10.2 billion by the end of the next century. Stability means that the population only replaces itself. If we fail to achieve these rates, there may be 14.9 billion people by the year 2100. The earth could sustain a good life for 10.2 billion people. However, if the number reaches 14.9 billion, we would place great stress on the environment. The problem is how to manage population growth to allow for a higher quality of life for all. Statistics show that population only stabilizes in a country when the quality of health, education, and social

This Brisbane, Australia, crowd has gathered for a union meeting.

ONE
WORLD

development is greatly improved. Sustainable development, then, is linked to issues of both the environment and population growth.

The real concern about current population statistics is the distribution of people. Developed countries are approaching zero population growth. More of the annual increase is concentrated in underdeveloped countries. This is where life support systems are already overtaxed. Shortages of food, fodder, and fuel result when the local population exceeds supplies of food and material. In the past, the pressure of increased population was often eased by migration to new lands. In the nineteenth century, between 10 and 15 million people left Europe for the new world. This is no longer a choice. Between 1970 and 1980, emigration from Europe amounted to only 4 per cent of the population. The figure for Latin America was 2.5 per cent, and the percentages from Asia and Africa were even lower. Instead, much of the movement is now within countries, from rural to urban areas. Since 1950, the number of city dwellers has quadrupled in underdeveloped countries. This is an alarming increase. It puts unmanageable pressure on urban services.

Demands from an escalating population for a higher standard of living create political, economic, and social instability.

Eighty-one per cent of the world's population live in underdeveloped regions. Fully 90 per cent of the world's population growth over the next century will occur in these same regions. These areas cannot now support an adequate lifestyle for all their people. How can they be expected to provide for millions more? Already, 1 billion of the earth's people live in absolute poverty. This is a tragic waste of human potential. We must better manage our resources to improve the quality of life for many of our planet's people. This means that we must improve health care, housing, and education. Well managed economic growth and just access to resources for all are the keys to a prosperous future.

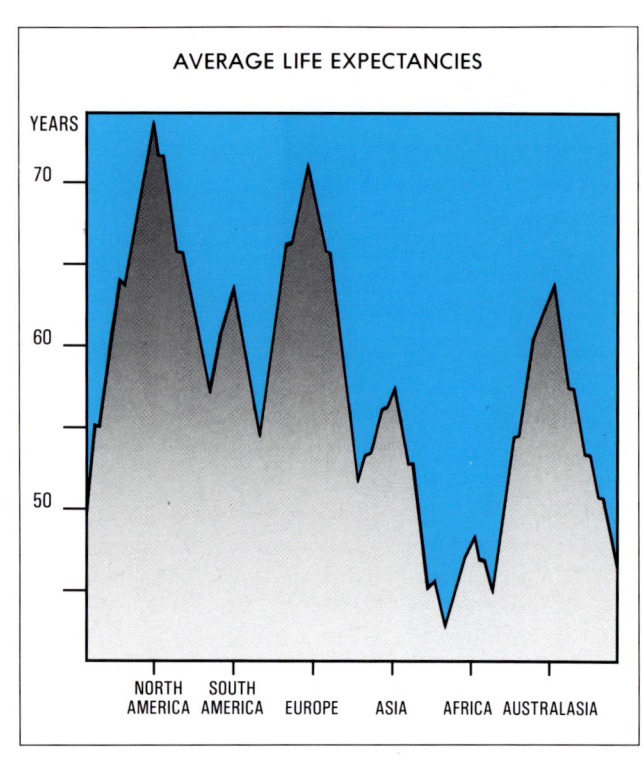

Industrialization means improved health care and more food. People in the developed world can expect to live much longer than people in the underdeveloped world.

THE GLOBAL POPULATION PERSPECTIVE

In the past, high death rates and short life expectancies held populations in check. In some areas famine, disease, or war reduced numbers. High birth rates were needed to maintain population growth. Large families were considered an economic necessity. Industrialization changed this for some people. Improvements in health care and the distribution of food helped reduce child mortality. Life expectancy increased. This, coupled with continuing high birth rates, first resulted in a large natural increase in population. The following dramatic decline in both birth and death rates resulted in slower if not stable growth. However, in the non-industrial nations high birth rates continued. The result was great pressure on natural resources.

Chapter 5

HUMAN RESOURCES

Basic needs, such as food and shelter, require a large supply of physical resources. This poses serious problems in countries like India, Bangladesh, and Pakistan. Here there are large, growing populations that strain limited amounts of fertile land and other resources. By contrast, countries like Brazil and Nigeria have a great deal of land as well as other resources (oil in Nigeria and minerals in Brazil). Nigeria and Brazil could perhaps have larger populations if their resources were better managed. Rural areas in underdeveloped countries are often regions which have high birth rates and an uneven distribution of land. This results in low productivity and often landlessness and unemployment.

Overpopulation is a concern for urban areas in these regions as well. Many people move away from rural areas in their search for a better life. Inadequate food and shelter and unemployment are usually in store for the unskilled rural worker who makes this move. Housed in a crowded shanty settlement, the migrant typically suffers from malnutrition and other afflictions common to the urban poor. Cities cannot cope with the influx and are unable to provide adequate services or employment.

Populations remain high for both cultural and economic reasons. The prestige of male virility and female fertility encourages large families. Wanting a male child also leads to repeat pregnancies in an attempt to have a son. Children are seen as an economic asset. Children contribute to family income

Clean water is a necessity unavailable to these Nepalese women.

ONE WORLD

and are a security for their parents' old age. These traditional practices are difficult to overcome. Even though overpopulation is now recognized as a global problem, some countries with smaller populations, Libya, for example, still support high growth rates for both prestige and economic development.

The number of human beings is now great enough to visibly affect the planet's life support systems. Care must be taken not to cross the threshold of irreversible degradation.

A key issue facing society today is how to provide a good quality of life for all. The world's resources are unevenly distributed. A good life seems to be an accident of birth. Some researchers, aware of the finite and frail nature of our resources, have come to question the future of our life on earth. Underdeveloped nations seek the high standard of living of the developed nations. Yet in many ways, striving to attain these standards is of questionable value.

People in developed nations currently enjoy a lifestyle characterized by mass materialism and waste. This quarter of the world's population consumes three-quarters of the earth's resources. In truth, a greater awareness of environmental protection is necessary if developed nations want to sustain their high standard of living. To halt pollution and the resulting contamination of our water, air, and food supplies, other production techniques and different fuels will have to be used. Although there is a growing awareness of the impact of our demands on the environment, there seems little desire to reduce our destructive lifestyle.

Can the pace of economic development in the industrial world continue side by side with an improving quality of life in the underdeveloped world? The challenges faced by underdeveloped countries are very different from those of developed countries. Improvements in nourishment, health care, housing, education, and employment are essential for a better life. To afford these improvements, there must be practical development projects. A vast reservoir of human potential lies waiting to be tapped in the underdeveloped nations. Failure to help threatens not only the environment but the stability of the world. Conflict over resources is a very real possibility.

Many people in developed countries enjoy a lifestyle that is characterized by luxury, excess, and materialism.

LIFESTYLE IN UNDERDEVELOPED COUNTRIES

Human population is unevenly distributed over the earth. The quality of life for any one individual depends on location, degree of industrial development, and density of population. Population growth can reduce the advantages of economic gain.

The diet of people living in underdeveloped countries is generally lacking both in quantity and quality. Life spans are considerably lower than those

Chapter 5
HUMAN RESOURCES

Life for this Bolivian man holds few promises. His clothes are torn and he sleeps in the street.

of people in more developed regions. The diet of people living in developed countries is abundant, sometimes excessive. In spite of this diet rich in fat and sugars, the life expectancy of a person from a developed region is half again as long as that of someone from an underdeveloped country. Many citizens of underdeveloped countries do not have the basic necessities of life. But **consumerism** is the standard of developed nations. Nine out of ten babies born today will live in the underdeveloped nations. However, if that tenth baby is born in Canada, it will in its lifetime consume six times more resources than the other nine babies combined. Both developed and underdeveloped regions place severe stress on our environment as an attempt is made to meet demands for improvements in quality of life.

Lack of food is only one of many health problems facing people in underdeveloped countries. Inadequate water supplies and poor sanitation cause widespread health problems. Among these problems are diarrhoea and worms. Improper drainage and waste water disposal contributes to malaria, which is common in tropical regions. Around 1.7 billion people lack clean water. Inadequate sanitation is endured by 1.2 billion people. In spite of these problems, the "health status" of underdeveloped countries has improved significantly since 1950. Two indicators of a society's health are rates of infant mortality and life expectancy. Both of these suggest that health has improved in virtually all areas of the underdeveloped world. Although these regions still fall short of developed regions in both, the gap has narrowed. Establishing health clinics has been the key element in the improvement of health. Medicine as it is practised in industrial nations is far too costly for nations still struggling to develop. However, by using traditional healers and midwives, the gap between large urban areas with doctors and villages lacking medical facilities and staff may be bridged. By involving the community, particularly traditional healers, most common illnesses can be treated. Immunization

---

DIET

A diet which provides essential nutrients plus adequate calories is needed for both physical and mental health. About 500 million people in underdeveloped countries are starving or ill-fed. Malnutrition means a lack of protein, vitamins, or minerals. Many diseases are caused by malnutrition. One such disease is kwashiorkor, a lack of amino acids found in protein. Blindness is caused by a lack of Vitamin A. Rickets is caused by a lack of Vitamin D. Scurvy is caused by a lack of Vitamin C. Undernutrition means a shortage of calories. Insufficient caloric intake is the most common problem facing a child in an underdeveloped country. It results in a lack of energy and ultimately in impaired growth, particularly of the brain. Women and young children are most susceptible to this problem. When the food supply of a family is limited, women and young children allow the men and older children to eat first. The UN estimates that the number of children who die from malnutrition or preventable disease before their fifth birthday is 15 million per year. The first step in improving the quality of life must be to eliminate hunger.

ONE WORLD

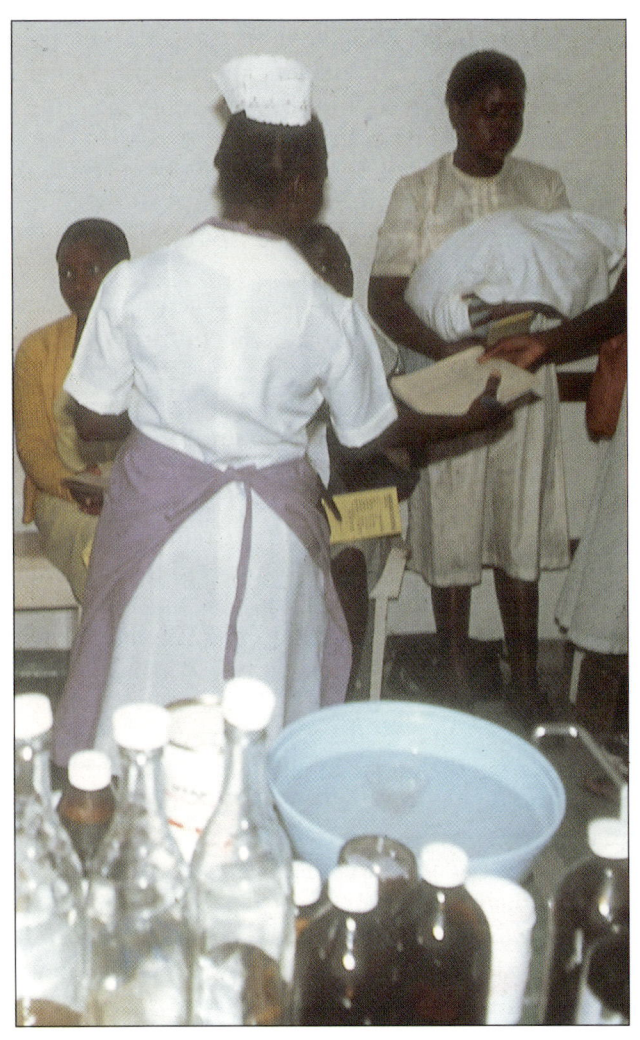

Pregnant women are treated at an antenatal clinic in Zimbabwe.

programs and oral rehydration therapy (a mixture of sugar and salts in water to cure diarrhoea) have saved many lives.

Twenty per cent of the world's population, a staggering 1 billion people, live in absolute poverty. These people exist without any of the basics of life. Their housing lacks ventilation, windows, piped water, and furniture. In rural areas their home may be a mud hut, while in urban areas it may be a makeshift shack of cardboard, scraps of wood, a drain-pipe, or whatever else is available. Life for these people is abject misery. A child born into this situation is destined to a life of extreme deprivation.

The problem of housing is another serious concern. There is neither the money nor the political will to build adequate housing on the scale necessary. These people are consigned to a life of malnutrition, illiteracy, disease, high infant mortality, and low life expectancy.

POPULATION MANAGEMENT

Despite the lowering fertility rates (i.e., the number of children born per female) worldwide, the number of humans still increases every year. In 1987 the global population increased by 83 million. By the year 2000, this annual increase could swell to 92 million. It is estimated that Brazil, China, India, Indonesia, and Mexico will increase the world's population by 700 million by the year 2007. High population growth rates threaten to reduce local standards of living as more people draw on limited natural resources for food and shelter. Unless fertility rates decline further, it will be more difficult for the earth to continue to fulfill even the most basic human needs. Twenty countries have shown a decline in fertility rates, ranging from 21 per cent to 75 per cent since 1960. Despite this impressive gain, the overall numbers continue to grow. Fertility rates ranging from 6.1 in Zaire to 8 in Kenya exist in 15 countries in Africa, and the Middle East. As well, Bangladesh and Pakistan both have fertility rates above 6.

POPULATION GROWTH

Some experts do not view population growth in the underdeveloped nations as a problem. They oppose population control for various political, economic, social, and religious reasons. Julian Simon, professor of economics and business administration at the University of Illinois, has a different approach. He has argued that more people means more potential knowledge. Because people can invent and carry out improvements, Simon claims that the number of improvements depends on the number of people available. The more people there are, the more brains there are to solve the earth's problems.

Chapter 5
HUMAN RESOURCES

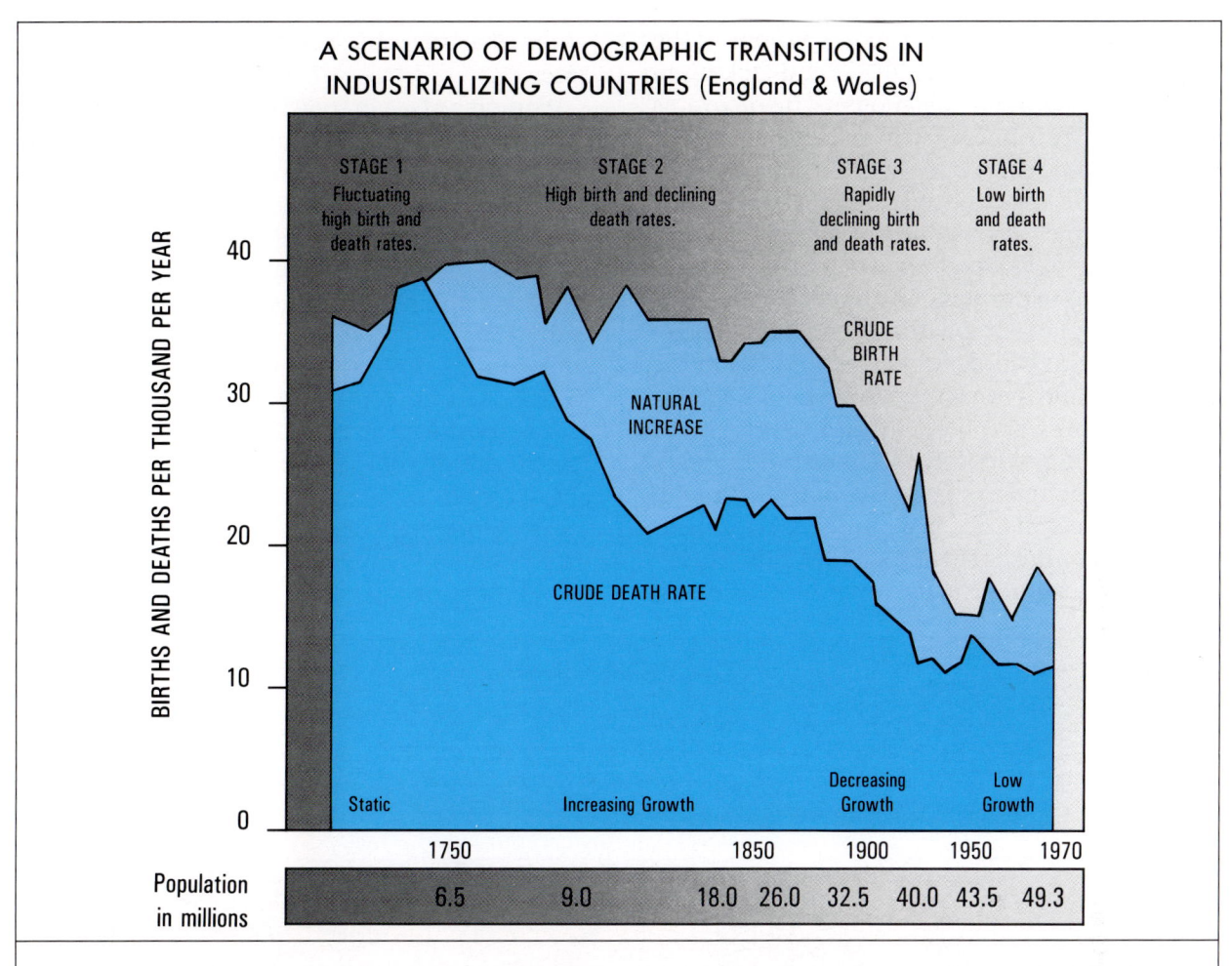

A SCENARIO OF DEMOGRAPHIC TRANSITIONS IN INDUSTRIALIZING COUNTRIES (England & Wales)

STAGE 1 Fluctuating high birth and death rates.
STAGE 2 High birth and declining death rates.
STAGE 3 Rapidly declining birth and death rates.
STAGE 4 Low birth and death rates.

Y-axis: BIRTHS AND DEATHS PER THOUSAND PER YEAR (0–40)

Curves shown: CRUDE BIRTH RATE, CRUDE DEATH RATE, with NATURAL INCREASE between them.

Static | Increasing Growth | Decreasing Growth | Low Growth

Year	1750		1850	1900	1950	1970
Population in millions	6.5	9.0	18.0 26.0	32.5	40.0	43.5 49.3

This chart of demographic transition illustrates the birth and death rate changes which have occurred in developed countries. Four stages can be identified:
1. High birth and death rates.
2. Improved living conditions such as better housing and more food, and improved medicine resulting in a lowering of the death rate. Birth rates continue to be high.
3. Higher standard of living and improved medical technology encouraging family planning. Death rates continue to decline and birth rates drop.
4. Low birth and death rates stabilizing population growth.

Studies show that when a family's standard of living rises, the number of children per family declines. Improvements in health care, living conditions, and education all improve the quality of life. Although this trend has been seen in developed countries, it is now clear that to wait for this same trend to occur in underdeveloped countries will be self-defeating. Most developed countries have been industrialized for well over a century. However, it was not until 1960 that significant declines in fertility rates began to take effect. Reducing birth rates could speed the development process through the reduction of pressure on natural resources. The quality of life in underdeveloped areas would be enhanced.

Political, economic, cultural, and social policies affect population growth.

ONE WORLD

Population management in many nations in the 1950s and 1960s was paternalistic and lacking in understanding. Developed nations set up programs which mainly distributed birth control devices. Social and cultural reasons for high birth rates were largely ignored. Many people in underdeveloped regions saw the birth control campaign as an attempt by the developed regions to destroy their cultures. High birth rates continued as these programs were ignored. On the other hand, today countries such as China, Sri Lanka, and Colombia have government-sponsored family planning programs which mix social policy and development plans. These countries have demonstrated quick and effective action in crisis situations. Although some problems still exist, in a number of countries population growth has slowed significantly. Social, cultural, and economic factors must be considered when starting any program to reduce fertility rates.

Women's place in society seems to have the most profound affect on fertility rates. In many underdeveloped countries, women have little education. They bear almost full responsibility for agricultural work, getting water, preparing meals, gathering firewood, and raising children. They marry at an early age and change from being chattels of their fathers to chattels of their husbands. Lacking in status, women's only source of prestige is the production of children, especially sons. This is particularly true in most African countries. The status of women has the greatest impact on fertility rates. Providing equal access to education and assuring women the basic human right of self-determination are key requirements in countries now experiencing rapid population growth.

WOMEN IN ACTION

Women in Gujarat, India, founded the Self-Employed Women's Association (SEWA) in 1972. The association is a co-operative that has helped over 12 000 of India's poorest women with training schemes, special credit programs, welfare, and negotiated minimum wages. Members of the SEWA include women employed in a wide range of trades, from vegetable sellers to weavers.

Education may provide the key to a better future for millions of people.

Chapter 5
HUMAN RESOURCES

CASE STUDY:

PROGRESS IN CHINA

Most children in China will grow up without brothers or sisters.

China recognizes that it needs stabilized population growth. The country is faced with feeding 22 per cent of the world's population with only 7 per cent of the world's arable land. In 1979, China's single child family policy was introduced. Always controversial, the single child concept is an attempt to slow population growth. This will allow the modernization process to continue. Resources will be used to improve the standard of living and further industrialization.

The single child family policy has three parts: propaganda messages, rewards, and disincentives. In propaganda on radio, tv, books, billboards, or party messages, the single child is always a girl. In spite of this, the traditional desire to have a male child persists. Rewards for following the policy may be improved housing, cash, priority placement in school or day-care, and six months leave for the new mother instead of the usual 56 days. Greater rewards are usually given in urban areas. Disincentives are also more serious in the city because there is an ongoing penalty as opposed to a one-time fine in rural areas. City workers may lose good assignments, bonuses, or even be demoted. Sometimes the second child may not be registered until the parents agree to sterilization or to use contraceptives. Failures in contraception mean more abortions are performed each year.

There are serious concerns about the single child family policy. Rural inhabitants whose first child is a girl are allowed a second child in the hope a son will be born to assist with the family farm. The military is concerned because single children are not required to serve. It is possible that the number of recruits will decline. Perhaps the greatest concern, however, is the impact which this policy will have on the aged. Traditionally, the family in China cares for older members. By the year 2025, 16.4 per cent of China's population will be retired. In some cases, four grandparents and two parents could be dependent on a single child. This has led to more pressure on government to give greater support to the aged. The policy now allows couples who are both single children to have two children. China reached a population of 1 billion people ahead of projections. Their awareness of the increased pressure this places on natural resources encourages the continuation of a program as controversial as the single child family policy.

1. What is the relationship between China's population and its arable land?
2. Why did China start a single child per family policy? How can this be enforced? Has it been a success?
3. What are the benefits of this policy? What happens if the child is a female?
4. What are the alternatives to this policy? Why does it have international implications?

ONE

WORLD

A Maasai mother with her child. Notice the child's brown hair that is symptomatic of kwashiorkor.

CONCLUSION

We can no longer reasonably expect that the planet's environmental resources can support unlimited population growth. We recognize that growth beyond 10.2 billion people will require significant change in food production techniques. If we grow beyond 15 billion, the changes will require not only greater efficiencies in resource use but also significant changes in food choices and lifestyle. Surveys confirm that 235 million women in underdeveloped countries want no more children and millions more would like to delay their next pregnancy. However, contraceptive measures remain unavailable for these women. Governments must address this issue with a multi-faceted approach. Family planning programs do not work in isolation. Education, health care, and the entire process of development must be integrated in order to successfully reduce fertility rates and slow population growth. Global security and prosperity are dependent on international co-operation in this difficult area.

QUESTIONS

1. How does the growth in human population affect the physical resources of the biosphere?
2. What is the relationship between the quality of life and the rate of population growth?
3. Why is unchecked population growth in underdeveloped countries cause for concern?
4. How does industrialization affect birth rates and family size? Account for this.
5. What is the effect of overpopulation on lifestyle and the environment in rural and urban areas?
6. Why is population growth a global and not simply a regional problem? What is the relationship between population, developed and underdeveloped nations, physical resource use, and standards of living?
7. Should every human being have the same standard of living? Why is this not the case? Is this a possibility? Why or why not?
8. Compare and contrast the lifestyles of a developed and an underdeveloped nation. What are the effects on people of poverty and malnutrition?
9. What two factors measure a society's health services? What measures are being taken to improve world health conditions? What factor defeats most of these efforts?
10. Describe the living conditions of the absolute poor. Where are these people? Why is their standard of living permitted to continue?
11. Why have some societies zero population growth? Is this desirable?
12. What is the key factor in reducing birth rates?
13. What is the relationship between birth rates and standards of living?
14. How does the cultural and social status of women and men affect family size?
15. How can population growth rates be reduced?
16. What are the five most populous countries? What are the five countries with the highest standard of living? (Refer to Mini-Atlas.)

Chapter 5

HUMAN RESOURCES

ACTIVITIES

1. **Diary:**
   Keep a detailed record of your food consumption for a period of one week. Note the time, specific quantity, and type of food. Include all beverages. At the end of the week, add up the number of calories consumed each day. Analyse the nutritional content of your food choices. Have you chosen food from each group in Canada's Food Guide? How much money did you spend on "junk food" during the week? How many meals did you eat outside the home?

2. **Class Dinner:**
   Plan a class dinner which will bring together people of both developed and underdeveloped regions (randomly select 25 per cent of the class to represent the developed world and the other 75 per cent to represent underdeveloped regions). Serve a three or four course meal to the rich 25 per cent. The 75 per cent from the underdeveloped regions will get only a bowl of rice and a glass of water. Have the students describe how they felt about their share of the dinner. This could then lead to a class discussion on the current inequity of food distribution. Brainstorm possibilities for solving the problem of hunger.

3. **Picture Collage:**
   Find pictures of material goods which a Canadian teenager would likely own. Make a collage illustrating the lifestyle of this individual. Contrast this with a picture collage of a teenager from a village in Africa.

4. **Conference:**
   Structure a conference to deal with global population growth. Choose delegates to represent countries from all parts of the world. Each delegate must come prepared to express the concerns which face his or her particular country. Consider population increases, resource availability, age structure of population, and the ability of the country to supply its population with basic services like health care and education. How will the world meet the demands of future population growth? Should countries consider mandatory programs of family planning? How will countries deal with aging populations?

5. **Poem, Song, or Short Story:**
   "Women's place in society seems to have the most profound affect on fertility rates."
   Research the role of women in either Canada or the underdeveloped world in the 1980s. Consider their role in the family, the work force, and the community. What status do women have in the society in which they live? What problems do they face? What rewards do they receive? Present your findings in a poem, a song, or a short story.

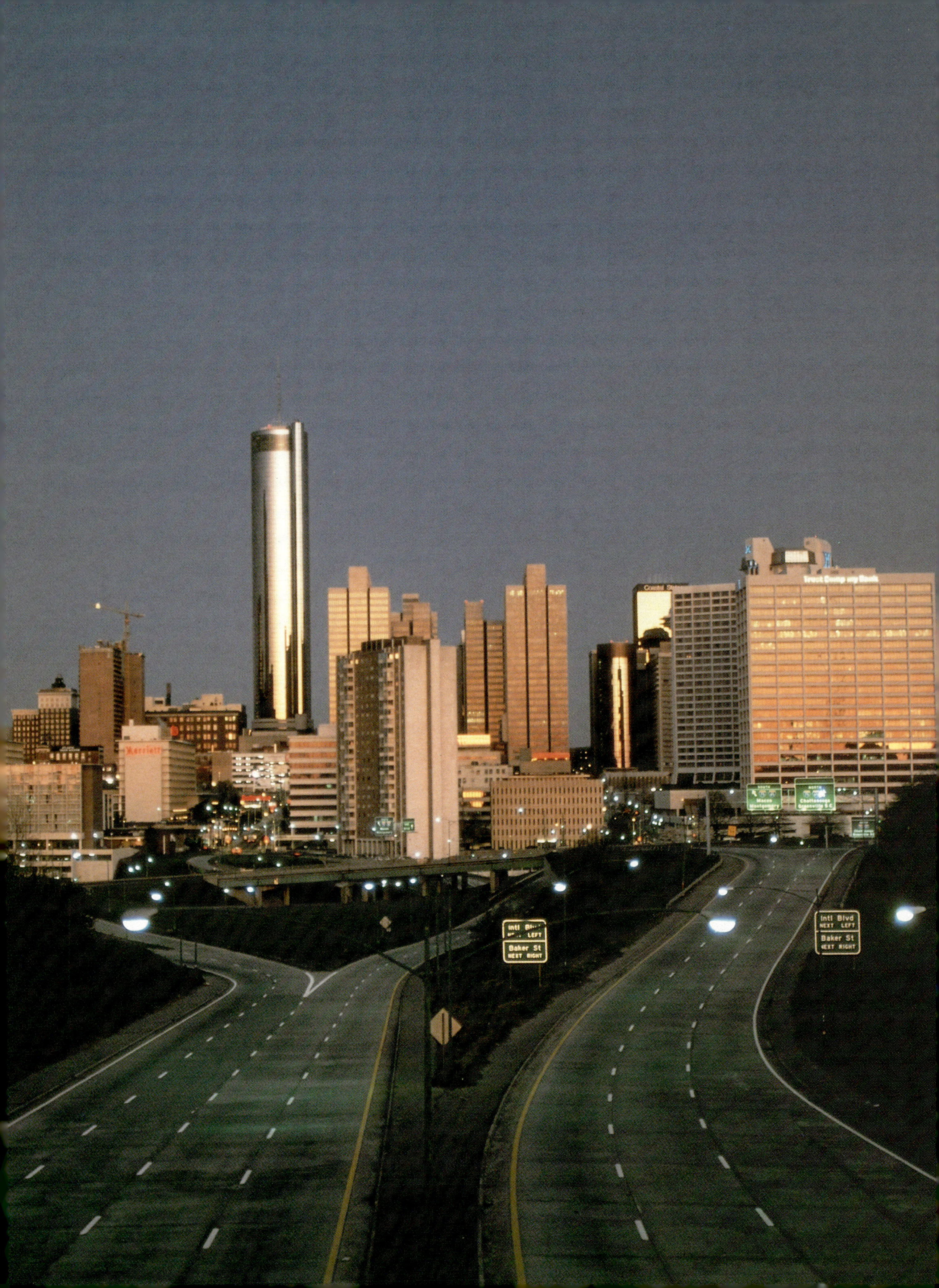
Intl Blvd
NEXT LEFT
Baker St
NEXT RIGHT

6

URBAN CULTURE

ONE OF THE LITTLE recognized phenomena of the modern world has been the unprecedented growth of the world's urban population. A global urban culture has been superimposed on the system of nation states. Cosmopolitanism is replacing nationalism as the world's cities are being transformed into homogeneous units. Whether one of the cities of North America or one of the older cities around the world, a sameness is being created to cater to the needs of international business people and tourists. Often referred to as a westernizing of the world, this transformation is designed to provide the daily services demanded by an industrial people. Apart from similarities in food, entertainment, and accommodations, the world's cities also share the same problems. Congested transportation, an inflow of tens of thousands from the rural areas seeking employment, and an inability to provide basic services for the urban poor are common characteristics of a global urban environment.

Today North America is close to 80 per cent urban with Western Europe not far behind. In some parts of the developed world cities have merged into neighbouring cities into what are termed agglomerations. The agglomeration of urban dwellers between Boston and Washington is called BOSNYWASH. In Third World countries the pattern of migration is

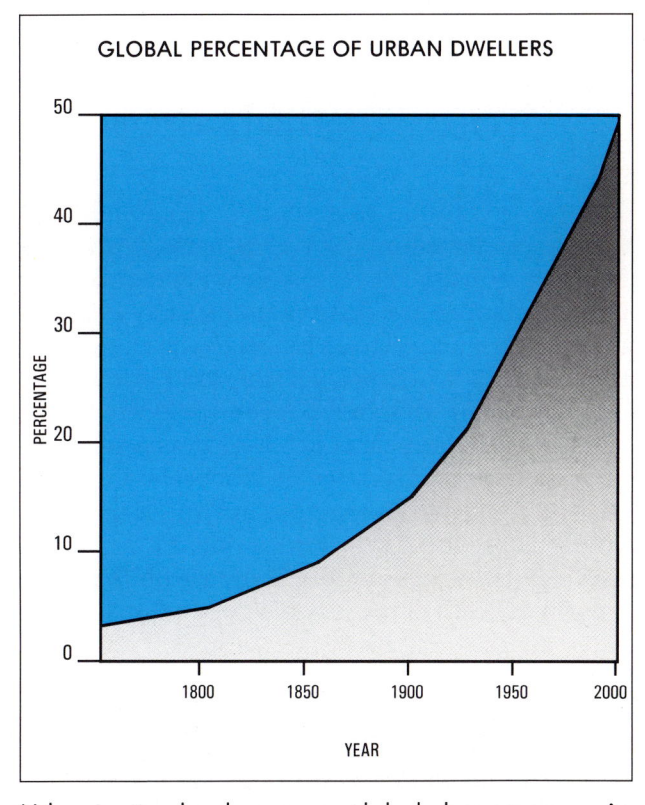

Urbanization has become a global phenomenon. As this chart shows, in 1900 only 14 per cent of the world's people lived in cities. By the year 2000, half the earth's population will live in urban areas.

ONE WORLD

to congregate in only one city. This places additional pressures to provide services and leaves the rural areas denuded of youth and manpower. Most of the national budget is spent in the city where local elites live luxurious lives in comparison to the abject poverty of the vast majority of the people.

In 1950, only seven cities in the world had a population larger than 5 million. By the year 2000 there could be fifty-seven such mega-cities, forty-two of them in the underdeveloped world. Of these, twenty-five could have more than 10 million people, with all but three in the underdeveloped world. Mexico City will probably be the world's largest city, with 30 million people. How will such enormous concentrations of people be fed, housed, transported, and given services? One of the greatest challenges facing mankind in the future will be managing urban populations.

Urbanization requires a restructuring of human political, social, cultural, and economic relationships.

GLOBAL URBANIZATION

Urbanization concentrates a country's population in large communities rather than spreading it throughout the countryside. There is a direct link between industrial development and urbanization. Urbanization is greatest when a society changes from an agricultural to an industrial base. Agriculture scatters workers over the land. However, manufacturing requires concentrated groups of potential workers near at hand. Also, as agriculture becomes mechanized, fewer labourers are needed, leading surplus workers to migrate to the cities in search of jobs. The world is now so urbanized that a global urban culture is emerging. In 1900, only 14 per cent of the world's population lived in cities. By the year 2000, the world will be 50 per cent urbanized.

Similar lifestyles in many of the world's cities have resulted in the creation of a global urban culture.

In the past, large cities developed distinctive characters, based upon their culture, religion, industry, or perhaps their architecture. Cities were isolated and their societies reflected the aspirations of a particular civilization. Today, however, cities are connected by a web of transport and communication networks. The transfer of industry and technology has made cities seem the same. Urban middle classes around the world wear the same clothes, eat the same foods, listen to the same music, and watch the same television programs. Linked by finance and trade, these cities are parts of a whole. For example, London, Zurich, Tokyo, and New York are all attached to the same financial network. Paris, Nairobi, and Rome connect with New York via their common activities. A Toronto resident may feel more at home in the centre of Tokyo than in a small town in rural Canada.

Urbanization is greatest when a society changes from an agricultural to an industrial base.

Chapter 6

URBAN CULTURE

> **SUPER-SKYSCRAPERS?**
>
> *As cities increase in size, land becomes increasingly valuable. One solution to the problem of scarce land is to build upwards instead of outwards. A super-skyscraper, housing a complete community, is an innovative approach to urban land use. This tower could be designed to accommodate business offices, service industries, daycare, educational facilities, recreation facilities, and apartments. Green areas on balconies and sun rooms on the outside walls could eliminate the need to go outside for long periods of time. Is this the urban future?*

By 1965, all industrial nations were highly urbanized. Great cities became centres of finance, trade, transportation, and entertainment. Urbanization is now a characteristic of underdeveloped regions as well. Urbanization in these areas, however, does not mirror that of the developed regions. Growth is generally faster in cities in the underdeveloped nations. The high fertility rate of a very young urban population adds to the growth resulting from rural migration. The inequality between the developed and the underdeveloped world is sharply defined in urban centres. Developed countries spend 97 per cent of the world's research and

Cities in underdeveloped countries are often peopled with unskilled workers. The result? Crowded urban areas with extremely high rates of unemployment.

development budget. In 1980, the 10 richest nations generated 83 per cent of the world's industrial production. During the late 1960s and early 1970s, the world economy changed to take advantage of the huge pool of cheap labour in underdeveloped regions. Multinational corporations shifted production to these regions. However, they kept management, research, and development in the industrial countries. Many of the benefits of industrialization thus go to the developed world. The underdeveloped regions are left to struggle with rapidly growing cities peopled with large numbers of unskilled labourers.

There are great differences between cities in the underdeveloped world and the developed world. One of the main differences is that in the nations of the underdeveloped world, people tend to concentrate in only one city, usually the capital. Singapore and Hong Kong are prime examples. However, this is also common in all other areas of the underdeveloped world. The largest city in most of these countries has 10 to 25 per cent of the entire population. Montevideo, for example, has 50 per cent of the population of Uruguay. In the Imperial age of the nineteenth century, most of these cities depended on trading primary products for manufactured goods. They have maintained this dominant position. Today they keep their importance as trading links with the developed world.

The high density of human populations in cities places tremendous pressure on the biosphere.

The entire structure of cities is different too. Cities in the developed world usually have a central business district. Skyscrapers dominate. In comparison, religious or government buildings often dominate the central district of cities in the underdeveloped regions. Housing for the urban elite in an underdeveloped region will be in the centre of the city. On the other hand, the poor live in large sprawling slums on the outskirts. Although there are some luxury apartments in an industrial city's centre, most affluent housing is in the suburbs. The urban poor live in inner city slums which result from the decay of older neighbourhoods. Thus, the housing pattern is reversed. People living in urban squatter settlements in the undeveloped nations do have more room than those crowded into the city slums of industrialized countries. However, they are generally far from both jobs and services.

URBANIZATION IN UNDERDEVELOPED REGIONS

The origin of the mega-city can be related in some ways to industrial colonialism. During this period, urban primacy began because economic and political power concentrated in only one area. Manufacturing was limited, but many businesses and services developed to meet the needs of the colonial power. After decolonization, many rural people came to the city hoping for a better life. This rural to urban migration has continued and is a major part of urban population growth. People in underdeveloped nations usually leave their rural home because of some event which they cannot control. Sometimes the move is intended to be temporary, but as time passes, it becomes permanent. The move may be because of climate. For example, in the Calcutta region of India, drought has driven many subsistence farmers off the land. Sometimes the move is the result of political or social pressures. Most often, however, people move because of the perceived advantages of the city. Hourly rates of pay are usually higher in the city. Casual labourers might be able to work eight months of the year instead of only four.

Work in the cities of the underdeveloped world is either formal or informal. The formal sector is capital-intensive, uses imported technology, and has protected markets through tariffs, quotas, or licensing. It typically exists on private property controlled by large businesses which may have ties to the developed world. Work in the formal sector is very difficult for the average urban worker to obtain. It requires formally acquired skills. As a result, usually only the educated and trained upper classes can work in this sector. Advances in technology have made the problem even worse. Machines now replace many semi-skilled and unskilled urban jobs.

This lack of opportunity in the formal sector leads many to seek employment opportunities in the informal sector. The informal sector is highly competitive but easy to enter. This is because it has no rules about working hours, rates of pay, or pensions. It is made up mainly of small businesses

Chapter 6
URBAN CULTURE

This marketplace in Peshawar, Pakistan, is an example of a local "bazaar" economy. The marketplace is highly competitive, but easy to enter.

both sectors. The informal sector includes services such as hair care, laundry, photography, and a large "bazaar" economy. This includes selling food, crafts, or clothing. People may work for little pay 10 to 15 hours per day, six or seven days per week. At the bottom of the informal sector are those who scavenge and beg. A beggar in Cairo or Manila may in fact do better than a rural landless labourer.

There are great differences in housing in underdeveloped countries between the small numbers of middle and upper class people and the majority who live in poverty. The upper classes live in elite neighbourhoods which are serviced fully and supplied with all amenities. These areas are often in the city centre. The poor, on the other hand, live in outlying squatter settlements or inner-city, high-density slums. This housing lacks space, furnishings, basic services, and security of tenure. Decrepit shanty towns also provide housing for the poor. Houses are typically in very bad condition and are usually on small rented plots.

Squatting is ill-planned, illegal, and unorganized. It is based on individual initiative. Since 1945 it has become a large part of the urbanization process in underdeveloped regions. People squat because they cannot pay rent or buy housing. There is also a lack of public funds to provide low-cost housing. As a result, many urban poor have neither piped water nor adequate waste disposal and sanitation facilities. Hunger and crowding lead to widespread incidents of disease.

Squatter settlements are often built on land that is unsuitable for development. The land may be on a flood plain, a desert, a hillside prone to land slippage, or next to polluting factories. People have described these settlements as an "urban cancer." In spite of this, squatter settlements are a permanent feature of urbanization in the underdeveloped regions. The largest and most established squatter settlements house diverse groups of people. These sometimes include factory workers and even white collar workers. This shows the essential poverty of the entire lower class. Local government response to squatter settlements varies. In Africa if urban poor people develop squatter settlements,

which need little or no capital and consist of self-employed or family labour. The skills needed can usually be obtained outside the school system. Sometimes people in informal urban jobs are linked to highly organized businesses. Occasionally only an official licence distinguishes a formal from an informal activity. Many of the urban poor work in

---

Nearly half of the world's population will soon be living in cities. This will create major problems in the areas of food supply, the provision of shelter and adequate transportation, and in the quality of life.

THE GROWTH OF THE WORLD'S 12 LARGEST CITIES (Estimates)

1975	POP. IN MILLIONS	1990	POP. IN MILLIONS	2000	POP. IN MILLIONS
Greater New York	19.8	Tokyo-Yokohama	23.4	Mexico City	31.0
Tokyo-Yokohama	17.7	Mexico City	22.9	Sao Paulo	25.8
Mexico City	11.9	Greater New York	21.8	Tokyo-Yokohama	24.2
Shanghai	11.6	Sao Paulo	19.9	Greater New York	22.8
Los Angeles-Long Beach	10.8	Shanghai	17.7	Shanghai	22.7
Sao Paulo	10.7	Beijing	15.3	Beijing	19.9
London	10.4	Rio de Janeiro	14.7	Rio de Janeiro	19.0
Buenos Aires	9.3	Los Angeles-Long Beach	13.3	Bombay	17.1
Rhein-Ruhr	9.3	Bombay	12.0	Calcutta	16.7
Paris	9.2	Calcutta	11.9	Jakarta	16.6
Rio de Janeiro	8.9	Buenos Airies	11.4	Seoul	14.2
Beijing	8.7	Seoul	11.3	Los Angeles-Long Beach	14.2

This chart portrays population figures and projections for the world's 12 largest cities. The civic governments in each of these cities face an enormous challenge.

they are not tolerated. There, it is common to simply bulldoze the area, forcing people to move. In Latin America, squatter settlements have changed and improved, largely as a result of some positive government programs. Many areas now see that private initiatives must be encouraged. It is recognized that squatter settlements fill a need which cannot otherwise be met due to the high cost of public housing. About one-half of Mexico City's 17 million people live in illegal settlements. As many as 40 per cent of the people in Ankara, Lima, and Casablanca are squatters.

As urban populations increase, more pressure will be applied on the resources of cities. Sprawling cities take over valuable farmland because rural and urban development are not coordinated. This is not possible when farmland is limited as it is, for example, in Egypt. Uncontrolled growth and lack of architectural planning makes providing even basic services too costly. Local governments face a challenge as large as their populations.

URBAN PROBLEMS

In spite of the vast differences between the developed and underdeveloped worlds, some problems for the urban environment are common to both. Governments must co-operate in urban planning and resource sharing if we are to solve these problems. Urban pollution is one of our most pressing shared global problems.

This facet of urban culture, perhaps more than any other, highlights our global interdependence.

Cities are growing so rapidly that they often cannot provide the standard of living demanded by their citizens.

Urban pollution is a result of industrial and human waste. Hazardous waste dumping, inadequate sanitation and disposal of solid wastes, open brown-coal smoke stacks, and contaminated water supplies all contribute to disease and ill-health. The cities of the developed nations have many of the same problems. There, a failure to act may be traced to a lack of will.

Chapter 6

URBAN CULTURE

North American families face challenges quite different from those experienced by people in underdeveloped countries. For these children the future looks bright.

In the underdeveloped nations, the problem is made worse by a lack of funds. In developed nations, bottled water is used if shortages occur or if a local water supply is contaminated. If noise pollution is a problem, sound barriers are built. Pollution controls on factories and vehicles reduce air pollution. Such responses are impossible in most of the underdeveloped world.

Transportation is another problem common to urban areas. How do we move millions of people around a city daily? Industrial cities have spent billions of dollars on rapid transit systems. Many people in most larger cities now depend on public transport to get to work. However, many people still insist on travelling by private car. Cars carrying one or two people take up much road space. The result is high density smog and traffic jams during the morning and evening rush hours. Although 20 per cent or more of all North American adults are without cars, many households have two or three cars. This car-dominated society poses challenges for urban planners.

Most underdeveloped cities lack sophisticated transportation systems because they do not have the funds to build them. Many people living in these cities consider transportation their most critical problem. Most urban poor live in outlying areas, while most jobs are in the central cores. The poor must endure long trips on crowded and inadequate trains or buses to get to work. Even when transportation is available, it is sometimes too costly for many people. Surveys suggest that over half of the trips taken by poor families are on foot. More fortunate people travel by bicycle.

Poor and inadequate systems of urban transport lead to greater crowding. Urban planners must cope with the distance between work and home and community life. Advances in communications make possible a new alternative. This concept would combine rural and urban living by establishing urban centres in the outlying areas of large cities. These urban centres would then be linked by roads and rapid transit to the city core.

Transportation is a problem common to all cities. The Metro efficiently moves thousands of people around Montreal every day.

71

ONE WORLD

CASE STUDY:
TOKYO–TAMA NEW TOWN EXPERIMENT

High-speed transportation helps to move people from outlying communities to the city centre and back again.

Japan has developed a system of planned population dispersal to deal with the 25 million people who live within 48 kilometres of Tokyo. The regional transit system must cope with large numbers of urban workers, as well as 40 per cent of the nation's total freight. Transit problems between Tokyo and Kobe have led to long and overcrowded trips for commuters. Attempts to solve this problem have caused a serious drain on urban resources. A possible solution involves the creation of a national network of new communities These would be serviced by telecommunications, air services, high-speed rail lines, roads, and harbours. The effect would be to decentralize economic development. Most new residents would work in or near their community.

Tama New Town is one such development. Almost 13 kilometres long and 1.6 – 3 kilometres wide, Tama has all the necessary services, including businesses. Smaller neighbourhoods within Tama are protected from vehicular traffic; instead, they have a complex network of walkways. Sixty per cent of Tama's workers work within the community. The other 40 per cent commute to Tokyo on high speed trains.

Tsukuba New Town is another project near Tokyo. This is a centre of learning for 120 000 people. About 28 000 hectares of land have been reserved for this project. The planned city will occupy about 15 per cent of the allotted land. An automated bus system will service it. In addition, fast travel to Tokyo may be possible via an experimental magnetic levitation train.

Japan's challenge is to shift its urban population away from the congestion of Tokyo, Kobe, and Osaka. New city developments are planned for the coastal area of the Sea of Japan. High-speed rail and communications networks must be given top priority in these developments.

1. Describe the strategy behind the new self-contained suburbs in Tokyo. How has this affected lifestyles?
2. Explain how Tokyo is attempting to solve its transportation problems.

CONCLUSION

Urbanization is now a major characteristic of world development. This global urban culture imparts a sameness of life for those involved in the transnational business which supports it. As mega-cities develop, new problems emerge in terms of housing, employment, social services, and transportation. In the developed world, urban renewal projects may take place in neighbourhoods which regenerate older neighbourhoods, create pedways and bike paths, and preserve historic buildings. In the underdeveloped world, cities do not have the funds to adequately house or service the current population, yet face the additional challenge of having to increase urban services by 65 per cent by 2000. It appears an insurmountable task without help from the developed nations. Forty-two per cent of Japan's exports and 33 per cent of the USA's exports go to the underdeveloped world. Interdependence is a part of life in the latter stages of the twentieth century. It is in the interests of all nations to solve the urban problems of the underdeveloped nations.

Chapter 6
URBAN CULTURE

Urbanization has become a striking global phenomenon.

QUESTIONS

1. Define the term urbanization.
2. How were the cities of the past different from those of today?
3. What has led to a global urban culture?
4. Define the term *primacy* in relation to urban growth.
5. What are the advantages and disadvantages to underdeveloped nations in having only one major city?
6. What are the three main reasons that people migrate from rural to urban regions?
7. What will be the lifestyle of the rural migrants to the cities of the underdeveloped regions? Knowing this, why do they come?
8. How can the standard of living for the urban poor be raised?
9. What is the informal economic sector?
10. How do squatter settlements differ from shanty towns? Why are they permitted to exist?
11. Name and explain two problems associated with urbanization.
12. Transporting large numbers of goods and people is vital to an urban society. What are some of the approaches to transportation adopted by the modern city?

ACTIVITIES

1. **Picture Collage:**
   Compose a picture collage which compares and contrasts two cities, one from the developed world and one from the underdeveloped world. What buildings form the central core? What housing is available? What entertainment and sports facilities are there? Parks? Transportation? Shopping?
   Consider the buildings at the central core, type of housing, transportation, entertainment and sports facilities, parks, shopping and other commercial establishments, religious buildings, educational facilities, and public services.

2. **Oral Report:**
   You have just returned from a week's holiday in the major city of your choice. Relate your experiences of sightseeing, eating out, shopping, and perhaps talking to local people. If possible, find pictures of this city to illustrate your talk. What did you find most interesting about this city? Was anything either difficult or disturbing?

3. **Research Proposal:**
   Draw up a proposal for a new urban subdivision which will accommodate about 100 000 people. You may assume that most residents will work in the nearby mega-city. How will your subdivision relate to this mega-city? Consider housing, transportation, education, health care, leisure time activities, park areas, and commercial establishments. Your proposal can be a drawing which identifies all the subdivision's features and shows its relationship to the parent city. A brief written summary should clarify the main features of your proposal.

4. **Resource Calculation:**
   Mega-cities use tremendous amounts of resources daily. They must also dispose of the waste. Using your family as a base unit, calculate the daily requirements of food for a city of 30 million people. How many tonnes of garbage would be produced in one day in a city of this size?

5. **Research Report:**
   Research the environmental impact of the use of automobiles for transportation in a large city. Consider fuel consumption, exhaust, and land use.

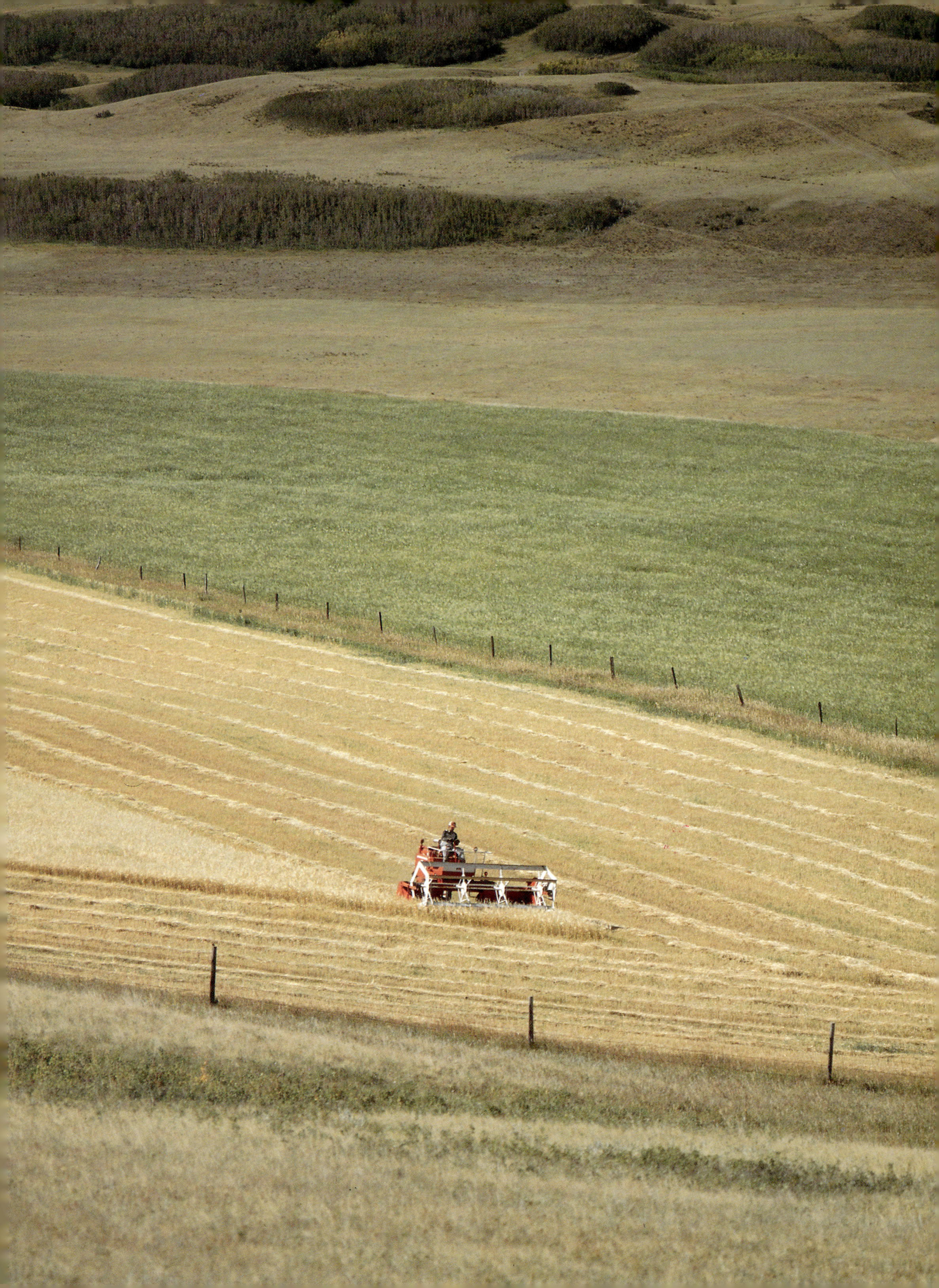

7

FOOD AND AGRICULTURAL RESOURCES

Humans can produce more food than the present world population needs. Starvation is caused by political and economic decisions.

EACH YEAR 40 MILLION PEOPLE die from hunger and hunger-related diseases. Most of these deaths occur in underdeveloped regions. This is in spite of large increases in global food supplies since 1961. Between 1961 and 1980, food production grew by 3.1 per cent, while population grew by 2.4 per cent per year. However, great disparity exists because of unequal distribution. Industrial nations subsidize farming, which results in huge surpluses. At the same time, many underdeveloped regions have turned food producing land into cash crops produced for export. This is at the expense of local food production. These cash crops earn much-needed foreign currency. However, once land is converted to the growing of cotton, coffee, or tobacco, it is unlikely to be used again for producing food. Crop choices, land use, and land distribution are political and economic problems that need to be tackled if everyone in the world is to be fed. It is essential that these political and economic decisions on food production and distribution be made with regard to global welfare.

WORLD FOOD CONSUMPTION

Four crops—wheat, rice, maize, and potato—contribute more tonnage to the world's total food production than all other food crops combined. Food choices vary significantly from one part of the world to another and attempts to influence these choices have been largely unsuccessful. Thus, dried milk powder or North American wheat are often left in storage while people go hungry.

Urbanization and industrialization change eating habits and encourage a desire for greater variety.

People in industrial nations spend a smaller portion of their total income on food than do people living elsewhere. At the same time, they have access to large quantities and wide varieties of food. In 1980, humans ate about 140 million tonnes of meat, or about 30 kilograms per person. People in industrialized countries ate most of this meat. Americans ate an average of 110 kilograms per person, the Japanese 30 kilograms per person. By contrast, people in India each ate only 1.1 kilograms per year on average. Ten or more calories of grain are required to produce just one calorie of grain-fed beef. The meat-rich diet of the developed world draws heavily on global grain production.

ONE WORLD

Modern farming techniques have increased crop yields but these techniques have also contributed to soil erosion. In the USA, the massive use of fertilizers and pesticides causes over half its water pollution. Progress has real costs.

MEAT EATERS

Americans eat about 800 kilograms of grain a year, almost all indirectly in the meat they eat. This amount has increased 160 kilograms since 1960. If people in developed nations simply ate the same amount of meat that they ate 20 years ago, they would improve their health, free large amounts of grain, and release pasture land for other uses.

Other food choices industrialized nations make are also costly. More than three-quarters of North American food is processed. For example, a fresh potato costs about 64¢. It will cost around $5.69 when made into potato chips. A wide variety of fresh fruit and vegetables is now available year round. In spite of this, North Americans eat one-third less of these than they did in 1910. Diet is a matter for concern in developed countries. Quantities of "empty calories" are consumed daily. People choose to eat processed food lacking essential vitamins and minerals. Diets characterized by excessive fat, sugar, and calories lead to a wide range of health problems, including heart attacks and cancer. In the United States, at least 33 per cent of people over 40 are obese. Millions of dollars are spent each year on slimming aids.

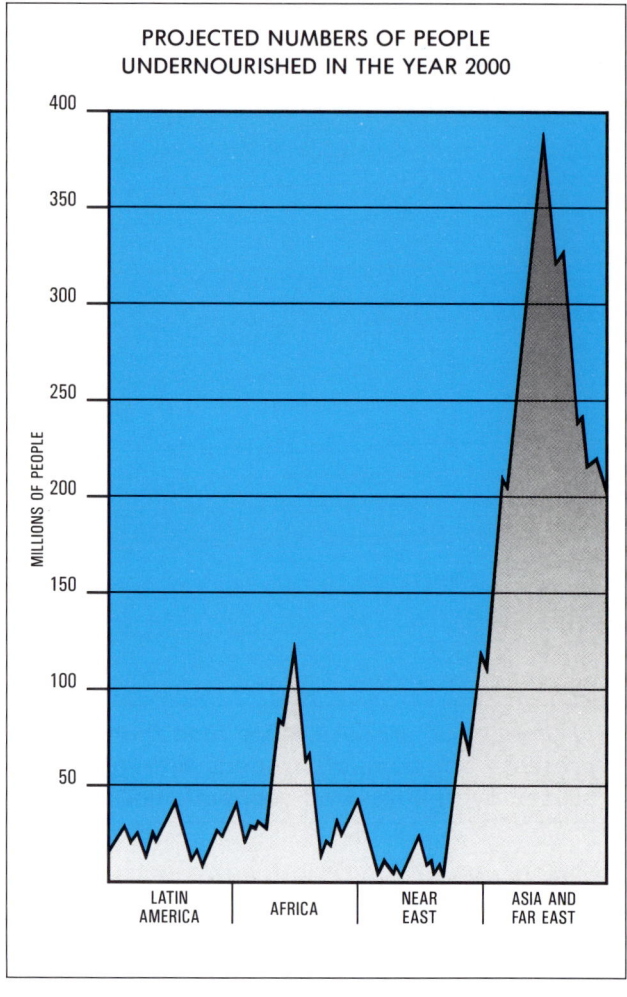

A human being needs 2400 calories a day for general well-being. Europeans and North Americans average 3000 calories a day, while people in underdeveloped nations average less than 2100 calories.

There are limits to the numbers of people the biosphere can feed.

While North Americans and Europeans average 3000 calories per person per day, people living in Haiti, Nepal, and nine other underdeveloped countries average less than 2100 calories per day. Disparity within these countries makes these figures much worse on a local basis. While the privileged eat to excess, the poor starve. Food choices for the rich in underdeveloped countries are just as wide as for those in developed countries. For most, however, the primary concern is food availability. Poverty means a diet that lacks variety and, often,

Chapter 7
FOOD AND AGRICULTURAL RESOURCES

calories and nutrients. Hunger, disease, and finally death can result. Can we increase global food supplies to include both the food needs of the poor and the food desires of the rich? Can we make the food choices of the developed world available to all parts of the world?

GLOBAL FOOD SUPPLIES

Global food supplies are unevenly distributed around the world.

There is not a world food shortage. If evenly distributed, there is more than enough food for all. Seventy-five nations have achieved some increase in per-person calorie intake since 1961. The global food supply rose from 2340 to 2630 calories per person. This is above the 2400 required for general well-being. However, these figures are deceptive as food distribution is so uneven. In 1985, famine in Ethiopia killed large numbers, while 12 other African countries produced cereal surpluses of 3.5 million tonnes. These surpluses were not made available to Ethiopia.

Africa, with 11 per cent of the world's population, produces only 7 per cent of its staple crops. The overall picture in Africa is bleak. From 1980 to 1986, food production increased by 2.9 per cent. However, population growth was at least 3 per cent. Since 1970, the average amount of food available per head has declined in sub-Saharan Africa. In Kenya, 40 per cent of the rural population lacks about 640 calories per day.

Population growth increases demands on the biosphere to provide more food.

By contrast, since 1961, India and China have become self-sufficient in grain and cereal production. China, with 30 per cent of the world's population, produces 35 per cent of the world's food and is starting to export. Western Europe and North America are the world leaders in food production. Here most of the world's food surplus is grown.

Optimistic projections suggest that a high level of technology in agriculture can increase the earth's growing capacity. A more realistic picture comes from looking at distribution as well. In the underdeveloped world, with their currently low levels of technology, 64 countries cannot feed themselves. Using the most advanced technology, all but 19 countries could become self-sufficient. This would still leave about 100 million people in countries with a food deficit. Globally, the problem seems to be one of distribution as well as production. We must recognize the fragility of agricultural resources. It is becoming harder to raise world agricultural output. In the mid-1950s, production levels consistently rose by 3 per cent per year. In the 1980s,

When farming techniques changed from human to horse powered, a substantial increase in agricultural yield was steadily measured. With the change to mechanized farming, the yields were even greater, but we are reaching limits to the increases in production we might expect.

HYDROPONICS

Hydroponics is the science of growing plants without soil. The plants are put in either gravel or water, then nutrients are added. Initially, this process was used to study what nutrients plants required. The technique is now used to grow plants commercially. Hydroponics could solve the problem of soil shortages or of soil contamination. Lettuce, tomatoes, and many other vegetables are currently grown by this process.

In the past 50 years, around 650 000 square kilometres have been added to the southern edge of the Sahara Desert. Globally, desertification could affect the land of 628 million people.

such production level increases are possible only with the expense of increased technology.

GLOBAL LAND USE

Of the earth's 13 billion hectares of total land area, only 1.5 billion hectares or about 11 per cent can be cultivated. With improved management and high expense, we could add another 1.7 billion hectares. This would bring the total arable land to 24 per cent, substantially increasing our annual food production. However, the underdeveloped world is most in need of increased food supplies. Machinery and technology, which are necessary to make the best use of land resources, are currently unavailable in these areas and in most cases are too expensive to import. Are industrial nations willing to fund land development projects to reduce world hunger?

Food supplies must be carefully managed. We must prevent degradation of both the land and the oceans to protect future food sources.

Do we fully appreciate the precious quality of land? Just 2.5 centimetres of topsoil can take from 100 to 2500 years to form. This amount of topsoil can be destroyed in as little as 10 years. Disappearance of our soil is a crucial problem. There is a "land crisis." Billions of tonnes of soil are carried away by the wind or washed into the sea each year. Europe, the area least affected by erosion, loses about 1 billion tonnes of soil per year. Asia loses about 25 billion tonnes. Cultivating steep slopes without adequate terracing, overworking the soil, inexpert irrigation, allowing livestock to overgraze grasslands, and getting rid of tree cover all cause erosion. This soil eventually ends up in the ocean and is lost forever. Unless this erosion is checked,

Chapter 7

FOOD AND AGRICULTURAL RESOURCES

any other cropland made productive by the year 2000 will simply replace land lost instead of adding to land area.

Another serious problem associated with this land crisis is desertification. It occurs not in the deserts themselves but in arid or semi-arid lands.

Desertification is defined as desert created by humans. It is caused by over-cultivation, deforestation, over-grazing, and poor irrigation. Excessive human numbers compound the problem by increased pressure on the land. Over one-third of the earth's ice-free land area is already affected or likely

An irrigation project allows crops to be planted along the riverbank in the rocky Dades Valley, Atlas, Morocco.

> **STERILIZATION OF THE SAHEL**
>
> A semi-arid belt of poor soils, ranging from 300 to 1200 kilometres in width, the Sahel stretches across Africa to the immediate south of the Sahara. Average rainfall varies from 8 to 50 millimetres a year. When—and if—it rains, up to 90 percent of the moisture evaporates. Drought is natural to the Sahel. What is not, is the over-grazing and deforestation that have allowed the desert to overrun an area roughly the size of France and Austria combined, all in the space of 50 years.
>
> For centuries, nomads in this huge territory lived in balance on marginal resources. The balance shifted in the 1950s and 1960s. The political policies of new African nations restricted the movements of nomads. Independence also brought foreign aid. Economic aid brought new strains of crops, like cotton and peanuts, that could survive a short growing season. Expanding agriculture and population overwhelmed grazing land. Thousands of new wells penetrate the aquifer (the underground layer that contains water) each year. Livestock strips vegetation around wells, topsoil blows away, and bare patches fuse into desert. The result? The steady encroachment of desert onto lands once capable of sustaining significant human, animal, and plant life. Unfortunately, this is a global phenomenon. Each year, human misuse denudes 40 000 square kilometres of the earth's surface.

to be affected by desertification. Since 1950, the desert in Sudan has pushed south by 100 kilometres. Although drought has been blamed for the Sahel disaster in the 1970s when at least 100 000 people and millions of animals died, the root of the problem lay in the past. Better than average rainfall had encouraged the cultivation of marginal lands. Livestock were crowded onto smaller areas of pasture. These people managed to survive as long as rainfall was plentiful. However, when the rains stopped, they were deprived of their livelihood. Their livestock perished and their crops failed. Famine ensued and thousands died.

AGRICULTURE IN UNDERDEVELOPED NATIONS

Agricultural exports are a major source of revenue for underdeveloped regions today. Cash crops such as coffee, cocoa, tobacco, or sugar provide the foreign currency needed to buy tools and technology for development. The production of cash crops makes large amounts of land unavailable for the production of food. In underdeveloped regions these cash crops are often grown on large plantations controlled by multinational corporations.

Local food production, however, is still labour-intensive. Traditional farming practices characterize the agricultural economy in the underdeveloped world. On average, 60 per cent of the people in underdeveloped areas work in agriculture. In some regions the percentage is even higher. For example, Africa averages about 80 per cent employment in agriculture. While domesticated animals in the developed world provide meat and milk, in underdeveloped regions they provide draft power. In India alone, there are over 80 million draft animals. These provide power equal to 30 megawatts. Farms are typically small and allow only a subsistence living. Fertilizers and pesticides are too costly, and technology capable of overcoming the problems of fragile soil is unavailable to these farmers. Yields are therefore much lower than in developed countries. The average production of wheat is 62 per cent of that in developed regions. Yields of maize at 23 per cent and rice at 35 per cent are even lower. A combination of factors leads to these low yields. Environment, seed quality, and exhausted and eroded soil all contribute.

Social and economic inequality leads large numbers of poor people to degrade the land by overcropping and destroying the forests in searching for fuel. This desperate effort to survive eliminates any possibility of improving quality of life or providing future security. Instead of increased yields and more food per capita, hunger persists.

Land reform is one of the most contentious issues in food production. In many countries in the underdeveloped world, tenant farmers till large sectors of land for the owners. These tenant farmers often have a very small amount of land for themselves that provides only a bare living. The upper classes control large landholdings and resist any

Chapter 7

FOOD AND AGRICULTURAL RESOURCES

change in the status quo. However, land rights and secure tenure are serious concerns. Land rights must also recognize the role of women in food production. In many countries, only men can hold land titles. Women, especially heads of households, must have landholding rights in the interests of food security.

One of the major problems of the underdeveloped world is the dilemma of cash crop production. Many countries have long grown coffee, sugar, cocoa, and other products desired by industrial nations. The export of these products provides needed foreign currency. In 1980, global export earnings from the sale of coffee totalled $12 billion, second only to petroleum. Of this, only 27 per cent goes to the underdeveloped producing countries. This revenue is earned at the expense of local food production.

Heavy food subsidies by governments in the developed countries affect local food markets even more dramatically. In 1983, these subsidies amounted to $14 billion in the European Common Market and $40 billion in the USA. These subsidies encourage over-production, leading to enormous surpluses. It is cheaper to give this food away than to store it. The subsidized food thus competes in underdeveloped countries with local products, driving the price down. The **World Bank** estimates that $8 billion per year in subsidies to subsistence farmers in the underdeveloped regions would relieve their poverty. However, this $8 billion is currently unavailable.

Cash crops, such as coffee, are purchased by developed nations. However, the growth of such cash crops leaves little arable land for the production of food for local people.

81

ONE WORLD

CASE STUDY:

KENYA — AN AGRICULTURAL SUCCESS

Since its independence in December 1963, Kenya has enjoyed an agricultural growth which is the envy of sub-Saharan Africa. It has the most advanced agricultural economy of any independent African country. This has been achieved by policies which encourage private land ownership, fair prices for producers, and a flexible foreign exchange rate. Kenya's government went through a crisis period in the early 1980s. It is now stabilized and committed to a program of social and economic growth.

Kenya's agricultural growth rate has averaged 3 per cent per year for the past decade. This is very significant when one considers that of Kenya's total land area of 582 750 square kilometres, only one-fifth is reasonably fertile. In addition, since Kenya's population is now 20 million, the country has a density of 35 persons per square kilometre of cultivatable land. In spite of such population pressure, Kenya has become one of the world's leading exporters of tea and coffee. In 1984, 107 933 tonnes of coffee, earning $285 million, were exported. Tea exports of 105 212 tonnes earned Kenya $266 million. These agricultural earnings have led to the establishment of a viable manufacturing sector.

Kenya's success seems to be directly related to its land policy. At independence, British settlers held about 25 per cent of its fertile land. On this land, tea was produced for export and cattle were raised. Africans who grew food crops such as maize, peas, beans, millet, and sorghum farmed the other 75 per cent of the land. The foreign holdings were mechanized while the local farms were traditional peasant operations. The foreign sector had been heavily subsidized by the local farmers during colonial times, as the small farmers paid most of the taxes. African farmers suffered overcrowding and extreme poverty. At independence, peasant farmers put extreme pressure on the government to redistribute land. The government felt that large-scale land redistribution would be economically damaging.

Between 1961 and 1965, funding from the UK and the World Bank did help to buy about 600 000 hectares of land from British settlers. This land was then sold to 35 000 African families. Otherwise, the majority of land farmed by Africans has been awarded to individual farmers who have valid claims to land parcels. The government is committed to a system of free market land distribution which allows successful farmers to increase their holdings. This policy of private land ownership has affected production of cash crops. In 1963, small-holders accounted for only 2 per cent of total production. Large estates produced the remaining 98 per cent. Foreign corporations owned many of these. In 1982, small-holders accounted for more than half of Kenya's tea exports.

To encourage agricultural production, pricing policies reward the producer. In many underdeveloped countries prices subsidize urban dwellers. The result is a price so low that the agricultural producer is forced out of the market. This pricing policy is particularly important in the pricing of local foodstuffs. Kenya closely regulates the pricing of maize, its most valuable domestic food. Maize accounts for 50 to 70 per cent of the caloric intake of Kenyans. Between 35 and 40 per cent of Kenya's cultivated area is devoted to maize. In order to become self-sufficient in maize, Kenya sets the price slightly below import parity to encourage a domestic supply.

Another factor in Kenya's success is maintaining a flexible foreign exchange rate. Many other African countries overvalue their currency. This leads to a large difference in the official and unofficial exchange rates. Kenya devalues its currency when necessary,

▶

82

Chapter 7

FOOD AND AGRICULTURAL RESOURCES

CASE STUDY

KENYA — AN AGRICULTURAL SUCCESS

The need for foreign currency drives many underdeveloped countries to cultivate their land for the production of cash crops. Kenya, for example, exports tea.

and therefore very little difference exists between the official and the unofficial rates. This allows local people to get fair value for goods which they sell and enables them to buy imported consumer goods.

Kenya has overcome a period of extreme political instability between 1980 and 1982. President Daniel arap Moi tried to erase the regional disparities which were the cause of much dissension. Central province, where most agricultural exports are grown, is much wealthier than other regions. To balance this wealth, outlying regions have been given more educational and employment opportunities. Agricultural growth has been given top priority in government planning.

One of Kenya's greatest challenges will be to deal with a rapidly growing population. Some problems of landlessness and unemployment still exist, but most people have been absorbed into the agricultural sector. Kenya has achieved a high degree of food self-sufficiency. It takes care of most of its domestic food needs, including maize, beef/dairy products, and poultry. In 1980 and 1984, when severe drought occurred, Kenya bought food imports with cash crop earnings. Tea and coffee account for 80 per cent of these earnings, while horticultural products and tobacco make up the rest. Kenya can now take advantage of a booming coffee market. This is the result of severe drought in Brazil, which is expected to affect its coffee industry for several years. Increased coffee revenues could allow for the manufacturing sector to expand. Increased numbers of jobs in this area could relieve some of the pressure of a population growing at a rate of 4 per cent per year. Population growth will be an area of vital concern for Kenya. Without some reduction in the rate of population increase, little improvement can be expected in the lifestyle of its people. Attention to this problem, however, could lead to a promising future for Kenya. Economic prosperity and political stability seem to be on the horizon.

1. What is the basis for Kenya's successful agricultural growth since independence? Explain your answer.

2. Discuss Kenya's food pricing policy and its effect on agriculture.

ONE WORLD

"AGRIBUSINESS"

Farming in the developed nations is now referred to as agribusiness. A few large corporations control the global food market. These provide the network that links all sectors of food production. For example, these large corporations monopolize the seed and fertilizer businesses. Mega-corporations shape consumer tastes even in underdeveloped regions. Their first concern is profit, and the poor are sometimes susceptible to questionable marketing strategies. An example was the campaign by Nestlé, a huge multinational food company, to sell infant formula as a substitute for mother's milk. People in underdeveloped countries often do not have access to clean water for making up formula, rendering the formula dangerous for babies. Citizen activists in industrial nations persuaded Nestlé to follow a UN-sponsored code of practice for selling baby food. Clearly the consumer can make a difference. In this instance, consumer advocates from industrial nations demanded corporate responsibility in areas where people were unable to speak for themselves.

More efficient food production can ease predicted food shortages.

In North America, large-scale farming operations have replaced less efficient and competitive smaller farms. In the USA, the number of family farms has decreased by 50 per cent in the last 25 years. Many surviving farms find their profits greatly reduced. In spite of this, American farmers are very productive. Only 2 per cent of the American population works in agriculture. Yet they feed their fellow citizens and produce more than one-half of all the food available on the international market. From 1950 to 1983, grain production increased from 623 million tonnes to 1447 million tonnes.

However, there has been a significant decrease in momentum due to the long-term costs of "high-tech" agriculture. One of the most alarming costs results from depletion of our land resources. Soil loss in the USA is 80 million hectares, or a land area almost twice the size of California. Industrial farming practices have made this land unproductive. A second cost is the effect of modern farming practices on our water supply. Fertilizers and pesticides

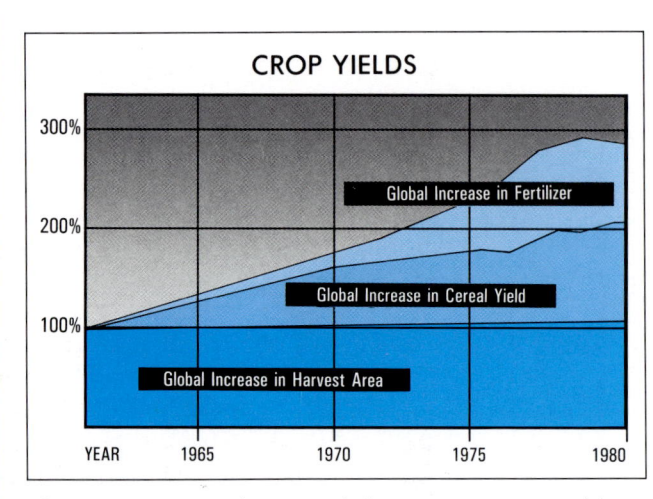

The "Green Revolution" did increase crop yields in certain underdeveloped countries but also greatly increased the use of fertilizers. Since the late 1970s the crop yields have started to level off.

create much of the increased productivity. However, they also cause over half of all water pollution in the USA. An allied problem is that of water availability, which is affected by irrigation. Irrigation now accounts for over 80 per cent of American water use. The American government has pressed Canada to divert some of its fresh water supply southward to avoid water shortages. This is a contentious issue which is yet to be worked out.

Expanding farm size and mechanizing operations are also costly. Rising costs have driven many farmers in Canada deeply into debt. The average debt in 1983 was about $70 000. Many farmers have been driven into bankruptcy.

AGRICULTURAL POSSIBILITIES

The standard of living relates directly to both the quantity and the quality of available food supplies.

Food security depends on a number of factors. As our population increases, so must food production. An even greater problem is distribution. How can the poor get the resources to feed themselves? Land reform is needed. Land distributed unfairly in many countries drives the poor onto marginal land.

Chapter 7
FOOD AND AGRICULTURAL RESOURCES

People in underdeveloped countries often must rely on local food sources for sustenance. This Egyptian street vendor signals that his fruit is for sale.

There they eke out a living at the expense of the environment and their future. With land reform must also come development of human resources. People can be taught to use land, water, and forests efficiently. We must also explore new food choices. Nutrients from the sea or alternative crops could replace meat and divert some of the grain now used as animal feed to hungry people.

The **"Green Revolution"** drew on advanced technology to vastly improve crop yields. It began with record crop yields in North America in the 1950s. However, it achieved its most dramatic success in the underdeveloped world in the 1960s in India. In the early 1950s, India produced about 50 million tonnes of cereals. By 1970 production had increased to 108 million tonnes. This meant an increase of roughly 35 to 40 per cent in annual food supplies for the average Indian. These gains were made possible by planting "high-yield" varieties of wheat and other cereal crops. These crops matured earlier, making several harvests possible. Sometimes as many as three crops could be grown in only one year. For optimum production, farmers used large amounts of fertilizer, pesticides, and irrigation water.

Green Revolution farming techniques demanded large amounts of capital. At first, developed countries helped research and develop new plant strains. However, when oil prices began to climb in 1973, it was clear that underdeveloped countries could

85

not afford the Green Revolution. The excitement of the early success of the Green Revolution has been dampened by its long-term costs. For example, because farmers planted only high yield crops, many kinds of rice are no longer grown. Their loss will be felt in the future. In addition, the initial gains of the revolution have peaked as the biological limits of new hybrid strains have been reached.

The worst effect of the Green Revolution has been its impact on the environment. Widespread use of chemical fertilizers and pesticides contaminates the soil, water, and air. The long-term effect on human health is not yet known. These agents may be responsible for cancer and birth defects.

Concern about using chemicals and pesticides has led to a small but growing movement called organic farming. Organic farmers rely on "natural" controls. For example, they rely on the ladybug to do the work of pesticides, and manure to do the work of fertilizer. Organic food now sells to a small but loyal group who fear the long-term results of eating chemicals. Organic farmers are also trying new techniques to reduce soil erosion and fuel cost. Ridge-till cultivating draws the soil up into ridges, uprooting and covering weeds. Instead of cultivating after a harvest, farmers leave the plant residue to provide ground cover during the winter and spring erosion seasons. Making fewer trips over the field conserves fuel and cuts the costs of production. The movement towards organic farming is growing as the underdeveloped world sees the potential for this type of agriculture. Intensive farming which nurtures the soil is one of our hopes for the future. Although it is doubtful that sustainable development could occur without also using fertilizers and modern agricultural techniques, organic farming could still be a valuable part of that development.

Livestock currently consumes nearly 40 per cent of the world's grain to serve the meat-rich diet of industrial nations. This source of protein could be replaced with fish. However, a high level of pollution contaminates fish supplies. Aquaculture, or "fish farming," is an alternative to naturally available fresh water fish. Yields from fish farming now are about 10 per cent of the world's fish production. With financial and scientific support, this could increase five to ten times by the year 2000. Research must also be done on new seed varieties and seed bank programs. Planting vast areas with the same crops has eroded genetic diversity. This lack of diversity could lead to crop failure, as common strains become more susceptible to pests and disease. Many of our genetic resources have been lost forever. This is true of both plants and animals.

CONCLUSION

Agriculture is a critical feature of development. In all industrial nations, mechanization of agriculture preceded the industrial revolution. These changes substantially increased food production to feed rural and urban populations and provide a surplus for export.

Farmers from various countries march through the streets of Montreal to show concern because many farmers fear losing their farms.

Chapter 7
FOOD AND AGRICULTURAL RESOURCES

Our agricultural systems are currently experiencing severe stress. Lack of attention to issues of land reform, technological innovations, and genetic diversity could propel us into a crisis of immense proportions.

By the end of the next century, we will need to feed at least twice as many people. Properly managed, the world's land could provide for these additional numbers. However, in doing so we must combine our knowledge of technology with an awareness of the fragility of our resources and the growing inequities which yield large numbers of disadvantaged people. We live in an interdependent world. Are we ready to share the responsibility of securing a future for all?

QUESTIONS

1. If there is a surplus of food in the world, why do so many people die of hunger each year?
2. What are the three basic problems that must be solved to eliminate starvation?
3. Compare and contrast the diets of people in developed and underdeveloped countries in both quantity and quality of food consumed.
4. What is the relationship between global food supplies and population densities?
5. How can global food supplies be increased?
6. How much of the land surface is arable? How much is used?
7. What are the major problems of the global land crisis? Explain each.
8. What are the results of farming marginal land?
9. Why do many nations in underdeveloped regions import foods?
10. Explain what is meant by the term agribusiness.
11. How have mechanization and high technology affected food production on land and at sea?
12. What is the dilemma of cash-crop production?
13. How have modern farming practices affected the quality of soil and water reserves?
14. What was the Green Revolution? Explain its affect on agriculture.
15. What were the disadvantages of the Green Revolution?
16. What is organic farming? What are its advantages?
17. What are the political and social roadblocks to land reform in the underdeveloped countries? Can they be overcome? Explain.
18. Name three alternative food sources.
19. How can the world's food supplies be increased?
20. Why is genetic diversity important to our food supplies?

ACTIVITIES

1. **Research Report:**
   Write a research report on the Green Revolution. Give specific details on new crops, production yields, and the impact on lifestyle in a particular area. Evaluate the revolution in India.

2. **Planning a Menu:**
   Plan a nutritious and economical menu for a family of four for one week. Consult Canada's Food Guide for suggested nutritional choices. Calculate the cost of your menu.

3. **Recommendations Report:**
   You are a scientist with the Food and Agriculture Organization (FAO) of the UN. Write a report on your recommendations for feeding the world's people in the year 2000. What new food sources have you discovered? How will you make this food available?

4. **Designing an Advertisement:**
   Design an advertisement for a new source of protein being promoted in the developed world. You must name it and describe it in a way which will make it highly desirable. You may draw the advertisement to promote it through newspapers or magazines, or you may make up a radio commercial, complete with music.

5. **Research Report:**
   Write a research report on the effects of food on our physical and mental well-being.

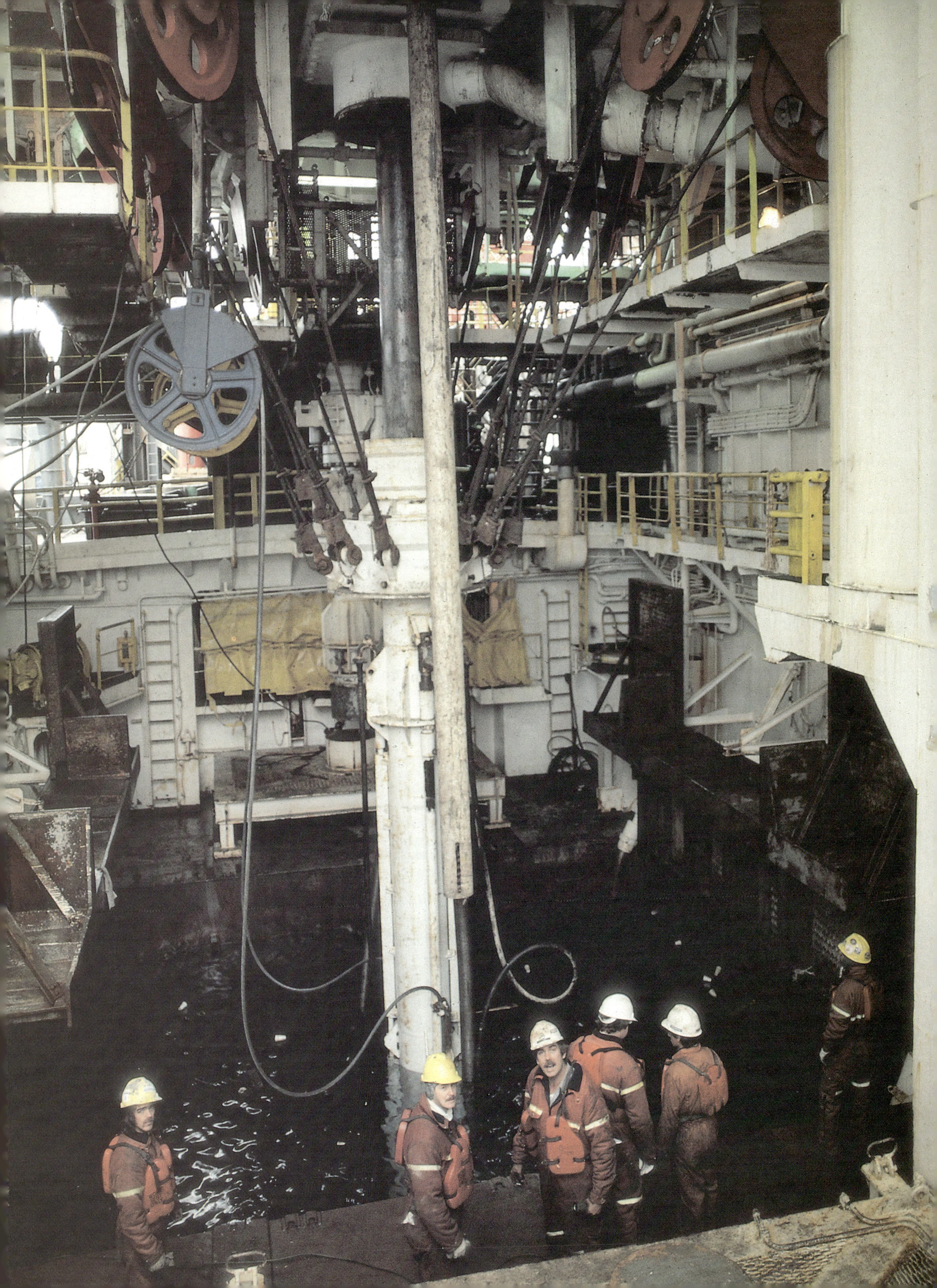

8

ENERGY AND DEVELOPMENT

Energy is one of the basic forces in the universe. Providing all the essential goods and services for mankind, energy is the source of motion and power. It fuels the human body. It stokes our factories and powers our cities. Capable of conversion into heat and warmth, it can change materials into different states and shapes. Energy lies at the heart of our standard of living. Without energy, we would not have the goods and services we expect as part of our daily lives. Our future industrial development depends on a safe and sustainable energy flow. Indeed, without energy, life could not exist.

THE ULTIMATE RESOURCE

There is endless energy in the universe.

There is an endless supply of energy in the universe. It is all around us, either as a force or stored as matter. We must decide what kind of energy we want, and then design the technology that will convert it for our use. Almost all our usable energy comes from the sun as solar radiation. Plants use about 3 per cent of this in making food. Some of the rest is reflected back into space, some is used for heat, and some is stored in water, winds, tides, and fossil fuels.

Over the centuries humans have come to rely almost exclusively on fossil fuels, such as wood, coal, oil, and gas for their energy needs. These are versatile, quick to burn, easy to get at, and easily controlled. Until now people have not needed to look elsewhere, as fossil fuels were abundant. However, not only are fossil fuels inefficient, they are dirty and give off a great amount of smoke and pollution. Only about 30 per cent of the energy released in combustion is recoverable. Despite this, over 80 per cent of the energy used today comes from wood, coal, oil, and gas. The rest comes from other sources, such as nuclear, hydro-electric, **geothermal**, wind, solar, or bio-mass systems. Using more of these systems would help to meet growing energy demands, and reduce the polluting effect of fossil fuels.

WORLD ENERGY DEVELOPMENT

Since wood was first used in fires people have taken forests, beds of coal, oil, and gas for granted. People, thinking energy was unlimited, paid little or no attention to conservation or energy efficiency because it was believed that nature would continue to provide everything needed. The same beliefs still hold sway today. Today, huge supertankers carry oil to refineries around the world. Each year thousands of trainloads of coal leave the mines to heat

ONE WORLD

Humans have developed elaborate ways to extract and distribute fossil fuels such as can be seen in this oil refinery at Pointe Aux Trembles, Quebec.

Many city skylines are brightly lit and demonstrate a tremendous waste of energy.

homes and fuel power plants hundreds of kilometres away. Pipelines crisscross continents, bringing oil and gas to centres of population and production. But this cannot go on forever. Sooner or later conventional supplies of fossil fuels are going to give out.

The small number of advanced industrial nations use most of the energy produced in the world today. Industrialized nations depend so heavily on fossil fuels for their high standard of living that disruption of supply would lead to extreme hardship. This is why these countries are willing to consider the use of military force to keep open international supply lines.

Ever-increasing energy usage helps fuel the extravagant lifestyles enjoyed by many people in the developed world. Comfortable surroundings that defy nature, stylish clothing, and high-tech communication networks; fresh or frozen, sanitized, and packaged foods; and many lavish leisure activities all drain the world's energy reserves. Plastics take more energy to make than steel, and synthetics take more energy to make than natural fibres. Urban living takes far more energy than rural life. Mega-cities, such as New York, Tokyo, and Singapore, have local energy demands that are so enormous that they must rely on distant suppliers for their energy requirements.

Industrial nations use a hundred times as much energy as the total used in the rest of the world. With 25 per cent of the planet's population, they use about 80 per cent of the world's energy. Canada and the United States, with only 8 per cent of the world's population, consume almost half the energy used in the world today. North Americans burn more energy in their cars alone than the total amount of energy used by the non-industrial nations. North Americans are the most energy-consuming people on earth. Their per capita demand is around 400 000 kilocalories each day. This is far above the 2000 kilocalories needed to sustain life. North American air conditioners alone use up more energy than the total energy consumption in all of

Chapter 8

ENERGY AND DEVELOPMENT

India. The rest of the world would need to increase its energy usage more than 20 times to catch up.

The modern cities' demands for lighting, space heating, refrigeration, and transportation gobble up energy at prodigious rates. Modern buildings are large, poorly insulated, and need costly temperature controls. Transportation corridors carry cars and trains from distant suburbs to city centres and back each day, at great energy costs. Brightly lit downtown areas draw people to high-energy entertainments, while costly eating out is common. The energy costs of such a lifestyle are staggering.

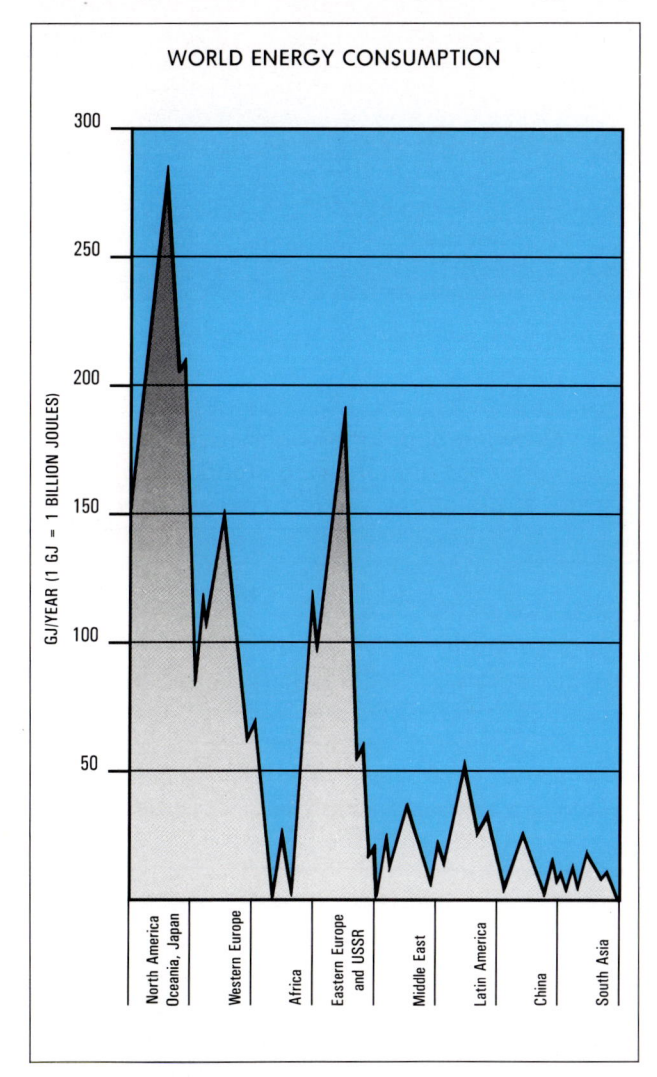

WORLD ENERGY CONSUMPTION

[Graph showing GJ/YEAR (1 GJ = 1 BILLION JOULES) from 0 to 300 across regions: North America Oceania, Japan; Western Europe; Africa; Eastern Europe and USSR; Middle East; Latin America; China; South Asia]

This graph compares world energy consumption. North America consumes the most, using twice as much as Western Europe and 17 times as much as South Asia.

It is a lifestyle which is also the envy of people in the non-industrial world. Their efforts to catch up are rapidly depleting our remaining fossil fuel reserves.

THE END IN SIGHT?

Uncontrolled human use of fossil fuels has led to environmental damage by pollution. The pollution is so great that we risk changing the composition of the atmosphere to one that life cannot tolerate.

How long can we keep up the growing rate of energy consumption? The planet cannot stand much more, yet future global energy needs will be very high. Without any increase in population or demand, the present levels can be sustained at about 12 billion watts of energy, an amount equal to 12 billion tonnes of coal. This is not realistic. Demands will not only keep rising, they will rise exponentially, likely doubling every 10 years. This means that in the final 10 years, the last half of the supplies will be used up. We would need 14 billion watts of energy to maintain our present standard of living given a world population of 8.2 billion. We could reach this population by early in the next century. A drastic increase to 55 billion watts would bring the whole world up to the living standard of the industrial societies. To do so we would have to double the amount of oil we use, quadruple the natural gas flow, use 5 times the coal, and increase the number of nuclear plants by at least 30 times. If the underdeveloped countries stay below industrial levels, we may survive the next half century with an increase to only 35 billion watts. Well before then, our fossil fuels will have run out.

Most people in the non-industrial world use wood as their main source of energy. Women and children routinely gather wood for cooking and heating. Due to large increases in population, the demand is so great that many regions have been completely deforested. Great Britain used up most of its forests long ago to build mighty imperial fleets. The United States has converted three-quarters of its forests to other uses. People everywhere now use up wood supplies faster than they can be replaced.

ONE WORLD

British Columbia's forests have been clear-cut for decades and now some areas are completely treeless.

RECYCLING PAPER

Fifty per cent of the world's paper could be recycled by the year 2000. We now recycle only 25 per cent, but an increase to 50 per cent would meet about 75 per cent of world demand for new paper. This would release about 8 million hectares of forest from paper production.

Similarly, we could recycle over 80 per cent of all aluminum, but now only about 30 per cent comes from scrap. Next time you are about to throw away an aluminum soft-drink container, consider the fact that you are throwing away the energy equivalent of several litres of gasoline.

About 2 billion people live in wood-deficient areas: where substitute fuels are not readily available, they burn dung, stubble, or weeds. This robs the soil of needed nutrients and adds to wind and water erosion. Those who are short of wood for fuel reduce the number of meals they eat and shorten the cooking time of their food. This leads to increased hunger and disease.

Growing populations and escalating demands for higher living standards place great strain on the world's energy reserves.

OIL EXTRACTION

Successful research into extracting oil from the existing oil shales of Colorado and the oil sands of Alberta will lengthen the time that humans have to perfect new energy systems based on fusion or solar power. Oil-rich soil deposits in Alberta and Colorado can supply the energy needs of North America until and after the new energy systems are ready for use.

Recoverable oil and gas supplies may last another 50 years. New ways of extracting about 3000 million barrels of synthetic oil from the Alberta oil sands and the Colorado oil shales should lengthen the life of this fuel by at least a century. Liquefying coal or adapting vehicles to run on alcohol are still in the early stages of development but hold promise. Brazil has replaced over half of the gasoline it needs with 10 billion litres of ethanol distilled from sugar cane.

Chapter 8

ENERGY AND DEVELOPMENT

CASE STUDY:

BRAZILIAN ALCOHOL ENERGY

The unstable nature of oil prices in combination with the threat of depleting oil reserves has led Brazil to look for new sources of energy. Ethanol's potential as a fuel was recognized early, but ethanol was never produced as cheaply as gasoline.

Brazil, the fifth largest landmass in the world, has based its transportation policies on road transportation. Its current fuel policy would convert motor transport to the use of alcohol as a fuel. The ethanol program is based largely on sugar cane, the most efficient of energy crops. Ethanol has been produced as an intoxicant from fruits and grains for centuries. Produced directly from sugar by fermentation, ethanol can be obtained from three main types of crop: sugar crops, root crops, and all major cereals. Sugar cane, however, yields 4000 decimetres per hectare or 65 per cent more than normal feedstock. Thus, large amounts of farmland have been converted to sugar cane production.

The use of alcohol as a fuel has several attractions. Automobile engines can readily run on a mixture of gasoline and alcohol. The commercial plants and processes necessary for production are already in place and require only expansion. Government incentives,

Sugar cane is a primary element in Brazilian ethanol production. Domestic ethanol will replace imported liquid fuels.

however, will be necessary to fund such an expansion program. The technology of distilling ethanol already exists. New distillers will be needed as will the conversion of millions of hectares of land to sugar cane production.

This will create thousands of jobs and ease the unemployment situation. The programme will also help to stem the tide of urban migration by keeping more growers on the land.

Brazil is not the only country to make the move away from petroleum products in its transportation sector. The technology of distilling ethanol is used around the world. Brazil is notable, however, in the ambitious nature of its conversion. To reach automobile fuel self-sufficiency Brazil plans to plant in excess of 20 million hectares of cane. This is more than all of the sugar cane grown in the 65 cane-producing nations. No longer will Brazil have to depend on imported liquid fuels.

1. What are the advantages to Brazil of converting their use of automotive fuels from petroleum products to alcohol?

2. What are the consequences for agriculture of this decision?

3. What are the alternatives to basing the state's transportation system on road transport?

4. Should Canada consider a similar policy? Why or why not?

ONE WORLD

Other nations are increasing coal production in the face of energy shortages. China, with a fifth of the world's population, intends to use coal to industrialize. The earth's coal beds may hold 7.6 trillion tonnes, which should last into the next century. But burning coal pollutes the environment. There is a limit to the pollution the air can safely handle before irrecoverable damage is done.

Air pollution from fossil fuels is already serious in many parts of the globe. The dependence of underdeveloped nations on these fuels to achieve gains in their standard of living only adds to the problem. Policies of industrial development at any cost could poison the biosphere. Smoke stacks and wood-burning ovens cast millions of tonnes of carbon dioxide, sulfur, and nitrogen oxides into the air. Carried aloft, they can remain in the atmosphere for months until scrubbed out by rain and snow when they fall to the ground. Air pollutants have a disastrous effect on the environment, destroying lakes, soils, and plant and animal habitats. They kill vegetation, cause severe land and water pollution, and damage buildings. Thousands of lakes in North America and Europe show a steady increase in acid levels from industrial pollution. This leads to the death of fish populations. These same acids will eventually enter the soil as groundwater, causing further environmental damage.

The greatest amount of damage is in central Europe, which receives more than 1 gram of sulfur pollution every year on each square metre of land and water. This is five times the natural level. Polish and East German forests have been all but destroyed. Air pollutants have penetrated the soils, affecting the roots' ability to take up soil water, making trees vulnerable to the mildest of droughts. Pollutants in the air have caused serious health problems, affecting asthmatics and elderly people most. Constantly breathing acidic air may have shortened the lifespan of the Polish people by at least a decade.

Rapid industrial development has placed the planet's fuel reserves in danger. Now, for the first time, humans have been forced to admit that these fuels are limited, and that the end of conventional supplies is in sight. People are simply using the fuels faster than they can be replaced. In about 300 years, we will likely use up all the fossil fuels on earth, fuels which took 600 million years to produce.

Pollution has caused this stream to decay.

Assuming we have only used up 1 per cent of all available fuel (when in fact we have used much more), and assuming that demands for more energy will double every 10 years, we should run out of reserves in 13 doublings, or 266 years. This is a hypothetical figure. It assumes that we have not yet used any fuel. One hundred years is a more realistic figure. We could likely extend this deadline by another 50 years if we become energy efficient. But if demands continue to grow, we would have less than a single lifetime to take action. We will have to develop an alternative energy supply that is inexhaustible, environmentally clean, and safe to use. There are many possibilities. Today, scientists see nuclear and solar power as the most promising answers to the question of future energy demands.

Chapter 8

ENERGY AND DEVELOPMENT

NUCLEAR ENERGY'S POWER AND PERILS

Nuclear energy is clean, though it can be dangerous. No energy system is without risks, but nuclear energy raises the risks to new levels. The possibility of a nuclear disaster is a legitimate matter of concern. An uncontained reactor meltdown would be a catastrophe for all animal and plant life for kilometres around. Scientists assure us that this could never happen. However, the incidents at Three Mile Island and Chernobyl remind us that accidents can happen.

Nuclear power is particularly attractive to nations with few alternative sources of power. France derives 65 per cent of its energy from nuclear sources, Canada only 13 per cent.

Nuclear energy can be released either by **fission** or **fusion**. Fission splits the nuclei of heavy elements such as uranium 235 in a chain reaction releasing large amounts of energy. The energy in 1 gram of uranium equals 13 barrels of crude oil or 2.7 tonnes of coal. However, if nuclear energy depended on the fissioning of U235, the nuclear age would be brief. The world does not have that much U235. The answer lies in the breeding reactors that create more fuel than they consume.

All energy systems are prone to accident. Nuclear systems have raised the level of danger because of the staggering effects of radiation pollution.

The neutrons released during nuclear fission bring about nuclear breeding. Each atom of a nuclear fission releases at least two fast, high-energy neutrons. One must trigger another fission to keep the chain reaction going. Others are lost. But the remainder

Electricity is produced in nuclear power plants. This photo shows the cooling towers on the Randro Seco power plant in California.

can be used to transform isotopes, such as thorium 232 into uranium 233, or uranium 238 into plutonium 239, both of which are fissionable. Thus, the process produces more fuel than is used in the initial reaction. This makes using large quantities of low grade ore possible. An efficient breeder can produce enough material to refuel itself and an identical reactor in about 10 years.

Technologies to control nuclear fusion are still quite far away. Fusion is the process by which the sun generates its energy. Fusion results when two light nuclei merge into a single nucleus of a heavier element. This only happens at very high temperatures and is accompanied by a great release of energy. Deuterium seems the most likely element for the fusioning process. If the process can be made to work, just 2 per cent of the deuterium in the ocean would supply a million times the energy of all the fossil fuels. In effect, the supply would be unlimited.

Test explosions of thermonuclear bombs prove that fusion energy can be released by raising the temperature of a high-density gas of charged plasma particles. The process needs a temperature range of about 50 million degrees Celsius. No solid matter can exist at that temperature, so the search is on for a way of containing the plasma. One possible solution is to use powerful magnetic fields as a "bottle." The cost of the research and the development of workable pilots will be enormous. But the results could be worth it. A single cubic kilometre of seawater has the potential energy of 300 billion tonnes of coal. In addition, only 1 per cent of the 1.5 billion cubic kilometres of water on the earth could sustain a doubling of energy demands forever.

Nuclear power is not without its drawbacks. In the first place, it is only about 35 per cent efficient. The chain reactions are a heat source that transform water into steam for generating electricity. Liquid coolants remove the heat, causing much of the heat to be lost in the process. In the second place, nuclear systems create large volumes of radioactive waste, and no one has yet solved the problem of radioactive waste disposal. What does one do with millions of **curies** of radioactive substances? The problem is worsened by the long **half lives** of the contaminants. For example, the half life of plutonium 239 is nearly 25 000 years. And many half lives are needed to make the wastes safe. We do not yet have the technology to deal with this problem. While we wait, the amount of nuclear waste continues to amass. In 1986, there were over 126 million tonnes of radioactive uranium mill tailings still left in the open. More than 1840 million cubic decimetres of low level wastes were stored in shallow earth-covered pits. At least 283 million cubic decimetres of high level liquid waste is stored above ground in steel drums. Some 30 000 spent fuel assemblies were stored in liquid pools. Ways must be found to make these wastes harmless, so they will no longer threaten human health and the environment.

Non-military nuclear technology is still relatively primitive, with most nuclear plant operators depending more on theory than actual field experience. The greatest danger involves a loss of coolant, which could result in a core meltdown that breaches the containment system, spewing out deadly radioactive particles. The worst case would see thousands dead within the immediate area, tens of thousands dying from cancer, and many thousands more inflicted with thyroid tumours and other genetic defects. Hundreds of square kilometres would be made uninhabitable and unfit for agriculture. Fortunately, no such accident has occurred. However, many accidents have raised grave concerns about the safety of the nuclear program. The fire at Brown's Ferry, Alabama, and the Three Mile Island incident were both close to meltdown. In the more recent accident at Chernobyl, radioactive gas did escape containment.

In some nations, nuclear power now accounts for a large amount of electrical power generation, although most nations remain nuclear free. In 1986, there were 366 nuclear plants in the world, with a further 140 in the design stage. There are 55 research reactors currently in use, of which 33 are in the developing nations. If nuclear power is the future, then adequate safeguards must be installed to protect the public and the environment from radioactive contamination.

ALTERNATIVE SOURCES

Other sources of energy will have to be developed to replace declining, nonrenewable fossil fuels. These new sources of energy should be environmentally safe, non-polluting, and in unlimited supply.

Chapter 8

ENERGY AND DEVELOPMENT

Our future energy needs may be met by harnessing the wind's energy.

Solar power may well be the answer to our future energy needs because solar radiation is a clean and endless source of energy. We do not have the technology now to harness this energy economically. The amount of sunlight falling on only 14 per cent of the North American deserts could supply the additional power North Americans will need to the end of the century. But we cannot cover that much land with solar panels. Another solution would be to place lightweight solar collectors in synchronous orbit. They could gather solar radiation and store it in space until needed. The energy could be beamed to earth by cloud-penetrating microwaves. A satellite station with a solar collector of only about 13 square kilometres could power New York City. The North American demand for additional power could be met by 250 stations. The system seems ideal, but actual development lies far in the future.

We can also buy time by making better use of other kinds of energy resources. Southeast Asia, Africa, and Latin America have tremendous hydropower potential. Tidal, wind, and geothermal power could also be brought on line. In total, they could add another 25 years before conventional sources run out.

THE VALUE OF CONSERVATION

In the meantime, we will have to conserve what fossil fuel resources we have left. Conservation can be achieved in several ways. But are we willing to change our lives to slow the drain? Would we be

ONE WORLD

Rush-hour traffic, like this congestion of cars in Toronto, uses up a tremendous amount of the fossil fuels we have available to us.

satisfied with smaller houses, fewer and smaller cars? Can we adapt to public transportation and give up our energy-consuming conveniences such as air conditioning? We will have to drive less and fly less. Our houses may not be as warm in winter and as cool in summer. We may have to do without some of our plastic and aluminum materials. Better building design and proper insulation can limit energy needs. The car industry has already designed smaller and more fuel-efficient cars. Thermostats could be turned down and lights turned off when not needed. Car pools and mass transit could add to the savings. People could work and play closer to their homes. Housing could be compacted, going up rather than spreading out in distant suburbs. Returning to natural materials would reduce the high energy costs of producing and consuming synthetics. There are many things we can do to lower our energy consumption. But will we do them?

The long-term solution lies in new technologies. Alternative sources will have to replace our fossil fuel dependence. Moving away from fossil fuels will be difficult and costly because these fuels are in such widespread use. Converting every furnace and industrial plant to new energy supplies would be a huge task. But we do not have a choice.

ENERGY CONSERVATION PROGRAMS

Once they were aware of the energy problem, the industrial nations started energy conservation programs to slash energy requirements by up to 50 per cent. New, more efficient car engines and lead-free gasolines began to appear on the market. Continent-wide programs of home insulation, including thermal windows and more efficient central heating, markedly reduced heating demands. New light bulb designs cut electrical demands by as much as 75 per cent, as did new and more efficient household appliances.

THE GREENHOUSE EFFECT

Burning fossil fuels pours an enormous amount of pollution into the atmosphere. Carbon dioxide has the greatest negative effect. Other pollutants, such as sulfur oxides, hydrocarbons, nitrogen oxides, chlorofluorocarbons, and solid particles also play a damaging role.

Sulfur is troublesome. When precipitation scrubs it out of the atmosphere, it forms sulfuric acid. This raises the acid level in soils and waters so that they become toxic. Hydrocarbons come from piston engines in cars and lawnmowers. They are also drawn into the air as methane gas. They react with nitrogen oxide in the presence of ultraviolet rays and produce the smog that so often layers our cities. This smog is usually a severe health hazard. It also forms ozone, which retards growth. Piston engines add to the amount of nitrous oxides in the air as well. Nitrogen dioxide absorbs ultra-violet rays and is a principal villain in forming urban smog. Nitric acid forms when nitrogen dioxide mixes with water. Solid particles enter the lower atmosphere from burning, soil drifting, and a wide range of other human and natural activities. These add millions of tonnes of smoke and dirt to the atmosphere each year. If combined with water vapour, they increase the amount of cloud cover and affect climates on a global scale.

The most critical pollutant of all is carbon dioxide. It regulates temperatures both in the atmosphere and on the earth's surface. It also absorbs some of the heat that radiates from the earth into space. By absorbing the earth's radiation, the gas

Chapter 8
ENERGY AND DEVELOPMENT

reduces the amount of energy the planet loses to outer space. This upsets the energy balance and causes temperatures to rise on the surface. This so-called greenhouse effect could result in a rise in temperatures of several degrees.

The heat islands created by cities show how habitation can dramatically affect climate and weather.

Since the industrial revolution, hundreds of millions of tonnes of pollutants have entered the atmosphere because of fossil fuel combustion. The carbon dioxide in the air has risen from 274 parts per million to 350 parts per million today. If the amount of carbon dioxide reaches 550 parts per million, the temperature would increase between 2 and 5 degrees Celsius. At the current rate of emission, this point could be reached as early as 2070. If we take into account the other pollutants and the growing use of coal, 2030 is a more likely date. If we do not move to other forms of energy, we will burn 250 per cent more fossil fuels in 2075 than today. This will mean a temperature increase of from 5 to 15 degrees Celsius. In the worst case (in which fossil fuel use, especially coal, increases five-fold) by 2073 temperatures could be 10 to 30 degrees Celsius higher.

Most of the world has no choice but to use fossil fuels, so it would be unrealistic to plan to immediately get rid of them. Thus, the warming will likely continue. Environmentalists hope to reduce the effects of fossil fuel combustion by limiting, if not reducing, use. They want to slow down the damage as much as possible by reducing the amount of pollution.

Warming the atmosphere would have drastic effects on plant and animal life which cannot withstand shifts in temperature. In the short-term, melting the ice caps would raise the levels of the world's oceans, flooding coastal cities and low-lying shorelines. About 40 million people would be affected. Losing the ice caps and warming land and surface water would produce unpredictable shifts in climate. There could be a complete reversal of weather. The deserts could become wetlands, while the production of food crops could shift to the polar regions. The continents would warm faster than the oceans and the interiors would become hotter and drier. Some scientists believe that the change is irreversible, will be rapid, and has already begun.

Others claim that the problem is more complex. The pollutants that cause the greenhouse effect also mix with water vapour in the atmosphere to form clouds. More solar radiation will be reflected into space without having reached the ground. In this way the planet's energy balance will automatically be restored. Cooling trends were noted when Mount St. Helens erupted and sent millions of tonnes of ash clouds into the air. The same cooling effect might take place as a result of fossil fuel combustion. In addition, high levels of carbon dioxide encourage the growth layers in plants and trees which help scrub the excess from the air. The oceans could also absorb large amounts of carbon dioxide in the short-term. Nature cannot cleanse the biosphere forever, but if we move away from fossil fuels while there is still time, the current damage could be repaired.

This cropland near Brandon, Manitoba, is dried-out and devastated, possibly because of the greenhouse effect.

CASE STUDY:

THERMAL GARBAGE

Changing matter into energy produces heat. No matter how efficient our machines are, heat is a byproduct of every reaction. We can use cooling towers and ponds, but overall, there will be more waste heat that will have to be absorbed by the atmosphere. We do not now have the ability to invent a 100 per cent efficient machine with no heat loss. Only imaginary perpetual motion machines can do this. In reality there is no technical fix for waste heat pollution.

Heat is the non-recyclable, non-returnable waste. Too often the effect of heat waste on the biosphere, which we cannot do much about, is lost in the publicity given the problem of air pollution, which we can do a considerable amount about. Standing close to an open fire gives an idea of the amount of heat waste given off by fossil fuel combustion. If we do not control the amount of waste heat it will affect climate far more than air

Urban heat islands, caused in part by people, vehicles, and buildings, pose a greater threat to earth's climate than air pollution.

Chapter 8
ENERGY AND DEVELOPMENT

CASE STUDY

THERMAL GARBAGE

pollution. By the end of the next century, waste heat may function like a second sun in the sky.

Heat waste currently concentrates in the heat islands of the cities. Modern industrial cities can radiate as much heat as the sun. This is especially true when air conditioners operate at their maximum and add their waste heat to that of the glass panes and baking concrete of the downtown cores. Urban heat islands are already several degrees hotter than their surrounding countrysides. Cities are warmer, have less snowfall, more rain, and because of smog, have less sunshine than their environs. In effect, they create a climate all their own.

Cities are the most unnatural environment. The tall vertical walls of their buildings greet the morning sun long before the natural landscape. The buildings' materials absorb and convey heat several times as fast as the countryside. Streets and rooftops radiate heat during the day and night, keeping temperatures high. The large numbers of people, vehicles, buildings, and factories all add to the heat. During weekends, when much of the city is shut down, there is a temperature drop of several degrees. This indicates just how much the climate is human-made.

The hottest part of a large city is the downtown core. The concentration of heat results in updrafts and a flow of fresh air in from the countryside. The rising columns fill with dust and dirt and industrial pollutants. They form a dome-shaped layer of smog which becomes more dense daily, until surface winds blow it away. Smog also slows down the outward flow of heat and adds to a city's high temperatures. Severe smog conditions are health hazards.

Cities use a great amount of electrical power to satisfy the comforts and luxuries of their inhabitants. Generating electricity results in more heat waste. Most generating plants are steam powered. Water enters large boilers where it is changed into superheated steam. It is discarded once used, but at a much higher temperature than before. This warmer water damages the eco-spheres of rivers and lakes. Warmer water decreases the level of oxygen, which directly affects aquatic life.

Warmer waters cannot take in organic wastes as easily as colder water can. Soon, over half the annual run-off in North America will be used in power generation, with subsequent environmental damage.

We can only guess at the total effect of heat waste on the biosphere. Perhaps it is only part of the natural balance, and nature will work it out. We only know that life cannot tolerate continued increases in temperature.

1. Explain how heat waste is created.

2. Why is heat waste more dangerous to the biosphere than air pollution?

3. Discuss ways to limit heat waste pollution.

4. Suggest ways in which heat waste could be converted into power.

5. Suggest ways to limit thermal garbage.

CONCLUSION

Energy is the source of all activity. Humans fulfill most of their energy needs through the combustion of fossil fuels. These fuels are finite and are rapidly being used up. Fossil fuels also add to the pollution of the environment. Air pollutants, particularly carbon dioxide, trap heat radiated from the earth towards space, causing a warming trend near the surface and upsetting the energy balance. Warming temperatures could have catastrophic results for humans. Ice caps would melt and weather and climate patterns would change.

A solution to the energy problem would be a move away from fossil fuels towards either fusion or solar power. In the meantime, energy conservation policies will have to be started. These would include more efficient uses of fuel and direct action to limit the effects of air pollution on the biosphere.

ONE
WORLD

The energy requirements of the modern industrial world are phenomenal. Could solar energy replace electricity?

QUESTIONS

1. Why is energy considered to be the ultimate resource?
2. How does the earth maintain an energy balance? What would be the result if this balance was broken down?
3. What are the advantages and disadvantages of fossil fuels?
4. Describe the use of energy in industrial societies.
5. Why are underdeveloped nations using coal to fuel industrial growth?
6. How can we meet the energy needs of double the present world's population? If shortages occur, how could energy be rationed?
7. The world's natural resources are unequally divided. Should those who have them share with those who do not? Why or why not?
8. How does sulfur pollution affect the environment? Why is it permitted to continue?
9. Name and explain three alternative energy choices. If there are cleaner energy supplies, why do humans still use fossil fuels?
10. What are the limits of fission power?
11. What are the technical difficulties in converting the world's energy needs to solar power?
12. Describe the results of further increases to surface temperatures. Can the greenhouse effect be controlled or eliminated?
13. How has nature attempted to compensate for the increase of carbon dioxide in the air? How has humanity tried to compensate?
14. What changes to building design could limit heat loss?

Chapter 8

ENERGY AND DEVELOPMENT

If the greenhouse effect runs its full course, these Inuit in northern Quebec will have to find some other form of transportation.

ACTIVITIES

1. **Debate:**

   Structure a debate on the following issues:
   Resolved that:
   "A nuclear waste storage facility will be built in your neighbourhood."

2. **Position Paper:**

   Write a position paper on the issue:
   "Should underdeveloped countries such as China fuel their industrial growth with coal?"

3. **Designing an Energy System:**

   Design an alternative energy system which produces energy without polluting the environment. Evaluate your system in terms of efficiency, cost, practicality, and disposal of waste by-products.

4. **Research Report:**

   Research the development of fusion power. Write a report which explains this development and highlights its implications for space travel.

5. **Designing an Advertisement:**

   Design an advertisement which will convince people to become energy-conscious.

6. **Display:**

   Make a display of energy-saving devices and practices that are common in your neighbourhood or city.

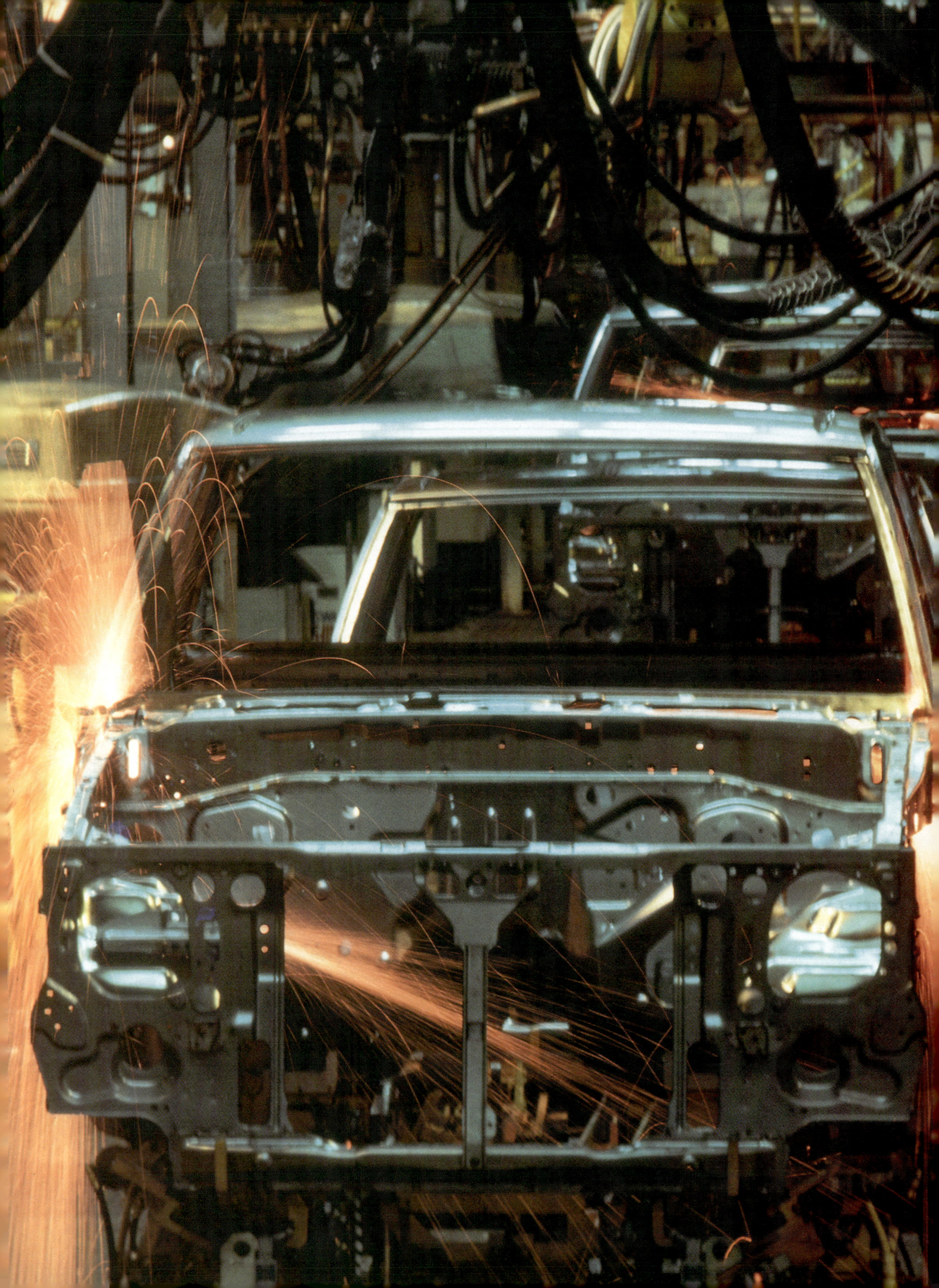

9

INDUSTRY AND LIVING STANDARDS

Industrialization is related directly to economic growth and the standard of living.

NOT EVERYONE BENEFITS equally from industrial growth. Natural resources and the wealth of the planet are unequally divided among its people. Only a handful of nations control the industrial heartlands. Seeing the link between industry and high standards of living, non-industrialized nations are trying to build their own industrial bases. They see industrialization as a way to produce the food and manufactured goods that will eliminate poverty and hunger.

Industrialization uses machines to change raw materials into manufactured goods. The speed and efficiency of the machines increase the volume of goods produced. This increase leads to more wealth and an easier lifestyle. People in the industrial nations lead more comfortable and longer lives than those in the non-industrialized nations.

THE INDUSTRIAL DEVELOPMENT GAP

People who live in industrial societies take for granted their very high standard of living. Assembly lines churn out the many material things that seem necessary for modern living. Sprawling industrial complexes use raw materials at a tremendous rate, creating the goods and services that make life easier. At the same time, they emit millions of tonnes of pollutants and waste. The industrial peoples often have short work weeks and long annual vacations. **Robotics** in the workplace will further reduce the time spent there. If machines do all the work, what will people do? Filling in leisure time will become the work of the future.

Most supermarkets in the developed world offer a variety of food choices.

ONE WORLD

Industrialization provides nations with enormous economic, military, and political power.

Urbanization is another characteristic of the developed countries. Most people in developed nations live in cities, where many services are concentrated. Public utilities abound. Health care, education, sanitation, telephones, and postal services are all fully available. All are important, but health and education are absolutely basic. All of the industrial nations have compulsory education systems. Workers need to absorb and react to the information dispersed through schools and universities, and by the press, radio, and television. Their abilities to read, understand, and communicate are fundamental to economic growth in the developed world.

THE CONTROL OF DEVELOPED NATIONS

The 70 per cent of the world's population who live in underdeveloped nations produce only 12 per cent of gross world product. Approximately 93 per cent of the world's industry, 80 per cent of its trade and investment, and almost 100 per cent of its research is controlled by the wealthy developed nations.

Industrial societies use large amounts of raw materials and energy. Most of these come from the rest of the world. They are then sold back to the non-industrial peoples at a higher price as finished goods. In order to ease the distribution of goods, multinational corporations have built worldwide networks of trade and finance which link many nations into a global economy. Fast and efficient transportation and communications speed the movement of goods and people around the world.

In contrast, apart from a very small elite, the standard of living for the peoples of the non-industrial world is dramatically lower. In these regions, few people have many material goods or machines. Rural people spend most of their time farming in a way that has changed little over the centuries. What they produce by their own labour they consume themselves in a subsistence lifestyle. Transportation is very poor or non-existent. In general, public services are inadequate. For the most part,

A vegetable market in Ecuador.

health services and education are not well developed. In addition, they are not spread evenly among classes of people. The governing elites are as well cared for as any of the industrial peoples. It is no wonder that their fellow citizens look at them and the developed world with envy.

THE HISTORY OF INDUSTRIAL DEVELOPMENT

The industrial revolution began in England in the eighteenth century. Discovering steam power and using it in mass production as well as replacing wood with coal in making coke gave England an edge over other nations. Coke is critical in the production of steel. Iron and steel were to be the wonder materials of the age. The use of steel vaulted Britain into a position of global supremacy. Attempts to keep the new processes secret were not successful, as apprentices and artisans travelling abroad carried the designs with them. Shortly after the Napoleonic Wars, industrial growth took root in Europe. The first developments took place along the band of iron fields and coalfields stretching from northern France and Belgium through Germany

Chapter 9
INDUSTRY AND LIVING STANDARDS

and beyond to Bohemia and Silesia. Canada and the USA followed suit, although the former was still part of the British system. At that time, factories and industrial cities had to be built close to the source of minerals. This is no longer true today. As a result of modern transportation networks, industrial facilities can be built anywhere, and raw materials brought to them.

Once begun, the pace of industrial growth continued to accelerate. At the turn of the century, only four nations controlled over 80 per cent of the world's industrial output: England, 35 per cent; the USA, 22 per cent; Germany, 16 per cent; and France, 11 per cent. Since then these four have been joined by Canada, the USSR, Japan, and the **newly industrializing countries (NICs)** of South Korea, Taiwan, Brazil, and the city-state of Singapore.

These North American children are learning to become computer literate. This skill gives them an industrial edge over the students from less advanced areas.

After they had used up their own raw materials, the industrial nations acquired new supplies through their empires. They needed the food, bauxite, petroleum, tungsten, rubber, nickel, and other ores of their colonies. Economic growth slowed because of the Great Depression of 1929 and the two world wars. The wars killed tens of millions of people, savaged Europe, Russia, and Japan, and wasted vast amounts of non-renewable resources. The political and social turmoil of these events severely dislocated the course of history. Political, economic, and social recovery did not take place until the 1950s.

GROWTH IN MANUFACTURING

In 1950, the world manufactured only one-seventh of the goods it does today, and used only one-third of the minerals. Between 1950 and 1973, world industrial production grew most quickly, with a 7 per cent annual growth in manufacturing and a 5 per cent growth in mining. Since 1973, annual growth rates have slowed to about 3 per cent in manufacturing and nearly zero in mining.

After 1955 the world economy had a period of unprecedented growth that lasted until the energy crisis of 1973. The developed nations were the beneficiaries of the global boom. These already had experienced management, skilled labour, transportation networks, and financing. Electrical power grids crossed landscapes to feed new plants. Paved, multi-laned highways linked production to markets in the mushrooming cities. Railways, seaways, and airports were enlarged to hasten the shipment of goods. The consumer society began in the 1960s when industrial capacity was turned to domestic goods for the average home owner. Many new products appeared on the shelves. Electrical appliances, modern housing, home furnishings, and cars became abundant. As machines took over more and more of the work, labour shifted into the tertiary service industries, improving the quality of life. Health and education began to experience rapid growth. No longer would a grade 8 education do. The testing of all school age children for immunizations and eye and hearing defects was the start of the present preventative health care programs. Dining out, entertainment, and sports became growth industries.

ONE
WORLD

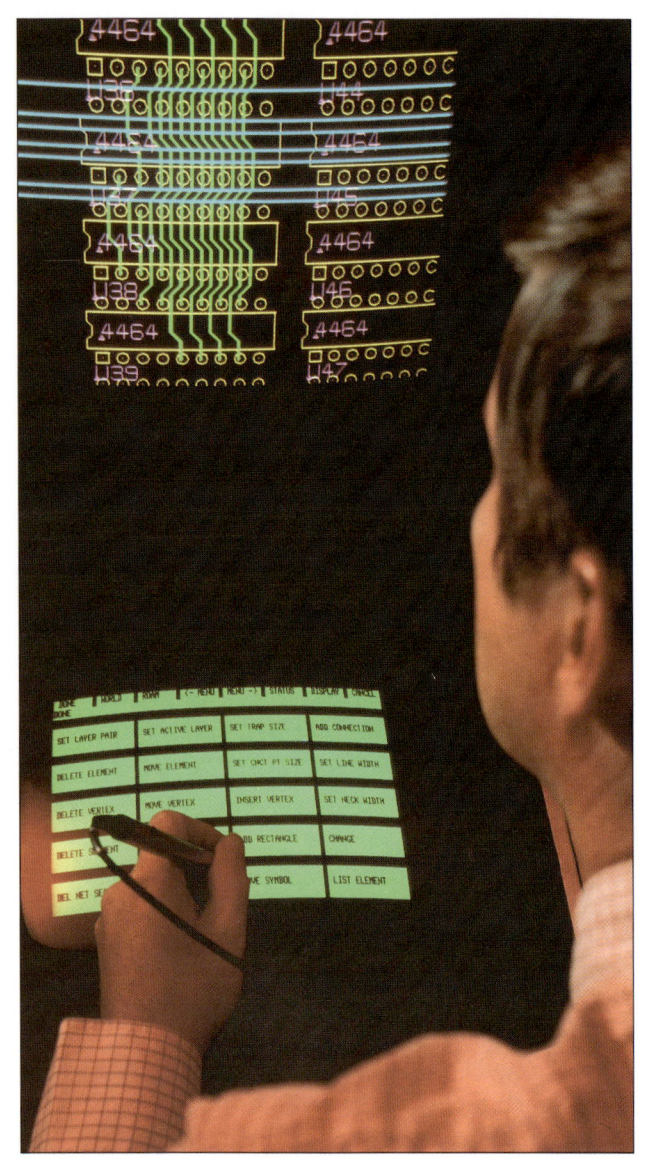

The advent of computer technology has vastly improved scientific research.

Synthetics are taking the place of depleted natural resources to maintain industrial growth.

New technologies created synthetics, fertilizers, cosmetics, and space exploration. Discoveries in medicine prolonged lifespans. In the meantime, the media took advantage of global tv and satellite transmission to begin shaping a world market for the goods and services of the developed world. The emergence of an urban culture within the world's major cities acted as a magnet for the Western, materialist, industrial culture.

In Western Europe, North America, and Japan, manufacturing grew over 8 per cent each year. In comparison, the non-industrial countries struggled to maintain a modest growth of 4 per cent. These were not real gains, however. The increase in production did not keep pace with increases in population. The overall effect was to lower already low living standards. The exceptions were the newly industrializing countries (NICs), where growth rates of 11 per cent were common.

The quadrupling of oil prices in the 1970s by the Organization of Petroleum Exporting Countries (OPEC) cartel shook the world's industrial systems, until 1980, when a slow recovery began. Oil-importing nations were hard pressed to pay for the increase in their energy costs. Underdeveloped nations were especially hard-hit as they were caught with major projects under construction. They borrowed heavily to complete them. They counted on the world market to absorb their products at a price to offset their borrowing. This did not happen. Today's sluggish market leaves them in a precarious position. They are forced to spend most of their budgets paying interest charges on their multi-billion dollar debts. At the same time, the underdeveloped nations' people, who were promised a better standard of living through development, want the change to happen. The situation is tense and becoming politically unstable.

THE COSTS OF INDUSTRIALIZATION

Buying technology and machines is not the only cost of industrialization. Industries reorganize society and change traditional lifestyles. The support systems of church and family are no longer available with traditional ties and rituals replaced by more urban ones. Cities have to be created to feed and shelter the thousands who have left their farms, searching for work and a new life. Public services have to be created for the swelling urban population. Entertainment, education, and financial systems are vital parts of the new scene. Transportation must be upgraded and, in many cases,

Chapter 9

INDUSTRY AND LIVING STANDARDS

Foreign aid may include industrial training programs.

created. It is difficult enough to change from an agrarian culture to an industrial one over decades. But today the change can take place within a generation. The results can be chaotic.

Underdeveloped countries need large amounts of money to industrialize. Modern factories are complex and expensive. These countries also need to acquire the technology of a modern society. Their peoples will have to acquire the knowledge needed by an industrial system. They also need access to world markets to sell their produce. Only China and India have populations large enough to sustain industrial growth solely at home.

Underdeveloped countries can obtain money from several sources. They can raise it themselves by selling raw materials and food. Some nations have turned to cash crops, such as cotton or tobacco. These crops are grown on what was once food-producing land. Underdeveloped countries are gambling that world markets will continue to be strong. If the markets collapsed, underdeveloped nations would not be able to feed themselves. Even now these nations are forced to import food. They can borrow from other nations, the World Bank, or from other regional banks, but the amounts are large and not every institution can handle the requests. Underdeveloped nations can receive military aid if they enter into alliances. They can also receive aid in the form of outright grants or loans. Direct foreign aid from all sources, government and volunteer, to the underdeveloped world has been $1500 billion since 1950.

Once they have the money, underdeveloped nations need to make political and economic decisions regarding industrial development. Politics might dictate building large industrial plants to promote national prestige. But these plants will do little good if they cannot sell their products in a saturated global market. The world does not need a major steel mill in every nation.

The 150 underdeveloped nations have taken many approaches to industrialization. Pressures are placed on the leaders of poor nations to produce better standards of living at any price. Yet the human and physical resources needed for growth may not be available. It is hard to set aside resources to develop energy, transportation, education, and research when people are starving.

The underdeveloped world's struggle to industrialize often fails, and only infrequently succeeds. There is no magic formula to guarantee success. No pattern for development is apparent. It does not seem to matter whether populations are large or small, educated or illiterate, rich in resources or not. The only common factor in success seems to be a desire of government and people to succeed together.

CASE STUDY:
SOUTH KOREA'S ECONOMIC "MIRACLE"

South Korea is one of the NICs whose economic development over the last 30 years seems a miracle. In 1953, three-quarters of South Korea's people were poor farmers. The Korean War had left the peninsula in a shambles. The major cities were in ruin and the nation was in mourning for its 1 million war dead. Today, South Korea is the world's twelfth largest trading nation, and has the seventeenth largest economy in the non-communist world. Three-quarters of the people living in modern housing have refrigerators, and almost everyone owns a tv. Ninety-seven per cent of the country's 42 million people are literate. Medical aid is available to the 11 per cent of the population who are poor. There is government-built housing for the needy and state help for food and rent. Social welfare accounts for 5 per cent of the annual budget. All of this has been achieved with the help of massive foreign aid.

In the decade after the war, American forces dominated the nation. They still maintain a strong presence in the country. The USA spent almost $2 billion on food and reconstruction. They rebuilt South Korea's cities and reorganized society. A land reform program got rid of the landlord class and most of the abuses of a feudal agrarian system. Nationwide energy and transportation networks were built. The USA saw South Korea as a bastion against communist aggression. For this reason they supplied almost all of the foreign aid during this initial period. A key feature of this effort was the development of a national education system.

The Rhee government wanted a self-contained industrial base so that South Korea could break free from her economic dependence on Japan. The Americans advised fostering only a few key export industries, such as tvs and other electronic machines. The Americans also wanted to put more effort into consumer goods and less into major projects such as shipbuilding.

Under the presidency of Park Chung Hee, a compromise was worked out. This has left South Korea with some heavy industry, but still far from self-sufficient. South Korea has one of the newest and largest steel making mills in the world, as well as efficient shipyards. Still, her energy supplies and component parts come from abroad.

Loans, from the World Bank and recently from Japan, replaced direct American financial aid after 1970. American indirect aid has always remained strong. This foreign investment led to the establishment of a few large export companies, such as Hyundai, Samsung, and Daewoo. These companies rely on exports which make up more than half their sales abroad. Because of the dependence on foreign sales, they are vulnerable to world market changes. The USA buys 40 per cent of their output.

The advantage South Korea has in manufacturing is its skilled and inexpensive labour pool. Koreans work 54 hours a week, much longer than North Americans. Some work 11 hours at a stretch in a workspace that is barely 35 square metres in area. Jobs are allocated on the basis of education. Those with a university degree receive four times the wages of others. Women receive half the wages of their male counterparts. Wages are still far behind those of other developing nations. Safety standards are ignored. South Korea has fatality rates three times those of Canada, and industrial injuries harm 3 per cent of the labour force each year.

South Korea has built its thriving economy on large-scale foreign loans and cheap labour. It is making some headway in paying its debts, but labour demands for higher wages and work strikes could cripple the fragile balance. Export sales of $10 billion a year to the USA could be lost if labour costs price exports out of the market. Some of South Korea's own companies have begun using less expensive labour in Taiwan and

▶

Chapter 9
INDUSTRY AND LIVING STANDARDS

CASE STUDY: SOUTH KOREA'S ECONOMIC "MIRACLE"

South Korea has built up its industrial base.

the Caribbean rather than assembling finished products at home.

The dash for rapid development has resulted in unpleasant side effects. The industries chosen for development, such as steel and petro-chemicals, create the worst pollution. These industries are all centred around the capital of Seoul, leading to a highly concentrated development region. Industrial air pollution and the addition of 300 cars a day to the capital's streets create smog concentrations four times those of Tokyo rates. The flood into the city by dispossessed rural workers has meant a growing number of people living in urban poverty. As long as the government continues its defence and export policies, there is little hope of the situation improving in the near future. Inner city violence is on the rise and burglaries have become a routine feature of city life.

The economic strategy for the next 25 years is to follow Japan. As Japan abandons its current markets in favour of high technology, South Korea hopes to step into the gap, making superconductors and plastics. A research city has been established at Taeduk to spearhead this new effort. But if this is to succeed, South Korea must maintain its advantage of skilled, low-cost labour. It must also start to make many of the $5 billion worth of component parts it now imports from Japan. It would also like to be rid of the licence fee which adds $10 to every VCR produced from Japanese parts. It must also find a way to enter the Japanese market. Last year, sales of radios, calculators, and electric fans to Japan increased 55 per cent.

South Korea's hopes rest on a shift from textiles to electronics. This will require a great deal of research and costly plant development at a time when the debt load is already heavy. Only large, government-supported companies can manage such an operation. Using their skilled labour force as an advantage, they hope to outsell their Japanese and Taiwanese rivals.

Like Japan, South Korea hopes to eventually become self-sufficient, relying more on a domestic than an export market for economic strength. The result would be an economy much less at the whim of North American buying demands. To do this, wages will have to rise in order to create a local demand for goods. This would destroy the wage advantage and could make South Korean products non-competitive on world markets.

1. How did South Korea successfully industrialize?
2. What are the weaknesses of South Korea's industrialization?
3. Why did South Korea not follow a policy of self-sufficiency?
4. How could world market prices affect the South Korean economy?
5. What would be the effect of increased wages or robotics?

ONE WORLD

THE LATIN AMERICA EXPERIENCE

The nations of Latin America have enormous potential for growth in both human and physical resources. The continent contains vast amounts of arable land, oil and mineral reserves, and hydro-electric power. Mexico, Brazil, and Argentina rank in the top 20 world economies. Brazil makes aircraft for export and Argentina sells turbines internationally. Brazil accounts for a third of the population and a third of the economic output of the region. But it is the only country that is even close to self-sufficiency.

The 1980s have been a lost decade for Latin America. Per capita income is lower today than in the mid 1960s. Unemployment has soared to more than 20 per cent of the urban labour force. Five million new jobs are needed each year to keep pace with a population growth of 3 per cent. Almost every country carries a heavy foreign debt burden. The total for the region amounts to some $700 billion. Interest payments on the debt total $30 billion each year. Many countries expend close to half of their income paying debts. Inflation has run rampant, reaching annual rates of 1200 per cent in Argentina and 500 per cent in Brazil. Unable to gain a larger share of the world's export markets due to a general global downturn, most countries have halted the flow of costly imports in order to survive. The only other region to have suffered so much in this decade is Africa.

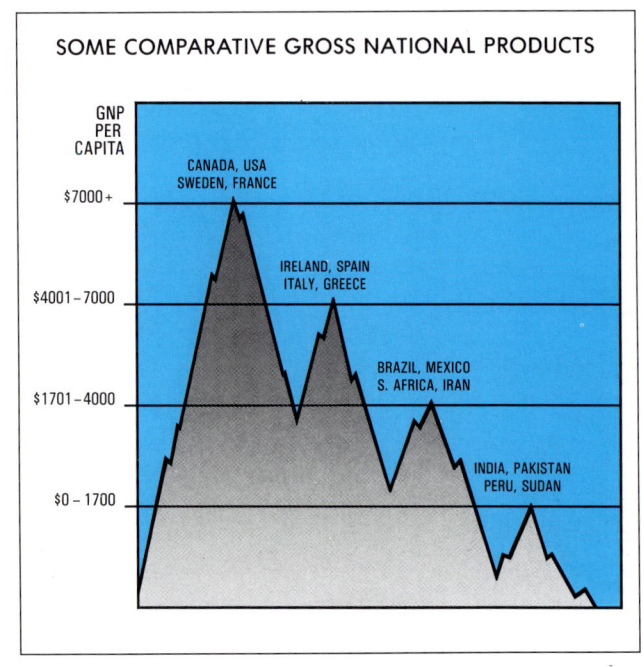

A country's gross national product (the total value of its goods and services) is a yardstick of its prosperity. The GNP in Western Europe and North America is far higher than that of the underdeveloped world.

TOTALITARIAN MADNESS

While many of the world's underdeveloped countries seem to face a never-ending series of natural setbacks and disasters, some nations have suffered equally at the hands of fellow humans.

Argentina is the world's eighth-largest country. The Pampas, a vastly rich breadbasket, boasts some of the deepest and richest topsoil on earth. The country is self-sufficient in oil, and has a relatively well-educated population. Blessed by nature, Argentina has every possiblity of being one of the greatest nations on earth — yet it is not. Why?

In the five years before the country's first democratically-elected leader in decades, Raul Alfonsin, came to power in 1983, foreign banks had lavished over $40 billion in development loans on Argentina. The generals who led the nation's military government siphoned off over $25 billion of this money to build South America's most powerful military force. Many of the remaining loans were diverted from their original purposes, into the generals' pet projects.

When they ran short of cash, the government simply printed new money to pay its workers and pay its bills. Inflation promptly soared to 1000 per cent per year. Ordinary people with decent jobs suddenly found their earning power slashed to virtually nothing. Meanwhile, wealthy Argentines secretly sent over $35 billion to private overseas accounts. By the early 1980s, the country that should have been one of the most prosperous in the world, had become "the richest poor nation on earth."

When the people of Argentina protested, their military rulers responded with a reign of terror which left thousands of innocent citizens dead, and tens of thousands of others simply "vanished" without a trace. The legacy of Argentina's military past has burdened the country with tremendous problems — all of them human-caused.

Chapter 9

INDUSTRY AND LIVING STANDARDS

The competitive market for all cereal products is a global market.

THE HISTORY OF DEVELOPMENT

Until World War II, the economic development of the region depended on exporting raw materials. Latin America competed on the world market for food sales with Canada, the United States, and Australia. South Africa was its main rival in exporting minerals. Expansion in exports was most rapid in Argentina and Uruguay (cereals), Chile (copper and nitrates), and Colombia (coffee). Although these nations escaped the ravages of two world wars, they were isolated from their traditional European markets. This slowed their growth until 1950. Then, in just one generation, all this changed. Economic disaster set in. Earnings from exports dropped to under $100 per capita, far below the $3000 average of industrial nations. In all, except Brazil, Venezuela, Mexico, and Ecuador, incomes tumbled.

Without the rising cost of oil in the 1970s, the situation would not have been as depressing. Only Sri Lanka and the sub-Saharan region of Africa had lower rates of growth.

The region decided to substitute domestic products for costly imports after World War II. High tariffs encouraged home-grown clothing, textile, furniture, and wood products industries. These required little skill to manufacture. By 1960, the region was self-sufficient in these sectors. Then various countries in the region began to produce cars, appliances, and other machinery, using costly processes and calling for economies of scale. They also required a large market to make unit costs reasonable. In 1958, a Latin American Common Market was proposed. The region also planned to build international transportation systems to service new industries. The idea of a common market failed because of intense national rivalries. In addition, the highly publicized Pan-American highway did not meet modern industrial needs.

Latin American nations were not able to develop a regional market of scale. This resulted in high, protectionist tariffs in each country. These tariffs, which averaged 500 per cent, supported the production of local goods at any cost. They also priced the goods out of any export markets. At the same time, the government decided to subsidize the price of food for political reasons. This resulted in so much being consumed at home that there was nothing left for export. Canada and the USA took over an increasing share of the world food market.

During the 1970s, economic growth declined dramatically. During this time, Japan and other fareastern NICs surpassed their Latin American rivals. Labour unions and industrialists opposed lowering the tariffs to gain a share of world markets. The unions would not accept wage reductions. Industrialists feared that they would not be able to compete under free trade.

All but Ecuador, Venezuela, Colombia, and Mexico suffered from the quadrupling of oil prices between 1973 and 1978. The affected countries borrowed heavily to offset the rise in petroleum costs. They continued large industrial development programs with the borrowed billions of dollars at interest rates reaching 20 per cent. This later crippled their economies. Even Mexico and Peru, which had newly found oil reserves, had to borrow heavily to develop them. By 1982, this heavy debt load led to economic crisis. Mexico was the first to announce it would no longer pay the interest on its debt. Since then, most of the development loans have been renegotiated at lower interest rates.

The trend for each nation to develop its own industrial complex did not improve standards of living in the 1970s. Large factories did not bring relief. They could not produce cheaply enough to compete in world markets. They also did not absorb nearly enough workers to ease unemployment. At the same time, mechanizing farms created a surplus of farm labour. Many young people left the rural areas for the cities. They came by the tens of thousands, looking for jobs, seeking shelter in the slums, and demanding a lifestyle which the cities could not provide. They were consumers and not producers. Unhappy with their lot, they have been the cause of political and social instability.

Industrialization led to population concentrations and mega-cities like Hong Kong.

Chapter 9

INDUSTRY AND LIVING STANDARDS

In 1985, interest payments on Latin America's total foreign debt were $35 billion. This has led to near-stagnation of most of the area's economies. The rapidly expanding role of state enterprise has been one cause of the debt dilemma. Foreign money increased public enterprise ten-fold. Almost 75 per cent of the debt was for expanding public enterprise. Apart from the efficient public utilities, most of the state-run companies proved inefficient, with low productivity. Underpaid bureaucrats ran them, and the potential for corruption was great. For example, the state-run Mages irrigation project in Peru cost $1 billion to irrigate 6000 hectares. The Brazilian nuclear program will need $3 billion more before any of its plants come on line. The state-constructed Mexico City subway cost $2500 per 2.5 centimetres to build. This is more than is spent on health care. Any productivity is gained at an abnormal cost. The result is that the combined GNP of all Latin American countries, including the Caribbean, does not equal that of West Germany.

REVERSING THE TREND

In 1985, new governments in Brazil and Mexico acted to reverse the downward trend. They have privatized many state enterprises and are selling many unprofitable, publicly owned companies. They intend to liquidate, dissolve, transfer, or sell as many public corporations as possible. Privatization has worked well in the UK. There, over a third of the (former) government workforce is now in the private sector. The British have sold $29 billion in state assets. Like the UK, Latin American countries want to retain state control over the efficiently run public utilities.

Some Latin American countries have acted to make foreign investment attractive. They have moved to reduce high tariffs, to get rid of subsidies, and to increase interest rates. This follows the successful examples of the Asian NICs and, more recently, Turkey. They hope to increase their share of the world market in selected sectors. They also hope to regain the technical and managerial skills they lost due to protected isolation.

They have made excellent progress in providing basic social services. Life expectancy has increased substantially, especially in the cities. The number of trained doctors and educators has continued to climb. And although far behind—Mexico spends $174 per student and Brazil only $74, compared with Spain at $849—progress in mass education is visible.

The lowering of tariffs and privatization of industry are strategies intended to make manufacturing competitive and increase Latin America's share of the world market from its meager 0.2%. But this objective will not be met as long as the developed nations continue to subsidize their products on the world market. Canada and the USA provide heavy financial assistance to their farming sectors, leading to what is in effect a dumping of export produce at low, non-competitive selling prices. The European Common Market encourages its own regional agricultural production by setting artificially high prices for home grown farm produce. The protection of agricultural products in Japan eliminates almost all imports. If everyone in Japan ate only 1 kilogram more of Argentine beef a year, Argentina would export 120 000 kilograms more. The costly rescue of bankrupt industries or the large subsidies given to industry by the USA and the Canadian provinces deny free competition to Latin American business. Legislative bans against produce contaminated by fruit flies have effectively arrested the export of fruits and vegetables. Because of this protection, which is not likely to disappear, Latin American nations will have to direct their

Many underdeveloped nations may have to shift to new export industries. Tanzania, for example, has become an exporter of tires.

export strategies into other sectors, as have the Asian NICs in the field of high technology. The NICs have successfully carved out a profitable export market despite suffering the same economic disasters as the rest of the world.

The developed countries also have a role to play in developing Latin America. Defaulting on the multi-billion dollar debt would cripple the world's financial institutions. Lending institutions lent heavily to the region during the boom years of the 1970s. Many of these loans have since been renegotiated. To maintain stability on the global money markets, all parties have to compromise. Part of this could be to increase the Latin American share of the world market for manufactured goods. Another part of the agreement would be to keep providing development funds for the region to improve people's living standards through industrialization. Despite the present high debt, one plan is to spend $20 billion more in the 15 poorest countries over the next three years. This seems a large amount, but it does not even meet the needs of the region for the current year.

CONCLUSION

The few industrially developed nations consume most of the world's energy and mineral resources.

Industrialization is directly linked to the standard of living. A small number of industrial nations control the world's manufacturing capabilities. The underdeveloped nations envy the high standard of living enjoyed by the developed nations. The underdeveloped nations are trying to industrialize but find they have neither the finances nor the knowledge and experience needed to build an industrial base. They have borrowed heavily at high interest rates to industrialize. This has led to crippling debt. Demands by their people for a better lifestyle could lead to political and economic instability.

QUESTIONS

1. What is the relationship between industrial development and the standard of living?

Industrial workers, like this welder, are an integral part of their country's industrial future.

2. How does industrialization provide a high standard of living? Why are not all nations industrially developed?
3. Why did England, along with parts of Western Europe, become the world's first industrial heartland? Where are the other industrial heartlands? (See the Mini-Atlas)
4. What are the characteristics of a developed state? A developing state?
5. What is the importance of education in an industrial society?
6. Why have international transportation and communications developed?
7. What part do the non-industrial nations play in global industrial enterprises?
8. What is the basis of the standard of living in western Canada?

Chapter 9
INDUSTRY AND LIVING STANDARDS

9. Why is western Canada not fully industrialized? Where does the West obtain its manufactured goods? Its finances? Its entertainment? Explain.
10. How did the OPEC cartel's dramatic increase in oil prices affect economic development?
11. What were the dangers of the decision by Latin American nations to use borrowed money for industrial growth? What is the result of their inability to get a large share of the world market?
12. What are the costs of industrial growth? How are those costs met? Who is responsible for developing the wide variety of support services?
13. How does the heavy debt load affect development in Latin America?
14. Why did the proposal for a Latin American free trade agreement fail?
15. How did the strategy of self-sufficiency affect Latin America's industrial growth? How did foreign investors react to the protective tariff barriers?
16. How did the expansion of the oil industry affect Mexico?
17. What are the advantages and disadvantages of government-owned businesses?
18. What is the aim of the privatization policy? What benefits do governments see in returning public enterprise to private control? Are there some public enterprises that should be kept? If so, which ones?
19. How do Canada's farm subsidies affect world markets? How do the countries of the European Common Market restrict the farm market? What is the effect of Japan closing her domestic markets to foreign goods?
20. How does the size of the world market affect plans by the underdeveloped states to industrialize?

ACTIVITIES

1. **Display:**
   Make a display which identifies material goods from around the world. Emphasize any similarities or differences which you discover. Consider all types of consumer goods — both practical and luxurious.

2. **Town Hall Meeting:**
   Hold a meeting of your local town or city council to solve the problem of chemical and toxic waste disposal. Choose a mayor and suitable number of council members. Select other people to act as citizens representing special interests like the environment and business. The remainder of participants could act as concerned citizens and taxpayers.

3. **Charting International Links:**
   On a map of the world, show the location of raw materials and various assembly points used in the manufacture of a car or any other finished product. Show the links of this international production network.

4. **Display:**
   Make a display which illustrates the interdependence of the world market. Show the source of raw materials like coffee, cocoa, sugar, wheat, and other foodstuffs, as well as raw materials used in the production of consumer goods. Show the exchange of goods from one part of the world to another.

5. **Research Report:**
   Research a multinational corporation of your choice. Identify its head office, branch offices, subsidiary companies, and the varieties of goods and services produced. Evaluate the effect of that corporation on the international marketplace, as well as on national economies.

6. **Development Strategies:**
   Design development strategies aimed at improving the standard of living for a non-industrialized country which has adequate raw materials, is deficient in energy supplies, and has a growing population. The nation has a surplus of food but cannot sell the surplus because world markets are saturated. The growth of slum areas around the major cities has created social problems. Because of a shortage of capital, the main harbour facilities, though of strategic value, are undeveloped.

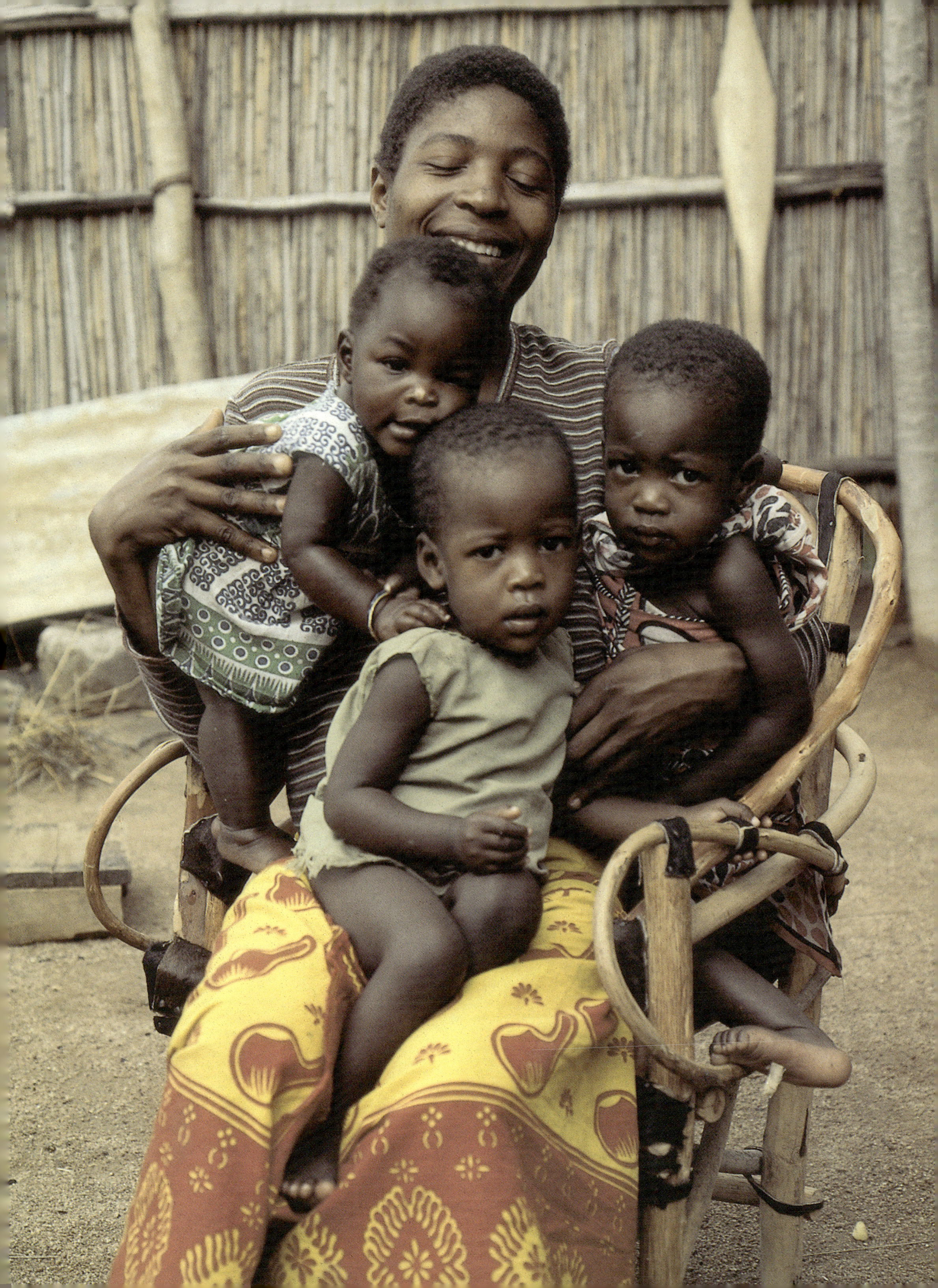

10

INTERNATIONAL CO-OPERATION

THE MODERN NATION state system was created by rivalry and war. Emphasis on security, prestige, and economic interests was fostered by rampant nationalism which today still outweighs the forces of international co-operation. Mutual suspicion brought on by different languages, customs, religion, ideology, and fear all contribute to deep rifts in international relations. The concept of interrelatedness has not yet become a compelling human instinct. There is yet but a limited momemtum towards internationalism in the face of the more dominant nationalism.

The competitive nation state system shows no signs of rapid decay. Nation states are reluctant to sacrifice any of their sovereignty in international agreements. Only when mutual interests occur can co-operation be achieved. Yet the growing interdependence of nations and national interests can lead to co-operative actions. The USA and the USSR, rivals in the Cold War, are now finding an increasing number of areas in which they can agree to participate for mutual advantage.

To a degree never before known, human beings are becoming more interdependent for their lives and welfare. Within the past decade there has been a growing movement towards international solutions to the global problems that affect standards of living. Acceptance of internationalism must be

UN soldiers on patrol in Cyprus.

ONE WORLD

accompanied by the assurance that any new arrangements must offer at least the same individual security as is now provided by the nation state. Nationalism is still the dominant factor in world affairs, but successful co-operation in the control and use of atomic energy, the treaty on outer space, the non-proliferation treaty, the strategic arms limitation treaties, and social and economic assistance to the underdeveloped world give hope for the future of humankind.

LAW OF THE SEA

The signing of the Law of the Sea agreements was a major success for international diplomacy and co-operation. Two competing sets of interests were at stake over the right to exploit the resources of the seas and the mineral wealth on the sea beds. On the one hand there was the belief that the wealth of the oceans should become a common heritage for all humans to share, thus restricting national claims to narrow bands along their shorelines. At the other extreme was the desire of the coastal states to expand their territorial claims far out to sea sweeping in 90 per cent of the mineral and fishing resources for their own use. The concept that coastal states could expand their jurisdiction if they had the means and the technology to do so was not viewed with favour by landlocked states that had no coastlines. With the technology now available, this makes legal the development of deep water petroleum extraction far beyond the continental shelves.

Attempts by the United Nations to secure some of the profits from seabed development for a common heritage foundered on the extreme and immovable posture of ultra-nationalism. Several nations are prepared to drill for oil and mine for copper and manganese far beyond the limit of the continental shelves. The possibility of establishing an international jurisdiction over the world's waters seems a remote ideal.

Having divided up the land surface of the globe, the nation states have turned their attention to dividing up the oceans. Coastal states want to claim the food and mineral resources that lie in the oceans and on the ocean floor and are extending their territorial limits outwards into the seas. The contest

Maritime countries demand and expect the right to exploit the seas' resources. These Canadian fishermen are unloading salmon.

Chapter 10
INTERNATIONAL CO-OPERATION

to possess the last of the earth's mineral and food resources is beginning. Will the contest be waged through co-operation, or conflict?

Superpowers have the military and economic strength to decide the use of the world's resources without consulting other peoples affected by their actions.

The oceans form overlapping and connecting links between the continents. Near the continents they form shallow seas that stretch out from the shorelines to depths of 200 metres. Far out to sea these shelves suddenly drop off as the seabed plunges to the ocean depths. These submerged shallow margins are called continental shelves and they are the home to rich fisheries. The shelves are of increasing value. This is due to finding oil and gas fields at a recoverable depth. Nations expand boundaries into the sea to control fisheries and the mineral wealth below. The question is who owns these natural resources?

Coastal states traditionally claimed an almost 5 kilometre seaward boundary of sole jurisdiction. Nations made exceptions for historical or previous continuous use. The great powers agreed to make some narrow straits international.

By 1980, most states had moved to 14.5 or 19 kilometre limits. More significantly, they also claimed special economic interests and the right to manage economic resources for an additional 302 kilometres. This extended territorial boundaries by some 320 kilometres. Within these limits, the coastal states managed the fisheries to ensure renewable harvests, policed pollution control, and established defence facilities.

Most coastal states support dividing the oceans into national territories. This division would mean further unequal distribution of global resources.

In 1945, the USA moved to regulate ocean fisheries, not only on the continental shelf, but in the high seas next to the shelf. They also claimed the seabed under the shelf to a depth of 200 metres. This led to the coastal states claiming about a third of the globe's seabed. At that time, the landlocked countries, who did not benefit, did not protest territorial expansion. The USA added about 2.5 million square kilometres to its east coast plus much of the shallow Arctic. A year later, Argentina, Chile, and Peru extended their boundaries to the 321 kilometre mark. Peru effectively cut off foreign fishing boats from the rich Humboldt fisheries. It was here that one of the first warning signs came that some of the fisheries were reaching their limits. The anchovy catch has dropped in the last 10 years from an annual 12.6 million tonnes to just under 2 million tonnes today. The trend is a warning that the oceans are being taxed to their limits and, in the case of some species, fished to extinction.

The UN convened several conferences of the maritime nations, hoping to get them to agree on the future of the world's oceans. The UN's efforts led to the signing of the Law of the Sea Treaty in Caracas in 1981. This agreement defined the concept of an **Exclusive Economic Zone (EEZ)**. These zones confirmed the 320 kilometre territorial expansion of the coastal states. Canada, the USA, the USSR, Japan, Australia, and New Zealand were the major winners. Where states are within 644 kilometres of each other, the mid point rule takes effect. Virtually all of the North Sea, Caribbean, and seas of Southeast Asia are affected by the mid point ruling and are totally under national control. The rest of the world's waters could be divided among the coastal states.

The richness of available fossil fuels encourages companies to develop off-shore drilling as part of their exploration and production.

ONE WORLD

CASE STUDY:

THE ANTARCTIC

International agreements are supposed to protect Antarctica from specific national claims. However, various nations have unofficially claimed slices of the Antarctic "pie." The whalebone in this photograph rests where once a Norwegian whaling station stood.

Antarctica is an example of another sort of supranational co-operation. However, its rich mineral and energy resources could tempt the superpowers to break the current agreements prohibiting ownership claims below the 60 degree latitude. The continent has a land surface of 14.2 million square kilometres and an average diameter of some 4000 kilometres. A 3000 metre thick dome of ice covers it, holding 2 per cent of the world's fresh water reserves. The ice sheet is not stable. If it slid off the land, the continent would rise several metres. The effect on the rest of the world's shorelines would be catastrophic. A rise of even a few metres would flood coastal cities.

International agreements protect the continent from any claims. However, establishing scientific and weather stations could be the basis for future claims. The unrecognized division of Antarctica into pie-shaped slices appears on some maps of the continent. Many nations, including West Germany, the USA, and the USSR have ignored these divisions and have established research stations at will. The ownership of gold, nickle, silver, cobalt, copper, and uranium ores could provoke conflict. Given the earth's depleting resources, commercial development must be tempting. Without agreement, the mineral wealth would go to the countries who can extract the ores and keep others away.

The waters around Antarctica are rich in seafood. The protein-rich meat from the tiny krill can now be extracted. Fishing ships from all over the world have appeared off the shores. Netting krill has doubled the amount of protein taken from the world's oceans. The annual catch is more than 50 million tonnes. Scientists are beginning to wonder how this affects other marine life and to caution against overharvesting. Nations, such as the USSR and Poland, who are always short of food, take little notice of long-range aims. Their goal is to feed their people. The blossoming of the krill fishery is partly due to the declining number of whales. Krill was a major source of food for whales. Until now whales kept krill numbers in balance. Perhaps people will now take over that role.

The natural resources of Antarctica could lead to confrontation because of increasing world population and food and energy needs. Overfishing krill could destroy the fisheries if the breeding stock is reduced. Using explosives or small-scale nuclear devices to extract precious minerals could damage the stability of the ice cap, causing it to sink into the ocean with worldwide effects. The political and economic future of the region is fraught with dangers.

1. What is the importance of Antarctica to global development?
2. How are national claims being established in Antarctica?
3. What are the terms of the international agreement on Antarctica?
4. What are the dangers of exploiting the resources in Antarctica?
5. Why is Canada not involved in Antarctica?

Chapter 10

INTERNATIONAL CO-OPERATION

Seafood-rich waters also feed Jackass penguins.

The mid point rule has already been used to divide the oil and gas resources of the North Sea. The UK, Norway, West Germany, the Netherlands, and Denmark have agreed to precise ocean boundaries. Pipelines and drilling platforms exploit the underwater fields in the interests of all. Prior to the development of the underwater oilfields, the UK had to import most of its energy supplies. Now the nation is an exporter of oil. There is much at stake in the ownership of the ocean floors.

High technology has made possible the mining of the ocean floors. Recovering pure nodules of manganese, nickle, and cobalt would help solve the world's mineral crisis. The oceans' annual catch of over 100 million tonnes of food could lead to political and economic power for the nations that own the rights. The nations that have ocean islands, such as Hawaii, the Canaries, and the Falklands, are

ONE WORLD

doubly fortunate. The UK fought the war in the Falklands partly to control the natural resources of most of the south Atlantic. The oceans are the frontier of the future, but who should benefit from their bounty?

FOREIGN ASSISTANCE

The most notable achievements in international co-operation have been in the field of social and industrial development aid to the developing world. This initiative has created more enthusiasm than any other area of global co-operation. The spread of world wide agencies directed at alleviating the problems of the peoples of the non-industrial world through technical assistance and economic and social development now encompasses three quarters of the planet. The sum total of government, non-government, and private organizations is clearly inadequate but they represent a very real response to the need to improve the lifestyle of billions of human beings. They are attempting to raise the standard of living for the great mass of the world's population. In a world sharply divided between rich and poor, foreign aid is directed at that segment of humanity which lives under the constant threat of starvation, poverty, and disease.

Foreign assistance has become one of the major characteristics of the growing interrelatedness between nations. Various kinds of aid and assistance help to carry out a redistribution of the world's wealth from the industrialized nations to the underdeveloped world. Aid can be tied to military and economic alliances, and is received from non-governmental organizations such as private charities or from the World Bank and other regional development agencies. The short term gains have produced a noticeable reduction in the numbers of the world's poor.

Assistance helps to keep many villagers clothed and fed.

This Moroccan man is watering a transplanted shrub as part of a reforestation project.

Foreign aid to developing countries is a major part of international relations. Aid aims to assist industrial development to eliminate poverty and hunger in the underdeveloped world.

Foreign aid became important in international relations in the mid 1950s. Since then, it has grown in both quantity and quality. Within only 40 years, some $1.5 trillion has gone to the underdeveloped world for industrial development. This figure does

Chapter 10
INTERNATIONAL CO-OPERATION

not include direct aid in food and medical supplies or aid through military assistance. Some people see the transfer of technology and industry to the underdeveloped world as a moral responsibility to share the resources of the world. Others see it as a matter of national self-interest in promoting economic and military strategies. Most governments, such as those of the UK and the USA, see aid as extending their own foreign policy. They wish to help their friends first. They do not give aid to those who do not support their policies.

SAMPLE OF CIDA CONTRIBUTIONS
1985-1986 (in Can. $)

Cyclone		Refugees, returnees, displaced persons	
Bangladesh	225 000	Benin	10 000
Drought		El Salvador	33 000
Angola	1 000 000	Ethiopia (varied humanitarian aid)	1 545 000
Chad	540 000	Nicaragua	76 000
Mali	40 000	Pakistan (Afghan refugees)	4 486 000
Mozambique	1 000 000	Sudan (varied humanitarian aid)	4 559 000
Earthquake		Thailand (varied humanitarian aid)	2 800 000
Chile	50 000	Uganda	50 000
Mexico	577 000	Zambia	23 000
Famine		**Orphans and widows**	
Mali	143 000	Guatemala	150 000
Flood		**Medicine**	
Brazil	20 000	Somalia	50 000
Chad	7 000	**Emergency food aid**	
India	10 000	Philippines	300 000
Typhoon		**Emergency assistance**	
Philippines	10 000	Mozambique	1 220 000
Viet Nam	50 000	**TOTAL**	**20 456 000**
Volcano			
Colombia	316 000		
Conflict			
Iran-Iraq	400 000		
Lebanon	516 000		
Philippines	250 000		

CIDA financially assists places that are afflicted by natural and political disasters.

Aid can and has speeded up development. Money and technical assistance can overcome stumbling blocks to industrialization. Aid offsets the high costs of building plants, research and development, worker training, health care, education, and transportation services. The underdeveloped countries cannot afford the time to go through the industrializing process. Developing nations can provide the industrial knowledge and processes needed to build an industrial base.

THE WORLD BANK

The World Bank has funded improvement projects worldwide. Nearly half of the bank's reserves now go to nutrition, education, population planning, small industries, and rural development. One World Bank project, the Francistown Project in Botswana, gave 95 per cent of households there roads, street lighting, and, most importantly, clean water.

Most people assume that aid is positive and helps to get rid of world poverty by promoting industrial development. This is true if the nations receiving it can make use of it and if population growth does not consume any potential gain. To benefit, recipient nations must be stable enough so that aid does not go to direct famine relief, military purposes, or corrupt officials. In about half of the cases, aid is used well. Marshall Plan aid, for reconstructing Europe, rebuilt the economies of a ravaged section of the globe. Successful aid has also been given to the NICs. Both Taiwan and South Korea received large-scale foreign aid for industrial growth. The knowledge, skill, and money needed to operate industrial complexes came from foreign aid. Without aid, West Germany and Japan would not be industrial giants today. Comparing East and West Berlin shows the value of aid. In the 1960s a wall had to be built around West Berlin to stop people in East Germany from fleeing to the more attractive city.

In other parts of the world, aid programs have not been as successful. A lack of food, material goods, technical skills, education, transportation, and health services undermines economic growth. Nor can aid overcome war, vagaries of weather, or exploding populations.

Some people question whether foreign aid actually reaches the poor. The 1970s were disastrous for the underdeveloped nations. Caught by rising energy prices, they showed little or no economic growth despite increased foreign aid. In many cases relief did not get through to those who needed it. Instead, it strengthened governments' control over the people. Widespread corruption and indifference misdirected much of the aid into other channels. The local governments' indifference to their peoples' plight seemed the greatest barrier to improving the standard of living, not the lack of

ONE WORLD

A Touareg man pours tea in northern Nigeria. In underdeveloped nations, only two out of five people have easy access to clean water and only one in four to proper sanitation.

material and resources. Poverty can result from political and economic decisions, not just resource scarcity.

The United Nations has determined that developed nations should allocate 1 per cent of their GNP to aid projects. This amount would substantially reduce global inequities. However, most nations fall short of this goal. Canada currently allocates .46 per cent of its GNP to a variety of foreign aid projects. The overall effect of aid is diminished by the escalating growth of population in the developing world. The millions of new people to feed and shelter use up a large proportion of aid funding, thus making real progress improbable. Startling success in foreign assistance was achieved, however, in the economic miracles of the NICs of Korea, Singapore, and Taiwan. Massive infusions of foreign aid are directly responsible for the current prosperity of these regions. Other examples of success lie in the field of direct aid for the survivors of natural disasters such as earthquakes, droughts, and floods.

The worst example of misuse of aid is Haiti, the world's poorest nation. Its 5 million people are poor compared with the rest of the world, and the number of people in absolute poverty is growing. Three-quarters of the people live at or below subsistence levels. In the urban areas tens of thousands live in rat-infested slums. These people have no access to safe water or adequate sewage disposal. In the countryside, soil erosion caused by deforestation and primitive farming practices has made a third of the land sterile. The nation cannot feed itself. More than 80 per cent of the children suffer from malnutrition. Infant mortality rates are over 20 per cent and most children get malaria or typhus before they are six years old.

Haiti appears beyond help. The tyranny and rapacity of the government are well-known. The

This is a Haitian slum. Haiti is the world's poorest nation.

Chapter 10

INTERNATIONAL CO-OPERATION

abuse of human rights is widespread. Despite recent changes in government, the ruling party remains in power. Since becoming a nation, there has never been an identifiable opposition. The Tons Tons Macout (the secret police) get rid of those opposed to the government by torture and killings. Changing the government by force is not likely to be any more successful than similar attempts in Afghanistan, Vietnam, Chile, Angola, or Nicaragua. Any change would only result in the same kind of administration.

Canada, the USA, West Germany, France, Taiwan, and Israel have supplied most aid to Haiti. The World Bank, FAO, UNICEF (United Nations Childrens' Fund), WHO, and a variety of non-governmental agencies have also provided help. None have achieved any kind of result. Fresh water projects end up in wealthy districts. Two-hundred million francs improved runways at the Duvalier International Airport. Canada cancelled one project after half of the $17.7 million disappeared as administrative costs. More than half of the 700 workers being paid did not exist. The World Bank concluded that about $15 million a month went to the president's Swiss bank accounts. No wonder many suggest abandoning aid to Haiti.

Much of the food and other products available in Haitian markets comes from outside of Haiti.

Withdrawing aid would most affect the poor. They would be expected to make up the difference through higher taxes. Withdrawing aid would only make matters worse. Now, aid is only slowing the decline in living standards. If it disappeared, it would result in abysmal conditions for the people. The economic prospects for the future are bleak. There seems to be no solution.

The role of the state in terms of economic development is dynamic in that it can accelerate growth through the extension of technical assistance and financial resources. Aid is a principal initiative in the foreign policies of industrial countries. Apart from the element of assistance to those less fortunate, they use aid as an instrument of foreign policy. Aid may be granted or withheld according to the willingness of the recipient to fall in with the donor country's expectations. In addition to the promotion of human welfare, then, aid can cement alliances and also open access to raw materials and low cost labour. The relationship established by aid projects is another example of interrelatedness amongst the world's nations.

PERSPECTIVE ON AID

PERSPECTIVE ONE

All human beings are entitled to a life of dignity free from hunger and material deprivation. A minimum standard of living that includes adequate supplies of food, shelter, and health service should be common to all humankind. To deny this opportunity to anyone when the world has adequate resources is immoral.

Aid can be the tool for eliminating the injustice of mass poverty. The more fortunate members of the global community have a compelling responsibility to eliminate poverty both at home and abroad. Foreign aid does improve the condition of the needy. Tens of millions of people have improved their lifestyle through development aid. In Jakarta, World Bank aid helped redevelop 10 000 hectares of housing bringing relief to 450 000 people over a period of a few years. In Morocco, aid funding has been used to teach mothers modern methods of hygiene and food preparation resulting in in healthier children. Educational projects through organizations like CUSO result in the preparation of young people for a more hopeful future.

One of the most successful uses of aid has been in the area of agriculture. In India, aid has assisted in developing high yield crops to the point where the sub-continent can now export foods. A decade ago India had to import food to feed her own people. Swamp reclamation projects in Asia have increased yields by six times. In Ethiopia, 30 000 farmers were given seed and new tools. In Gambia, water management programs have resulted in a 64 per cent increase in harvests. Clearly, these are areas where aid money can make a significant difference in the lives of local farmers.

Foreign aid can also be used for remote industrial development. Technological knowledge and equipment is sometimes beyond the ability of the underdeveloped nation to develop. Yet future economic viability depends on industrial development. The dramatic growth of the NICs and the high standards of living now enjoyed by their people attest to the possibilities of aid properly managed.

Aid is effective. We have a moral obligation to assist the millions of people who struggle to survive. To reduce or eliminate foreign aid programs because of the costs would be both immoral and counter-productive and would lead to political and economic instability.

PERSPECTIVE TWO

There may well be a right to life but one cannot expect that right to be accompanied by the right to a certain standard of living. There are now some two billion people in need of aid and their numbers are growing. They place relentless pressure on their governments for services that cannot be provided. Their lifestyle expectations are unrealistic in view of both the resource availability and development strategies in these areas.

Poverty is the result of local mismanagement of resources. Political and economic policies regarding land ownership, cash-crop production, repressive taxation of lower classes, and the support of a military and social elite are matters which foreign aid cannot address. Aid does not trickle down to the poor but is diverted for the use of those in power. Since foreign assistance consolidates the power of the elite over the people, it should be stopped. This money should be used instead to help the poor at home.

Aid is simply a crutch which retards normal development. Money is often squandered in projects which give status and prestige to those in power but which may in fact make life more miserable for the poor. The use of farm machinery can significantly improve the productive capacity of agriculture. However, in a weak economy, the majority of farmers displaced by machinery are unable to find employment and hence starve. A 20 year funding of cotton production in the Central African Republic has not resulted in a single bale being produced. The 75 kilometre Shiti-Niari railway was financed four times over to a total of some 34 million ecus. Twenty kilometres have been built but 15 of these are in disrepair from neglect and cannot be used. Tanzania, in 1960, was the bread basket of Africa. Today, after receiving more aid per capita than any other African nation, it is unable to feed itself. There are many people in the industrial world who are trapped in the cycles of poverty. Would aid money not be better spent at home?

Unrealistic promises of justice and equality raise expectations beyond the realm of possibility. When promises are not met, the result is too often instability and conflict. Aid should not be a matter of helping the poor. It should instead be seen as a matter of national security. Given to allies it can deter aggression and at the same time secure needed natural resources. The USA, Britain, and France are correct in directing foreign aid to their allies and former colonies.

In view of the above perspectives, should Canada continue a policy of foreign assistance? Why? Why not?

CONCLUSION

The land surface of the world is divided into nation states with various degrees of wealth and military power. The nation state system promotes confrontation rather than co-operation. Tension and conflict have been characteristic of international relations. New weapons have made war a terrifying alternative. Recent co-operation in the Antarctic, agreements on using outer space, and the Law of the Sea promise hope for the future.

Chapter 10
INTERNATIONAL CO-OPERATION

The major problems facing humankind, such as resource depletion and inequitable distribution of food and resources, are global in nature. Foreign assistance from developed to underdeveloped nations is now provided by both government and private agencies. The extent and nature of aid projects is an issue which demands attention. It is becoming increasingly clear that without assistance, underdeveloped nations cannot hope to solve their problems. The question is how to make aid more effective.

QUESTIONS

1. Why is nationalism still a dominant force?
2. Name three examples of international co-operation in world affairs.
3. Explain the competing interests which affect the exploitation of sea resources.
4. Explain the Law of the Sea Treaty.
5. Why is ownership of ocean resources an important issue? Explain who should own ocean resources.
6. Explain three types of foreign aid.
7. Explain how foreign aid affects the development process.
8. Give two examples of successful aid projects.
9. Explain why foreign aid is sometimes ineffective.
10. What percentage of GNP does the UN suggest developed nations allocate to foreign aid? How much does Canada allocate?
11. Explain how aid has been misused in Haiti.
12. What solution do you suggest for Haiti?
13. Name and explain how aid has been successful in any five countries.
14. Name five reasons which support the position that aid should not be given to underdeveloped countries.

ACTIVITIES

1. **Guest Speaker:**
   Invite a guest speaker to discuss the work of either a government or non-government agency's involvement in aid projects in the underdeveloped world.

2. **Debate:**
   Debate the issue of foreign aid.
   Resolved that:
   "Developed nations contribute at least 1 per cent of their GNP to underdeveloped nations in some form of foreign aid."

3. **Model UN Assembly:**
   Structure a model UN Assembly to discuss a current global crisis such as:
   a) The status of Antarctica
   b) Security in the Arctic
   c) The Law of the Sea and ocean resources.

4. **Research Report:**
   Select a country which has received foreign aid and write a research report. Identify the specific aid given, how the aid was used, and the effect of aid on the standard of living of the people.

5. **Scrapbook:**
   Collect 10 newspaper articles on nationalism and 10 newspaper articles on internationalism.
   What hope is there for international co-operation in the future? Write a paragraph explaining your perception of the global situation. Can internationalism prevail over nationalism?

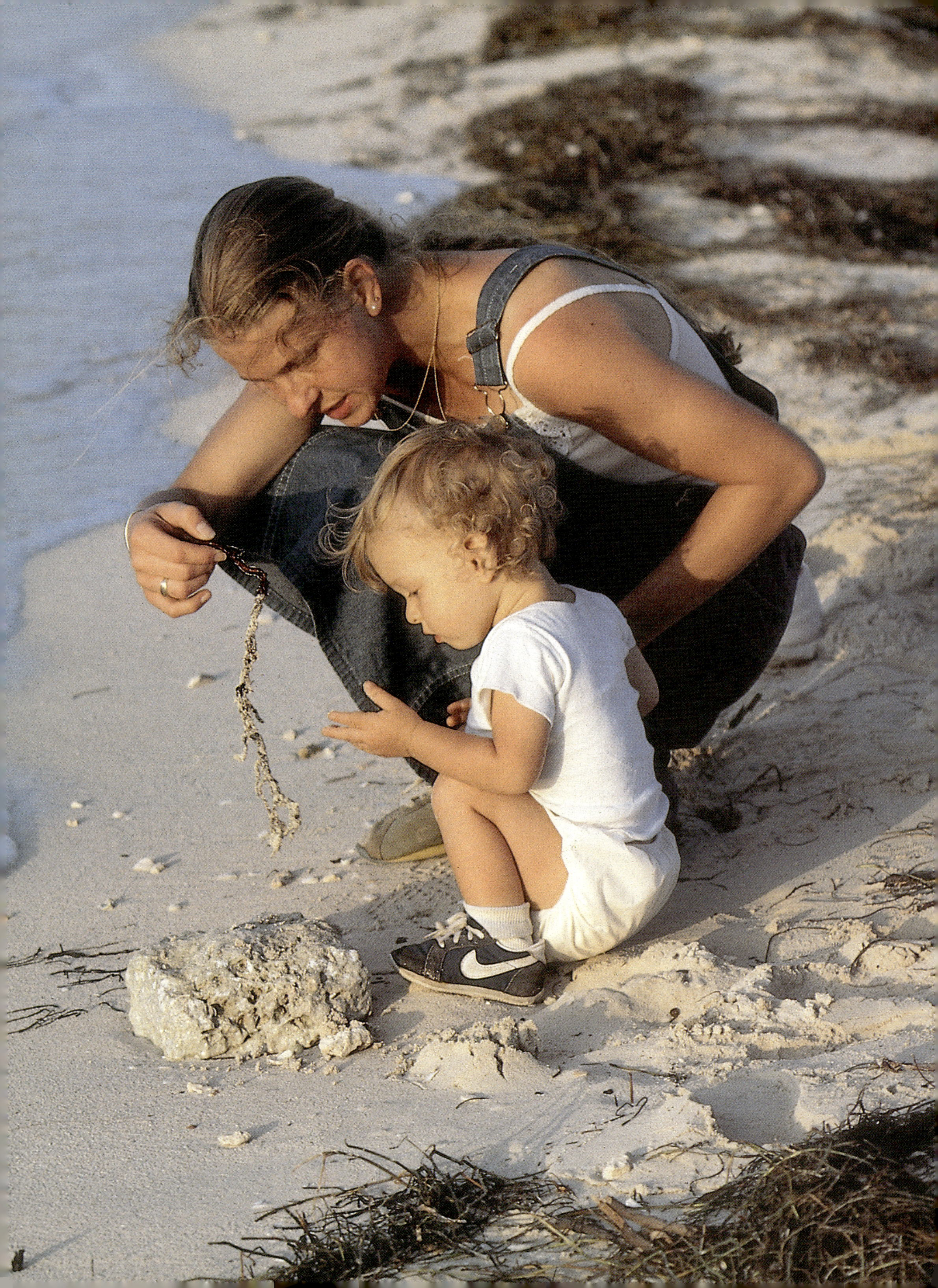

11

TOMORROW

WE CANNOT PREDICT the future. We can only guess what lies ahead. There are many possibilities. The future lies somewhere between survival and extinction. On the one hand, the earth's resources could balance out. Industrial societies could have lower birth rates and resource use could decline. On the other hand, we could end humanity in nuclear war or environmental catastrophe. The truth lies somewhere in between. Most forecasts assume that we must live out our future on earth. Should we leave earth, a whole new future opens up for us. Let us look at four scenarios of potential futures.

Humans currently stand on the threshold of a new age. As we approach the twenty-first century, we are faced with choices emanating from the technological developments which have enhanced the lifestyle of the developed world. The last century has been characterized by incredible changes in technology. Our quality of life has improved dramatically and has changed at an increasingly rapid pace. It is the envy of those still consigned to a life of misery in the underdeveloped countries. This radical change in lifestyle, however, has placed enormous pressure on the environment. We are depleting the earth's natural resources and degrading the environment. Can we continue to sustain the lifestyle which we have come to expect in the developed world while improving the lifestyle of

This tea party portrays a lifestyle millions of people in underdeveloped countries will never enjoy.

those currently denied even the most basic subsistence in the underdeveloped world? Will we find ourselves in conflict over the availability of resources or control of land? Would conflict tempt nuclear powers to use the most powerful and most terrifying weapon created by humans, the nuclear bomb? Could humans survive a nuclear confrontation?

Depleting resources and pollution endanger the biosphere. Environmentalists, scientists, politicians, and ordinary people are sounding the alarm. We have choices. We could keep using up natural resources with reckless abandon until they run out. The developed world could keep monopolizing the earth's gifts. The underdeveloped countries could allow their numbers to increase without regard for their support. Or we could enhance all our lives by better managing the planet.

Technology is developing so rapidly that it might produce new ways to protect the environment as well as a high-tech lifestyle. Can we harness technology for global prosperity? Will the future be full of new frontiers in human achievement? Let us explore four possible futures now:

1. Humanity continues to waste resources and pollute the environment.
2. A nuclear war produces "nuclear winter."
3. We learn how to live in harmony with the environment.
4. We try to solve our resource and overpopulation problems by founding colonies in space.

WASTEFUL HUMANITY

Despite becoming more aware of environmental problems, humanity's lifestyle still threatens the biosphere. What will the future be like if we keep ignoring the warnings? If the world's activities continue unchanged, what will life in 2050 be like?

Deciding the earth's **carrying capacity** is most vital. If we ignore the effect of population on the availability of resources, will we be able to continue our present lifestyle? UN figures show that failing to start population planning programs will mean that there will be more than 10 billion people by 2050. Ninety per cent of this increase will be in the underdeveloped regions. Many of these countries cannot now feed their people. How will they feed the extra people? Will the developed regions share?

We may be able to produce about 7.3 billion tonnes of grain. Eating as we do, this food could sustain about 11 billion people. Remember the developing nations' diet allows 730 million people to go hungry. Of these, 40 million die each year. Most of these deaths are in the underdeveloped regions. Many of these regions have already passed their carrying capacity. Struggling to survive means farming marginal cropland. This leads to erosion and ultimately exhausts the soil. Many of the world's new inhabitants will be too poor to have enough to eat and hunger will persist.

Using wood for fuel has led to cutting forests faster than nature can replace them. This practice could destroy our **rainforests**. People have cut down the forests of the Ivory Coast and Nigeria in the past 40 years. The remaining rainforests are in South America, tropical Asia, and central Africa. Deforestation also comes from dam and plantation projects and livestock-raising programs. About 100 000 square kilometres of rain forest are lost each year. At this rate we will have no rainforests on our planet within the next 50 years.

What will this mean for us? One-quarter of the earth's people depend on the tropical forests for their water supply. Tree roots protect precious topsoil. Forests provide many products, like timber, oils, fibres, and fruit. Many modern medicines come from plants available only in rainforests. Extinction is occurring so rapidly that some species may be forever gone from the planet before they are even identified.

Perhaps the most threatening result of deforestation is its effect on climate. Rainforests help to balance temperatures between temperate and tropical regions by recycling rainfall. They also absorb carbon dioxide. Deforestation has increased the release of both methane and carbon dioxide into the atmosphere. The earth has been gradually warmed. A "worst case scenario" is that between 2042 and 2080, temperature increases would melt the polar ice cap. Oceans would rise, flooding coastal areas. Flooding would be disastrous since many densely populated areas are on land now close to sea level.

Living standards in underdeveloped regions are declining as their populations grow. However, the developed world continues to demand an unequal share of the earth's resources. We plunder the earth's resources for material goods. Industrial societies seem to believe that "more is better." We have been conditioned to want the latest gadget. We discard items no longer fashionable. To make

Chapter 11

TOMORROW

The building of this Pan-African highway destroyed the precious rainforest growing there.

our life easier we use disposable diapers and dishes. Technology has produced indestructible products which now pose mammoth problems of disposal. One of our most pressing problems is garbage. We have even polluted space with garbage. How will future generations deal with the garbage legacy of this generation?

Industrialization has given us a lifestyle envied by the rest of the world. However, it has created problems which now threaten this lifestyle. Pollution is one of our most serious concerns. We have now polluted our groundwater in many areas of the world. As most major rivers are used as disposal systems, our water supply is at risk. Chemical pollution affects our food and the air we breathe. Using styrofoam and other materials with chlorofluorocarbons, such as aerosol spray cans, could further damage the ozone layer. Living as we have will end our resources sometime after 2050. What will happen when our resources are gone? Can we prevent collapse?

NUCLEAR WINTER

After the bombing of Japan in 1945, it was clear that a nuclear bomb could kill and maim large numbers of people as well as destroy tracts of land and buildings. Monitoring the Japanese population also showed that being exposed to radiation could cause long-term illness. Most early studies focused on the possibility of survival. Building bomb shelters and stockpiling food were the priorities in the late 1950s and early 1960s. People knew that the landscape would be contaminated. However, it was thought that damage would be temporary. Little thought was given to the fate of earth. In 1982, a Dutch scientist named Paul Crutzen dropped his own bombshell. All life could end in nuclear winter! This would not be because of nuclear bombs but because of their after-effect on the environment.

Detonating only 1 per cent of the global nuclear arsenal could be disastrous for global climate. The most likely targets would be cities, coalfields, oil fields or depots, and power plants. Within hours of a war starting between the superpowers, 4500 megatonnes could be detonated. A thousand cities could burn simultaneously. One million square kilometres of woodland could be set ablaze from the blast. About 363 million tonnes of smoke could

During a nuclear winter, black clouds would gather above the earth, blocking the sun.

darken the skies. As much as 99 per cent of the sun's light could be blocked out. Within two days, the earth would begin to chill rapidly. At first the northern hemisphere would suffer the most. Gradually, however, the smoke would be carried south by prevailing winds. By the end of two weeks, temperatures in the north would have dropped to as low as -60 degrees Celsius in the area under the densest cloud. Temperatures would not fall as low in the south. However, tropical eco-systems would still be unable to withstand the sudden cold.

The survivors of a nuclear holocaust would suffer cold, thirst, and hunger. Many would suffer from burns or radiation sickness. All inland bodies of water would ice over and the ground would freeze. It would be difficult to get food or shelter. Cold and darkness would be followed by toxic smog, radiation, and black acid rain. Burning cities could release deadly gases like ammonia, methane, hydrocarbons, and carbon monoxide, as well as asbestos particles, PCBs, and dioxins. Some scientists suggest that the radioactive particles falling in acid rain would deplete the ozone layer. There would be an ultraviolet spring following the nuclear winter. Even if humans survived a nuclear winter, could they survive the ultraviolet rays of the sun?

Mass extinction of species would occur, especially in tropical areas more vulnerable to cold. Photosynthesis would stop and food chains would fail. In the most pessimistic scenario, only giant worms and clams in the Galapagos and midsea ridges would survive. In the most optimistic scenario, some of the South Sea islands like Tahiti might be spared. These islands may be refuges, but how would one travel to them?

There seems to be no guaranteed "safe" level of nuclear war. Almost any level of combat would produce enough smoke to cause nuclear winter. A war in either spring or summer would be even more devastating as it would catch vegetation when it is most vulnerable. If war occurred in fall, the harvest would be contaminated. Survivors would be left to scavenge like prehistoric people. However, these survivors would be unused to scavenging and would be coping with a destroyed landscape. Even if any resources remained, the technology needed to mine them would have been destroyed. Humanity would not survive.

MANAGING OUR FUTURE

The **Gaia hypothesis** views humanity as an integral part of the universe. As a strand of life in the eco-system, humanity depends upon the earth for life support. Every one of our actions has an impact on this system. If we accept this theory and attempt to live in harmony with the environment, can we continue our life on earth? Are we willing to keep our numbers and activities in balance with earth's needs?

Family planning programs are already in place in some parts of the underdeveloped world. Suppose we looked at this issue at the global level and helped countries in an integrated way involving health care and education? The UN suggests that if **replacement level fertility** is reached in 2010, our global population would stabilize at 7.7 billion by 2060.

Current global food production methods could now sustain 7.5 billion people with an average of 9000 calories daily. This figure includes calories in seed and animal feed as well as human food consumption. This is substantially higher than the current average of 5940 calories (including the calories in seed and animal feed). By increasing the productivity and amount of land used for agriculture and by introducing new foods, we could feed even larger numbers. The most optimistic outlook suggests that high-technology farming and managing of resources wisely could sustain 27 billion people by the twenty-second century.

Industrial societies use great amounts of energy. Do we have enough energy to keep increased numbers warm, fed, entertained, and transported? The energy crisis of the 1970s made us aware of our vulnerability. Since then, energy conservation programs have led to greater efficiency and reduced waste. In addition, it is now clear that renewable energy sources could be the key to the future. Solar energy, wind power, and hydrogen-powered engines are just a few of the possibilities. These are still costly and unreliable. However, great strides are being made and new technology could unlock the potential. New technologies wisely managed can sustain growth at manageable levels.

Alternative energy sources will reduce the pollution which is now one of our most pressing concerns. Recycling programs could reduce the mountains of paper, glass, and aluminum garbage which we are currently facing. Reducing chemical fertilizers and pesticides in agriculture would decrease risks to health as well as to groundwater and air. Clearly, action must be taken now if we are to preserve our environment. Government restrictions on the use of pesticides exist in many parts of the developed world. In addition to these measures, the World Bank has now three criteria for its projects: economic growth, poverty reduction, and environmental protection.

Sustainable development can only occur if sound economic and political decisions are made considering the environment. The recent arms agreement between the USA and the USSR shows that there is some hope to redirect resources. Now, an average of $150 per person per annum is spent on the arms race. This totals $750 billion, or 6 per cent of

ONE WORLD

These geothermal geysers in New Zealand are used to generate electricity.

global GNP. We concentrate on destruction instead of development. Just seven months of military spending would provide clean water and sanitation facilities for 2 billion people. A mere eight hours' spending could get rid of malaria.

There are enough resources on earth for a much larger population. However, we need new approaches and global co-operation to avert disaster. We have been waging war on the environment for decades. We must now reassess our position on earth. Just as world leaders restructured their political and economic units after World War II, world leaders today must consider bold new programs to protect our future.

LIFE OFF EARTH

Leaving the planet to search for new colonies is one way to solve problems of depleting resources. Space might provide living space and new sources of resources. Although this may sound far-fetched, imagine how people reacted to this idea of jet aircraft only one generation ago. In 1960, when President John Kennedy announced the United States' determination to reach the moon by the end of the decade, technology to do so did not exist. Scientists now suggest that we could use ice from Saturn's rings as a source of water. Technology is now being developed for an expedition to Mars. Scientists

Chapter 11
TOMORROW

are now working on ways to completely alter the atmospheric conditions on Mars, so that it could support life. It may be possible to simulate the conditions on earth. After founding a base on Mars, why not space cities? Humanity's first step on the moon was one of the most exciting moments of our time. Since then, technology has advanced by leaps and bounds. Consider the possibility of exploration of the solar system. Perhaps we might even consider in the very distant future, the first robot interstellar probes.

Once people have started space stations, the next step could be great power stations in orbit 300 or 500 kilometres above earth. Microwave energy could be beamed to the earth's surface. Clean and efficient, this energy source could replace our current dependence on fossil fuels.

The technology of space missions could also be used for "floating cities." These cities would be in the atmosphere. They would not scar the landscape but rather would free the land area for parks and forests. This greenery could be enjoyed by residents of the cities. Renewed parts of the earth might once again be used responsibly.

Nuclear fusion, **bionics**, and extended **artificial intelligence** could be by-products of space technology. These developments might usher in a new age of machinery. Engines powered by nuclear fusion do not deplete our non-renewable resources or pollute the environment. Robots work cheaply, efficiently, and tirelessly. They could provide many services at home, at the office, or in the factory. Already there are "conscious computers" which respond to emotions. "Conscious computers" are only the beginning of our interaction with technology. In addition, our ability to control the weather will be advanced. We might be able to avoid droughts and increase food production. This type

An artist's depiction of a space colony, containing all the comforts of home, including trees, rivers, and lakes.

ONE WORLD

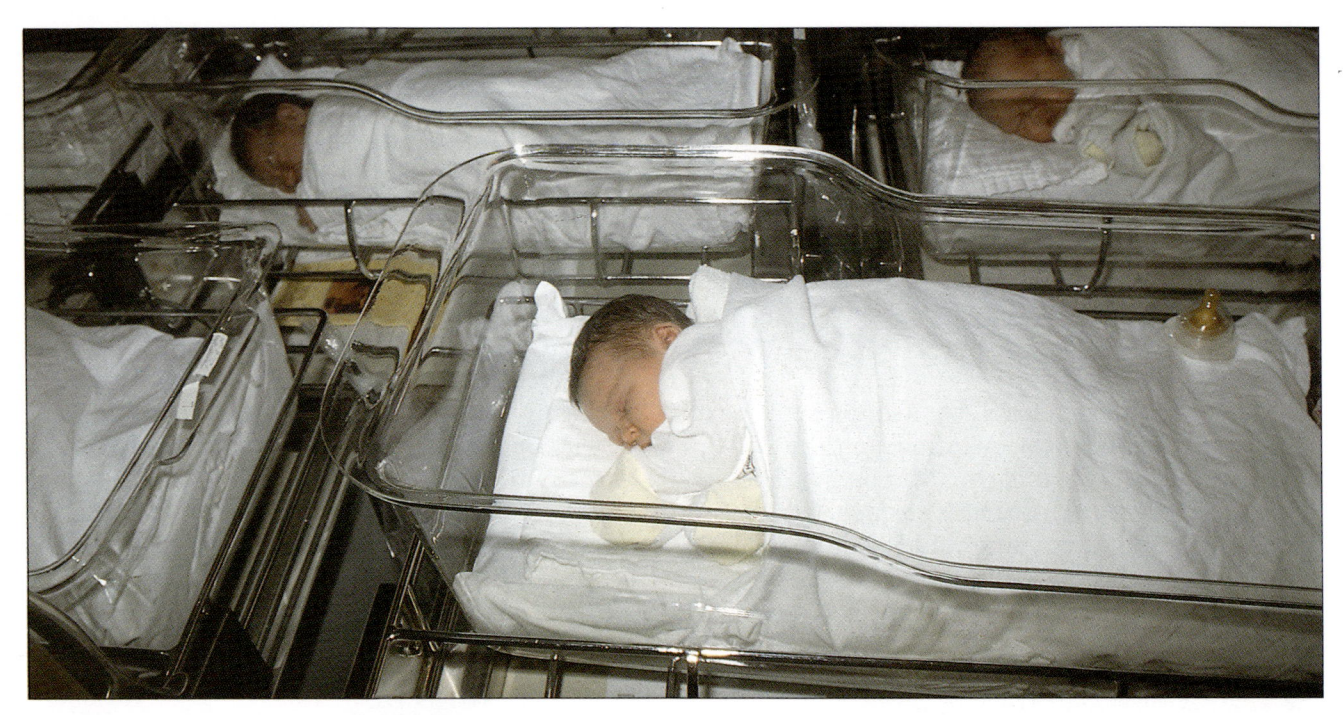

What sort of future will our children have?

of planetary engineering will have to be highly sensitive to the fragile condition of the eco-systems.

Sceptics could dismiss this type of speculation as nonsense. Consider, however, one of humanity's most prized possessions: the creative imagination. Since we first appeared on earth, we have used this ability to adapt to and fashion our environment. Our powers of observation, tenacity, and ingenuity also are part of this creativity. We have discovered the wheel, harnessed water power, produced the jet engine, and developed the computer. Can we doubt our ability since we have already shown such incredible creativity? Can we not expect equally great achievements in the future?

CONCLUSION

Gaia, the living planet, is our home. Being aware, finally, that we share this home with many other species, will we act to save our future? Today humanity faces the most serious challenge of its existence. It is a challenge, however, with a potential for great achievements. Already people are attempting to take up this challenge to chart a new course for this planet.

Children born this year in many parts of the world can expect to live longer and be better educated than their parents. Although great inequity still exists, there is a higher standard of living for larger numbers of people. Poverty is still a most serious problem for one-fifth of the world's people. Recent international conferences have led to renewed commitments by industrial nations to help solve the economic problems of the disadvantaged nations.

Human numbers could swell to 27 billion by the twenty-second century. Could we feed so many people? Scientists are already researching new sources of food. Aquaculture could provide another source of protein. Seed banks promise greater genetic diversity and higher yields. In addition, industrial nations are being encouraged to eat fewer calories in the interests of better health. Eating less meat in the industrial world would mean that cereal grains now used in meat production could be eaten by humans.

Urbanization has posed great problems in all parts of the globe. Some of these problems are now being addressed creatively. Governments have supported self-help projects in sprawling squatter settlements. Cities in industrial nations have decentralized. Self-contained suburbs now house large numbers of people outside large cities. New transportation systems link these suburbs to the city core.

Chapter 11

TOMORROW

This alternative geodesic home in North Carolina is the kind of home we may see more of if people choose to live with alternative sources of energy.

Large numbers of people need vast amounts of energy. Depleting energy resources have alerted us to conserving current energy reserves. More importantly, we are now aware of the need to develop new sources of energy. Future generations may meet their energy needs by harnessing the sun's power, the wind, or tidal waves. Nuclear energy and geothermal power (tapping the heat under the earth's surface) are two other choices.

Perhaps our interdependence shows itself most clearly in the industrial process. Multinational corporations have built a chain link around the world. An international assembly line has been established. Resources come from several countries. Industrial plants around the world assemble the resources before final assembly into a finished product takes place. Trade and travel have led to a global culture.

As we come into contact with people and products from many nations we are beginning to have a global consciousness. Can we use this global consciousness to transcend our national borders? Can we keep a sense of pride in our own culture and appreciate other cultures? Will this appreciation lead to co-operation internationally? The recent agreements between the superpowers to limit nuclear weaponry are encouraging. People are growing more aware of the cost of arms escalation. One hopes that these resources could be used for human progress instead.

Most encouraging of all has been humanity's realization of its place in the world. Our relationship with nature began with a childlike dependence on nature's gifts. In awe of the forces which controlled life, most ancient religions had a female deity representing the nurturing aspects of nature and a male deity who represented the harsher side. Like children, people were anxious to please and careful to obey nature's forces. Developing science and technology enabled people to control their environment. For a time, this power led to wanton disregard for nature as people delighted in each new technological development. We seem now, however, to be waking up. Nature cannot take such pressure from human activities. Being aware has in it the seeds of a new beginning. People no longer need to fear nature and they are able to control its most violent features. We may now become earth's guardian. Understanding our place in the eco-sphere may lead us to appreciate nature's gifts and protect them for future generations. Will we accept the role of steward of our environment? Are we ready for a life in harmony with nature?

Global alarm bells are sounding to alert people to the environmental crisis we now face. We are at a crossroads. It is a frightening yet an exciting time to be alive. Which path will we choose?

GLOSSARY

Acid rain is the fallout of industrial pollutants, sometimes as acidified rainfall and sometimes as dry deposits. Acid rain damages plant life; acidifies rivers, lakes, and groundwater; and corrodes buildings.

Artificial intelligence refers to the logical thought processes carried out by computers.

Bionics describes the study of human and animal biological functions, especially those of the brain, that could be used in developing electronic equipment such as computers.

The **biosphere** is the part of the earth where life can exist. The biosphere is made up of the atmosphere (the air that surrounds the earth), hydrosphere (the water on the earth's surface), and lithosphere (the solid outer shell of the earth, believed to be between 70 and 150 kilometres thick).

Carrying capacity is the largest number of people the earth's eco-system (see definition below) can maintain without damaging the eco-system's basic structure.

Chlorofluorocarbons (CFCs) are a synthetic chemical used in refrigerants, aerosol sprays, and cleansers of electronic parts. CFCs are broken down by ultraviolet rays in the stratosphere, freeing chlorine atoms that interfere with the formation of ozone.

Consumerism is the theory that it is economically good for a society to continually increase its consumption of goods.

Curies (named after Marie Curie, a French physicist and chemist) are units of radioactivity in which 3.7×10^{10} disintegration occurs per unit per second.

Eco-systems, a term coined by Oxford economist A.G. Tansley in 1934, describe the interaction of all living things of a particular environment with each other and with their habitat.

An **Exclusive Economic Zone** (EEZ) defines the area of the ocean that is under the jurisdiction of coastal states.

During **fission**, an atomic nucleus is split, releasing large amounts of energy.

Fossil fuels are fuels, such as coal, oil, and gas, which are derived from the remains of living things.

In **fusion**, atomic nuclei combine to form heavier nuclei, resulting in the release of large amounts of energy.

The **Gaia hypothesis** is an attempt to explain the ability of the biosphere (see definition above) to create an environment that most favours its own stability and which is able to keep that stability in spite of changes in the environment. Professor James Lovelock, the originator of the hypothesis, sees the biosphere as a single living system that he calls "Gaia," after the Greek goddess of the earth.

Geothermal energy is an increasingly common source of energy in volcanic areas. Geothermal steam may be used to produce electricity and is a source of heat.

The **greenhouse effect** takes place when heat waves, which are radiating out from the earth, are trapped near the earth's surface by layers of cloud or smog. This leads to an unnatural heating of the earth's lower atmosphere.

The **"Green Revolution"** was a program launched by the United Nations Food and Agriculture Organization (FAO) in the 1960s. The aim of the program was to increase food production in the underdeveloped world and so eradicate hunger. Agricultural yields did increase, but the program has been criticized on various counts, including the damage done to the environment by the massive use of pesticides and fertilizers and the large increase in the underdeveloped nations' debts due to the costs of the program.

Groundwater is the technical name for the water stored within soil and rock pores. Groundwater sources are being depleted by agricultural use at a dangerous rate. Groundwater depletion causes water tables to fall and can cause land subsidence. In addition, many sources of groundwater used for drinking are now being polluted by agricultural chemicals and hazardous wastes which are seeping through the soil.

Half-lives are the time needed for half of the atoms in a radioactive substance to decay.

Newly industrializing countries (NICs) are former underdeveloped countries which have industrialized rapidly and experienced high economic growth in recent years. South Korea, Brazil, Taiwan, and Singapore are examples of NICs.

The **ozone layer** is the earth's protective shield against ultraviolet rays. The ozone in the upper atmosphere reacts with these high-energy rays, filtering most of them out before they can reach the surface.

Rainforests are dense evergreen forests that have very tall trees, a heavy undergrowth, and receive a great amount of rainfall all year.

Replacement level fertility describes a situation in which a population is not growing but is simply replacing itself.

Robotics is the term used for machines that are able to replace workers on assembly lines.

Solar radiation is the wide spectrum of energy radiation given off by the sun.

The **World Bank**, established in 1944, refers to three closely related agencies of the UN: the International Bank for Reconstruction and Development; the International Development Association; and the International Finance Corporation, which makes loans to private companies in the underdeveloped world. The bank has been criticized for ignoring the environmental effects of projects it has funded. In 1987, the bank set out three new guidelines for its projects: economic growth, alleviation of poverty, and protection of the environment.

INDEX

acid rain, 13, 28, 94
Afghanistan, MA-15, 127
Africa, 13, 25, 44, 69, 132
   agriculture, 77, 80
   energy, 91, 97
   life expectancy, 54
   see also specific African countries
agribusiness, 84
agricultural revolution, 37, 40-42
agriculture, 77, 87, 93, 113
   cash crops, MA-16, 75, 80-83
   foreign aid, 128
   green revolution, 84-86
   land reform, 80-82, 84-85
   organic farming, 86
   soil degradation, 18, 76, 78-80, 84
air conditioners, 90, 101
alcohol. See ethanol
Algeria, MA-15
Angola, 125, 127
Ankara, Turkey, 70
Antarctica, 122
Argentina, MA-15, 70, 112-13, 115, 121
arms race, MA-5, 25-27, 135-36
Atlantic Ocean, 13, 124
atmosphere, 12-13
Atmosphere, World Conference on the Changing, 28
Australia, 14-15, 44, 53, 113, 121
Austria, MA-15, 32
automobiles, 71, 90, 93, 98

Bangladesh, MA-15, MA-17, 55, 58, 125
Beijing, China, 70
Belgian Congo (Zaire), 30
Belgium, MA-15, 32, 106
Benin, 125

biosphere, 9
Black Death, 44
Bolivia, MA-15, 57
Bombay, India, 70
Botswana, 15, 125
Brazil, 25, 48, 55, 58, 70, 83, 107, 125
   agriculture, 92-93
   education, 115
   energy, 92-93, 115
   Gross National Product, 112
   industry, 18, 92-93, 112
   standard of living, MA-15
   trade, 112-13
Britain. See Great Britain
Brundtland Report, 28
Buenos Aires, Argentina, 70

calories, 76-77, 82
Canada, 48, 107, 121
   energy, 90
   environment, 28, 84
   foreign aid, 126-27
   Gross National Product, 112, 126
   immigration, MA-11, 46
   industry, 32-33
   standard of living, MA-15
   trade, 33, 84, 113-15
Canadian Charter of Rights and Freedoms, 49
Canadian International Development Agency (CIDA), 125
Canadian University Service Overseas (CUSO), 128
CARE projects, 124
Caribbean Sea, 121
Casablanca, Morocco, 70
Central African Republic, MA-15, 128

Index

cereal grains, 77, 84, 93, 113
    maize, 41, 75, 80, 82
    oats, 41
    rice, 41, 75, 80, 86
    rye, 41
    wheat, 75, 80, 85
Chad, MA-15, 125
chemicals, production and use of, 19
Chernobyl, USSR, 95-96
children in society, MA-13, 49, 56-58, 126
Chile, MA-15, 33, 113, 121, 125, 127
China, MA-5, 44, 70, 109
    agriculture, 41, 77
    energy, 91, 94
    population, MA-4, 58, 60-61
    standard of living, MA-15
    trade, 33, 42
climate, 13-14, 132, 134
coal, 89, 91-92, 94, 99
Colombia, MA-15, 60, 113-14, 125
Comecon, 30
communications, 47
computers, 107-8, 137
conservation, 97-98, 101
consumerism, 57, 107
Cyprus, 119

Denmark, MA-15, 32, 123
desertification, 78-80
diet. *See* food
disease, 44, 57, 86

East Germany, 94, 125
Ecuador, 14, 106, 113
education, 106, 110, 115, 127
Egypt, MA-15, 30, 33, 70, 85
El Niño Current, 14-15
El Salvador, 125
employment in underdeveloped countries, 68-69
energy, MA-10, 135
    alcohol, 93
    conservation, 97-98
    consumption, 90-91
    fossil fuel, 89-92, 94, 98-101, 112, 114
    nuclear, 19, 91, 94-96
    solar, 11-12, 89, 94, 97
    water, 44
England, 34, 44-46, 66, 70, 106-7
    see also Great Britain
Environment, Task Force on the (Canada), 28
Environment and Development, World Commission on, 28
erosion, 17, 78, 86, 92, 126
ethanol, MA-10, 92-93
Ethiopia, MA-15, MA-17, 24, 77, 125, 128
Europe, 47, 54, 76, 78, 94, 106-7, 125
    see also specific European countries
Europe, Eastern, 91

Europe, Western, MA-10, 48, 65, 77, 91, 108
European Common Market, 30, 81, 115
Exclusive Economic Zone (EEZ), 121

Falkland Islands, 123-24
family planning, 60-61
Federal Republic of Germany. *See* West Germany
fertility rates, 58-60, 67
Finland, MA-15, 29
fisheries, 14, 121-22
    aquaculture, 86
fission, nuclear, 95-96
food, MA-16-17, 40, 82-85, 135
    distribution, 77
    quality and variety, 57, 75-76
    subsidies, 81
Food and Agriculture Organization (FAO), 30, 127
food chain, 14, 17, 19
foreign aid, 48, 80, 109-10, 124-28
foreign debt of Latin America, 114-16
forest, 91-94
    rainforest, 132-33
fossil fuels, 99-101
    coal, 89, 91-92, 94, 99
    petroleum products, 89-92, 98, 112, 114, 121, 123
France, MA-5, 24, 34, 66, 70
    energy, 95
    foreign aid, 127-28
    Gross National Product, 112
    industry, 32, 44-45, 106-7
    standard of living, MA-15
Francistown Project (Botswana), 125
fusion, nuclear, 96

Gaia hypothesis, 135
Gambia, 128
genetic diversity, 86
German Democratic Republic. *See* East Germany
Germany, 24, 29, 45, 106-7
    see also East Germany *and* West Germany
Ghana, MA-15
global urban culture, 23, 33, 65-66, 72, 108
Great Britain, MA-5, 91, 91, 115, 123-24
    foreign aid, 82, 125, 128
    industry, 32, 46
    standard of living, MA-15
    transportation, 47
    urbanization, 46
    see also England
Greece, 112
green revolution, 84-86
greenhouse effect, 11, 27, 98-99
Gross National Product, MA-15, 112, 115, 126
Guatemala, 125
gulf stream, 13

Haiti, MA-15, 76, 126-27
heat waste, 100-101

Helsinki Agreements, 49
Hong Kong, MA-15, 68, 114
housing, 68-70, 98, 139
human rights, 25, 48-50, 127
Hungary, MA-15, 48
hydroponics, 77
hydrosphere. See oceans

Iceland, 13
imperialism, 42-45, 107
imperialism, economic, 34
India, 41-42, 44, 48, 55, 58, 68, 91, 109
    agriculture, 77, 80, 85
    foreign aid recipient, 125, 128
    Gross National Product, 112
    standard of living, MA-15, 75
Indonesia, 14, 58, 70, 127
industrial revolution, 12, 37, 45-47, 106
industrialization, 44, 105, 107
    and the environment, MA-14, 18, 27
    and urbanization, 66-67, 114
    benefits, 33, 54
    costs, 68, 108-9, 114, 116
    of South Korea, 110-11
international co-operation, MA-4, 24-31, 33-34, 48, 119-24
    see also foreign aid
International Labour Organization, 29
Iran, 112, 125
Iraq, 125
Ireland, MA-15, 112
irrigation, 79, 84, 115
Israel, MA-15, 34, 127
Italy, MA-15, 32, 112
Ivory Coast, 48, 132

Jakarta, Indonesia, 70, 127
Japan, 13-14, 24, 29, 44, 114, 121, 134
    foreign aid recipient, 48, 125
    industry, 32, 107-8
    standard of living, MA-15, 75
    trade, 72, 110-11, 115
    urbanization, 66, 70, 72, 90
Jericho, 41

Kampuchea, MA-15
Kenya, MA-15, 58, 77, 82-83
Kuwait, MA-15

land, MA-2
    degradation, 80, 84
    reform, 80-82, 84-85
    use, MA-16-17, 67, 75, 78-79, 93
Latin America, 54, 112
    debt, 114-16
    energy, 91, 97
    housing, 70
    trade, 113-14
    see also Mexico and specific countries of South and Central America
Law of the Sea, 120-21
League of Nations, 29
Lebanon, 125
Libya, MA-15, 56
life expectancy, 54, 57, 115
Lima, Peru, 70
lithosphere. See land and soil
London, England, 66, 70
Los Angeles, USA, 70

Malaysia, MA-15
Mali, 125
Marshall Plan, 30, 48, 125
meat, 75, 86
Mexico, MA-15, 58, 66, 70, 112-15, 125
Mexico City, Mexico, 66, 70, 115
migration, MA-11-13, 46, 54, 65, 68
military spending. See arms race
minerals and mining, 18-19, 42-43, 112, 121-23
Morocco, 70, 79, 124, 127
Mozambique, 125
multinational corporations. See transnational corporations

National Indian Foundation (FUNAI) (Brazil), 25
nationalism, MA-4, 25-27, 29, 33, 119-20
Nepal, 55, 76
Netherlands, MA-15-16, 32, 123
New York, USA, 66, 70, 90
New Zealand, MA-15, 44, 121, 136
Nicaragua, MA-15, 125, 127
Nigeria, MA-15, 55, 126, 132
North America, 65, 71, 77, 108
    agriculture, 84-85
    diet, 76
    energy consumption, 90-92, 97
    pollution, 94
    see also Canada and United States and Mexico
North American Air Defence Command (NORAD), 30
North Atlantic Treaty Organization (NATO), 26, 30
North Sea, MA-10, 34, 121, 123
Norway, MA-15, 28, 32, 123
nuclear
    accidents, 96
    energy, MA-10, 19, 91, 94-96
    weapons, MA-5
    winter, MA-5, 134-35

oceans, MA-10, 13-15, 17, 19, 34, 120-24
Oman, MA-15
organic farming, 86
Organization of American States (OAS), 30
Organization of Petroleum Exporting Countries (OPEC), MA-10, 34, 108
ozone, 12, 27, 98

Index

Pacific Ocean, 13-14
Pakistan, MA-15, 55, 58, 69, 112, 125
Paris, France, 66, 70
peace-keeping, 30, 119
Permanent Court of International Justice, 29
Peru, 14-15, 70, 112, 114-15, 121
petroleum products, 114
    gasoline, 92, 98
    natural gas, 90-92, 121, 123
    oil, MA-10, 19, 34, 89-92, 112, 114, 121, 123
Philippines, 125
Poland, MA-15, 94, 122
pollution, 9, 27, 70-71, 89, 105
    atmospheric, 12-14, 19, 94, 98-99, 101, 111, 134
    soil, 86, 94
    water, MA-14, 16-18, 25, 76, 84, 86, 94, 134
population, MA-8-9, MA-13, 37-38, 40-41, 46, 56, 70, 75, 82-83
    distribution, 54-55
    fertility rates, 58-60
    life expectancy, 54, 57
    management, 53, 58-61, 132, 135
Portugal, MA-15
potatoes, 75-76

radioactive waste, 19, 96
rainforest, 133
    carbon dioxide cycle, 132
recycling, 19-20
    aluminum, 92
    paper, 92
research, 67-68, 111
Rio de Janeiro, Brazil, 70
Russia, 107
    see also USSR

Sahara Desert, 78
Sahel region, 80
St. Helens, Mount, 99
Sao Paulo, Brazil, 70
satellites, 10-11, 97
Saudi Arabia, MA-10, MA-15, 34
Self-Employed Women's Association (SEWA) (India), 60
Seoul, South Korea, 70, 111
Shanghai, China, 70
Singapore, MA-15, 68, 107, 126
smog, 98-99, 101, 111
soil, 17-18, 78-80, 84, 92, 112, 126
solar radiation and energy, 11-12, 89, 94, 97
Somalia, 125
South Africa, 14-15, 44, 112-13
South Korea, MA-15, 70, 107, 110-11, 125-26
space exploration, 48, 136-37
Spain, MA-15, 32, 34, 43, 112, 115
Sri Lanka, MA-15, 60, 114
standard of living, MA-6-8, MA-12-13, 30, 38, 40, 46, 56-59, 68-69, 105-8, 124
    and colonialism, 47

    and industrialization, 45, 89-90, 114-16, 132, 134
    chart, MA-15
steel, 90, 106
Sudan, 80, 112, 125
Suez Canal, 33
sugar into ethanol, 92-93
Sweden, MA-15, 32, 112
Switzerland, MA-15, 32
Syria, MA-15

Taiwan, 107, 110, 125-27
Tanzania, MA-15, 115, 128
Thailand, MA-15, 125
Tokyo, Japan, 66, 70, 72, 90
trade, MA-10, 33, 42, 44, 81-83, 110-16
transnational corporations, 31-33, 68, 80
    corporate responsibility, 84
    economic imperialism, 34
transportation, 23, 47, 71-72, 91, 93, 107
Turkey, MA-15

Uganda, 24, 125
Union of Socialist Soviet Republics. See USSR
United Arab Emirates, MA-15
United Kingdom. See Great Britain
United Nations, MA-4, 28-30, 48, 84, 119-21, 126, 132, 135
United Nations Childrens' Fund (UNICEF), 127
United Nations Educational, Scientific and Cultural Organization (UNESCO), 30
United States of America (USA), 24, 29, 34, 47, 121-22
    agriculture, 76, 81, 84
    arms race, MA-5, 26
    energy, 90
    environment, 28, 91
    foreign aid, 48, 125, 127-28
    Gross National Product, 112
    human rights, 49
    immigration, 46
    industry, 32, 45, 107
    international co-operation, 119, 135
    standard of living, MA-15, 75-76
    trade, 33, 72, 113-15
    urbanization, 65-66, 70
Universal Declaration of Human Rights, 48-49
urban planning, 71-72
urbanization, MA-12-13, 41-42, 46, 55, 65-72, 106, 111
Uruguay, 68
USSR, 24, 29, 48, 119, 121-22
    arms race, MA-5, 26, 135
    energy, 91
    industry, 107

Venezuela, MA-15, 113-14
Vietnam, 125, 127

Warsaw Pact, 26, 30
water, 13, 15-18, 42, 57, 80, 84, 126-28
    see also oceans

West Germany, MA-15, 32, 48, 122-23, 125, 127
women in society, 49, 60, 81, 110
wood fuel, 91, 94
World Bank, 81-82, 109-10, 125, 127, 135
World Commission on Environment and Development, 28, 34
World Conference on the Changing Atmosphere, 28
World Health Organization (WHO), 30, 127

Yokohama, Japan, 70
Yugoslavia, MA-15

Zaire, 30, 58
Zambia, MA-15, 125
zero population growth, 53-54
Zimbabwe, MA-15, 48, 58

CREDITS

Mini-Atlas maps: Esselte Map Services AB, Stockholm, Sweden and Pièce de Résistance Ltée., Edmonton, Canada

Charts: pp. 3, 54, 59, 65, 70, 76R, 84, 91, 112, 125 by Pièce de Résistance Ltée.

Chart: p. 27, The Linear Network, Edmonton, Canada

Design & Typesetting: Pièce de Résistance Ltée., Edmonton, Canada

Lithography: Color Graphics Alberta Ltd., Edmonton, Canada

Printing: Quality Color Press, Edmonton, Canada

Photo Credits:
L = Left R = Right T = Top B = Bottom
Large Cover Photo, Tom Grill/Miller Comstock Inc.
Small Cover Photo, Robin White/Fotolex
Back Cover Photo, Dr. A. Farquhar/VALAN
Credits are listed by page number.
6, 7, 15, 16, 33, 38L, 39, 40, 44, 52, 55, 62, 69, 79, 83, 93, 118, 124L, 124R, 126L, 133, 136, Robin White/Fotolex
2, 60, Roger Lemoyne/CIDA
4, J.R. Page/VALAN
5, 77, Francis Lepine/VALAN
8, NASA/Hot Shots
10, 11R, Finley Holiday/VALAN
11L, 14, Camerique/Hot Shots
13, Matthew Plexman/Hot Shots
17, 18T, 45, Thomas Kitchin/VALAN
18B, J. Erscott/Y.Momatiuk/VALAN
19, 34, 43, 61, 74, 76L, 78, 97, 102, 113, 114, 116, 131, 134, FOCUS
20, 22, 81, Anthony Scullion/VALAN
MA-1, 48, 64, Tom Grill/Miller Comstock Inc.
23, Jeff Maloney/FOCUS
24, TS/RED CANA Press Photo Service, London
26, 29, 35, 119, Canadian Department of National Defense
28, 86, CANA Press Photo Service
31, 105, Michael Stuckey/Miller Comstock Inc.
32, Ford Company, Canada
36, 71T, Jean Bruneau/VALAN
38R, 56, 67, 130, Kennon Cooke/VALAN
41, Bill Smith/Hot Shots
42, Aubrey Diem/VALAN
46T, Glenbow Archives NA-1960-1
46B, Glenbow Archives NA-2222-1
49, Fred Ward/Black Star
50, Miller Comstock Inc.
53, Dr. A. Farquhar/VALAN
58, Christine Osborne/VALAN
66, Chris Bruun/FOCUS
71B, Jean-Marie Jio/VALAN
72, Garth Roberts/Hot Shots
73, Allan Wilkinson/VALAN
85, Richard Howitz, VALAN
88, J. Eastcott/Y. Momatiuk/VALAN
90L, Val Wilkinson/VALAN
90R, DeWitt-Hartman/Miller Comstock Inc.
92, V. Whelan/VALAN
94, Gilbert Van Ryckevorsel/VALAN
95, Tom Myers/Hot Shots
98, Wm. J.S. Smith/Hot Shots
99, Chris Malazdrewicz/VALAN
100, B. Templeman/VALAN
103, Denis Roy/VALAN
104, 108, Jim Pickerell/Miller Comstock Inc.
106, Pam Hickman/VALAN
107, V. Wilkinson/VALAN
109, D. Austen/Hot Shots
111, Consulate General of the Republic of Korea
115, David Barbour/CIDA
120, K. Sommerer/Miller Comstock Inc.
121, Owen Colborne/Hot Shots
122, Miller Comstock Inc.
123, Fred Bruemmer/VALAN
126R, 127, Joshua Berson
137, NASA
138, VALAN
139, Gerard Fritz/Hot Shots

sommaire

10 Crumbles salés
30 Tartes Tatin salées
52 Crumbles sucrés
92 Tartes Tatin sucrées
112 Je veux la technique !
118 À garder sous le coude

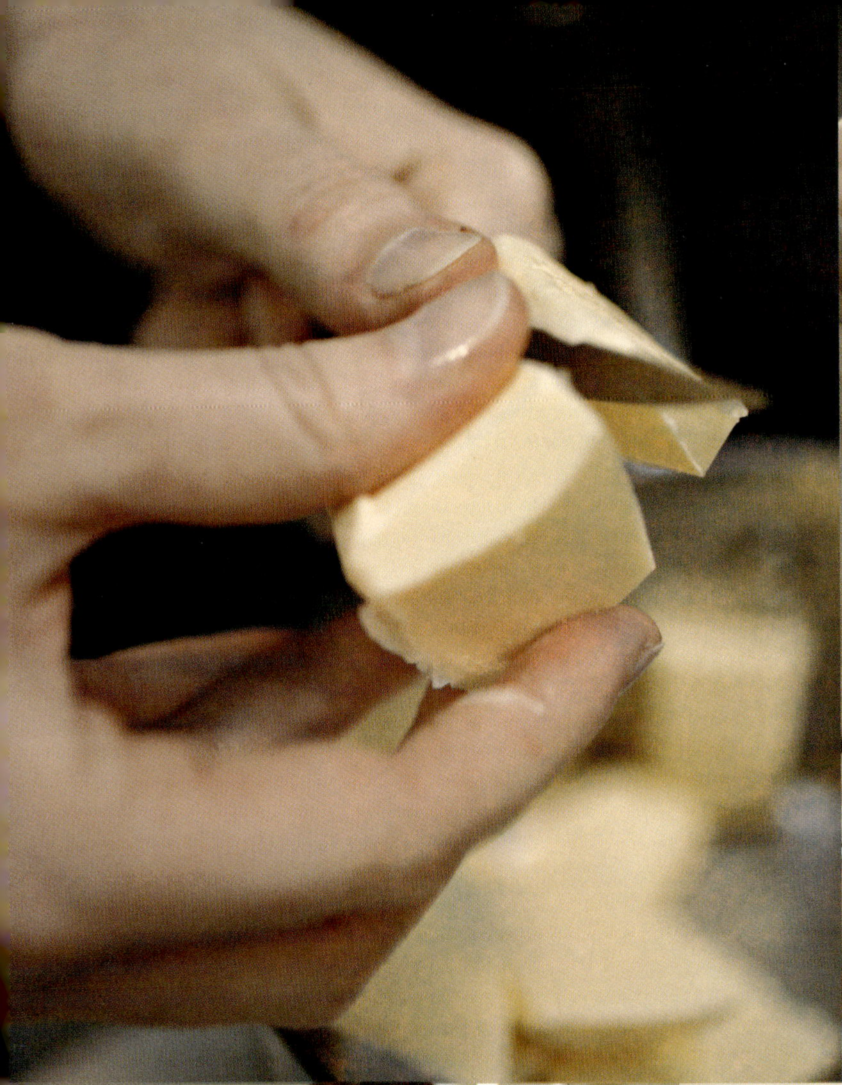
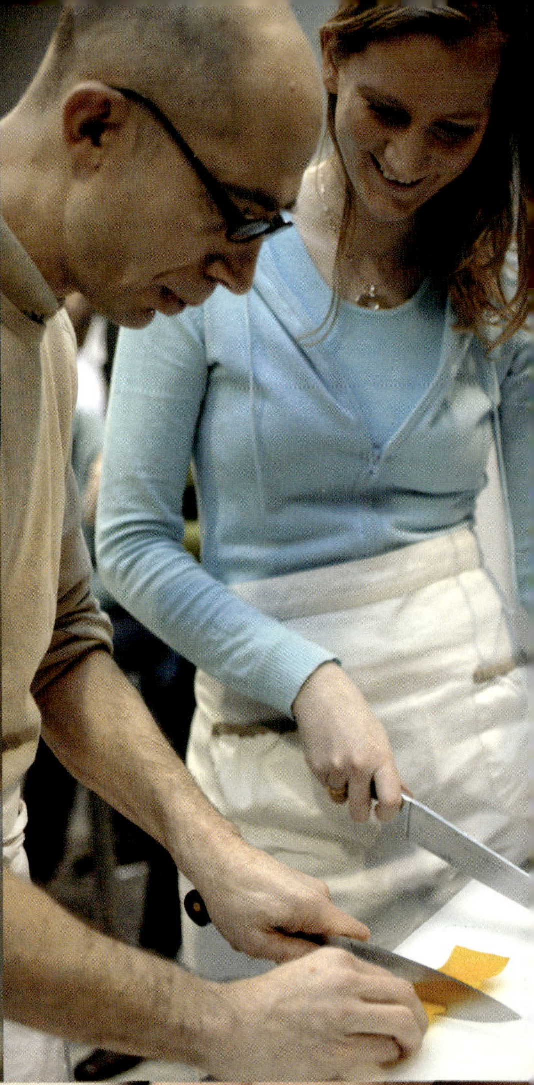
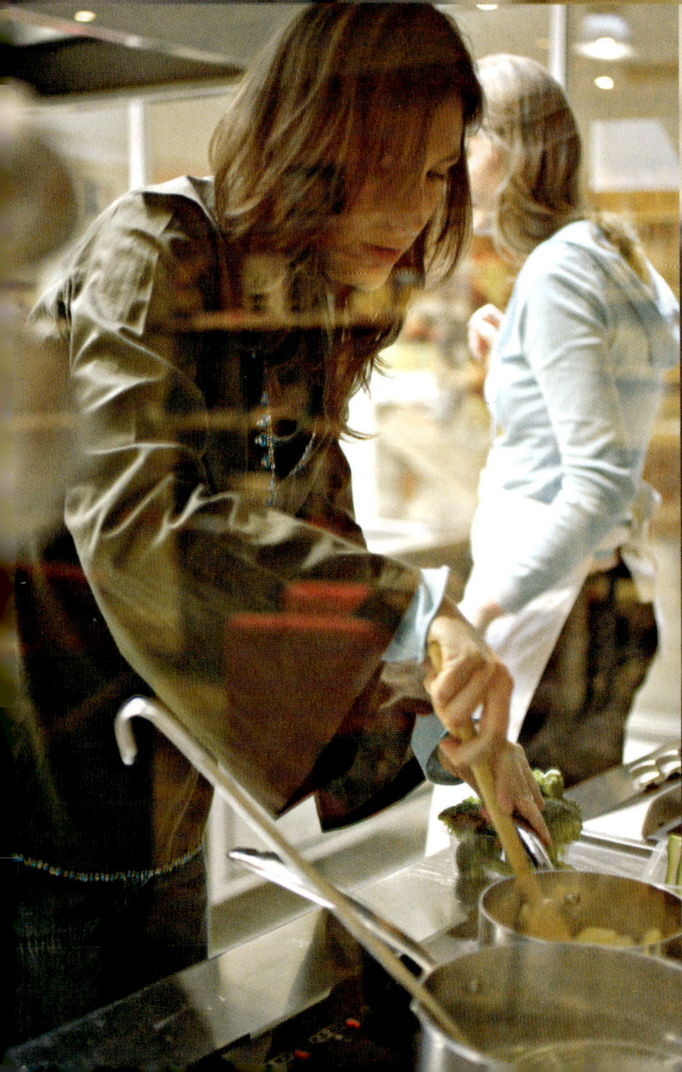
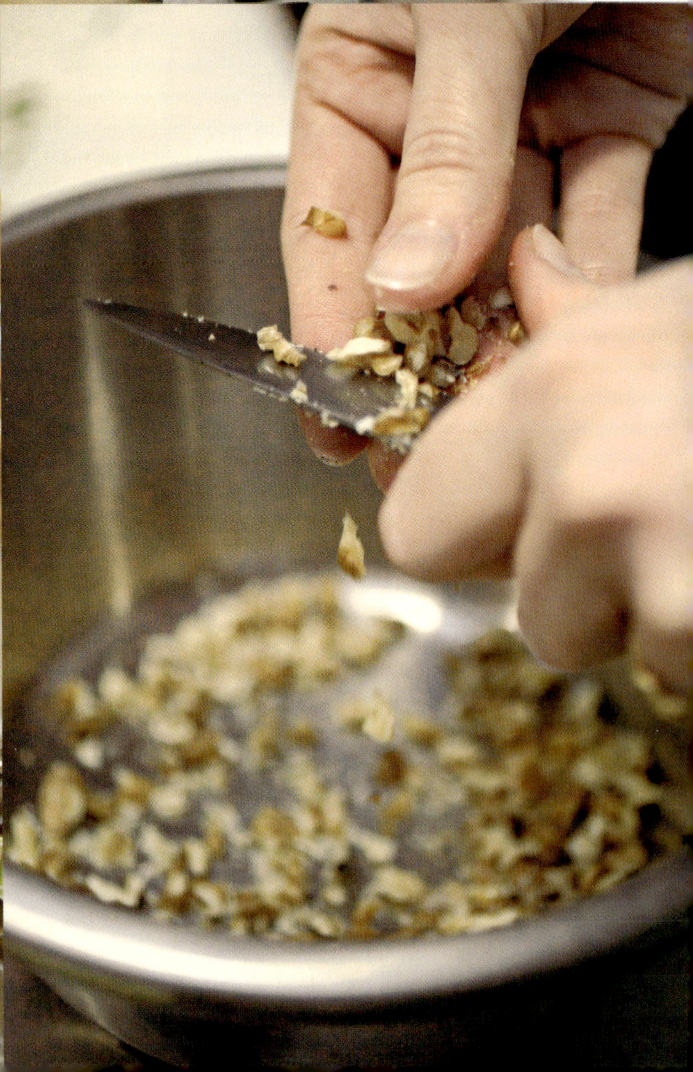

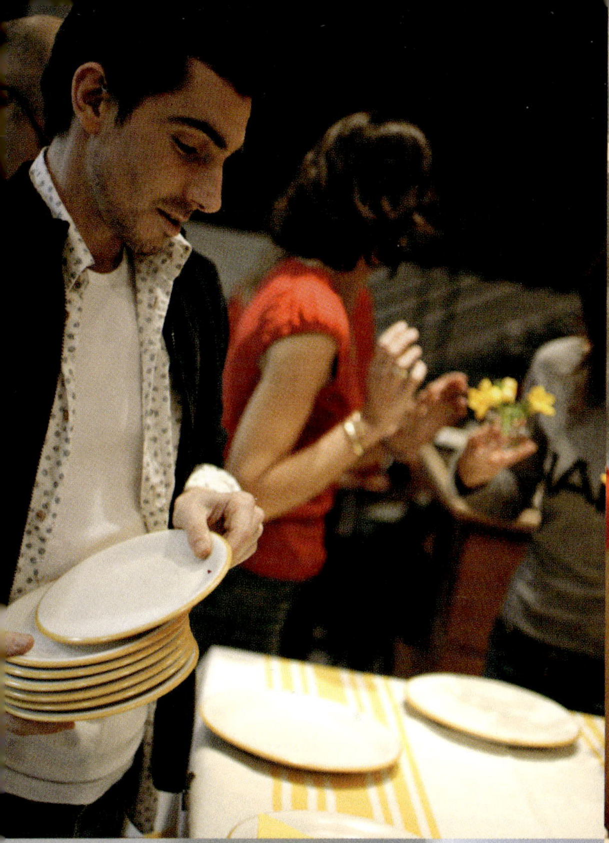
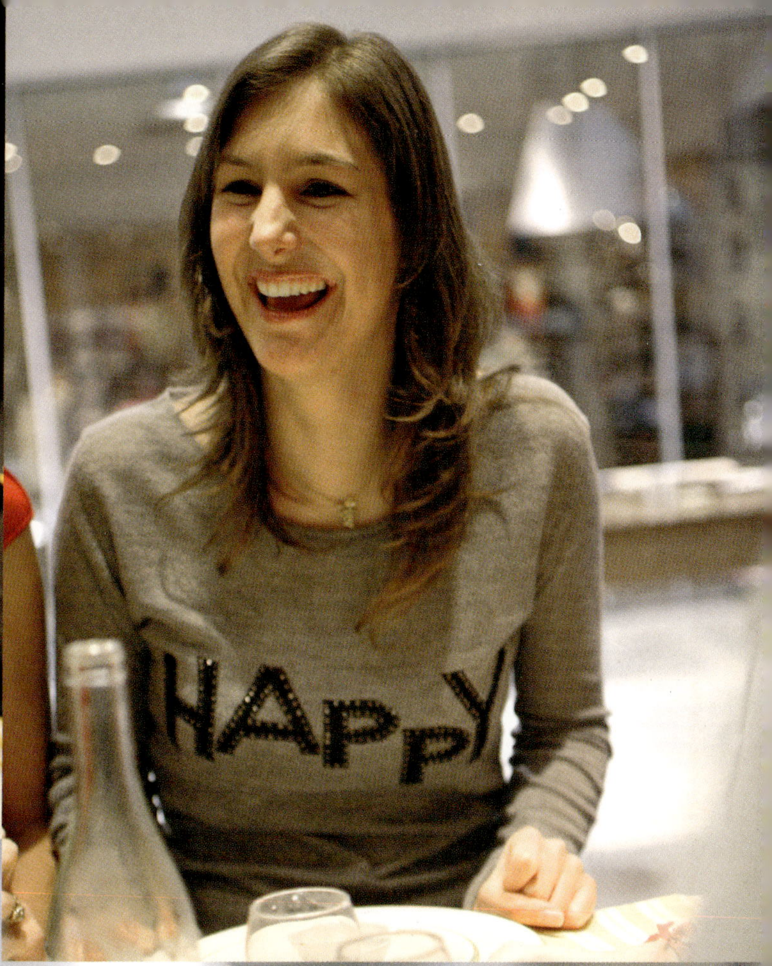
HAPPY
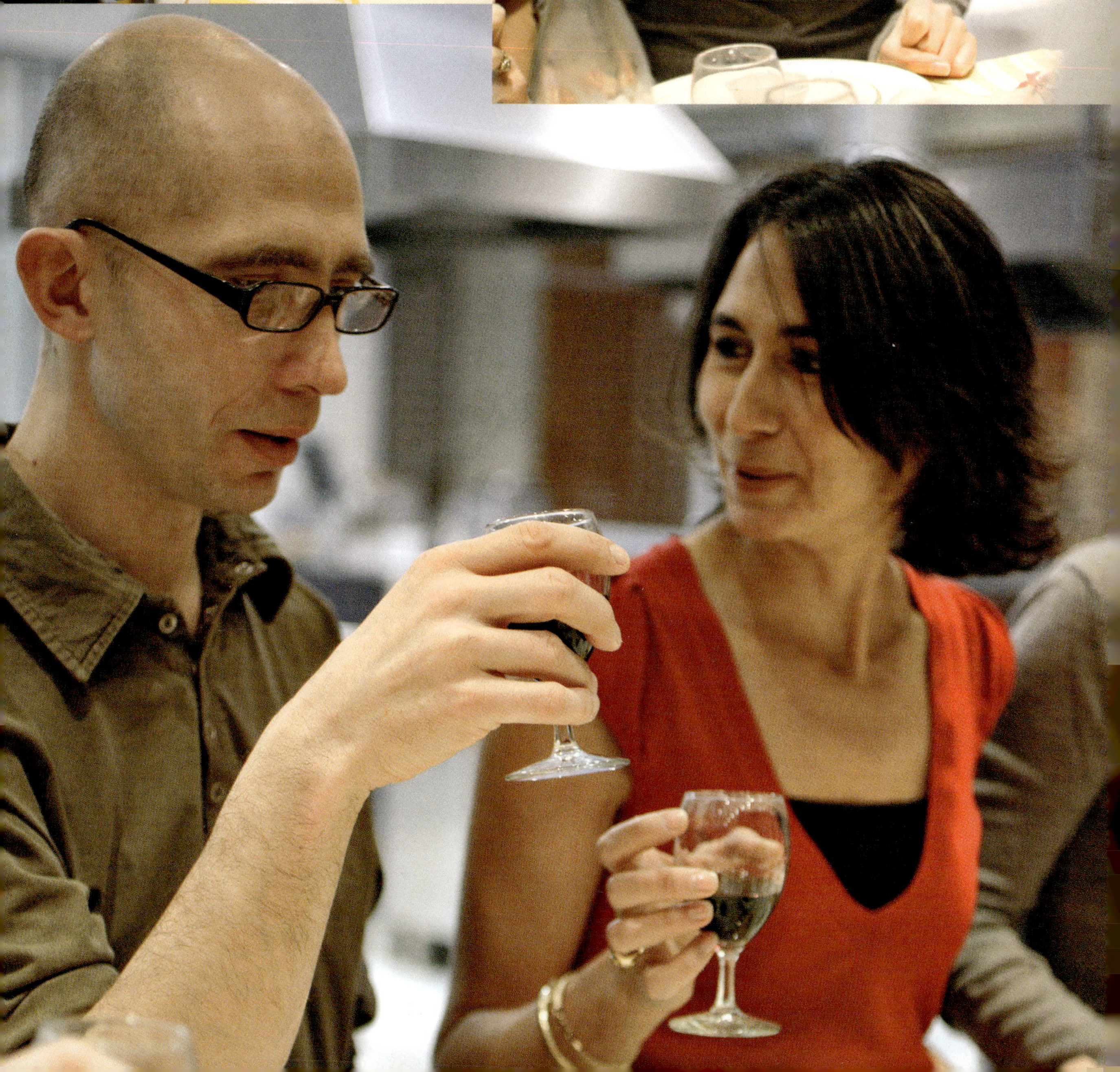

je veux la recette !

Pour la garniture / **Tatin de saumon aux épinards** / Cuisson 20 min / 90 g de farine / TATIN APHRODISIAQUE D'ANANAS AU GINGEMBRE / **émiettez-la du bout des doigts** / Épluchez l'oignon et l'ail / Les ingrédients pour 4 à 6 pers. / FAITES RAMOLLIR LE BEURRE AU MICRO-ONDES / **Pour varier** / Tatin au bleu et au bacon / Quand ce n'est plus la saison des prunes / RÂPEZ GROSSIÈREMENT LE PARMESAN / 9 tomates moyennes / **Le tuyau de Laurence** / Crumble au muesli / Une recette estivale / 1 SACHET DE SUCRE VANILLÉ / Si la pâte dore trop rapidement / CONCASSEZ FINEMENT LES AMANDES / **de retourner la tatin sur un plat pour la démouler** / Malaxez la préparation avec les mains / SERREZ BIEN VOS DEMI-TOMATES LES UNES CONTRE LES AUTRES / **versez le Cointreau dans la poêle** / TATIN DE COURGETTES AU BOURSIN / Quand la compote de rhubarbe est cuite / Pour accompagner ce délicieux crumble / RÉPARTISSEZ LES ÉPINARDS / Crumble de poulet à l'estragon / Pour une version plus light, / **un vin rouge de qualité, comme un negroamaro** / CRUMBLE ANANAS ET COCO / 2 pommes granny smith / la pâte aux palets bretons / Un crumble 100 % végétarien / DANS UNE GRANDE CASSEROLE

Crumble au saumon et à l'aneth

PRÉPARATION 20 MIN | **CUISSON** 20 MIN | **COÛT** ★★ | **DIFFICULTÉ** ★★ |
MATÉRIEL SPÉCIFIQUE 6 RAMEQUINS PLATS (CASSOLETTES)

1 Épluchez les échalotes et coupez-les finement. Dans une poêle, faites fondre le beurre. Ajoutez les échalotes et faites-les blondir quelques minutes. Ajoutez les épinards surgelés. Salez et poivrez. Laissez cuire 8 min environ en remuant régulièrement.

2 Pendant ce temps, préchauffez le four à 180 °C (th. 6). Ôtez la peau des pavés de saumon et les arêtes si nécessaire. Coupez les pavés en morceaux. Lavez l'aneth et coupez-le finement. Dans un bol, mélangez la crème fraîche avec l'aneth coupé et la ciboulette.

3 Beurrez les ramequins. Quand les épinards sont cuits, égouttez-les et répartissez-les dans le fond des 6 ramequins. Ajoutez le saumon puis la crème aux herbes sur le dessus. Réservez.

4 Pour la pâte à crumble, faites ramollir le beurre au micro-ondes. Râpez grossièrement le parmesan. Dans un saladier, mélangez la farine avec la chapelure, le parmesan râpé et le beurre ramolli.

5 Malaxez la préparation avec les mains puis émiettez-la du bout des doigts pour lui donner une consistance sableuse (comme une grosse semoule). Ajoutez la pâte sur le saumon aux épinards en une couche régulière. Faites cuire au four 15 à 20 min environ. Servez immédiatement.

Les ingrédients pour 6 personnes

Pour la garniture

2 échalotes
1 noisette de beurre pour la poêle
100 g d'épinards surgelés
sel et poivre
3 beaux pavés de saumon
1 bouquet d'aneth
15 cl de crème fraîche épaisse
2 cuil. à soupe de ciboulette coupée finement
1 noisette de beurre pour les ramequins

Pour la pâte

75 g de beurre
60 g de parmesan
90 g de farine
3 cuil. à soupe de chapelure

Pour varier_ **Crumble de thon et sésame.** Remplacez le saumon par du thon. Supprimez alors la crème à l'aneth et ajoutez 6 cuil. à café de sésame entre le thon et la pâte sableuse. Vous pouvez accompagner votre crumble d'un filet de sauce soja.

le truc de stéphan

Pour que votre saumon soit encore plus parfumé et si vous en avez le temps bien sûr, faites-le mariner pendant 1 h avec un peu de sel, de poivre, de jus de citron et d'huile d'olive. Cuisinez-le ensuite comme dans la recette.

crumbles salés

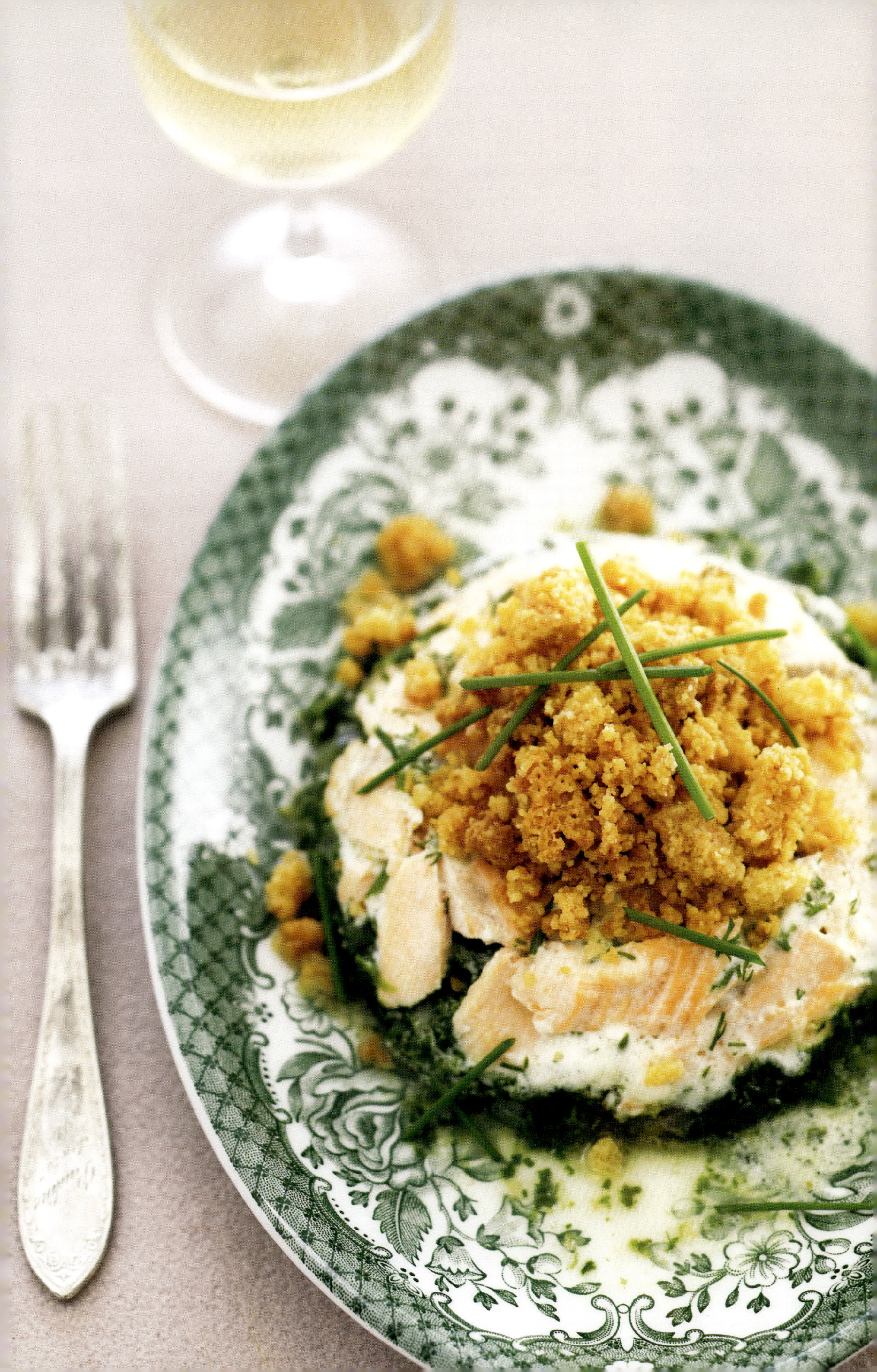

Crumble de tomates au chèvre frais

PRÉPARATION 25 MIN I **CUISSON** 25 MIN I **COÛT** ★★ I **DIFFICULTÉ** ★★

→ VOICI UNE RECETTE SUCCULENTE ET ORIGINALE DÉVOILÉE PAR NOTRE COPAIN STÉPHAN. ON NE VOUS EN DIT PAS PLUS MAIS ON VOUS LA RECOMMANDE VIVEMENT !

1. Épluchez les échalotes et coupez-les finement. Plongez les tomates 30 secondes environ dans de l'eau bouillante. Lorsque leur peau commence à se décoller, ressortez-les une à une à l'aide d'une louche. Pelez-les et coupez-les en morceaux.

2. Dans une sauteuse ou une grande poêle, faites chauffer l'huile. Ajoutez l'ail, les échalotes, les tomates, le chèvre frais, le basilic et le sucre. Salez et poivrez. Laissez cuire 8 min environ en remuant régulièrement. Beurrez un plat à gratin. Répartissez la préparation dans le fond du plat.

3. Préchauffez le four à 210 °C (th. 7). Ôtez la croûte des crottins de chèvre et coupez-les en morceaux. Ajoutez-les sur le lit de tomates.

4. Pour la pâte à crumble, faites ramollir le beurre au micro-ondes. Râpez grossièrement le parmesan. Dans un saladier, mélangez la farine avec la chapelure, le parmesan râpé, le beurre ramolli et le thym.

5. Malaxez la préparation avec les mains puis émiettez-la du bout des doigts pour lui donner une consistance sableuse (comme une grosse semoule). Ajoutez la pâte sur les tomates au chèvre en une couche régulière. Faites cuire au four 25 min environ. Servez immédiatement.

Les ingrédients pour 4 à 6 personnes

Pour la garniture
- 2 échalotes
- 9 tomates moyennes
- 2 cuil. à soupe d'huile d'olive
- 3 cuil. à soupe d'ail haché
- 75 g de chèvre frais (type Chavroux)
- 3 cuil. à soupe de basilic coupé finement
- 2 pincées de sucre
- sel et poivre
- 2 crottins de Chavignol
- 1 noisette de beurre pour le plat

Pour la pâte
- 75 g de beurre
- 75 g de parmesan
- 75 g de farine
- 3 cuil. à soupe de chapelure
- 1 cuil. à soupe de thym

la botte secrète d'aude et leslie

Vous pouvez ajouter 2 courgettes coupées en rondelles dans la sauteuse au même moment que les tomates. Dans ce cas-là, comptez 6 tomates au lieu de 9.

le tuyau de laurence

Ajoutez 5 tomates séchées à l'huile d'olive, égouttées et coupées en petits morceaux. Vous les trouverez en grande surface, au rayon traiteur ou en bocal.

crumbles salés

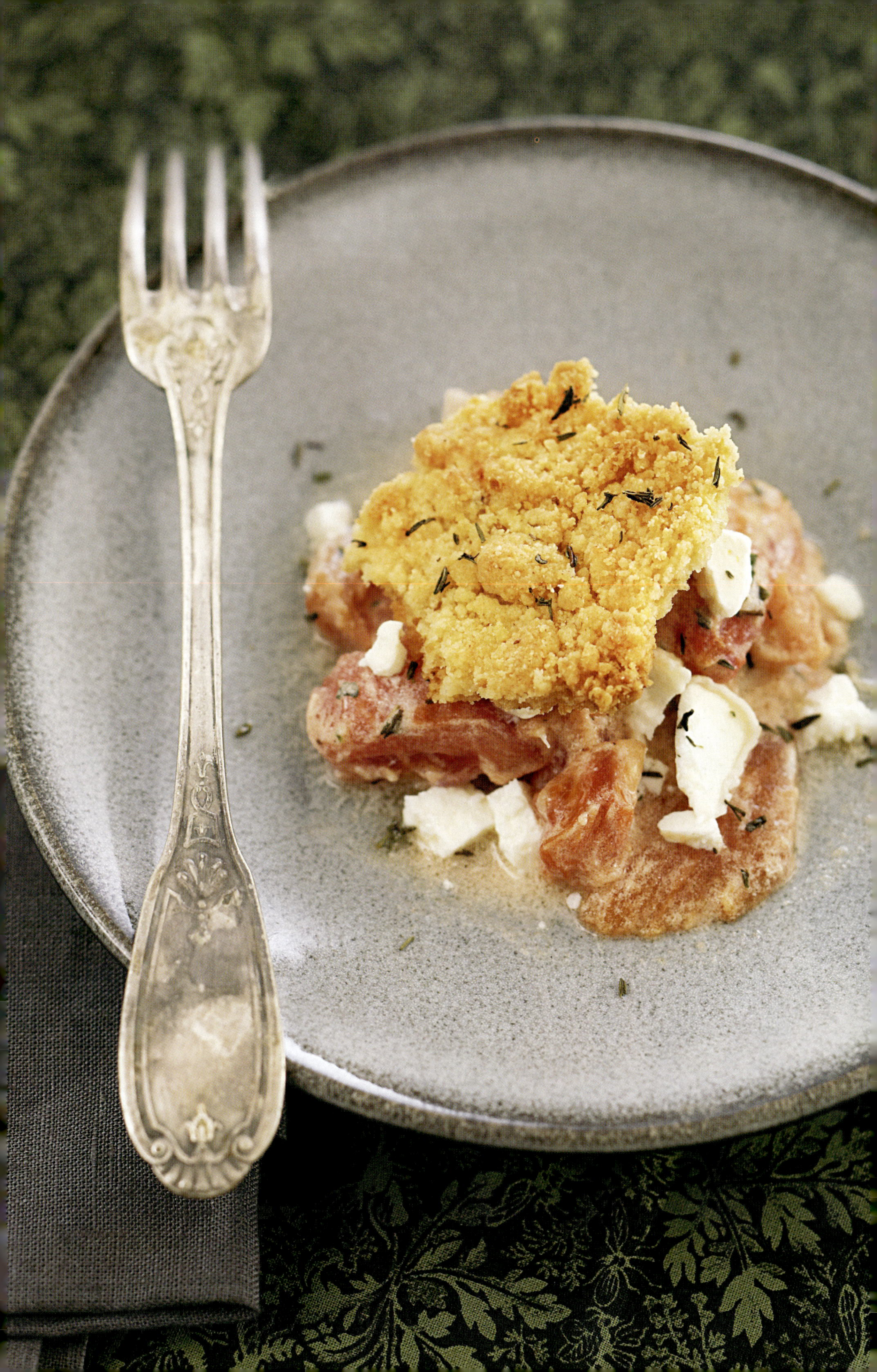

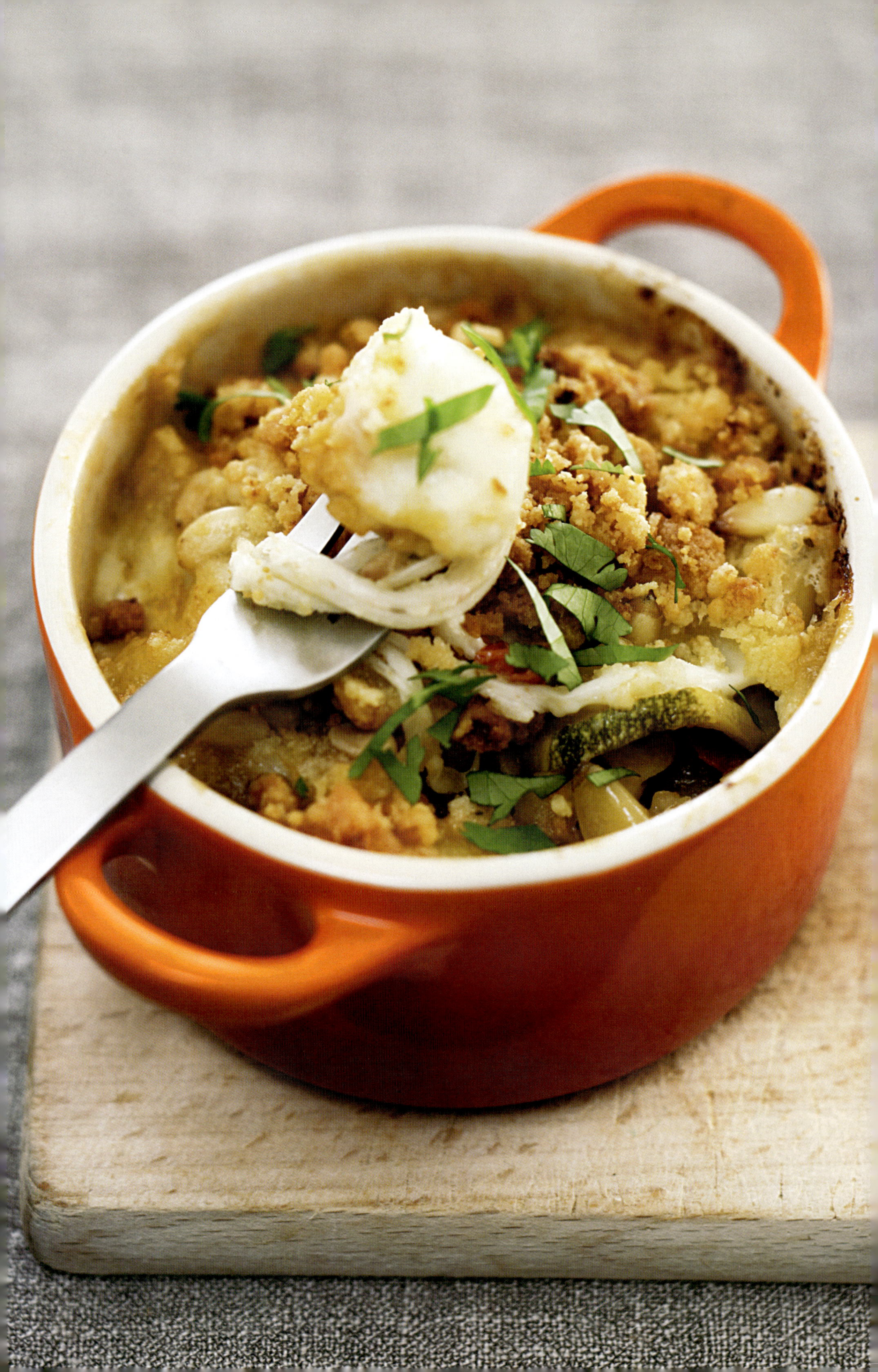

Crumble d'aubergines, mozzarella et pignons

PRÉPARATION 30 MIN | **CUISSON** 30 MIN | **COÛT** ★★ | **DIFFICULTÉ** ★★

→ UNE DE NOS RECETTES FÉTICHES, CERTES UN PEU LONGUE À RÉALISER MAIS, CROYEZ-NOUS, LE JEU EN VAUT LA CHANDELLE.

1 Épluchez l'oignon et l'ail et coupez-les finement. Épluchez les aubergines et coupez-les en petits morceaux. Dans une sauteuse ou une poêle, faites chauffer l'huile. Ajoutez l'oignon et l'ail et faites-les revenir 3 à 4 min environ en remuant régulièrement.

2 Ajoutez les aubergines, le thym et le romarin dans la sauteuse. Salez, poivrez et laissez cuire 15 min environ à feu doux et à couvert. Remuez régulièrement.

3 Pendant ce temps, lavez les courgettes puis épluchez-les à l'aide d'un économe en laissant une bande de peau sur deux. Coupez-les en rondelles. Lavez les tomates et coupez-les en rondelles.

4 Ajoutez les tomates et les courgettes dans la sauteuse. Versez 1/2 verre d'eau et laissez cuire à nouveau 15 min. Remuez régulièrement pour éviter que ça n'accroche. Rajoutez un peu d'eau si nécessaire.

5 Préchauffez le four à 180 °C (th. 6). Pour la pâte, faites ramollir le beurre au micro-ondes. Râpez grossièrement le parmesan et mélangez-le avec la farine, les pignons et le beurre ramolli.

6 Malaxez la préparation avec les mains puis émiettez-la du bout des doigts pour lui donner une consistance sableuse (comme une grosse semoule).

7 Beurrez un moule à gratin. Quand les légumes sont cuits, répartissez-les dans le fond du plat. Égouttez et coupez la mozzarella en fines rondelles et disposez-la sur le dessus des légumes, puis ajoutez la pâte sableuse en une couche régulière. Faites cuire au four 25 à 30 min environ. Servez immédiatement.

Les ingrédients pour 6 à 8 personnes

Pour la garniture
1 oignon
1 gousse d'ail
2 aubergines
4 cuil. à soupe d'huile d'olive
3 pincées de thym
3 pincées de romarin
sel et poivre
3 courgettes
3 tomates
150 g de mozzarella
1 noisette de beurre pour le plat

Pour la pâte
150 g de beurre
50 g de parmesan
250 g de farine
50 g de pignons

le verre de vin qui va bien

Avec cette recette très italienne dans son inspiration, pensez à servir un vin rouge de qualité, comme un negroamaro.

crumbles salés

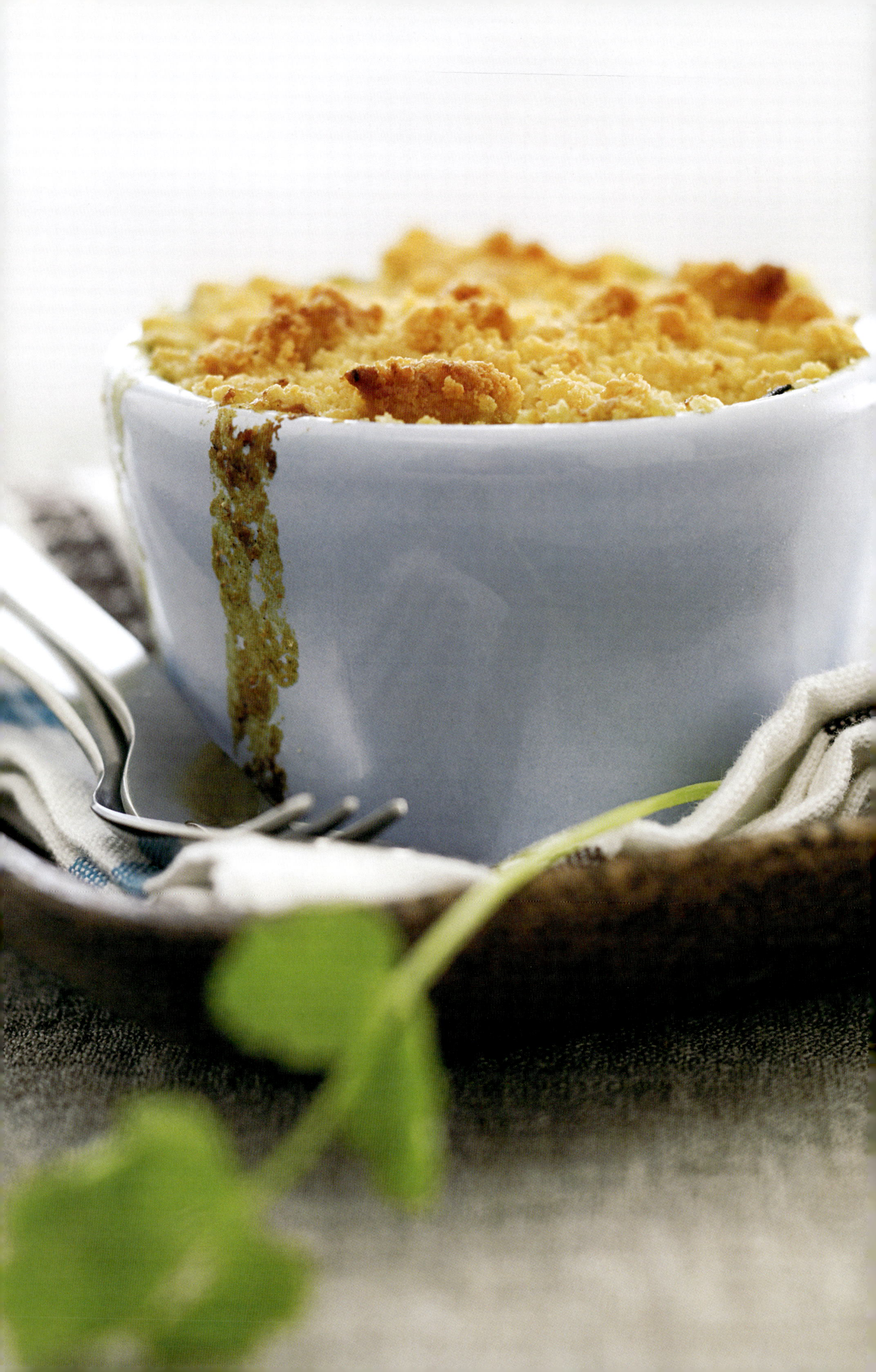

Crumble épinards, feta et raisins secs

PRÉPARATION 20 MIN | **CUISSON** 20 MIN | **COÛT** ★★ | **DIFFICULTÉ** ★

1 Dans une grande casserole, faites chauffer l'huile d'olive. Faites revenir les échalotes 3 à 4 min environ. Puis ajoutez les épinards surgelés et laissez-les cuire à feu moyen 10 min environ jusqu'à complète décongélation. Remuez régulièrement.

2 Préchauffez le four à 180 °C (th. 6). Dans un bol, écrasez la feta à la fourchette. Dans la casserole, ajoutez la crème fraîche, la moitié de la feta (100 g), les pignons et les raisins. Salez et poivrez. Mélangez bien. Répartissez les épinards dans le fond d'un plat à gratin. Ajoutez l'autre moitié de feta (100 g) émiettée par-dessus.

3 Pour la pâte à crumble, faites ramollir le beurre au micro-ondes. Râpez grossièrement le parmesan. Dans un saladier, mélangez la farine avec le parmesan râpé, la chapelure et le beurre ramolli.

4 Malaxez la préparation avec les mains puis émiettez-la du bout des doigts pour lui donner une consistance sableuse (comme une grosse semoule). Ajoutez-la sur les épinards à la feta en une couche régulière. Faites cuire au four 20 min environ. Servez immédiatement.

Les ingrédients pour 6 personnes

Pour la garniture
2 cuil. à soupe d'huile d'olive
1 cuil. à soupe d'échalote finement coupée
1 kg d'épinards surgelés
200 g de feta
4 cuil. à soupe de crème fraîche
1 poignée de pignons
1 poignée de raisins de Corinthe
sel et poivre

Pour la pâte
75 g de beurre
75 g de parmesan
75 g de farine
3 cuil. à soupe de chapelure

Astuces_ • Sachez que vous pouvez remplacer la feta par du chèvre frais. • Pour une version plus light, utilisez de la feta et de la crème fraîche allégées.

la botte secrète d'aude et leslie

Pour un crumble plus épicé, mélangez la crème fraîche avec 4 pincées de curry en poudre.

crumbles salés

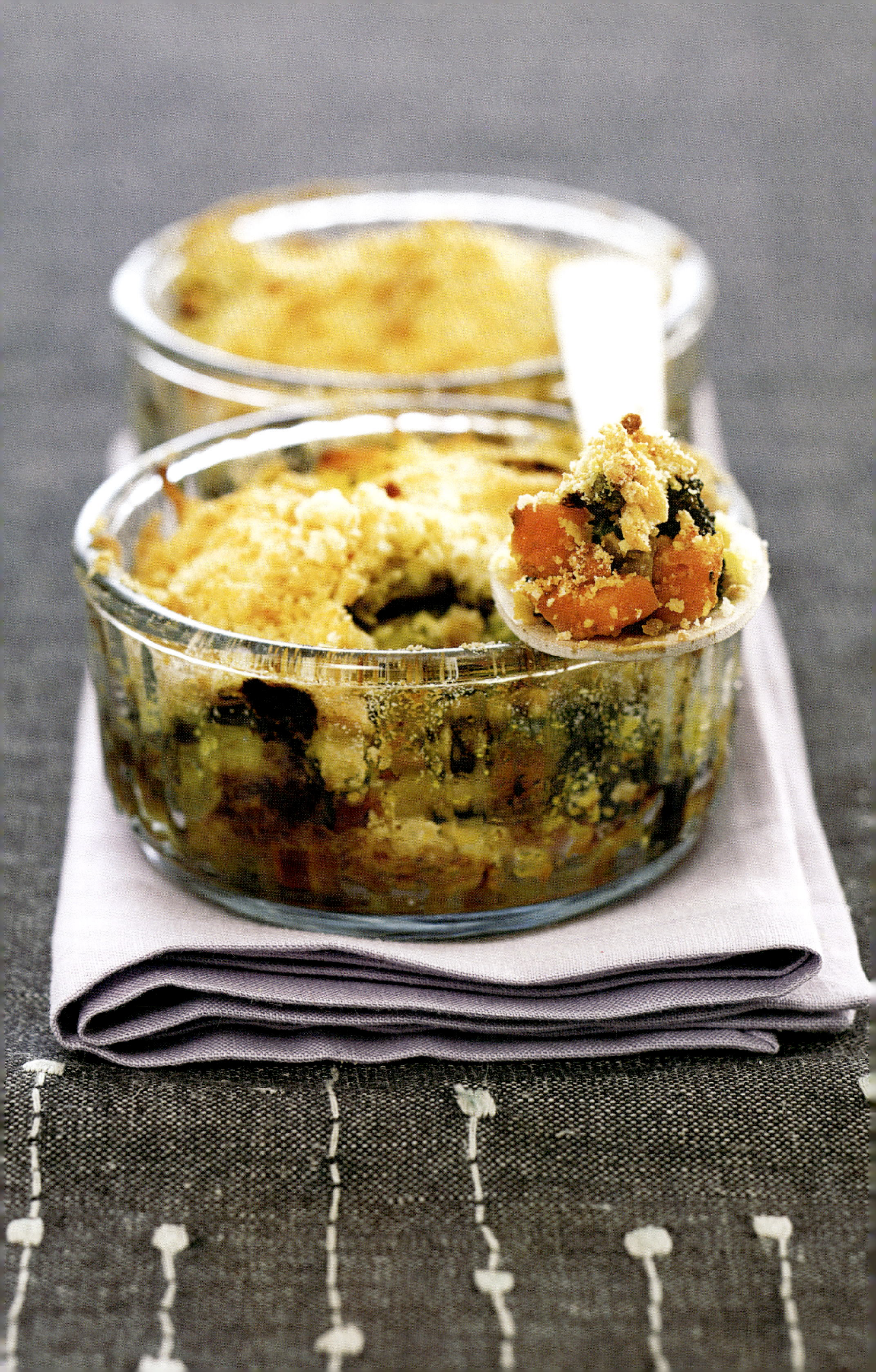

Crumble de légumes au curry

PRÉPARATION 25 MIN | **CUISSON** 25 MIN | **COÛT** ★★ | **DIFFICULTÉ** ★★

→ UN CRUMBLE 100 % VÉGÉTARIEN QUE VOUS POURREZ CUISINER SELON VOS ENVIES ET EN FONCTION DES LÉGUMES QUE VOUS AVEZ SOUS LA MAIN… PAS DE STRESS CONCERNANT LA LISTE DES INGRÉDIENTS, ELLE EST MODULABLE À SOUHAIT : CHOU ROMANESCO, POIVRONS, TOMATES, FÈVES, HARICOTS VERTS, CHAMPIGNONS DE PARIS…

1 Épluchez les oignons et l'ail et coupez-les finement. Ôtez le germe de la gousse d'ail s'il y en a un. Épluchez les carottes et coupez-les en petits morceaux. Rincez les navets et les courgettes. Coupez-les en fines rondelles. Lavez et coupez le brocoli en tout petits quartiers. Lavez la coriandre et coupez-la finement.

2 Dans une sauteuse, un wok ou une grande poêle, faites chauffer l'huile. Ajoutez l'ail, les oignons, le piment et le curry. Salez et poivrez. Laissez revenir 3 à 4 min en mélangeant bien. Ajoutez tous les légumes (petits pois compris) et la coriandre. Laissez cuire 10 à 12 min en mélangeant régulièrement. Beurrez un plat à gratin et répartissez-y les légumes.

3 Préchauffez le four à 180 °C (th. 6). Pour la pâte à crumble, faites ramollir le beurre au micro-ondes. Râpez grossièrement le parmesan. Dans un saladier, mélangez la farine complète avec le parmesan râpé, la chapelure et le beurre ramolli.

4 Malaxez la préparation avec les mains puis émiettez-la du bout des doigts pour lui donner une consistance sableuse (comme une grosse semoule). Ajoutez la pâte sur les légumes au curry en une couche régulière. Faites cuire au four 25 min environ. Servez immédiatement.

Les ingrédients pour 6 personnes

Pour la garniture
2 oignons
1 gousse d'ail
4 carottes
4 navets
3 courgettes
1 tête de brocoli
3 branches de coriandre
5 cuil. à soupe d'huile d'olive
1 cuil. à café de piment d'Espelette
2 cuil. à soupe de curry en poudre
sel et poivre
6 cuil. à soupe de petits pois surgelés
1 noisette de beurre pour le plat

Pour la pâte
75 g de beurre
70 g de parmesan
80 g de farine complète
3 cuil. à soupe de chapelure

Astuces_ • Si vous n'avez pas de farine complète, remplacez-la par de la farine blanche.
• Pour une version express, choisissez des poêlées de légumes surgelées toutes prêtes.
• Pour une entrée ludique, servez ce crumble végétarien dans des ramequins individuels, accompagné d'une salade de mâche.

Pour varier_ **Crumble de légumes au curry et bœuf haché.** Faites cuire 300 g de bœuf haché dans une poêle avant de l'ajouter sur les légumes. Une version idéale pour un plat unique à déguster en famille…

Crumble courgettes et Boursin

PRÉPARATION 20 MIN I **CUISSON** 30 MIN I **REPOS** 3 H I **COÛT** ★ I **DIFFICULTÉ** ★

1 Lavez les courgettes et épluchez-les avec un couteau économe en laissant une bande de peau sur deux. Râpez-les à l'aide d'un robot ou d'une râpe, mettez-les dans une passoire avec du gros sel et laissez-les dégorger 3 h.

2 Beurrez un plat à gratin. Quand les courgettes sont dégorgées, répartissez-les dans le fond du plat. Poivrez. Coupez le Boursin en fines rondelles et déposez-le sur les courgettes.

3 Préchauffez le four à 200 °C (th. 6-7). Pour la pâte à crumble, faites ramollir le beurre au micro-ondes. Râpez grossièrement le parmesan. Dans un saladier, mélangez la farine avec le parmesan râpé, la chapelure, le thym et le beurre ramolli.

4 Malaxez la préparation avec les mains puis émiettez-la du bout des doigts pour lui donner une consistance sableuse (comme une grosse semoule). Ajoutez la pâte sur les courgettes au Boursin en une couche régulière. Faites cuire au four 30 min environ. Servez immédiatement.

Les ingrédients pour 4 personnes

Pour la garniture
3 courgettes
gros sel
poivre
1 Boursin
1 noisette de beurre pour le plat

Pour la pâte
75 g de beurre
80 g de parmesan
75 g de farine
3 cuil. à soupe de chapelure
1 cuil. à café de thym

Astuce_ Quand vous n'avez pas le temps de faire dégorger vos courgettes, râpez-les et pressez-les immédiatement entre vos mains pour enlever l'excédent d'eau.

Pour varier_ **Crumble courgettes et chèvre.** Remplacez le Boursin par un Chavroux ou 2 crottins de Chavignol. Rajoutez alors 1 cuil. à soupe d'herbes de Provence dans les courgettes râpées.

le verre de vin qui va bien
Servez tout simplement un anjou rouge avec cette recette.

crumbles salés

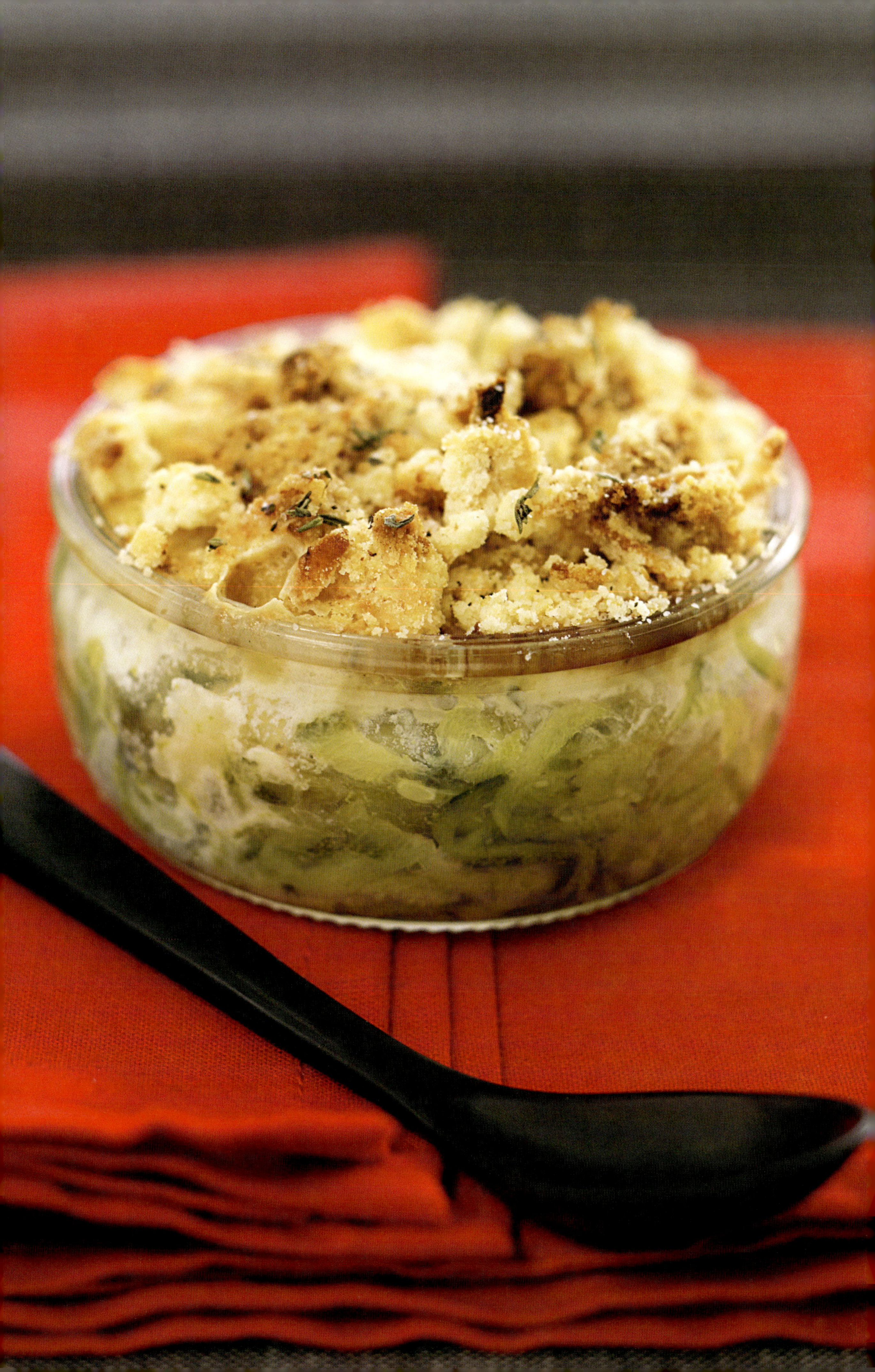

crumbles salés

recette pour épater...

Crumble d'agneau, origan et parmesan

PRÉPARATION 30 MIN | **CUISSON** 25 MIN | **COÛT** ★★ | **DIFFICULTÉ** ★★

1 Dans une casserole d'eau bouillante salée, faites cuire les pommes de terre 20 min environ. Pendant ce temps, épluchez et coupez l'oignon et l'ail en quatre. Ôtez le germe de la gousse d'ail s'il y en a un. Dans un robot, hachez l'agneau avec l'ail, l'oignon et l'origan.

2 Dans une poêle, faites chauffer l'huile. Ajoutez la viande hachée et laissez-la cuire 4 min en remuant régulièrement. Râpez la moitié du cube de bouillon aux herbes dans 1/2 verre d'eau chaude et mélangez bien pour obtenir un bouillon. Versez-le sur l'agneau et laissez cuire 5 min à nouveau.

3 Préchauffez le four à 200 °C (th. 6-7). Beurrez un plat à gratin. Quand les pommes de terre sont cuites, égouttez-les et épluchez-les. Coupez-les en fines rondelles. Répartissez-les dans le fond du plat, puis tartinez-les de moutarde. Ajoutez la viande cuite par-dessus.

4 Pour la pâte à crumble, faites ramollir le beurre au micro-ondes. Râpez grossièrement le parmesan. Dans un saladier, mélangez la farine avec le parmesan râpé, la chapelure et le beurre ramolli.

5 Malaxez la préparation avec les mains puis émiettez-la du bout des doigts pour lui donner une consistance sableuse (comme une grosse semoule). Ajoutez la pâte sur l'agneau en une couche régulière. Faites cuire au four 20 à 25 min environ. Servez immédiatement.

Les ingrédients pour 6 personnes

Pour la garniture
4 pommes de terre
1 oignon
1 gousse d'ail
1 cuil. à soupe d'origan
600 g d'épaule d'agneau désossée et coupée en morceaux
2 cuil. à soupe d'huile d'olive
1/2 cube de bouillon aux herbes
1 cuil. à soupe de moutarde forte
sel et poivre
1 noisette de beurre pour le plat

Pour la pâte
100 g de beurre
80 g de parmesan
120 g de farine
4 cuil. à soupe de chapelure

la botte secrète d'aude et leslie

Pour varier les plaisirs, sachez que vous pouvez remplacer l'origan par de la menthe finement coupée. Variez aussi les parfums des moutardes : estragon, poivre vert...

le verre de vin qui va bien

Si vous sortez le grand jeu en proposant cette recette à vos amis, surprenez-les également avec une bonne bouteille étrangère. Proposez un vin libanais, produit dans la vallée de la Bekaa par exemple.

Crumble poires, roquefort et noix

PRÉPARATION 15 MIN I **CUISSON** 15 MIN I **COÛT** ★ I **DIFFICULTÉ** ★ I
MATÉRIEL SPÉCIFIQUE 4 RAMEQUINS PLATS (CASSOLETTES)

→ UN CRUMBLE AUX SAVEURS SUCRÉ-SALÉ, DÉLICIEUX EN ENTRÉE ACCOMPAGNÉ D'UNE PETITE SALADE DE MÂCHE OU DE CRESSON, ASSAISONNÉE À L'HUILE DE NOIX.

1 Préchauffez le four à 200 °C (th. 6-7). Épluchez et coupez les poires en fines lamelles. Répartissez-les dans le fond de 4 ramequins plats (cassolettes). Coupez le roquefort en cubes et déposez-le sur les poires. Poivrez.

2 Pour la pâte à crumble, faites ramollir le beurre au micro-ondes. Dans un bol, battez les œufs avec une fourchette. Dans un saladier, mélangez la farine avec la chapelure, les œufs battus et le beurre ramolli à l'aide d'une fourchette.

3 Ajoutez la pâte à crumble sur les poires au roquefort en une fine couche. Faites cuire au four 15 min environ. Concassez les noix à l'aide d'un mortier ou avec le manche d'un couteau et ajoutez-les juste avant de servir.

Les ingrédients pour 4 personnes

Pour la garniture
4 petites poires mûres
200 g de roquefort
poivre

Pour la pâte
60 g de beurre
2 œufs
4 cuil. à soupe de farine
6 cuil. à soupe de chapelure
8 cerneaux de noix

Astuce_ Pour une version 100 % salée, remplacez les poires par des épinards surgelés que vous ferez préalablement cuire 8 min environ dans une casserole.

le tuyau de laurence

Pour varier les plaisirs, pensez à remplacer le roquefort par de la fourme d'Ambert, du bleu de Bresse ou du gorgonzola.

crumbles salés

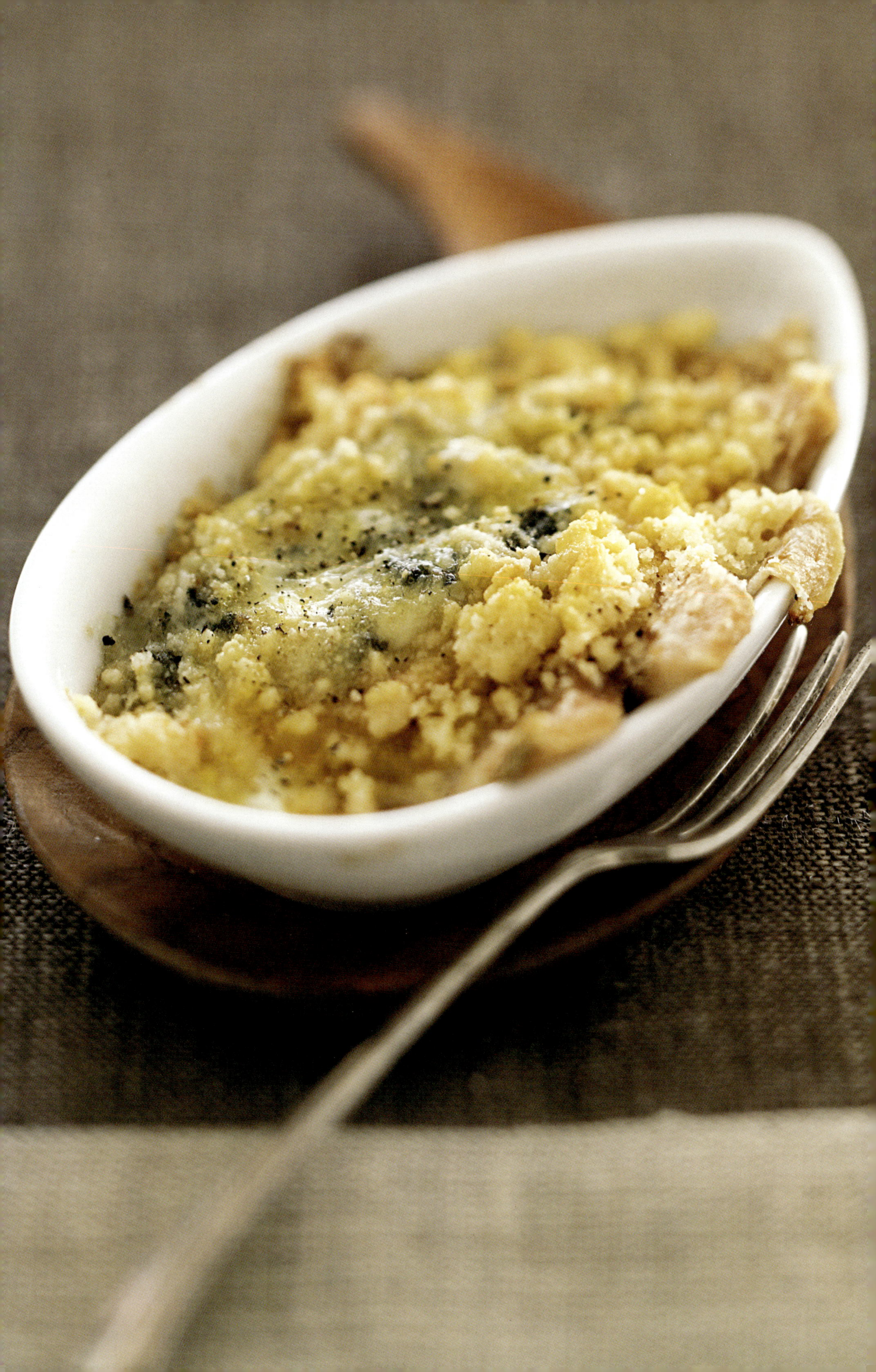

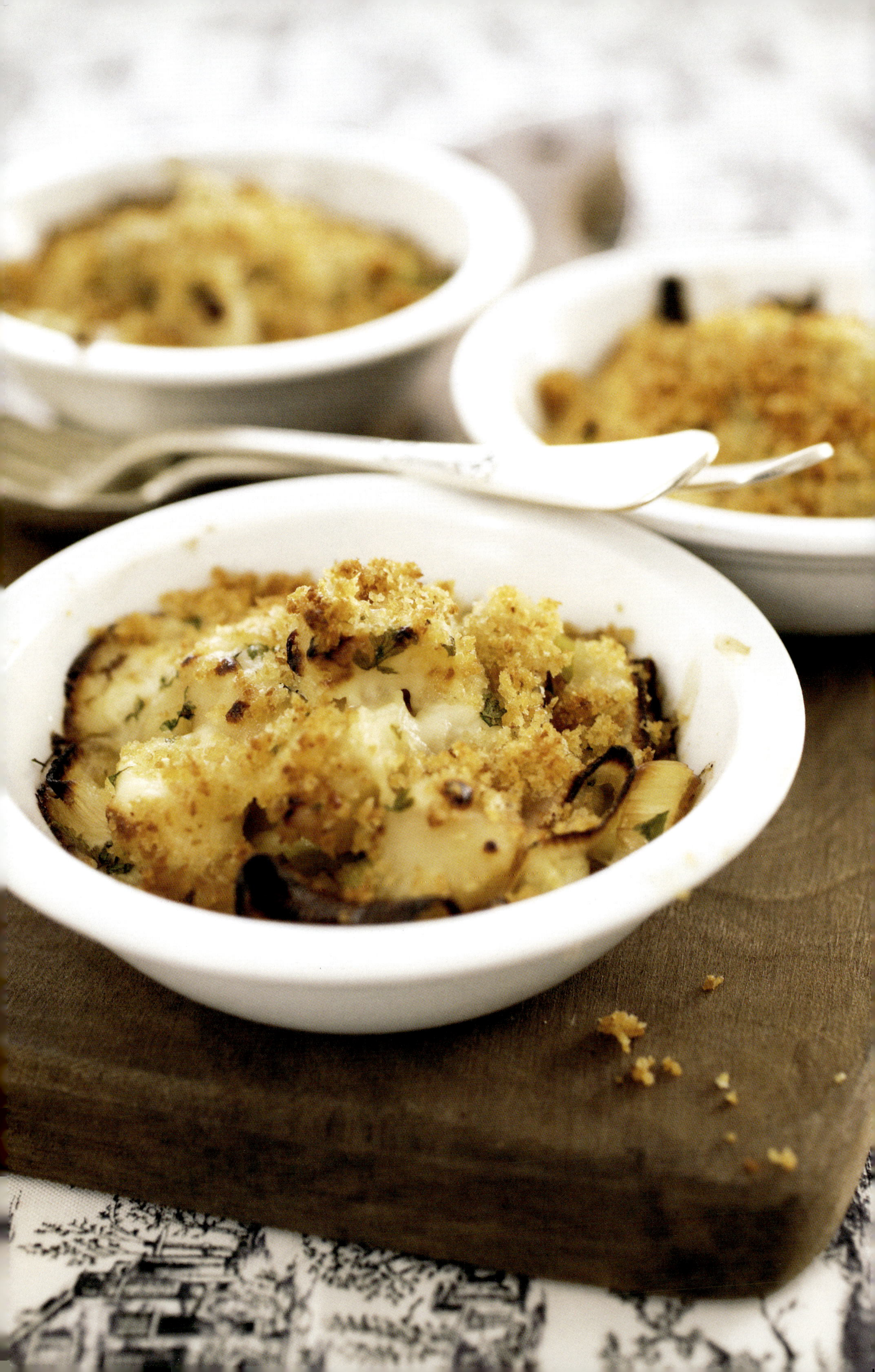

Mini-crumbles de saint-jacques aux poireaux

PRÉPARATION 30 MIN | **CUISSON** 35 MIN | **COÛT** ★★★ | **DIFFICULTÉ** ★★ |
MATÉRIEL SPÉCIFIQUE 4 RAMEQUINS PLATS (CASSOLETTES)

1 Lavez le cerfeuil et coupez-le finement. Épluchez les blancs de poireaux et coupez-les en fines rondelles. Dans une casserole, faites chauffer 3 cuil. à soupe d'huile. Ajoutez les poireaux et la moitié du cerfeuil. Laissez cuire 15 min environ à feu doux et à couvert en remuant régulièrement. Salez et poivrez.

2 Pendant ce temps, nettoyez les saint-jacques en retirant le corail et la veine noire qui entoure la chair. Passez-les à l'eau claire et séchez-les délicatement sur du papier absorbant. Coupez chaque noix en deux dans le sens de la longueur.

3 Dans une poêle, faites chauffer 1 cuil. à soupe d'huile d'olive et ajoutez les noix de saint-jacques. Saisissez-les 20 secondes de chaque côté.

4 Préchauffez le four à 180 °C (th. 6). Beurrez 4 ramequins. Répartissez les poireaux cuits dans le fond des ramequins et ajoutez les saint-jacques. Mélangez la crème fraîche, la moutarde et l'autre moitié du cerfeuil. Versez cette crème sur les noix de saint-jacques. Faites cuire au four 25 min environ.

5 Pour la pâte, ramollissez le beurre au micro-ondes puis mélangez-le à la chapelure.

6 À la fin des 25 min de cuisson, émiettez un peu de pâte sur le dessus de chaque ramequin. Faites cuire à nouveau 10 min au four. Terminez la cuisson en passant vos mini-crumbles 2 min sous le gril du four.

Les ingrédients pour 6 personnes

Pour la garniture
3 branches de cerfeuil
3 blancs de poireaux
4 cuil. à soupe d'huile d'olive
sel et poivre
12 noix de saint-jacques
15 cl de crème fraîche
1 cuil. à café de moutarde forte
1 noisette de beurre pour les ramequins

Pour la pâte
100 g de beurre
10 cuil. à soupe de chapelure

le tuyau de laurence

Saupoudrez un peu de curry sur votre préparation de poireaux, le mariage est succulent.

le verre de vin qui va bien

Pour accompagner ce crumble, servez un vin rouge qui se marie bien avec les coquilles Saint-Jacques : le chiroubles.

Crumble de poulet à l'estragon

PRÉPARATION 25 MIN | **CUISSON** 25 MIN | **COÛT** ★★ | **DIFFICULTÉ** ★★

1 Lavez l'estragon et coupez-le finement. Coupez les blancs de poulet en lamelles. Dans une poêle, faites chauffer la noisette de beurre. Ajoutez l'oignon coupé et faites-le revenir 3 à 4 min. Ajoutez le poulet et laissez-le cuire 10 min.

2 Pendant ce temps, lavez et effilez les pois gourmands (équeutez-les et le fil viendra en coupant les deux extrémités). Lavez et coupez le brocoli en tout petits quartiers. Dans une casserole d'eau bouillante salée, faites cuire les légumes 5 min environ.

3 Préchauffez le four à 200 °C (th. 6-7). À la fin des 10 min de cuisson, ajoutez dans la poêle la crème fraîche et l'estragon coupé. Poivrez. Mélangez à l'aide d'une cuillère en bois jusqu'à ce que la crème soit bien lisse. Répartissez le poulet à la crème dans le fond d'un moule à gratin. Ajoutez les légumes bien égouttés sur le poulet.

4 Pour la pâte à crumble, concassez finement les amandes dans un mortier (ou à l'aide d'un manche de couteau). Faites ramollir le beurre au micro-ondes. Râpez grossièrement le parmesan. Dans un saladier, mélangez la farine avec le parmesan râpé, les amandes et le beurre ramolli.

5 Malaxez la préparation avec les mains puis émiettez-la du bout des doigts pour lui donner une consistance sableuse (comme une grosse semoule). Ajoutez-la sur les légumes en une couche régulière. Faites cuire 25 min environ. Servez immédiatement.

Les ingrédients pour 4 personnes

Pour la garniture

4 branches d'estragon
3 blancs de poulet
1 grosse noisette de beurre pour la poêle
1 oignon finement coupé
150 g de pois gourmands
1 tête de brocoli
3 cuil. à soupe de crème fraîche épaisse
sel et poivre

Pour la pâte

50 g d'amandes salées
80 g de beurre
50 g de parmesan
100 g de farine

Astuces • Vous trouvez des oignons finement coupés déjà tout prêts au rayon des surgelés ; comptez alors 2 cuil. à soupe. • Vous pouvez remplacer l'estragon par du basilic.

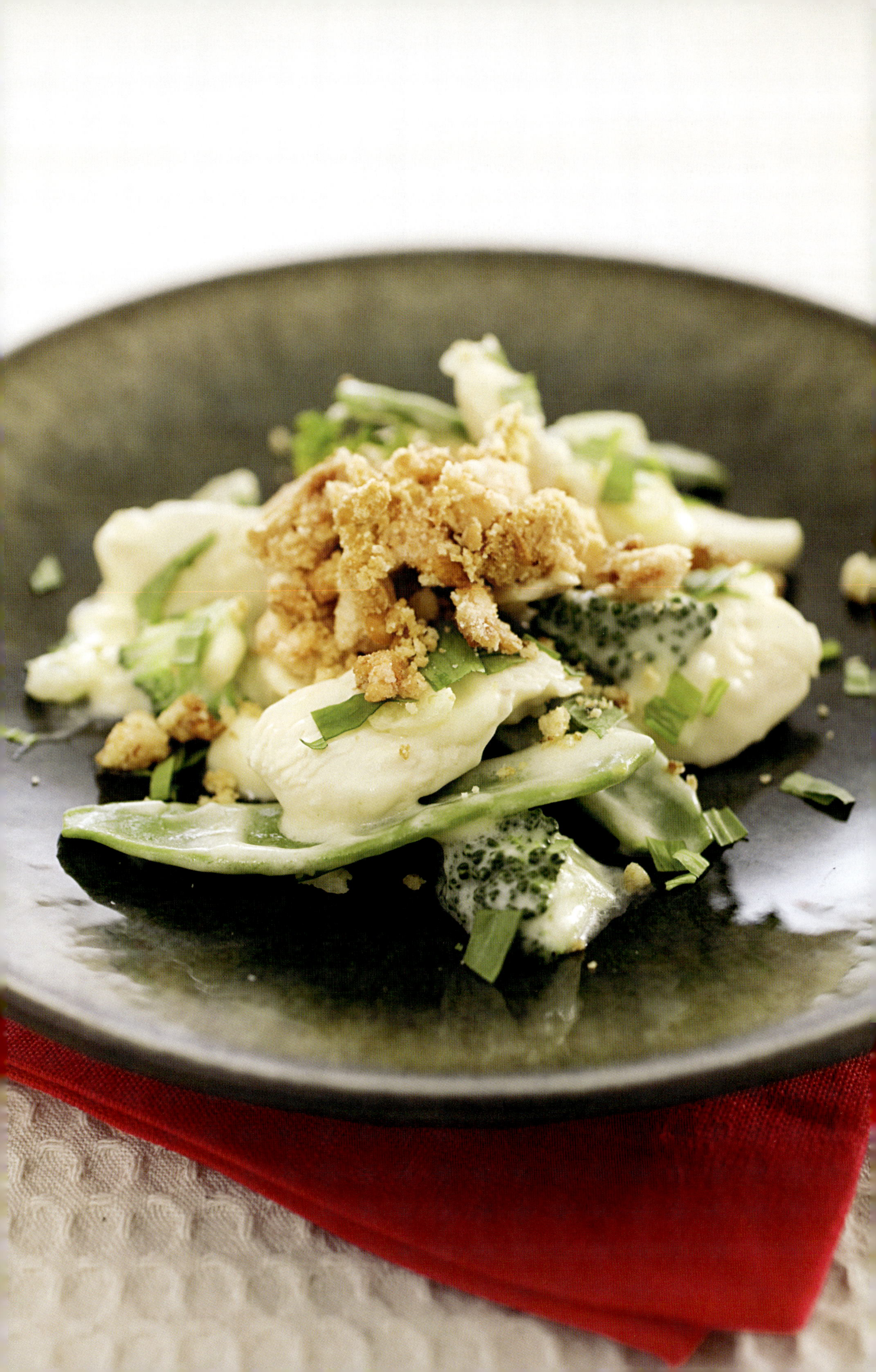

Tatin de pommes de terre au brie

PRÉPARATION 20 MIN | **CUISSON** 30 MIN | **COÛT** ★ | **DIFFICULTÉ** ★★

→ ACCOMPAGNÉE D'UNE BELLE SALADE VERTE, CETTE TATIN DES SOIRS D'HIVER SERA UN PLAT UNIQUE IDÉAL POUR VOS DÎNERS ENTRE COPAINS.

1 Épluchez les pommes de terre. Faites-les cuire 10 min environ à l'eau bouillante salée. Pendant ce temps, faites dorer à la poêle les échalotes et l'ail dans un filet d'huile d'olive. Réservez hors du feu. Coupez le brie en lamelles sans ôter la croûte.

2 Quand les pommes de terre sont cuites, égouttez-les et coupez-les en rondelles. Préchauffez le four à 180 °C (th. 6). Beurrez un moule à bord haut (moule à manqué) et répartissez la moitié des pommes de terre en rosace dans le fond. Recouvrez-les de lamelles de brie puis ajoutez l'autre moitié des pommes de terre. Parsemez le tout d'échalote et d'ail.

3 Dans un bol, battez en omelette l'œuf avec la crème et le persil. Salez et poivrez. Versez la préparation dans le moule. Faites cuire au four 10 min environ.

4 Sortez le moule du four, étalez la pâte sur la préparation et aplatissez-la pour qu'elle adhère bien. Coupez l'excédent de pâte si nécessaire. Faites cuire au four 20 min à nouveau. À la sortie du four, attendez 30 secondes avant de passer la lame d'un couteau le long du moule pour décoller la tarte Tatin. Puis retournez-la sur un plat pour la démouler. Servez immédiatement.

Les ingrédients pour 4 à 6 personnes

- 1,2 kg de pommes de terre
- 3 cuil. à soupe d'échalote finement coupée
- 2 cuil. à soupe d'ail finement coupé
- 1 filet d'huile d'olive
- 400 g de brie
- 1 noisette de beurre pour le moule
- 1 œuf
- 10 cl de crème liquide
- 3 cuil. à soupe de persil finement coupé
- sel et poivre
- 1 pâte brisée pur beurre

Pour varier_ Tatin de pommes au camembert. Faites revenir dans une poêle 4 pommes rouges, épluchées et coupées en quartiers, avec une belle noisette de beurre (10 min environ). Déposez-les ensuite dans le fond d'un moule beurré et aplatissez la pâte feuilletée par-dessus. Faites cuire au four 30 min à 180 °C (th. 6). Démoulez la tarte Tatin et repassez-la sous le gril du four quelques minutes recouverte de lamelles de camembert.

la botte secrète d'aude et leslie

Pour un petit plus gourmand, rajoutez des lardons dans cette tarte Tatin. Faites-les revenir à la poêle en même temps que les échalotes et l'ail.

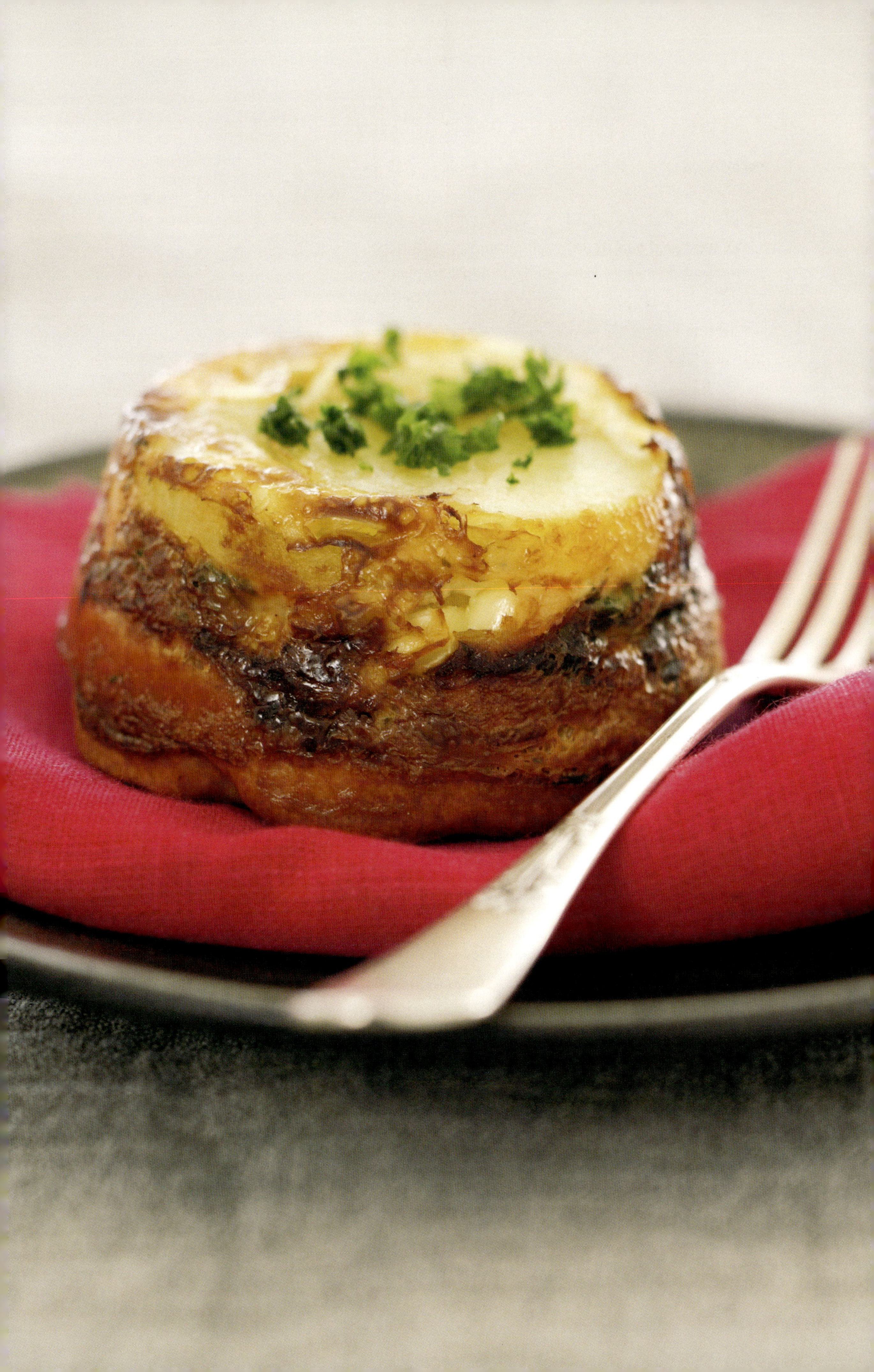

Tatin de tomates au chèvre et au basilic

PRÉPARATION 25 MIN | **CUISSON** 35 MIN | **COÛT** ★ | **DIFFICULTÉ** ★★

1 Préchauffez le four à 230 °C (th. 7-8). Dans une casserole d'eau bouillante, plongez les tomates 30 secondes environ. Lorsque leur peau commence à se décoller, ressortez-les une à une à l'aide d'une louche.

2 Épluchez les tomates, coupez-les en deux et épépinez-les. Huilez la plaque du four et déposez-y les demi-tomates. Salez et poivrez. Faites cuire au four 10 à 15 min ; vous obtenez ainsi des tomates confites.

3 Pendant ce temps, huilez un moule à bord haut (moule à manqué). Ôtez la croûte des crottins de Chavignol et coupez-les en rondelles. Lavez le basilic, séchez-le et coupez-le finement.

4 Quand les tomates sont prêtes, déposez-les dans le fond du moule (côté bombé contre le fond), en laissant un espace entre la garniture et le bord du moule. Saupoudrez-les de basilic. Recouvrez le tout de rondelles de chèvre.

5 Déroulez la pâte feuilletée et badigeonnez-la de moutarde avec le dos d'une cuillère. Aplatissez la pâte sur la tarte, côté moutarde sur le chèvre. Recourbez les bords à l'intérieur et faites cuire au four 35 min environ en réduisant la température du four à 210 °C (th. 7).

6 À la sortie du four, attendez 30 secondes avant de retourner la tarte sur un plat pour la démouler. Ajoutez les pignons sur le dessus juste avant de servir.

Les ingrédients pour 6 personnes

- 12 à 14 tomates (selon leur grosseur)
- 1 filet d'huile d'olive pour la plaque du four et le moule
- sel et poivre
- 1 filet d'huile d'olive pour le moule
- 2 crottins de Chavignol
- 10 feuilles de basilic
- 1 pâte feuilletée
- 2 cuil. à soupe de moutarde forte
- 1 belle poignée de pignons

Astuces_ • La clé de la réussite : serrez bien vos demi-tomates les unes contre les autres avant de les recouvrir de chèvre. • Pensez à arroser votre tarte Tatin d'un filet de vinaigre balsamique juste avant de servir.

Pour varier_ Vous pouvez remplacer le basilic par des herbes de Provence et le chèvre par de la mozzarella. **Version provençale.** Troquez la moutarde contre de la tapenade d'olives noires.

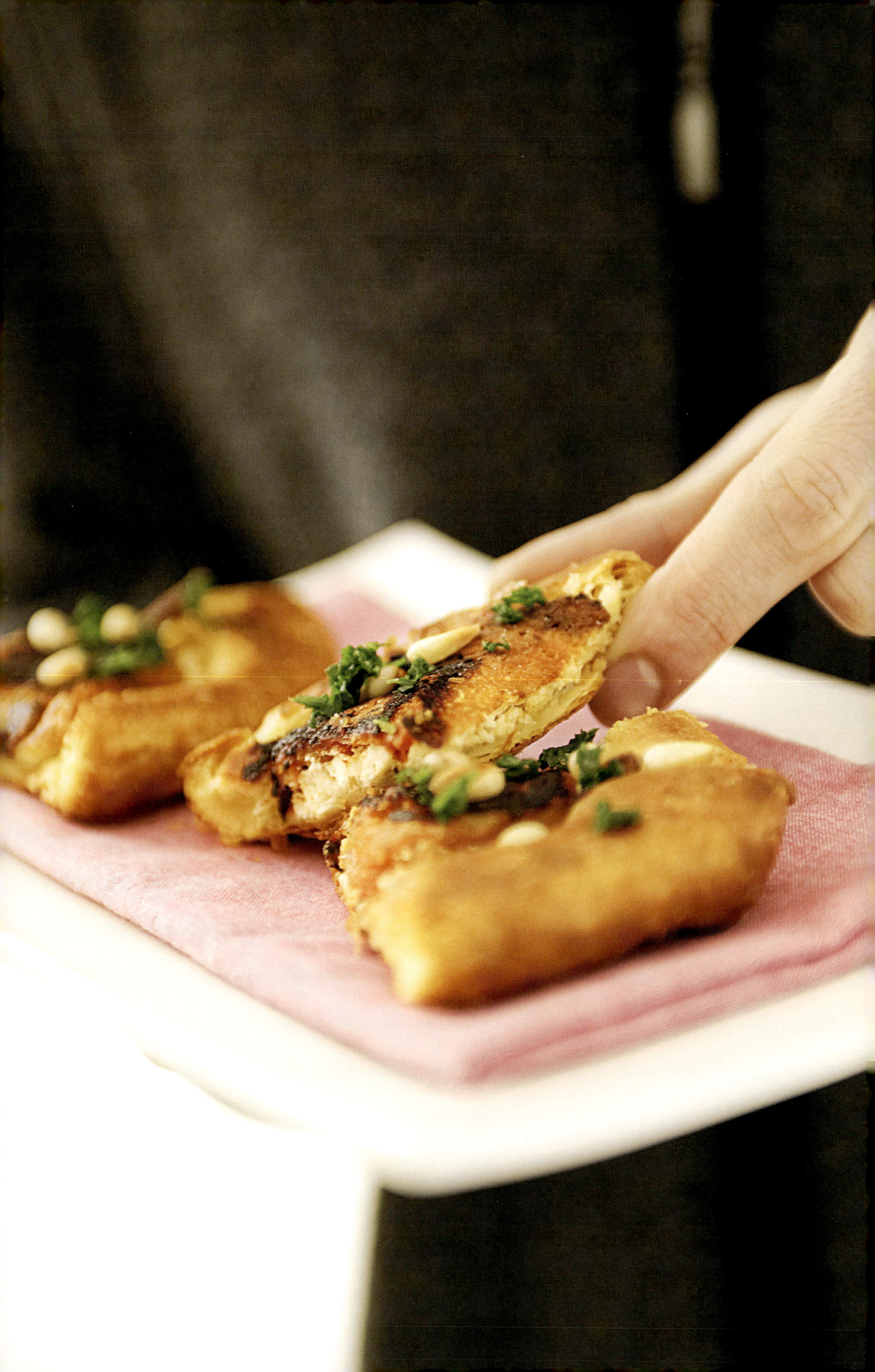

tartes Tatin salées

recette**pour**épater...

Tartelettes Tatin de foie gras aux pommes vertes

PRÉPARATION 25 MIN | **CUISSON** 15 MIN | **RÉFRIGÉRATION** 15 MIN | **COÛT** ★★★ | **DIFFICULTÉ** ★★★ |
MATÉRIEL SPÉCIFIQUE 4 MOULES INDIVIDUELS

1 Épluchez les pommes et coupez-les en lamelles épaisses. Dans une poêle, faites-les revenir avec le beurre (6 à 7 min). Beurrez les moules individuels, et répartissez-y les pommes en rosace.

2 Coupez le foie gras frais en 4 tranches égales. Dans une poêle antiadhésive, faites-le poêler quelques secondes de chaque côté. Puis déposez-en une tranche dans chaque moule. Salez et poivrez.

3 Déroulez la pâte brisée et découpez-y 4 disques de diamètre légèrement supérieur aux moules. Étalez les disques de pâte sur le foie gras et aplatissez-les pour qu'ils adhèrent bien. Puis recourbez les bords à l'intérieur. Placez-les 15 min au réfrigérateur.

4 Préchauffez le four à 210 °C (th. 7). Faites cuire au four les tartelettes Tatin 15 min environ. 5 min avant la fin de la cuisson, réalisez des copeaux avec la tranche de foie gras mi-cuit : à l'aide d'un couteau de cuisine, découpez de très fines tranches, elles vont « se casser » d'elles-mêmes en copeaux.

5 À la sortie du four, attendez 30 secondes avant de démouler les tatins. Ajoutez les copeaux de foie gras juste avant de servir.

Les ingrédients pour 4 personnes
- 4 pommes granny smith
- 1 belle noisette de beurre pour la poêle
- 1 noisette de beurre pour les moules
- 400 g de foie gras de canard frais
- sel et poivre
- 1 pâte brisée
- 1 tranche de foie gras mi-cuit

Astuce_ Quand vous poêlez votre foie gras, n'ajoutez aucune matière grasse et ne le saisissez pas plus de quelques secondes sinon il risque de fondre.

la **botte secrète** d'aude et leslie

Pensez à faire revenir vos tranches de pomme dans de la graisse d'oie à la place du beurre. C'est à se damner !

tartes Tatin salées

Tatin d'endives au curry

PRÉPARATION 35 MIN I **CUISSON** 25 MIN I **COÛT** ★ I **DIFFICULTÉ** ★★

1. Ôtez les premières feuilles abîmées des endives. Lavez-les et coupez-les en gros tronçons.
2. Dans une sauteuse, faites-les revenir dans les 2/3 du beurre (50 g) à feu doux 25 à 30 min jusqu'à ce qu'elles soient cuites et dorées. Ajoutez le curry et mélangez délicatement pour conserver de beaux tronçons.
3. Préchauffez le four à 200 °C (th. 6-7). Coupez le reste du beurre en petits morceaux (25 g) et déposez-les dans le fond du moule, puis saupoudrez de sucre avant d'ajouter les endives au curry en laissant un espace entre la garniture et le bord du moule. Poivrez.
4. Étalez la pâte sur les endives et aplatissez-la pour qu'elle adhère bien. Puis recourbez les bords à l'intérieur. Faites cuire au four 20 à 25 min environ. 10 min avant la fin du temps de cuisson, faites revenir les lardons dans une poêle antiadhésive jusqu'à ce qu'ils soient bien dorés.
5. À la sortie du four, attendez 30 secondes avant de passer la lame d'un couteau le long des bords et de retourner la tarte sur un plat pour la démouler. Ajoutez les lardons grillés sur le dessus juste avant de servir.

Les ingrédients pour 4 à 6 personnes
- 1 kg d'endives
- 75 g de beurre
- 4 pincées de curry en poudre
- 2 cuil. à soupe de sucre
- poivre
- 1 pâte feuilletée
- 100 g de lardons

Astuce_ Avant de déposer les endives dans le fond du moule, égouttez-les bien si elles ont rendu un peu d'eau.

le tuyau de laurence

Quand vous faites revenir vos endives, saupoudrez-les de 1 cuil. à soupe de sucre en poudre, elles caraméliseront légèrement et n'auront plus aucune amertume.

le verre de vin qui va bien
Servez cette tarte aux endives avec un verre de vin blanc de Savoie, juste frais.

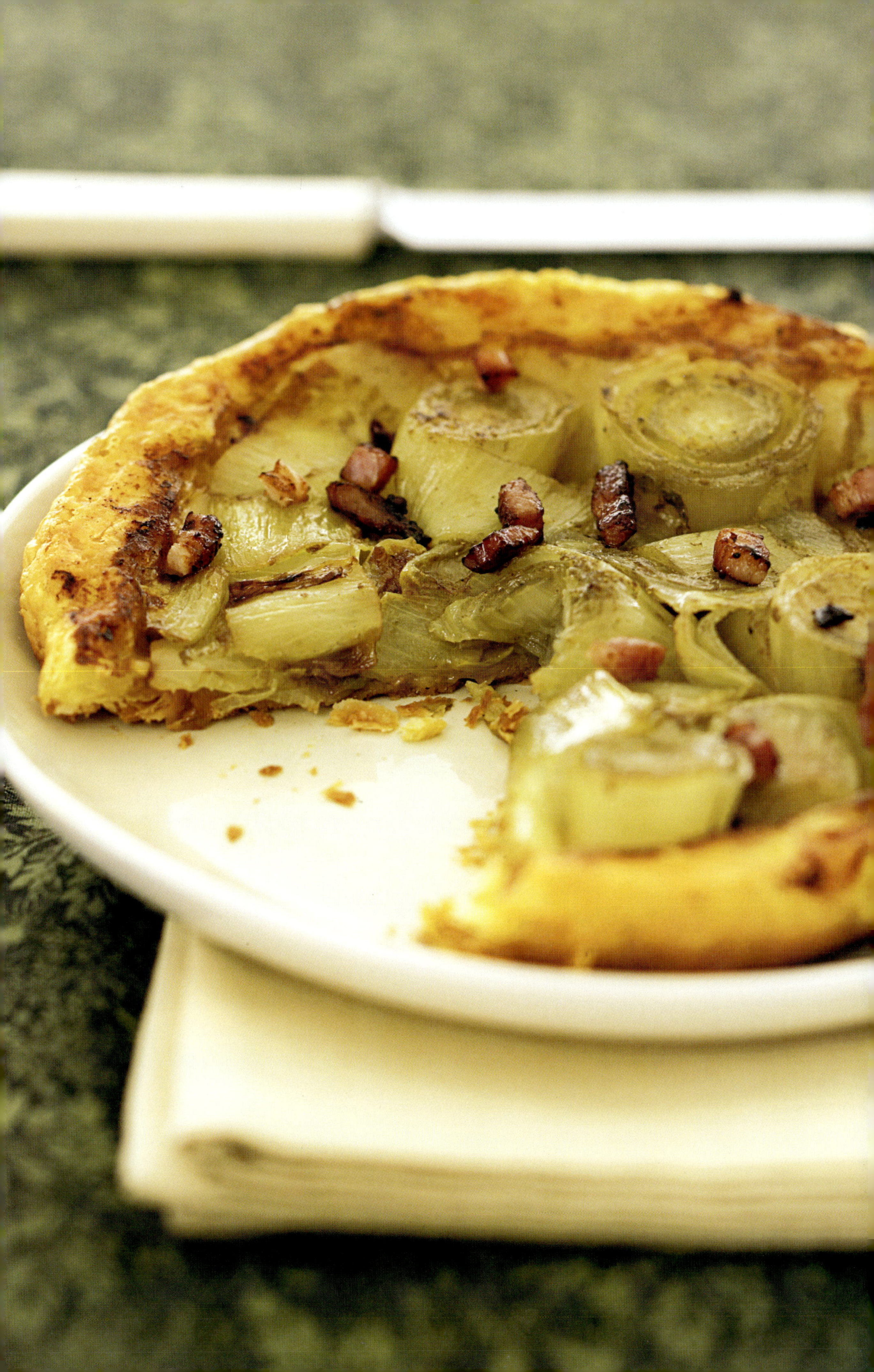

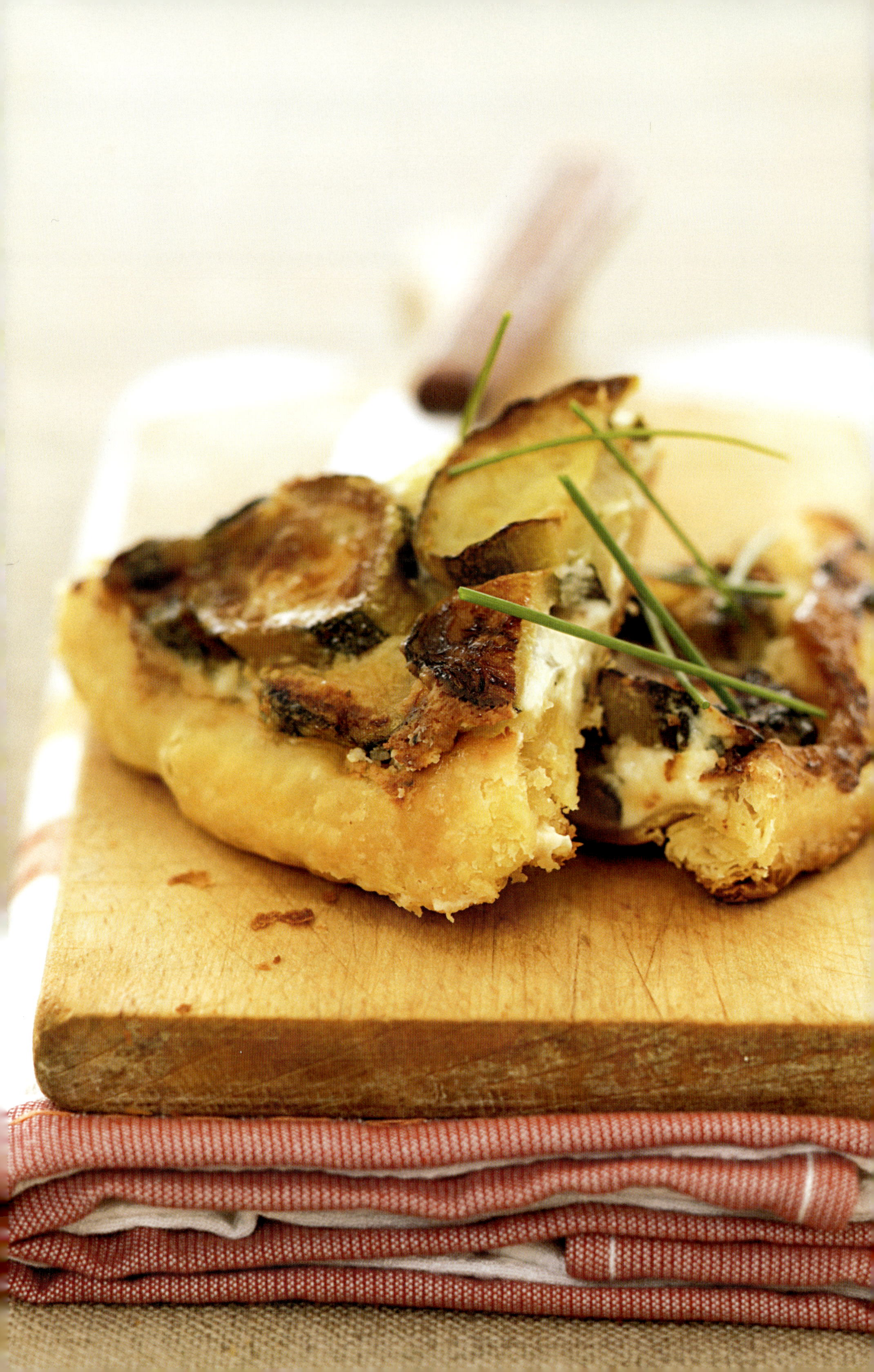

Tatin de courgettes au Boursin

PRÉPARATION 15 MIN I **CUISSON** 25 MIN I **COÛT** ★ I **DIFFICULTÉ** ★

1 Beurrez un moule à bord haut (moule à manqué). Lavez et épluchez les courgettes avec un couteau économe en laissant une bande de peau sur deux. Coupez-les en rondelles pas trop fines. Dans une sauteuse ou une grande poêle, faites revenir les courgettes dans l'huile d'olive à feu moyen 10 min environ. Salez et poivrez.

2 Préchauffez le four à 210 °C (th. 7). Déposez les courgettes dans le fond du moule en laissant un espace entre les légumes et le bord du moule. Coupez le Boursin en rondelles et répartissez-le sur les courgettes.

3 Étalez la pâte feuilletée sur les rondelles de Boursin et aplatissez-la pour qu'elle adhère bien. Puis recourbez les bords à l'intérieur. Faites cuire au four 25 min environ. À la sortie du four, attendez 30 secondes avant de retourner la tarte sur un plat pour la démouler. Parsemez de brins de ciboulette avant de servir.

Les ingrédients pour 4 à 6 personnes

1 noisette de beurre pour le moule
1 kg de courgettes
4 cuil. à soupe d'huile d'olive
 pour la sauteuse
sel et poivre
1 Boursin
1 pâte feuilletée
quelques brins de ciboulette
 pour la décoration

Pour varier_ Tatin de courgettes au chèvre et à la menthe. Remplacez le Boursin par du chèvre frais et ajoutez 1/2 bouquet de menthe finement coupée entre les courgettes et le chèvre.

le tuyau de laurence

Pour une version plus light, mettez les courgettes sur du papier absorbant juste après leur cuisson dans la sauteuse, afin d'éliminer toute la graisse.

tartes Tatin salées

Tartelettes Tatin au magret de canard

PRÉPARATION 20 MIN I **CUISSON** 25 MIN I **COÛT** ★★ I **DIFFICULTÉ** ★★ I
MATÉRIEL SPÉCIFIQUE 4 MOULES INDIVIDUELS

1 Préchauffez le four à 180 °C (th. 6). Épluchez les pommes et coupez-les en lamelles. Dans une poêle, faites-les revenir avec la noisette de beurre (6 à 7 min).

2 Beurrez généreusement 4 petits moules individuels et répartissez-y la moitié des pommes en rosace. Déposez dans chaque moule 4 tranches de magret puis rajoutez par-dessus le reste des pommes. Salez et poivrez.

3 Étalez la pâte sur les pommes et aplatissez-la pour qu'elle adhère bien. Puis recourbez les bords à l'intérieur. Faites cuire au four 20 à 25 min environ.

4 Pendant ce temps, concassez les noisettes dans un mortier.

5 À la sortie du four, attendez 30 secondes avant de retourner les tatins sur les assiettes pour les démouler. Ajoutez quelques noisettes concassées et le thym en branche juste avant de servir.

Les ingrédients pour 4 personnes
4 pommes
1 belle noisette de beurre pour la poêle
1 belle noisette de beurre pour les moules
16 tranches de magret de canard fumé
sel et poivre
1 pâte feuilletée
1 poignée de noisettes
75 cl de vinaigre balsamique (facultatif)
branches de thym pour la décoration

Astuces_ • Si vos pommes ont tendance à se dessécher quand vous les faites poêler, n'hésitez pas à rajouter un peu de beurre. • Si vous n'avez pas de mortier, placez vos noisettes dans un torchon et écrasez-les à l'aide d'un rouleau à pâtisserie ou d'un petit marteau.

la botte secrète d'aude et leslie
Cette recette est une merveille si vous accompagnez vos tartelettes Tatin d'un caramel de vinaigre balsamique. Pour cela, faites réduire 75 cl de vinaigre balsamique, en le faisant chauffer à feu doux dans une casserole jusqu'à ce qu'il devienne sirupeux comme du caramel (1 h 15 environ). Vous pouvez en préparer à l'avance et le conserver au réfrigérateur.

le tuyau de laurence
Saupoudrez cette délicieuse tatin de pignons de pin, leur saveur se marie étonnamment bien à celle des pommes et du magret.

40 tartes Tatin salées

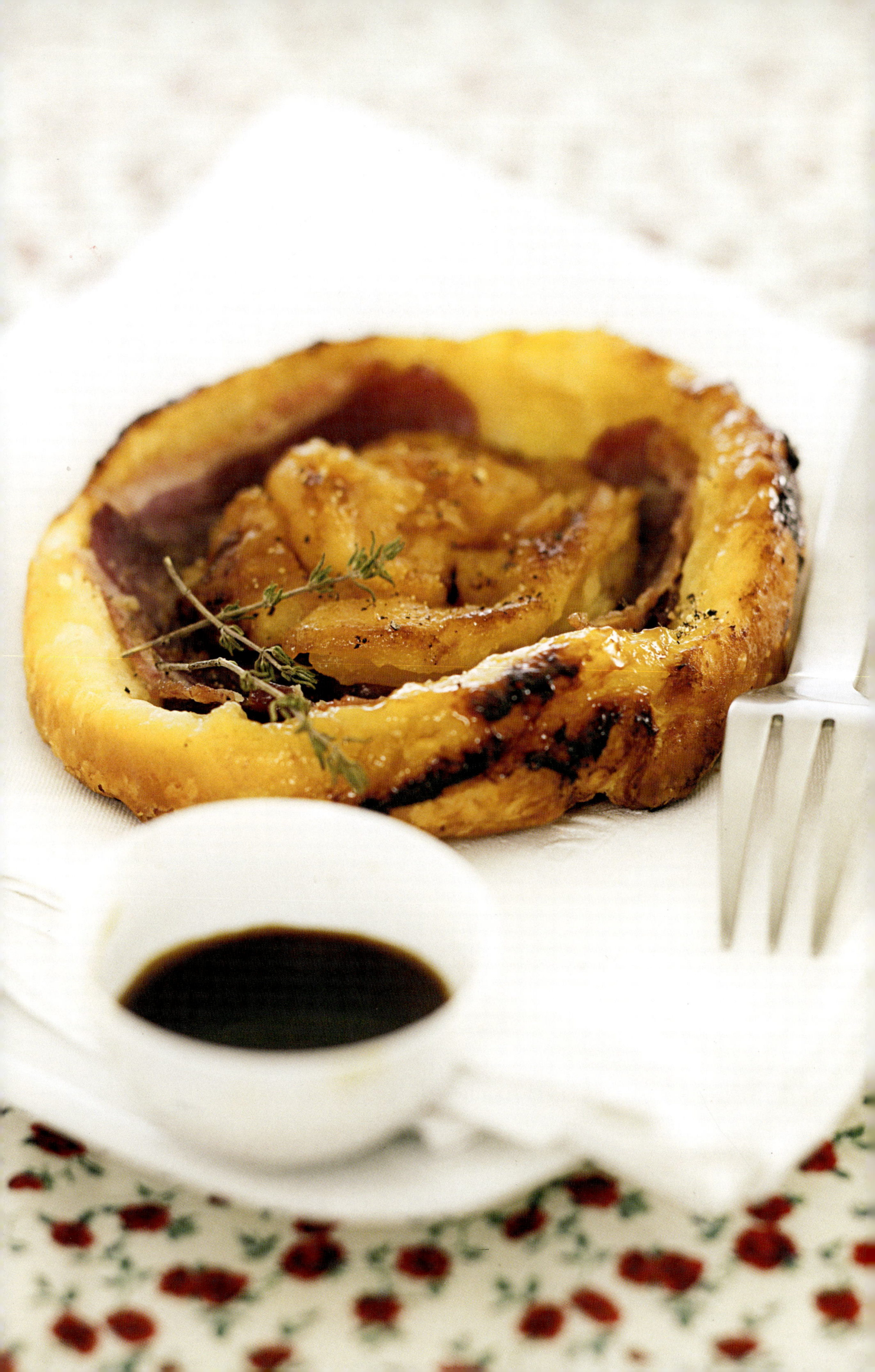

Tatin de saumon aux épinards

PRÉPARATION 20 MIN | **CUISSON** 25 MIN | **COÛT** ★★ | **DIFFICULTÉ** ★

1 Dans une sauteuse ou une grande poêle, faites fondre les épinards dans l'huile d'olive. Laissez-les cuire jusqu'à ce que l'eau soit bien évaporée (10 min environ). Égouttez-les bien. Salez et poivrez.

2 Arrosez le saumon avec le 1/2 jus de citron. Dans un saladier, battez en omelette les œufs avec la crème et la ciboulette. Poivrez. Beurrez un moule à bord haut (tourtière). Ajoutez les épinards dans la préparation aux œufs et versez le tout dans le fond du moule. Recouvrez le tout de dés de saumon.

3 Étalez la pâte brisée sur le saumon et aplatissez-la pour qu'elle adhère bien. Puis recourbez les bords à l'intérieur. Faites cuire au four 20 à 25 min environ. À la sortie du four, attendez 30 secondes avant de retourner la tarte sur un plat pour la démouler. Parsemez de brins de persil avant de servir.

Les ingrédients pour 4 à 6 personnes

- 500 g d'épinards surgelés
- 2 cuil. à soupe d'huile d'olive
- sel et poivre
- le jus de 1/2 citron
- 150 g de dés de saumon frais
- 2 œufs
- 10 cl de crème liquide
- 2 cuil. à soupe de ciboulette finement coupée
- 1 noisette de beurre pour le moule
- 1 pâte brisée
- quelques brins de persil pour la décoration

Astuce_ Pensez à bien égoutter les épinards en les pressant dans le fond de la passoire avant de les ajouter dans la préparation aux œufs.

la botte secrète d'aude et leslie
Vous pouvez rajouter un peu de feta écrasée dans la préparation aux œufs. Un délice !

le verre de vin qui va bien
Vous pouvez bien sûr servir cette tatin originale avec un vin blanc sec mais vous pouvez aussi proposer de la vodka glacée, servie dans des shots.

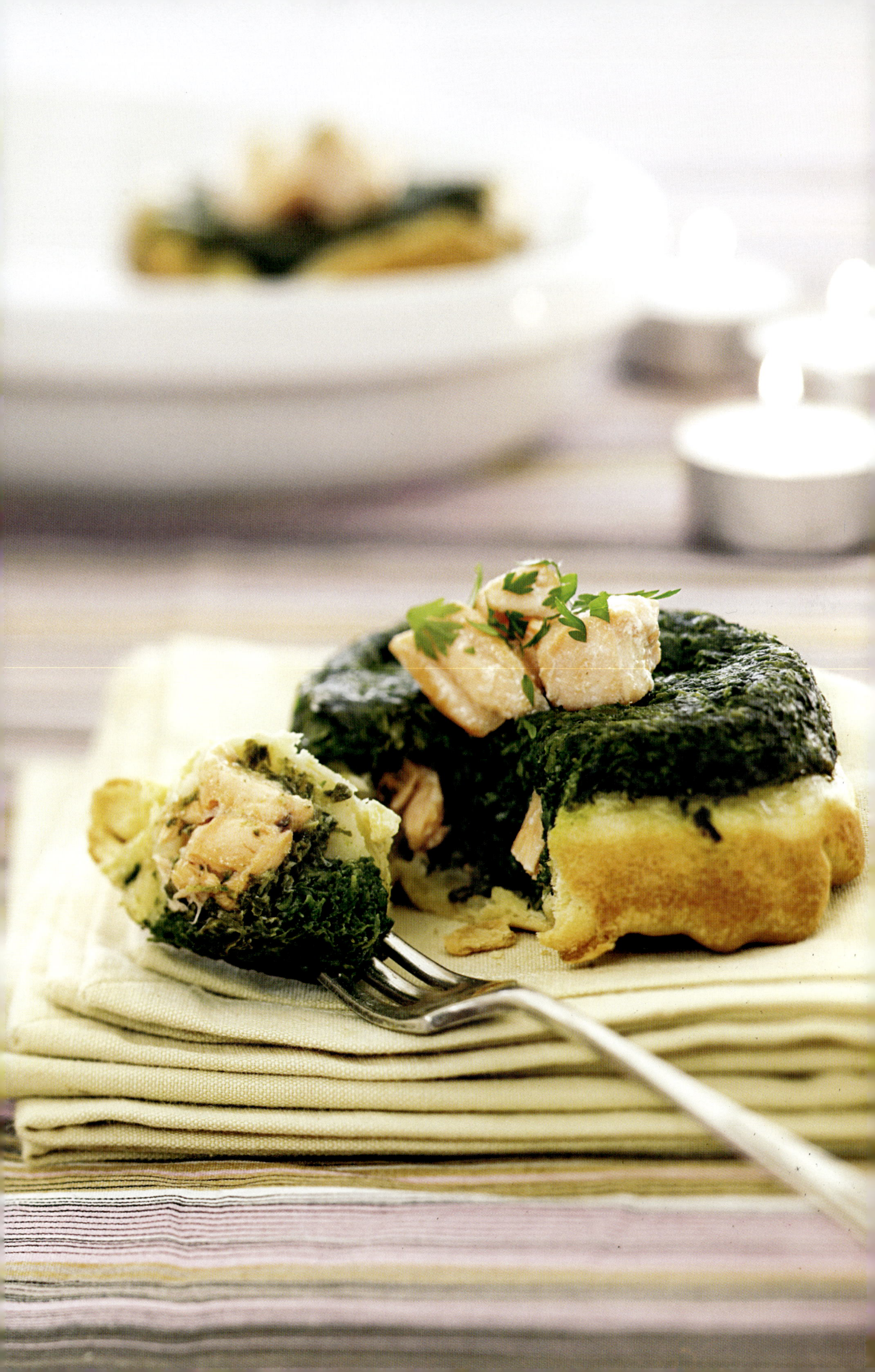

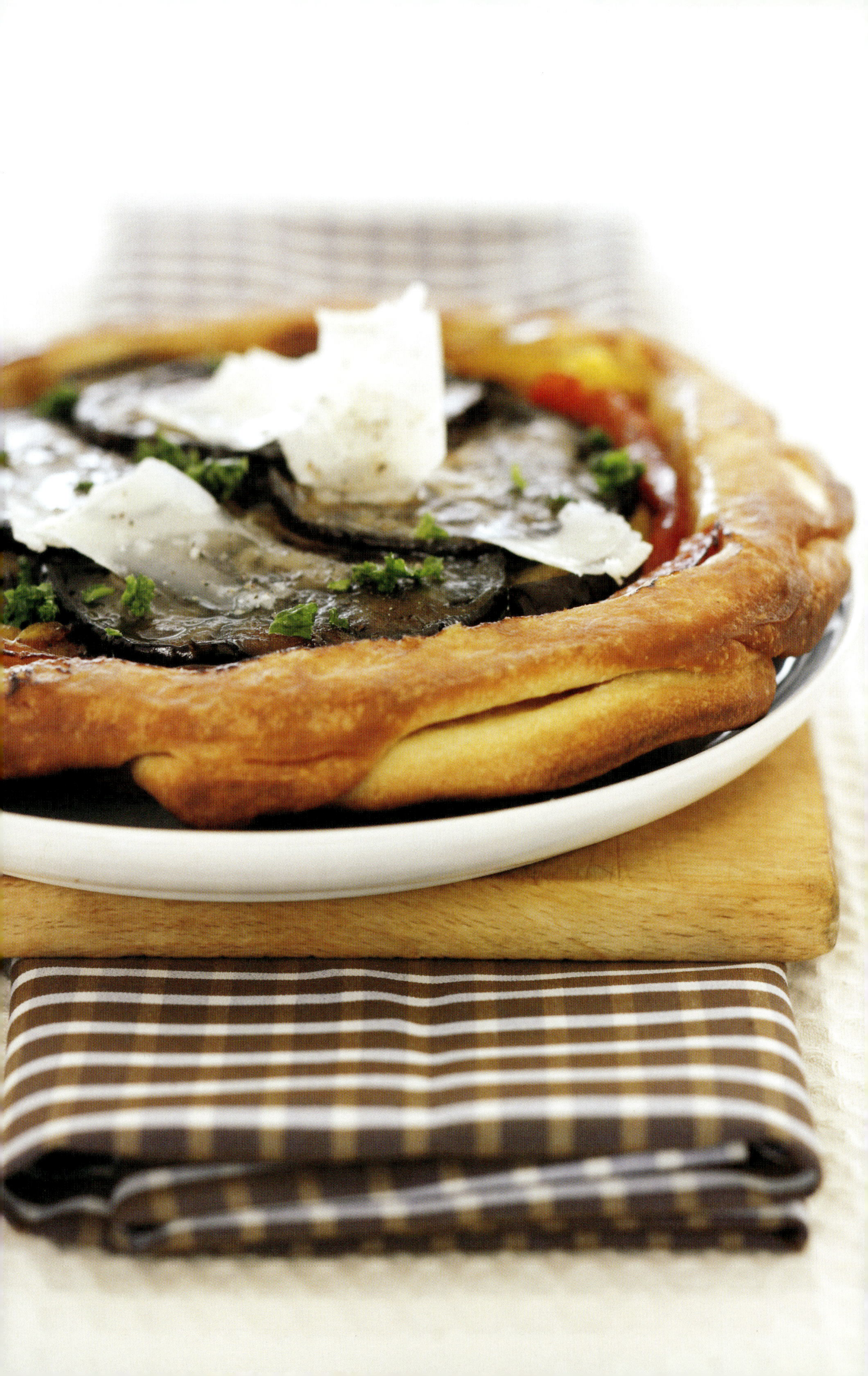

Tatin d'aubergines aux poivrons

PRÉPARATION 25 MIN I **CUISSON** 40 MIN + 40 MIN I **COÛT** ★★ I **DIFFICULTÉ** ★★★

1 Préchauffez le four à 210 °C (th. 7). Recouvrez la plaque du four de papier sulfurisé. Lavez les aubergines et les poivrons. Coupez les aubergines en rondelles pas trop épaisses. Disposez le tout sur la plaque du four. Arrosez généreusement d'huile d'olive et faites cuire au four 35 à 40 min environ.

2 À la sortie du four, ôtez la peau et les pépins des poivrons et coupez-les en lamelles.

3 Huilez un moule à bord haut (tourtière). Dans le fond du moule, répartissez en couches successives la moitié des aubergines en rosace, le caviar d'aubergines, les poivrons, la tapenade puis le reste des aubergines. Poivrez. Faites cuire au four 10 min environ.

4 Puis, sortez le moule du four, étalez la pâte sur les aubergines et aplatissez-la pour qu'elle adhère bien. Puis recourbez les bords à l'intérieur. Faites cuire au four 30 min à nouveau jusqu'à ce que la pâte soit bien dorée. À la sortie du four, attendez 30 secondes avant de retourner la tarte sur un plat pour la démouler.

Les ingrédients pour 4 à 6 personnes
2 aubergines
2 poivrons rouges
1 poivron jaune
1 beau filet d'huile d'olive pour les légumes
1 filet d'huile pour le moule
4 cuil. à soupe de caviar d'aubergines
3 cuil. à soupe de tapenade d'olives noires
poivre
1 pâte brisée pur beurre

Astuce_ Pour gagner du temps, sachez qu'il existe des aubergines et des poivrons grillés surgelés.

la botte secrète aude et leslie
Pour une tatin encore plus gourmande, vous pouvez rajouter du chèvre frais ou de la mozzarella entre les aubergines et la pâte.

le tuyau de laurence
À tester de toute urgence avec de beaux copeaux de parmesan sur le dessus avant de servir !

tartes Tatin salées

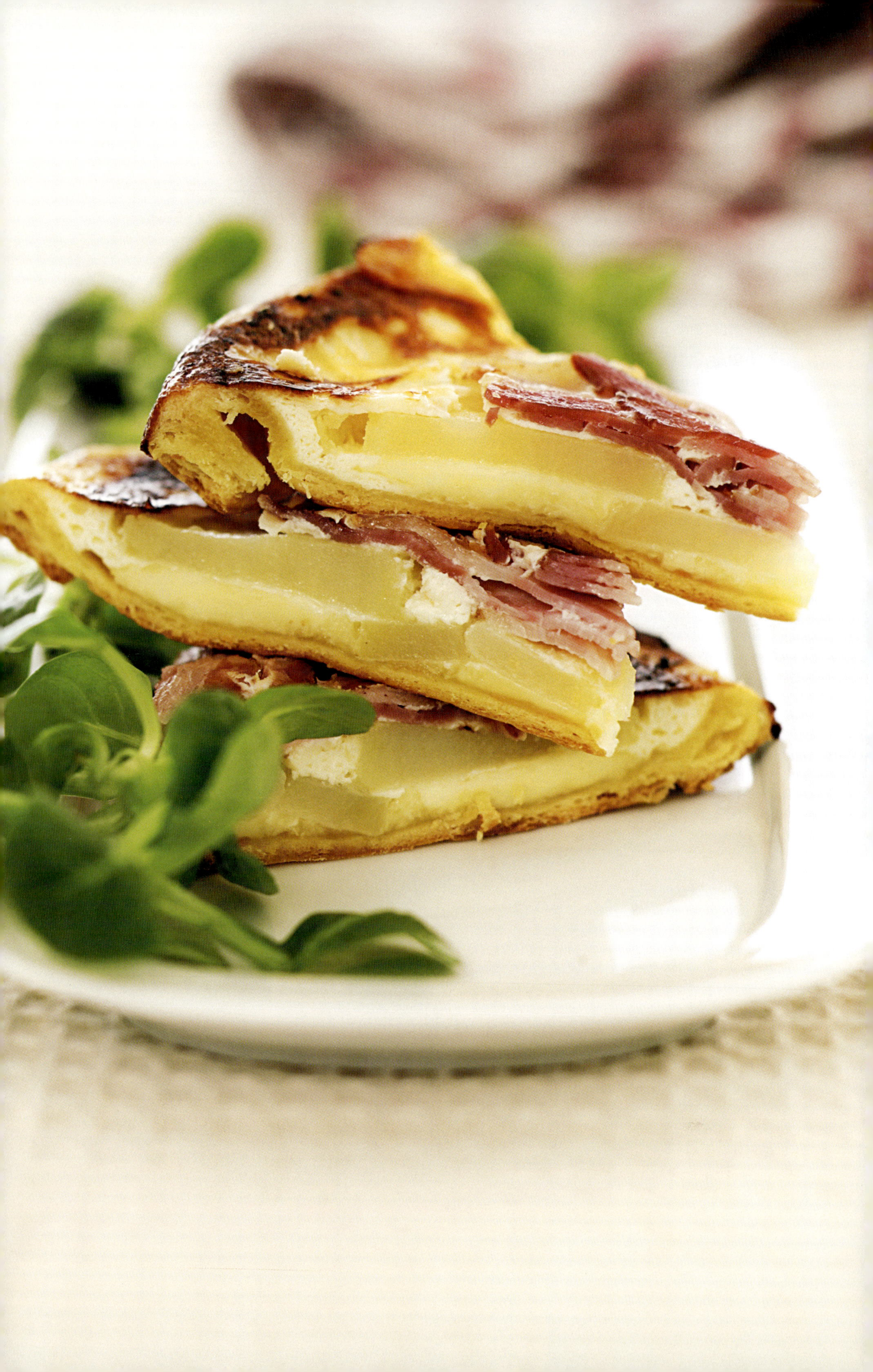

Tatin façon tartiflette

PRÉPARATION 25 MIN I **CUISSON** 30 MIN I **COÛT** ★★ I **DIFFICULTÉ** ★

→ À DÉGUSTER EN PLAT UNIQUE AVEC DES CORNICHONS ET UNE GROSSE SALADE VERTE.

1 Dans une casserole d'eau bouillante salée, faites cuire les pommes de terre entières 15 à 20 min (selon leur grosseur). Pendant ce temps, ôtez la croûte du fromage à raclette. Dans un saladier, battez en omelette les œufs avec la crème fraîche. Ajoutez le comté râpé.

2 Préchauffez le four à 210 °C (th. 7). Quand les pommes de terre sont cuites, égouttez-les, épluchez-les et coupez-les en rondelles pas trop épaisses. Beurrez généreusement un moule à bord haut (tourtière). Dans une poêle antiadhésive, faites revenir les tranches de lard 3-4 min environ, puis déposez-les en étoile dans le fond du moule.

3 Puis ajoutez les pommes de terre bien serrées en rosace. Salez et poivrez. Puis ajoutez le fromage à raclette. Versez la préparation aux œufs. Étalez la pâte brisée dessus, puis piquez-la à l'aide d'une fourchette. Recourbez les bords à l'intérieur. Faites cuire au four 30 min environ.

4 À la sortie du four, attendez 30 secondes avant de retourner la tarte sur un plat pour la démouler. Servez chaud, tiède ou froid.

Les ingrédients pour 6 personnes

- 4 belles pommes de terre
- 8 petites tranches de fromage à raclette
- 3 œufs
- 20 cl de crème fraîche épaisse
- 100 g de comté râpé
- 1 noisette de beurre pour le moule
- 6 belles tranches de lard
- sel et poivre
- 1 pâte brisée

Astuce_ Pour un résultat au top, faites cuire vos pommes de terre à la vapeur.

Pour varier_ **Tatin au bleu et au bacon.** Remplacez le fromage à raclette par du bleu d'Auvergne et le lard par du bacon. **Tatin au saumon fumé et chèvre frais.** Remplacez le fromage à raclette par 1 Chavroux et le lard par des lamelles de saumon fumé.

tartes Tatin salées

Tatin de boudin noir

PRÉPARATION 25 MIN | **CUISSON** 25 MIN | **COÛT** ★★ | **DIFFICULTÉ** ★★★

1. Épluchez les oignons et coupez-les finement. Dans une poêle, faites-les revenir dans une grosse noisette de beurre jusqu'à ce qu'ils soient fondants et dorés. Salez et poivrez. Remuez régulièrement.

2. Pendant ce temps, dans une autre poêle, faites revenir le boudin en rondelles dans une noisette de beurre 5 min environ en le retournant à mi-cuisson. Épluchez les pommes entières, évidez le cœur à l'aide d'un vide-pomme ou de la pointe d'un couteau, et coupez-les en rondelles pas trop épaisses.

3. Quand les oignons et le boudin noir sont prêts, réservez-les hors du feu. Préchauffez le four à 200 °C (th. 6-7). Dans la poêle utilisée pour les oignons, faites revenir les pommes dans une noisette de beurre (6 à 7 min environ).

4. Beurrez un moule à bord haut (tourtière). Déposez les rondelles de boudin dans le fond du moule en laissant un espace entre la garniture et le bord du moule. Puis ajoutez successivement les pommes en rosace et les oignons.

5. Étalez la pâte sur les oignons et aplatissez-la pour qu'elle adhère bien. Puis recourbez les bords à l'intérieur. Faites cuire au four 20 à 25 min environ, jusqu'à ce que la pâte soit bien dorée. À la sortie du four, attendez 30 secondes avant de retourner la tatin sur un plat pour la démouler. Servez-la immédiatement parsemée de persil finement coupé.

Les ingrédients pour 4 à 6 personnes

3 oignons
3 belles noisettes de beurre pour les poêles
sel et poivre
600 g de boudin antillais
2 pommes
1 noisette de beurre pour le moule
1 pâte feuilletée
3 brins de persil pour la présentation

Astuce_ Pensez à accompagner votre tatin au boudin de compote de pommes servie chaude ou d'une purée de légumes.

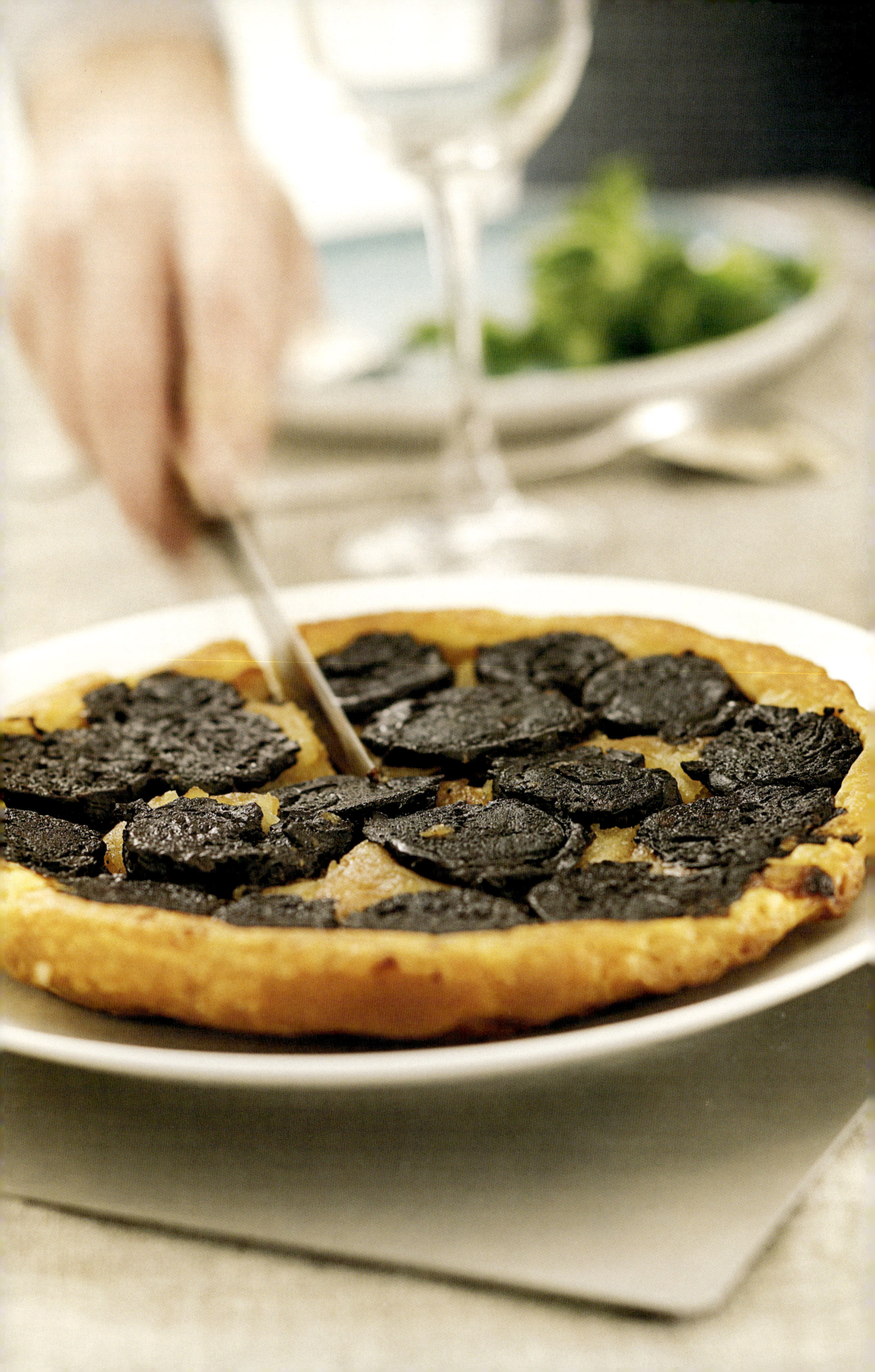

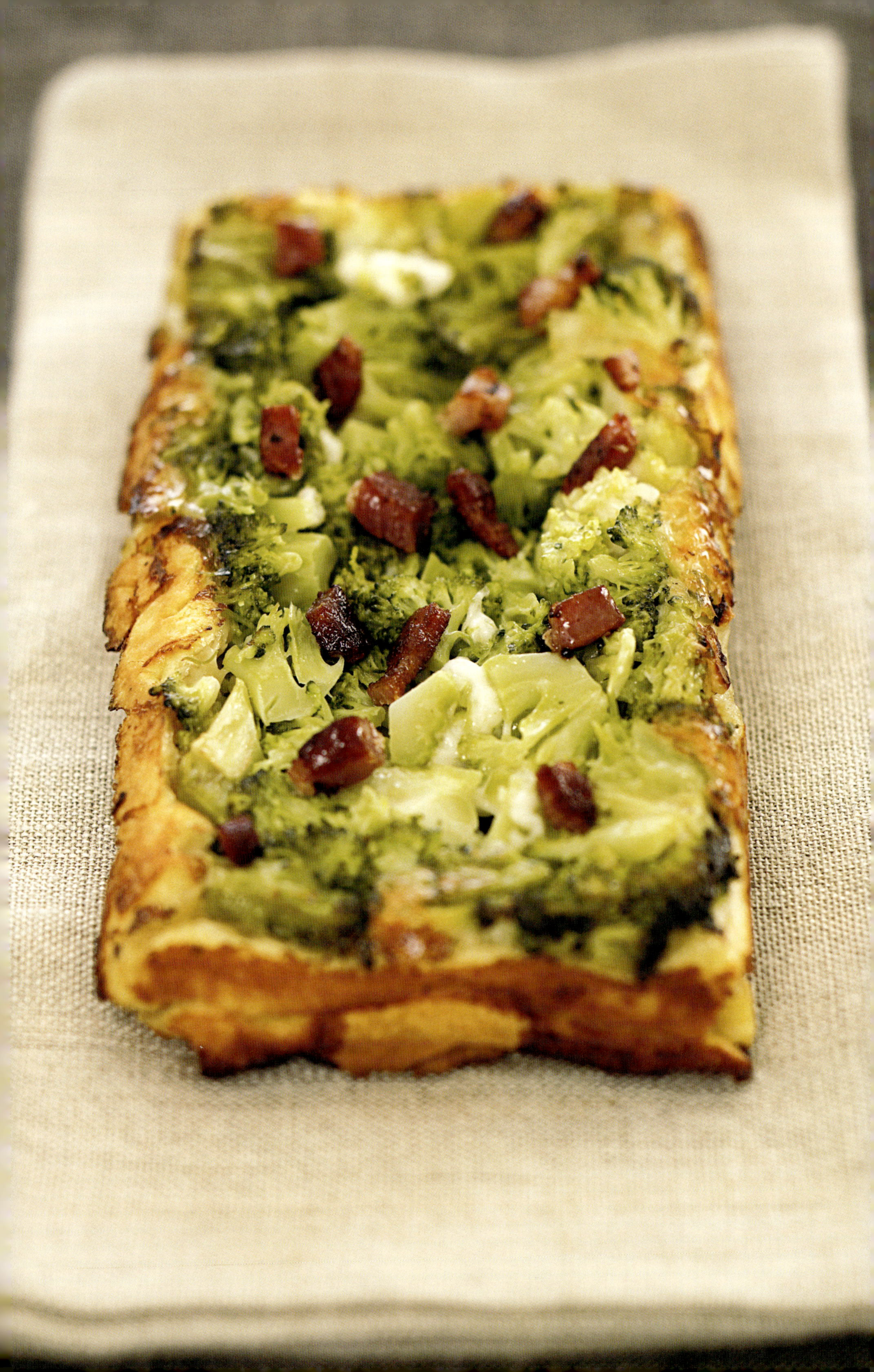

Tatin de brocoli, mozzarella et petits lardons

PRÉPARATION 20 MIN | **CUISSON** 25 MIN | **COÛT** ★ | **DIFFICULTÉ** ★

→ UNE TARTE TATIN QUI SE RÉALISE EN UN TOUR DE MAIN. À LA FOIS ÉQUILIBRÉE ET GOURMANDE, ELLE SERA UN MOYEN IDÉAL DE FAIRE AIMER LES LÉGUMES À VOS ENFANTS.

1 Huilez un moule à bord haut (moule à manqué). Dans une grande casserole d'eau bouillante salée, faites cuire les têtes de brocoli 10 à 12 min, jusqu'à ce qu'elles soient cuites mais encore croquantes. Pendant ce temps, coupez la mozzarella en tranches.

2 Préchauffez le four à 180 °C (th. 6). Quand les brocolis sont cuits, égouttez-les et déposez-les dans le fond du moule en laissant un espace entre la garniture et le bord du moule. Ajoutez la mozzarella. Poivrez.

3 Étalez la pâte sur la mozzarella et aplatissez-la pour qu'elle adhère bien. Puis recourbez les bords à l'intérieur. Faites cuire au four 25 min environ, jusqu'à ce que la pâte soit bien dorée.

4 10 min avant la fin du temps de cuisson, faites revenir les lardons dans une poêle antiadhésive jusqu'à ce qu'ils soient bien dorés. À la sortie du four, attendez 30 secondes avant de retourner la tatin sur un plat pour la démouler. Servez-la immédiatement parsemée de petits lardons grillés.

Les ingrédients pour 4 à 6 personnes
1 filet d'huile d'olive pour le moule
600 g de petites têtes de brocoli surgelées
1 boule de mozzarella
sel et poivre
1 pâte brisée
100 g de lardons

Astuce_ Vous pouvez remplacer la mozzarella par du chèvre frais.

le verre de vin qui va bien

Avec cette délicieuse tatin, jouez sur les contrastes et servez un bon beaujolais village.

Crumble poires, prunes et noisettes

PRÉPARATION 15 MIN | **CUISSON** 25 MIN | **COÛT** ★ | **DIFFICULTÉ** ★

1 Lavez et dénoyautez les prunes. Coupez-les en petits morceaux. Répartissez-les dans le fond d'un moule. Épluchez et coupez les poires en petits morceaux. Ajoutez-les sur les prunes.

2 Préchauffez le four à 210 °C (th. 7). Pour la pâte à crumble, coupez le beurre doux et le beurre salé en morceaux et faites-les ramollir au micro-ondes. Dans un saladier, mélangez la farine avec le sucre roux, la poudre de noisettes et le beurre ramolli.

3 Malaxez la préparation avec les mains puis émiettez-la du bout des doigts pour lui donner une consistance sableuse (comme une grosse semoule). Ajoutez la pâte sur les fruits en une couche régulière. Faites cuire au four 25 min environ. Servez tiède ou froid.

Les ingrédients pour 6 personnes

Pour les fruits
8 prunes jaunes
4 poires mûres

Pour la pâte
60 g de beurre doux
60 g de beurre salé
90 g de farine
100 g de sucre roux
100 g de poudre de noisettes

Astuce_ Quand ce n'est plus la saison des prunes, remplacez-les par des quetsches surgelées.

le truc de stéphan

Faites sauter les fruits à la poêle dans un peu de beurre salé avec quelques pincées de sucre roux, ils auront encore plus de saveur.

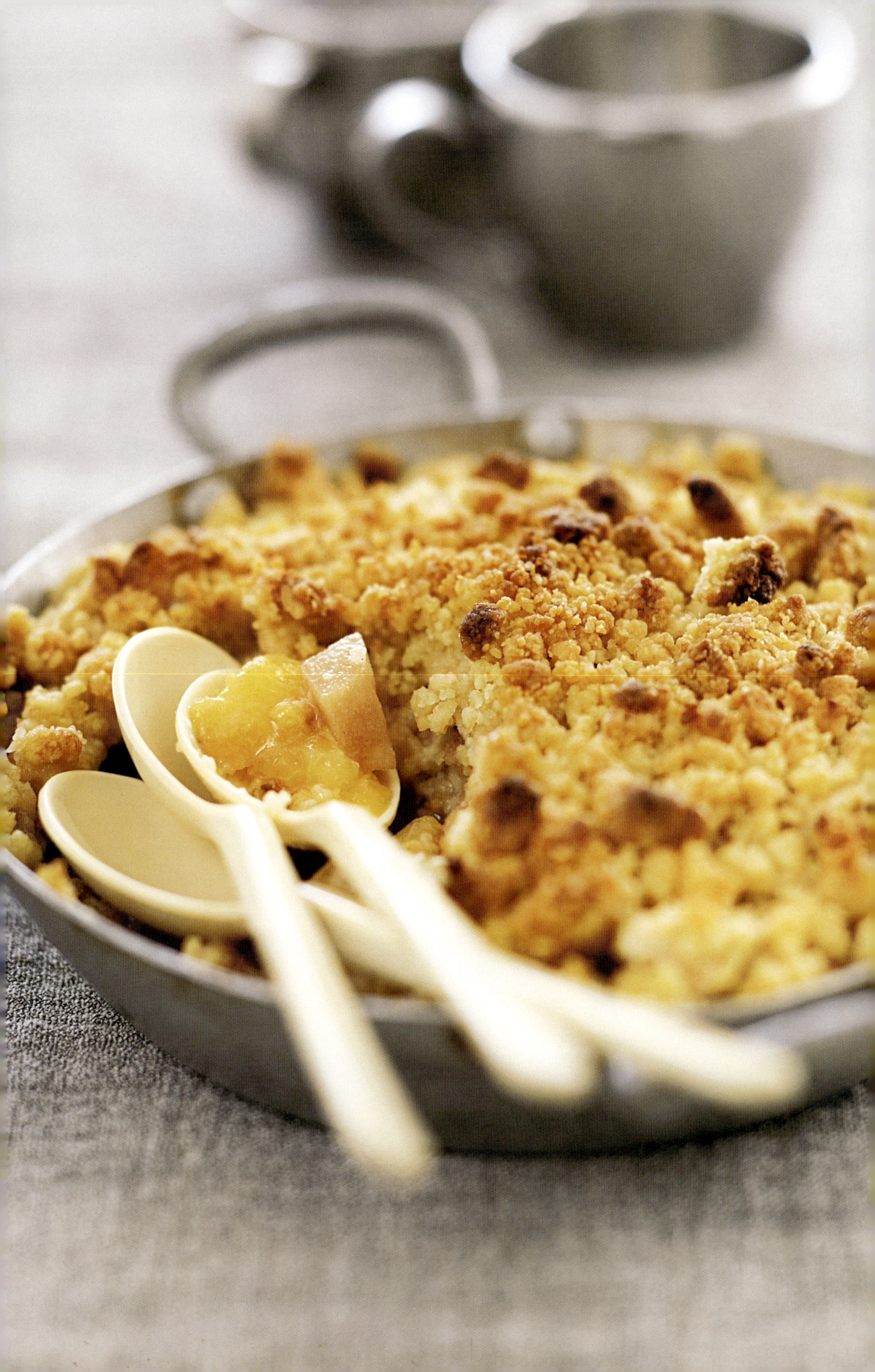

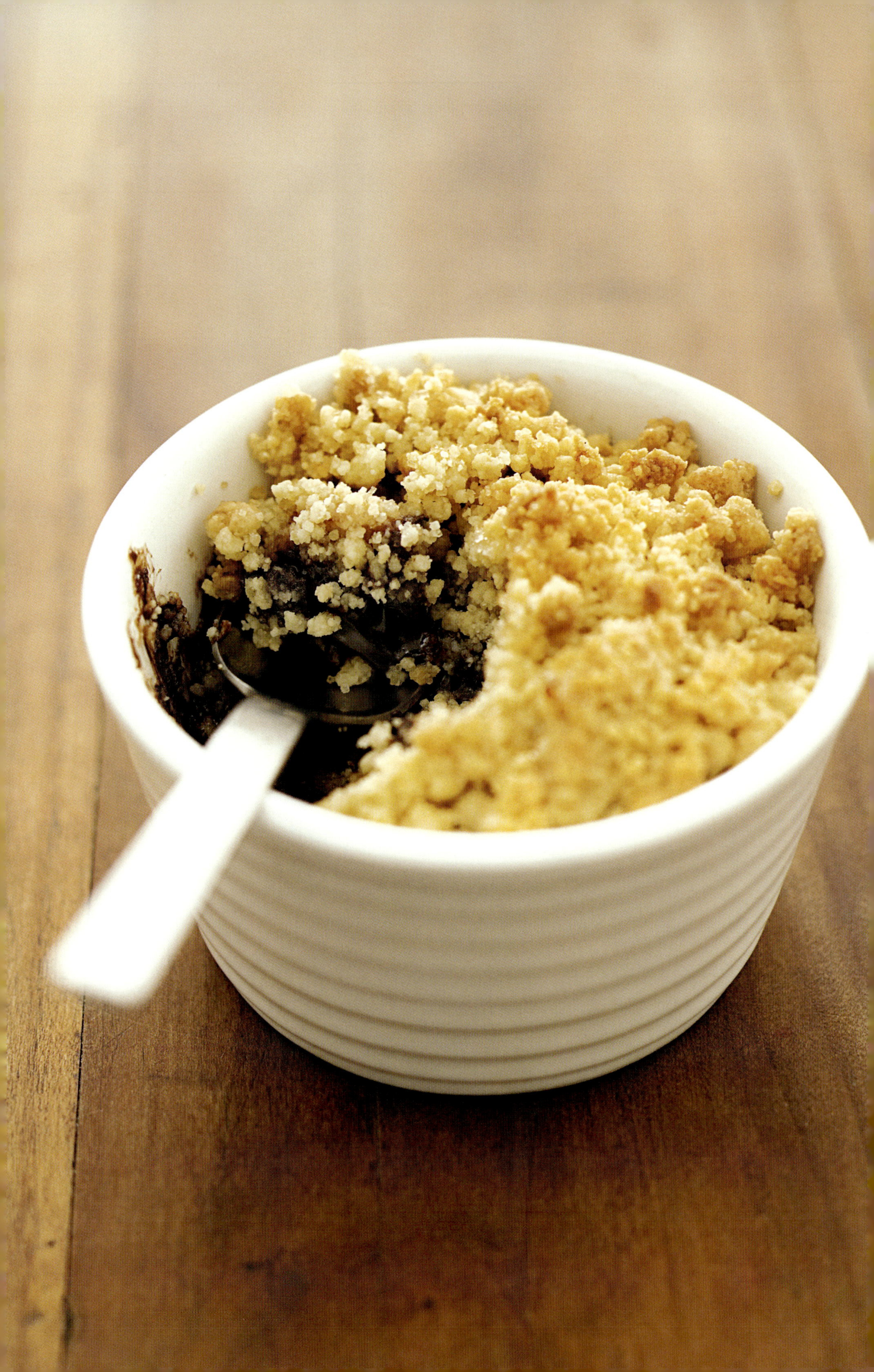

Mini-crumbles de poires aux deux chocolats

PRÉPARATION 20 MIN I **CUISSON** 25 MIN I **COÛT** ★ I **DIFFICULTÉ** ★ I
MATÉRIEL SPÉCIFIQUE 6 RAMEQUINS

→ PENSEZ À JOUER SUR LE CONTRASTE CHAUD-FROID EN ACCOMPAGNANT VOTRE CRUMBLE TIÈDE D'UNE BOULE DE SORBET À LA POIRE POSÉE DIRECTEMENT SUR LE DESSUS DE CHAQUE RAMEQUIN. SI VOUS PRÉPAREZ LE CRUMBLE LA VEILLE, PASSEZ-LE QUELQUES INSTANTS AU FOUR, IL RETROUVERA TOUT SON CROUSTILLANT.

1 Formez des copeaux de chocolat au lait à l'aide d'un couteau économe. Épluchez et coupez les poires en petits morceaux et déposez-les dans 6 ramequins. Saupoudrez-les de sucre vanillé puis ajoutez par-dessus les pépites de chocolat noir et les copeaux de chocolat au lait.

2 Préchauffez le four à 210 °C (th. 7). Pour la pâte à crumble, coupez le beurre en morceaux et faites-le ramollir au micro-ondes.

3 Dans un saladier, mélangez la farine, le sel, le sucre roux et le beurre ramolli. Malaxez la préparation avec les mains puis émiettez-la du bout des doigts pour lui donner une consistance sableuse (comme une grosse semoule). Ajoutez la pâte sur les fruits en une couche régulière. Faites cuire au four 25 min environ, jusqu'à ce que la pâte soit bien dorée. Servez tiède.

Les ingrédients pour 6 personnes

Pour les fruits
50 g de chocolat au lait
6 poires
1 sachet de sucre vanillé
50 g de pépites de chocolat noir

Pour la pâte
80 g de beurre
150 g de farine
1 pincée de sel
80 g de sucre roux

la botte secrète d'aude et leslie

Pour une version encore plus chocolatée, vous pouvez déposer quelques carrés de chocolat noir et au lait dans le fond des ramequins avant d'ajouter les poires.

crumbles sucrés

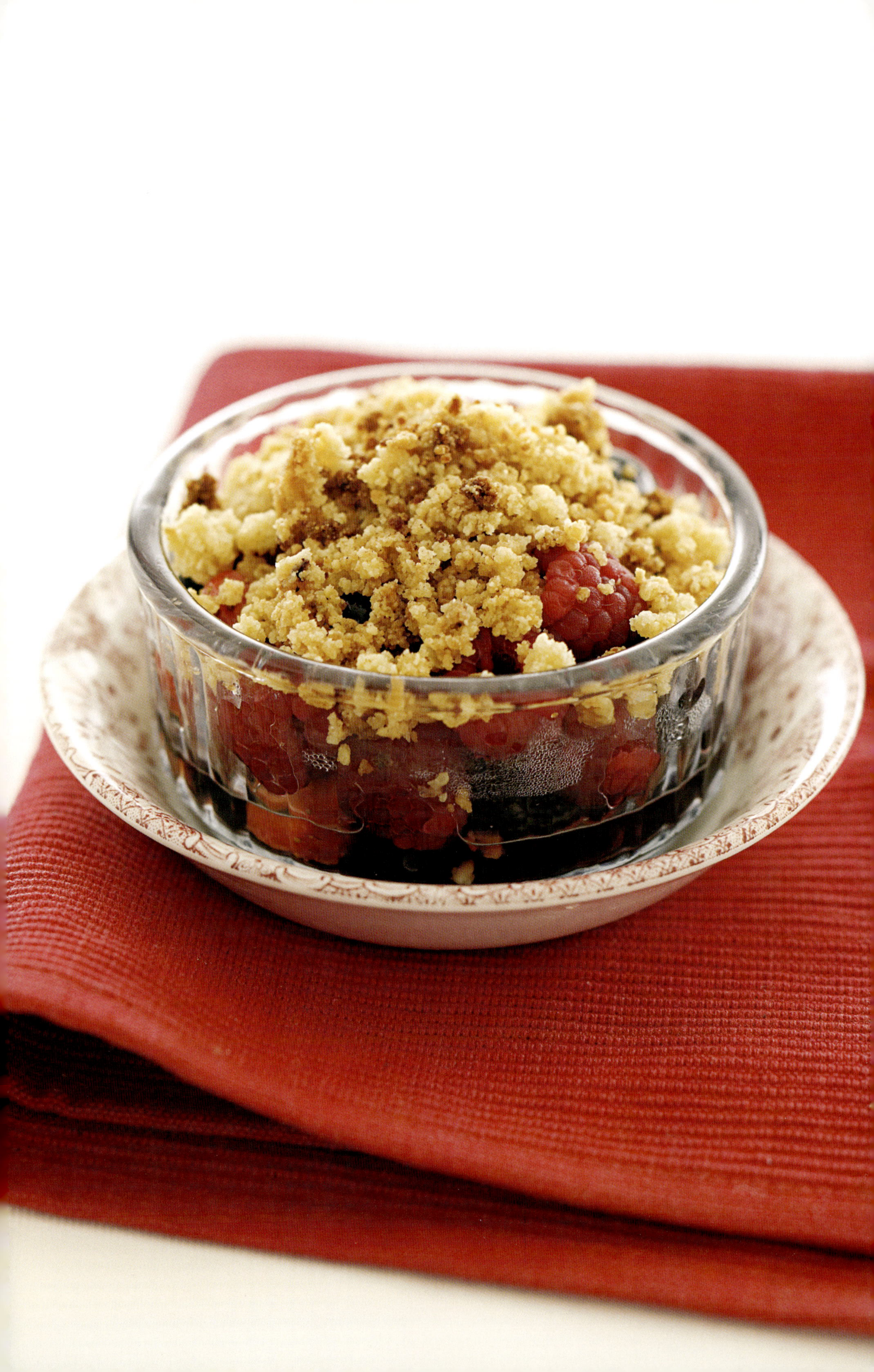

Crumble aux fruits rouges

PRÉPARATION 20 MIN I **CUISSON** 30 MIN I **COÛT** ★★ I **DIFFICULTÉ** ★★

1 Lavez les fruits rouges et séchez-les délicatement en les posant sur du papier absorbant. Équeutez les fraises et coupez-les en quatre. Dans une casserole à feu vif, versez les fruits et le sucre vanillé et faites-les cuire 2 à 3 min environ. Hors du feu, ajoutez les 30 g de sucre roux dans les fruits tièdes et mélangez délicatement. Répartissez-les dans le fond d'un moule beurré.

2 Préchauffez le four à 180 °C (th. 6). Pour la pâte à crumble, coupez le beurre en morceaux et ramollissez-le au micro-ondes. Dans un saladier, mélangez bien la farine avec la poudre d'amandes, les 100 g de sucre roux, la cannelle et les pincées de sel. Puis ajoutez le beurre ramolli.

3 Malaxez la préparation avec les mains puis émiettez-la du bout des doigts pour lui donner une consistance sableuse (comme une grosse semoule). Ajoutez la pâte sur les fruits rouges en une couche régulière. Faites cuire au four 30 min environ jusqu'à ce que la pâte soit bien dorée. Servez tiède.

Les ingrédients pour 6 personnes

Pour les fruits
200 g de fraises
150 g de framboises
150 g de mûres
100 g de myrtilles
1 sachet de sucre vanillé
30 g de sucre roux
1 noisette de beurre pour le moule

Pour la pâte
125 g de beurre
90 g de farine
90 g de poudre d'amandes
100 g de sucre roux
3 pincées de cannelle en poudre
2 pincées de sel

Astuce_ Quand ce n'est plus la saison des fruits rouges frais, pensez aux mélanges de fruits rouges surgelés.

Pour varier_ **Crumble pommes et fruits rouges**. Remplacez les fraises par 2 pommes (type jonagold ou pink lady) coupées en petits morceaux.

le tuyau de laurence

Ajoutez 2 cuil. à soupe de pastis à vos fruits rouges pendant la cuisson. Ce petit goût anisé se marie divinement bien à la saveur des fruits rouges.

crumbles sucrés

Crumble aux kiwis

PRÉPARATION 15 MIN | **CUISSON** 30 MIN | **COÛT** ★ | **DIFFICULTÉ** ★

1. Préchauffez le four à 210 °C (th. 7). Épluchez les kiwis et coupez-les en petits dés. Répartissez les fruits dans le fond d'un moule. Saupoudrez-les de gingembre et de sucre vanillé.

2. Pour la pâte à crumble, coupez le beurre doux en morceaux et faites-le ramollir au micro-ondes. Dans un saladier, mélangez bien la farine avec la poudre d'amandes, la noix de coco râpée, le sucre en poudre et le sucre roux. Puis ajoutez le beurre ramolli.

3. Malaxez la préparation avec les mains puis émiettez-la du bout des doigts pour lui donner une consistance sableuse (comme une grosse semoule). Ajoutez la pâte sur les kiwis en une couche régulière. Faites cuire au four 30 min environ jusqu'à ce que la pâte soit bien dorée. Servez tiède.

Les ingrédients pour 6 personnes

Pour les fruits
8 kiwis mûrs
2 pincées de gingembre en poudre
1 sachet de sucre vanillé

Pour la pâte
120 g de beurre doux
80 g de farine
80 g de poudre d'amandes
30 g de noix de coco râpée
40 g de sucre en poudre
60 g de sucre roux

Astuce_ Si la pâte dore trop rapidement en cours de cuisson, abaissez la température du four à 180 °C (th. 6) et couvrez votre crumble d'une feuille de papier d'aluminium.

la botte secrète d'aude et leslie

Pour une petite touche originale, ajoutez 1 poignée de raisins secs entre les kiwis et la pâte. Dans ce cas-là, laissez-les tremper quelques instants dans un petit verre de rhum pour leur donner du moelleux et du goût. Un délice !

le tuyau de laurence

Remplacez le gingembre en poudre par des éclats de gingembre confit. C'est un peu plus relevé et c'est exquis.

le verre de vin qui va bien

Avec ce crumble délicatement acidulé, servez un saint-croix-du-mont dont les arômes souligneront bien ceux des kiwis et du gingembre.

crumbles sucrés

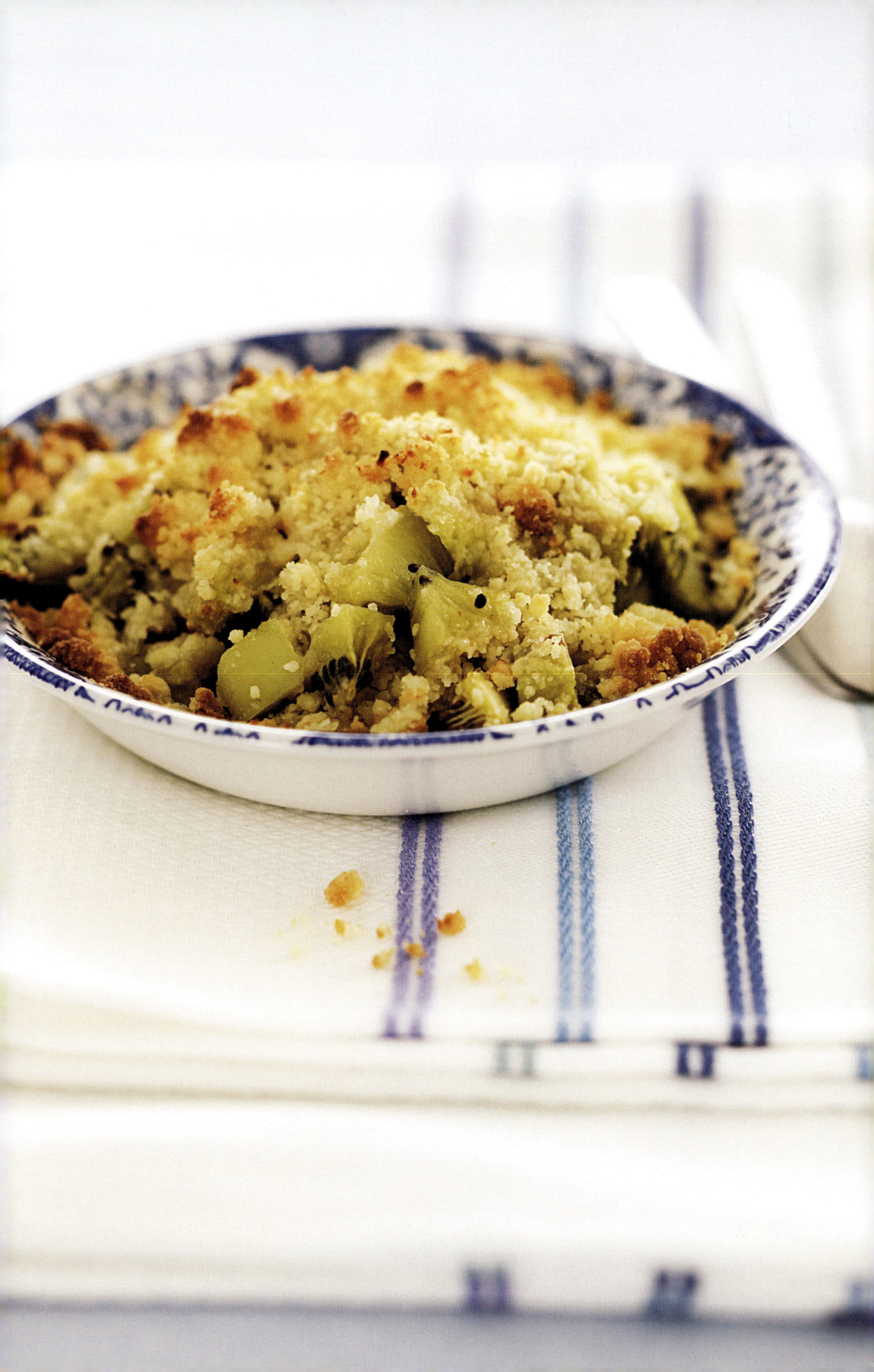

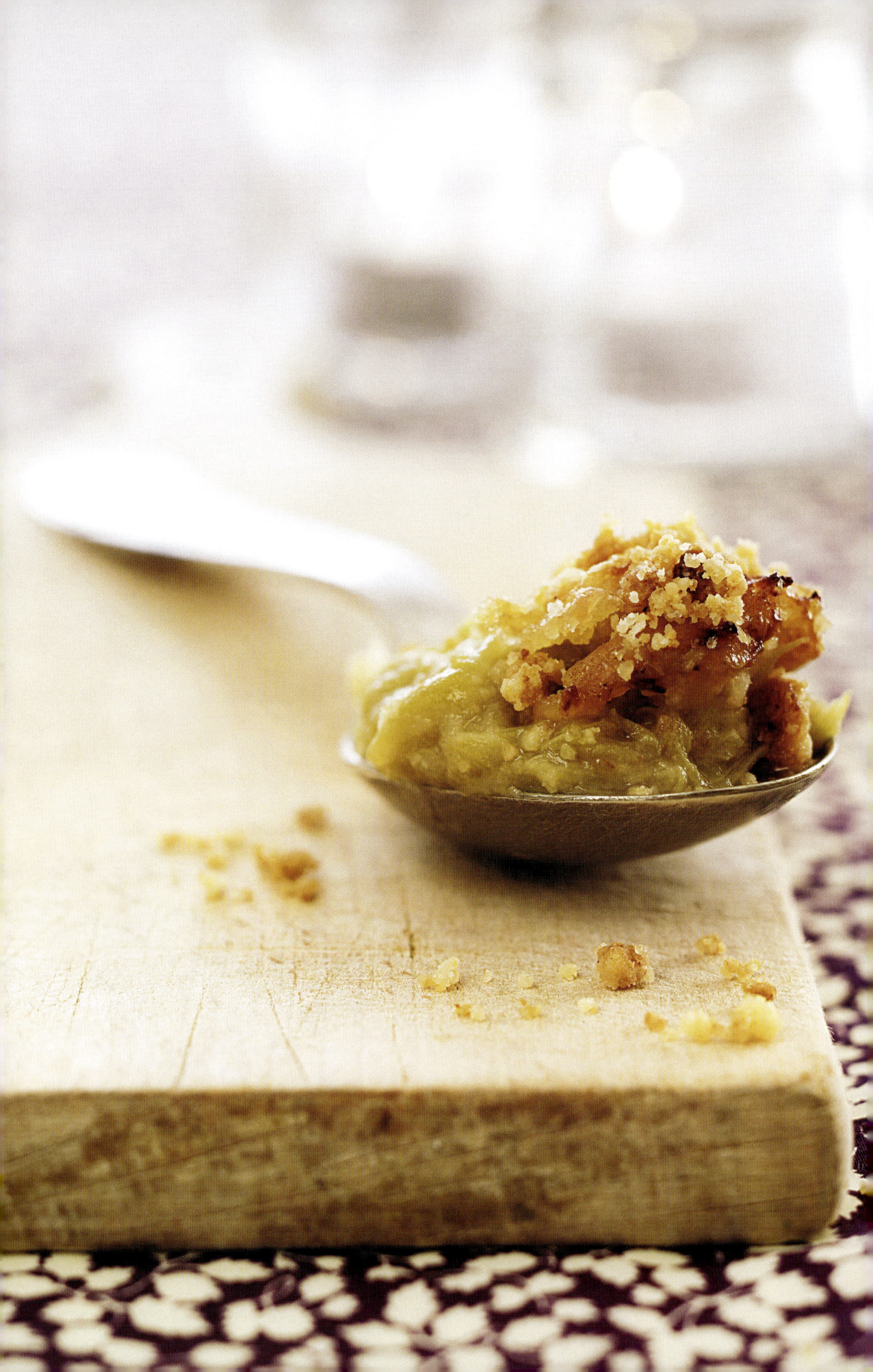

Crumble à la rhubarbe

PRÉPARATION 25 MIN I **CUISSON** 30 MIN I **COÛT** ★ I **DIFFICULTÉ** ★★

→ CE DÉLICIEUX CRUMBLE SE MARIE À MERVEILLE AVEC UNE GROSSE NOISETTE DE CRÈME FRAÎCHE ÉPAISSE OU UNE TRADITIONNELLE BOULE DE GLACE À LA VANILLE.

1 Préchauffez le four à 210 °C (th. 7). Épluchez la rhubarbe puis coupez-la en petits tronçons. Dans une casserole à feu doux, mettez-la avec les 100 g de sucre roux et le sucre vanillé dans un fond d'eau (1 verre environ). Laissez cuire à couvert 20 min en remuant régulièrement.

2 Pendant ce temps, pour la pâte à crumble, coupez le beurre en morceaux et faites-le ramollir au micro-ondes. Dans un saladier, mélangez la farine avec la poudre de noisettes et le sucre roux. Puis ajoutez le beurre ramolli.

3 Malaxez la préparation avec les mains puis émiettez-la du bout des doigts pour lui donner une consistance sableuse (comme une grosse semoule).

4 Quand la compote de rhubarbe est cuite, versez-la dans le fond d'un moule. Ajoutez la pâte sableuse sur les fruits en une couche régulière. Faites cuire au four 20 min environ. Sortez le crumble du four et parsemez-le d'amandes effilées. Faites à nouveau cuire au four 10 min, jusqu'à ce que la pâte et les amandes soient bien dorées. Servez tiède.

Les ingrédients pour 6 personnes

Pour les fruits
1 kg de rhubarbe
100 g de sucre roux
1 sachet de sucre vanillé

Pour la pâte
150 g de beurre
150 g de farine
60 g de poudre de noisettes
150 g de sucre roux
3 cuil. à soupe d'amandes effilées (facultatif)

Astuce_ Sachez que vous pouvez utiliser de la rhubarbe surgelée pour cette recette. Un bon moyen d'échapper à la corvée de l'épluchage !

le tuyau de laurence

Si votre rhubarbe est un peu trop acide, remplacez-en la moitié par 500 g de fraises. Un mariage subtil !

le truc de stéphan

La rhubarbe est très riche en fibres et en pectine, deux substances proches et excellentes pour la santé et la digestion, consommez-la sans modération.

crumbles sucrés

Le vrai crumble aux pommes

PRÉPARATION 15 MIN | **CUISSON** 30 MIN | **COÛT** ★ | **DIFFICULTÉ** ★

→ VOICI L'INRATABLE RECETTE D'*APPLE CRUMBLE*, RAPPORTÉE PAR MAMAN DANS SES VALISES, LORS DE SON PREMIER SÉJOUR LINGUISTIQUE À PORTSMOUTH… TESTÉE ET APPROUVÉE DEPUIS 40 ANS !

1 Préchauffez le four à 210 °C (th. 7). Épluchez et coupez les pommes en petits morceaux. Répartissez-les dans le fond d'un moule. Puis arrosez-les de jus de citron et saupoudrez-les de sucre vanillé et de cannelle.

2 Pour la pâte à crumble, coupez le beurre en morceaux et faites-le ramollir au micro-ondes. Dans un saladier, mélangez bien la farine avec le sucre roux. Puis ajoutez le beurre ramolli.

3 Malaxez la préparation avec les mains puis émiettez-la du bout des doigts pour lui donner une consistance sableuse (comme une grosse semoule). Ajoutez la pâte sur les fruits en une couche régulière. Faites cuire au four 30 min environ. Servez tiède.

Les ingrédients pour 6 personnes

Pour les fruits
6 belles pommes
le jus de 1/2 citron
1 sachet de sucre vanillé
3 pincées de cannelle en poudre

Pour la pâte
125 g de beurre
200 g de farine
150 g de sucre roux

Astuce_ Vous pouvez augmenter les doses de cannelle (5 pincées) sur les pommes pour un crumble plus épicé.

Pour varier_ Sachez que vous pouvez troquer les 200 g de farine par 50 g de poudre d'amandes et 150 g de farine.

la botte secrète d'aude et leslie

Pour un crumble haut en saveurs, à l'aide d'un pinceau alimentaire, badigeonnez vos pommes avec 100 g de confiture de framboises avant d'ajouter la pâte sableuse et de mettre au four.

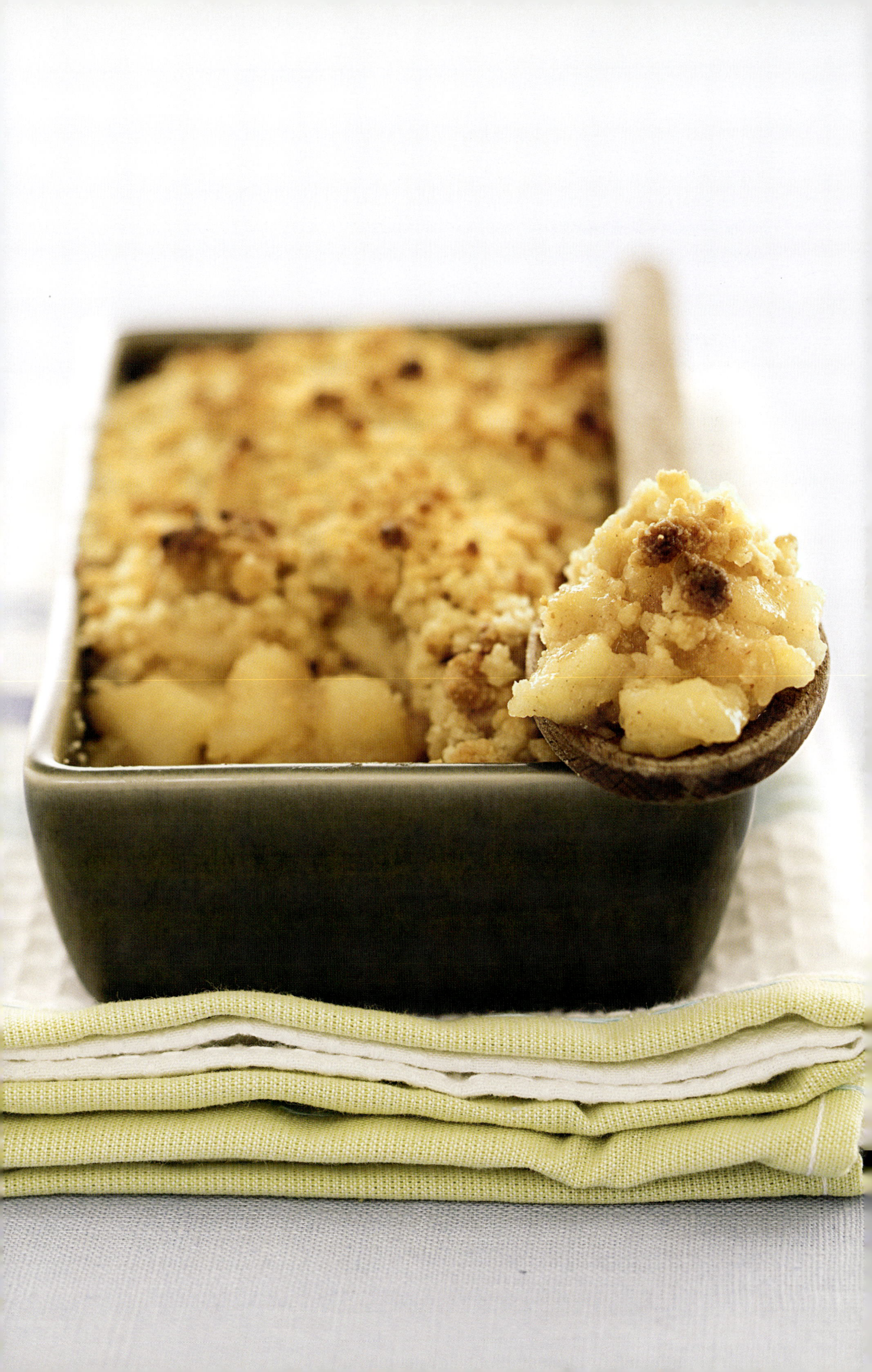

Mini-crumbles mangues, fruits de la Passion et coco

PRÉPARATION 15 MIN | **CUISSON** 30 MIN | **COÛT** ★★ | **DIFFICULTÉ** ★ |
MATÉRIEL SPÉCIFIQUE 4 RAMEQUINS

1 Préchauffez le four à 210 °C (th. 7). Épluchez les mangues et coupez leur chair en petits dés. Répartissez-les dans le fond des 4 ramequins. Coupez les fruits de la Passion en deux et ôtez-en les graines et le jus à l'aide d'une petite cuillère. Puis ajoutez-les sur les mangues. Saupoudrez le tout de gingembre en poudre.

2 Pour la pâte à crumble, coupez le beurre en morceaux et faites-le ramollir au micro-ondes. Dans un saladier, mélangez bien la farine avec le sucre roux et la poudre d'amandes. Puis ajoutez le beurre ramolli.

3 Malaxez la préparation avec les mains puis émiettez-la du bout des doigts pour lui donner une consistance sableuse (comme une grosse semoule). Ajoutez la pâte sur les fruits en une couche régulière. Faites cuire au four 30 min environ.

4 Servez ces mini-crumbles chauds accompagnés d'une boule de glace à la noix de coco posée au centre de chaque ramequin. Dégustez immédiatement.

Les ingrédients pour 4 personnes

Pour les fruits
3 mangues mûres
2 fruits de la Passion
2 pincées de gingembre en poudre
4 boules de glace à la noix de coco

Pour la pâte
80 g de beurre
150 g de farine
80 g de sucre roux
2 cuil. à soupe de poudre d'amandes (facultatif)

Astuce_ Si vos mangues ne sont pas suffisamment mûres, coupez-les en lamelles puis faites-les cuire dans une poêle à feu doux avec une noisette de beurre et 2 cuil. à soupe de sucre jusqu'à ce qu'elles deviennent tendres (5 min environ).

le tuyau de laurence

Ajoutez les zestes fins de 1/2 citron vert. Cela dégage un arôme exotique très subtil.

le truc de stéphan

La mangue et le fruit de la Passion sont truffés de vitamines et donc bons pour la santé. N'hésitez pas à déguster ce crumble d'Aude et Leslie en toute occasion.

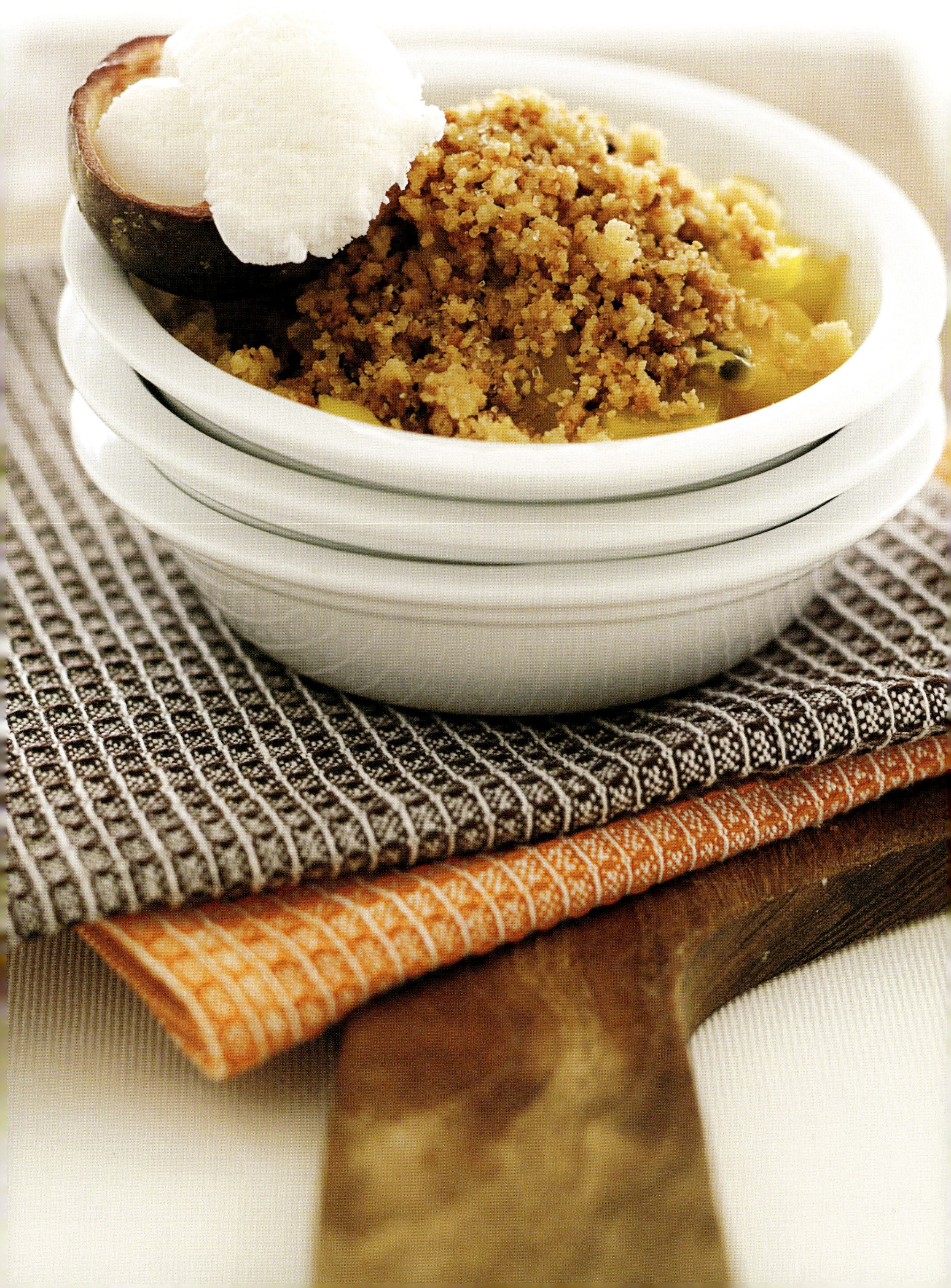

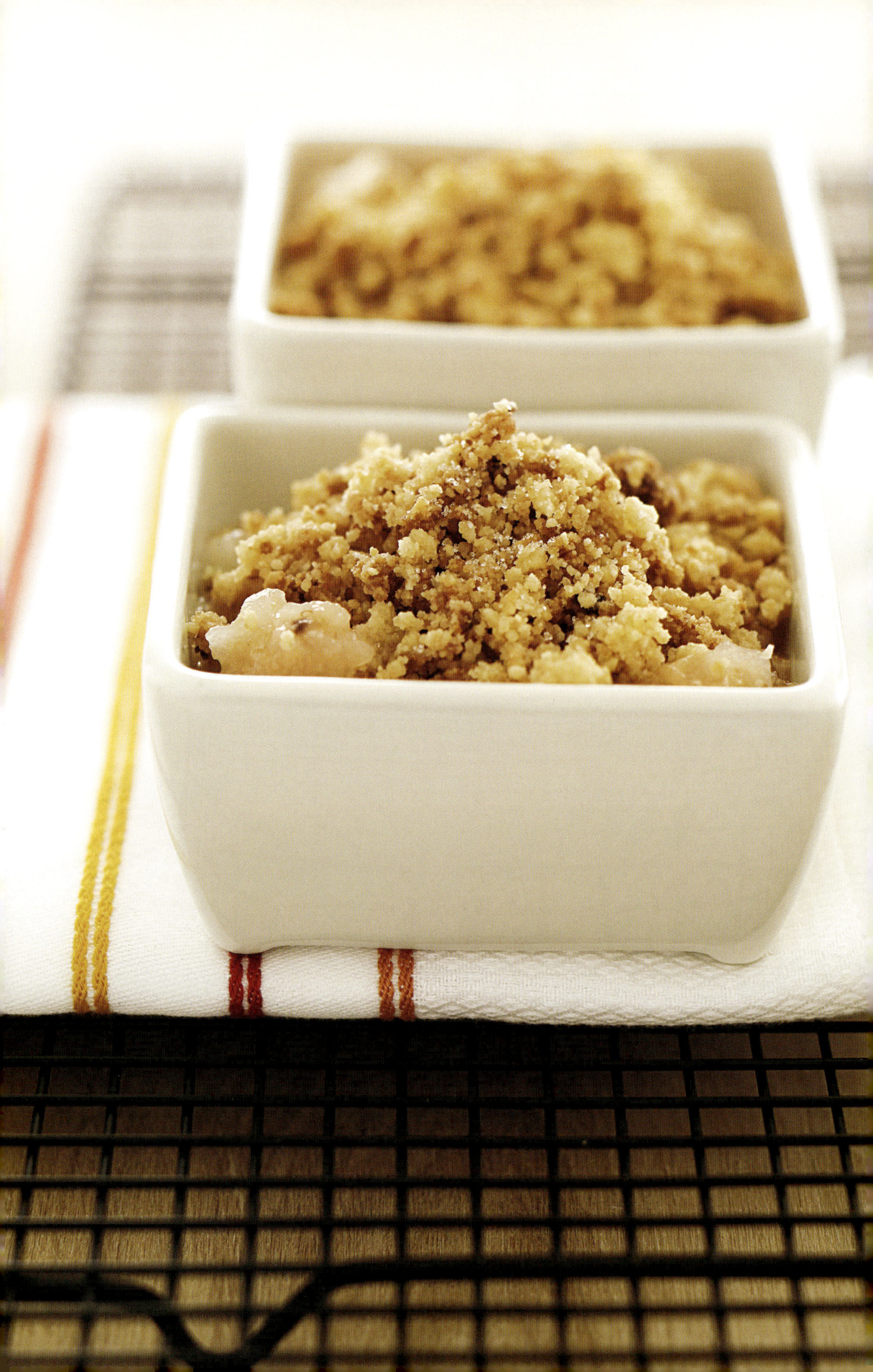

Crumble figues et cannelle

PRÉPARATION 25 MIN I **CUISSON** 25 MIN I **COÛT** ★★ I **DIFFICULTÉ** ★★

1 Préchauffez le four à 200 °C (th. 6-7). Épluchez les figues et récupérez la chair. Épluchez et coupez les poires en morceaux. Dans une casserole, faites cuire les poires dans 1/2 verre d'eau 5 à 7 min environ à feu moyen.

2 Ajoutez la chair des figues et laissez cuire 5 à 7 min à nouveau jusqu'à l'obtention d'une compote. Mélangez régulièrement pour éviter qu'elle n'accroche. Rajoutez un peu d'eau si c'est le cas.

3 Pendant ce temps, pour la pâte à crumble, coupez le beurre en morceaux et faites-le ramollir au micro-ondes. Dans un saladier, mélangez bien la farine avec le sucre roux et la cannelle. Puis ajoutez le beurre ramolli.

4 Quand la compote de figues aux poires est prête, égouttez-la légèrement et ajoutez le sucre glace. Mélangez bien et répartissez-la dans le fond d'un moule.

5 Malaxez la préparation avec les mains puis émiettez-la du bout des doigts pour lui donner une consistance sableuse (comme une grosse semoule). Ajoutez la pâte sur les fruits en une couche régulière. Faites cuire au four 20 à 25 min environ. Servez tiède ou froid.

Les ingrédients pour 6 personnes

Pour les fruits
10 figues fraîches
2 poires
4 cuil. à soupe de sucre glace

Pour la pâte
80 g de beurre
150 g de farine
80 g de sucre roux
1 cuil. à café de cannelle en poudre

le verre de vin qui va bien
Soulignez les saveurs de ce crumble avec un petit verre de sauternes juste frais.

crumbles sucrés

Crumble pommes, coings et abricots secs

PRÉPARATION 25 MIN | **CUISSON** 30 MIN | **COÛT** ★★ | **DIFFICULTÉ** ★

1 Préchauffez le four à 210 °C (th. 7). Coupez les abricots secs en tout petits dés et réservez. Épluchez et coupez les pommes et les coings en petits morceaux. Dans une poêle, faites chauffer les 40 g de beurre. Ajoutez les fruits et les 40 g de sucre. Laissez cuire 15 min environ en remuant régulièrement.

2 Pendant ce temps, pour la pâte à crumble, coupez le beurre salé et le beurre doux en morceaux et faites-les ramollir au micro-ondes. Dans un saladier, mélangez bien la farine avec la poudre de noisettes et les 80 g sucre roux. Puis ajoutez les morceaux de beurre ramollis. Malaxez la préparation avec les mains puis émiettez-la du bout des doigts pour lui donner une consistance sableuse (comme une grosse semoule).

3 À la fin de la cuisson des pommes et des coings, hors du feu, ajoutez les dés d'abricots secs et mélangez bien. Répartissez le tout dans le fond d'un moule. Ajoutez la pâte sur les fruits en une couche régulière. Faites cuire au four 30 min environ. Servez tiède.

Les ingrédients pour 6 personnes

Pour les fruits
12 abricots secs
400 g de pommes
600 g de coings
40 g de beurre doux
40 g de sucre en poudre

Pour la pâte
40 g de beurre salé
50 g de beurre doux
100 g de farine
50 g de poudre de noisettes
80 g de sucre roux

Astuce_ 10 min avant la fin de la cuisson, vous pouvez parsemer votre crumble d'amandes effilées.

le tuyau de laurence

Présentez vos crumbles dans des verres transparents, effet gourmand garanti.

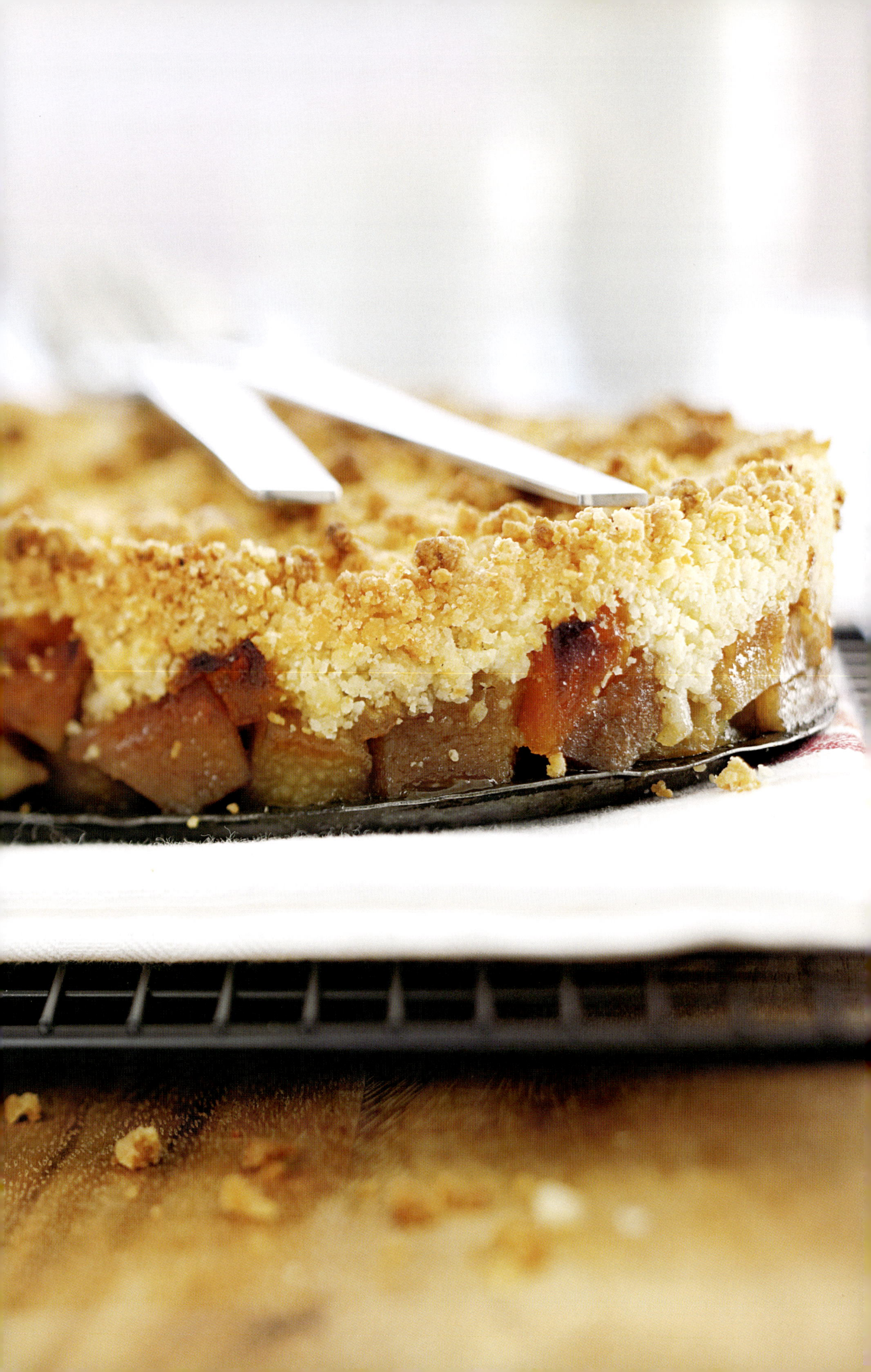

Crumble aux quetsches, noisettes et pain d'épice

PRÉPARATION 15 MIN | **CUISSON** 30 MIN | **COÛT** ★★ | **DIFFICULTÉ** ★ |
MATÉRIEL SPÉCIFIQUE 6 RAMEQUINS

1. Préchauffez le four à 210 °C (th. 7). Concassez les noisettes dans un mortier (ou à l'aide d'un manche de couteau). Lavez les quetsches. Coupez-les en deux puis dénoyautez-les. Répartissez-les dans le fond des 6 ramequins. Saupoudrez le tout de noisettes concassées, de sucre vanillé et de cannelle.

2. Pour la pâte à crumble, coupez le beurre en morceaux et faites-le ramollir au micro-ondes. Dans un saladier, mélangez bien la farine avec la poudre de noisettes et le sucre roux. Puis ajoutez le beurre ramolli.

3. Malaxez la préparation avec les mains puis émiettez-la du bout des doigts pour lui donner une consistance sableuse (comme une grosse semoule). Ajoutez la pâte sur les quetsches en une couche régulière. Faites cuire au four 30 min environ. Servez immédiatement avec une boule de glace au pain d'épice posée au centre de chaque ramequin.

Les ingrédients pour 6 personnes

Pour les fruits
1 poignée de noisettes non salées
800 g de quetsches
1 sachet de sucre vanillé
4 pincées de cannelle en poudre
6 boules de glace au pain d'épice

Pour la pâte
120 g de beurre
150 g de farine
60 g de poudre de noisettes
120 g de sucre roux

Astuce_ Si vous ne trouvez pas de glace au pain d'épice, sachez que ce crumble se marie à merveille avec de la glace à la noisette, au nougat ou évidemment avec l'incontournable boule de vanille.

Pour varier_ **Crumble pommes-quetsches.** Il suffit de réduire la quantité de quetsches à 600 g et d'ajouter 2 pommes ; coupez-les en petits morceaux pour qu'elles soient cuites en même temps que les quetsches.

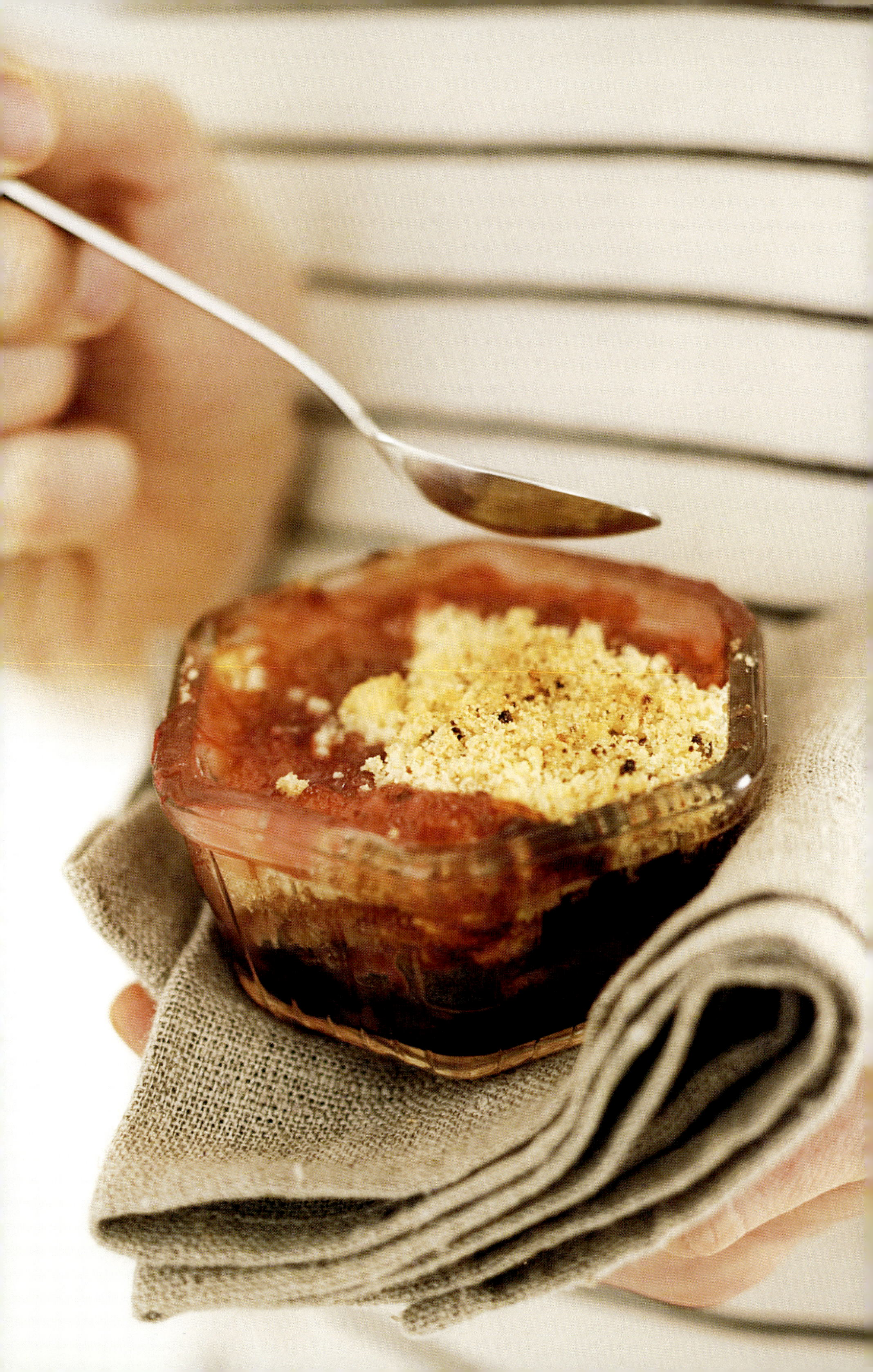

Crumble aux mûres simplissime

PRÉPARATION 15 MIN | **CUISSON** 25 MIN | **COÛT** ★★ | **DIFFICULTÉ** ★

→ N'HÉSITEZ PAS À PRÉPARER CE DÉLICIEUX CRUMBLE À LA DERNIÈRE MINUTE, LORS DE VOS DÎNERS À L'IMPROVISTE. CETTE RECETTE RÉUSSIT À TOUS LES COUPS… SACHEZ AUSSI QUE VOUS POUVEZ UTILISER DES MÛRES SURGELÉES POUR RÉALISER CE DESSERT EN TOUTE SAISON.

1. Préchauffez le four à 200 °C (th. 6-7). Rincez rapidement les mûres à l'eau claire puis séchez-les en les posant sur du papier absorbant. Répartissez-les dans le fond d'un moule. Tartinez le dessus des fruits de confiture de framboises avec le dos d'une cuillère.

2. Pour la pâte à crumble, coupez le beurre en morceaux et faites-le ramollir au micro-ondes. Dans un saladier, mélangez bien la farine avec la poudre d'amandes et le sucre roux. Puis ajoutez le beurre ramolli.

3. Malaxez la préparation avec les mains puis émiettez-la du bout des doigts pour lui donner une consistance sableuse (comme une grosse semoule). Ajoutez la pâte sur les fruits nappés de confiture en une couche régulière. Faites cuire au four 25 min environ, jusqu'à ce que le crumble soit bien doré. Servez tiède.

Les ingrédients pour 6 personnes

Pour les fruits
800 g de mûres
4 cuil. à soupe de confiture de framboises

Pour la pâte
120 g de beurre
90 g de farine
90 g de poudre d'amandes
100 g de sucre roux

Astuce_ Si vos mûres sont très acides, mélangez-les avec un sachet de sucre vanillé avant d'ajouter la confiture de framboises et rajoutez 2 pommes ou 2 poires coupées en petits morceaux en même temps que les mûres.

la botte secrète d'aude et leslie

Pour varier les saveurs, pensez à réaliser un crumble mi-mûres, mi-groseilles (400 g de mûres, 400 g de groseilles). Troquez alors la confiture de framboises contre de la confiture de fraises. Testée et approuvée tout l'été, cette recette est à se damner…

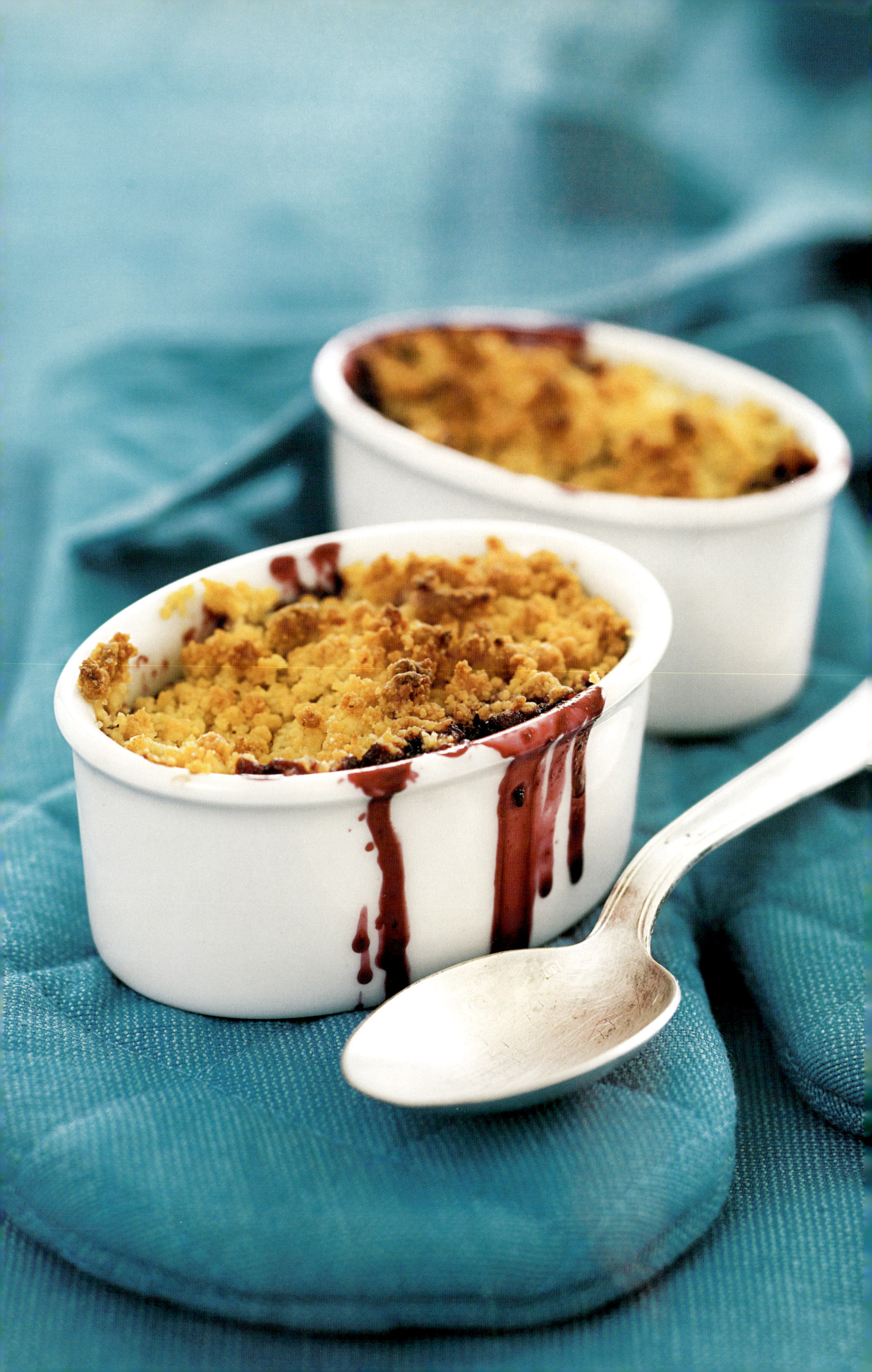

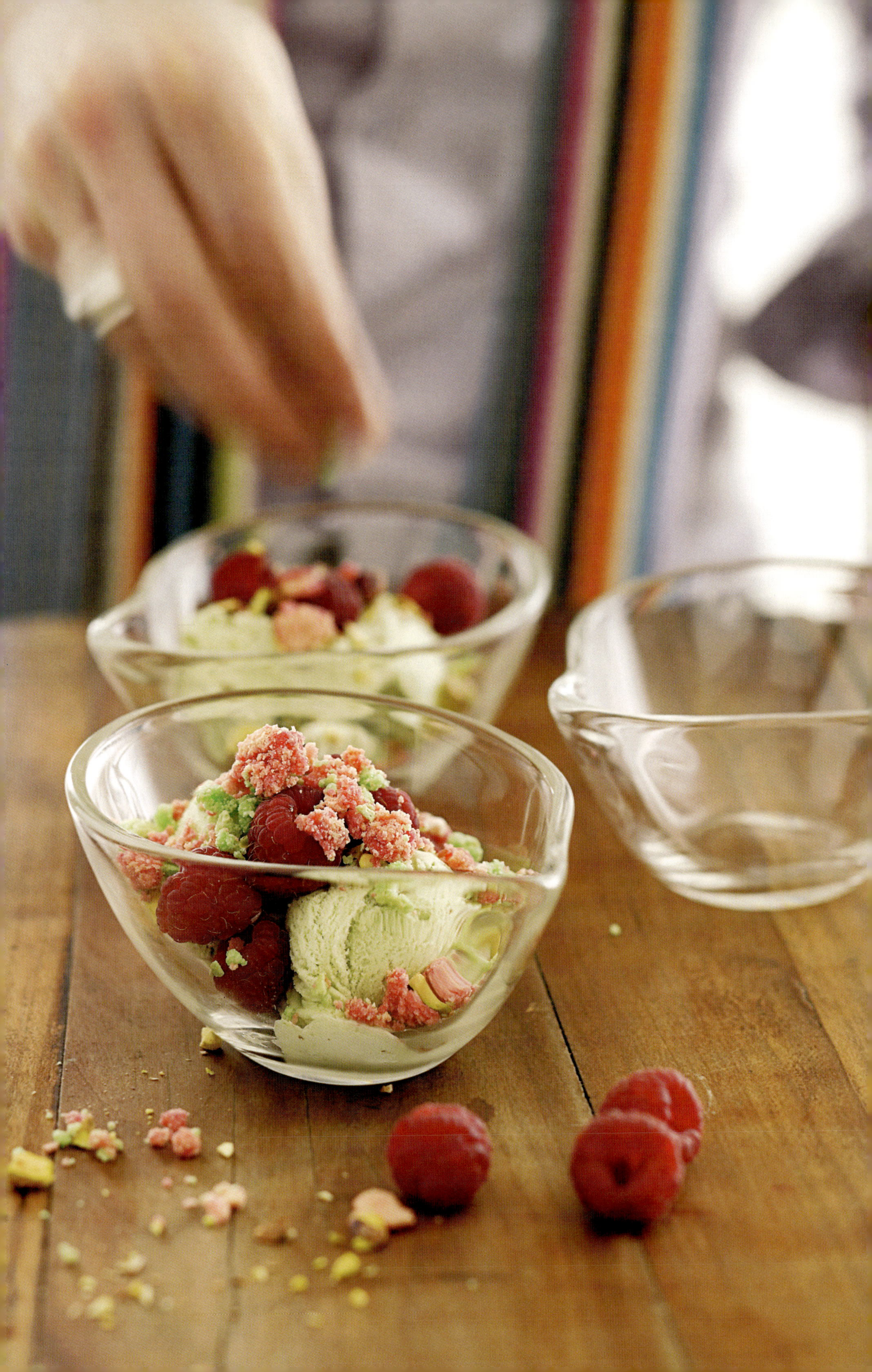

Crumble express glacé

PRÉPARATION 15 MIN | **COÛT** ★★ | **DIFFICULTÉ** ★

→ « PETITS EFFORTS POUR GRANDS EFFETS » POURRAIT ÊTRE LA DEVISE DE CETTE RECETTE EXPRESS. VOUS N'AUREZ EN EFFET PAS BESOIN DE PRÉPARER LA PÂTE À CRUMBLE QUI EST ICI REMPLACÉE PAR DES MACARONS ÉMIETTÉS. UN BONHEUR POUR LES PAPILLES !

1 Passez les framboises rapidement sous l'eau claire et séchez-les délicatement en les posant sur du papier absorbant. Concassez les pistaches dans un mortier (ou à l'aide d'un manche de couteau). Émiettez grossièrement les macarons.

2 Répartissez les 8 boules de glace à la pistache dans 4 grands verres transparents. Ajoutez les framboises, puis les pistaches concassées. Recouvrez le tout de macarons émiettés. Servez immédiatement.

Les ingrédients pour 4 personnes

Pour les fruits
250 g de framboises
4 cuil. à café de pistaches décortiquées et non salées
8 boules de glace à la pistache

Pour la pâte
8 mini-macarons à la framboise
8 mini-macarons à la pistache

Pour varier_ Laissez libre cours à vos envies pour les parfums... Toutes les combinaisons sont possibles, ou presque. En voici deux qui fonctionnent à merveille. **Crumble express vanille-fraise**. Il suffit de remplacer les framboises par des fraises et la glace à la pistache par de la glace à la vanille. Pour les macarons, choisissez-les parfumés à la vanille et à la framboise. **Crumble express poires-chocolat**. Il suffit de remplacer les framboises par des poires coupées en morceaux et arrosées de jus de citron, et la glace à la pistache par de la glace au chocolat. Pour les macarons, choisissez-les au chocolat et au praliné.

le tuyau de laurence

À essayer avec des spéculoos émiettés, fameux !

Crumble ananas et coco

PRÉPARATION 20 MIN | **CUISSON** 35 MIN | **COÛT** ★★ | **DIFFICULTÉ** ★

1 Préchauffez le four à 200 °C (th. 6-7). Dans un bol, versez le rhum et ajoutez les raisins secs. Laissez-les tremper quelques minutes pour leur donner du moelleux et du goût.

2 Pendant ce temps, tranchez les deux extrémités de l'ananas puis coupez-le en 4 dans le sens de la longueur pour former 4 quartiers. Éliminez la partie dure centrale (la pointe en triangle de chaque quartier) puis ôtez l'écorce à l'aide d'un couteau. Coupez ensuite la pulpe en petits morceaux et répartissez-la dans le fond d'un moule. Égouttez les raisins secs et ajoutez-les sur l'ananas. Saupoudrez le tout des 2 cuil. à soupe de noix de coco râpée.

3 Pour la pâte à crumble, coupez le beurre en morceaux et faites-le ramollir au micro-ondes. Dans un saladier, mélangez bien la farine avec les 60 g de noix de coco râpée et le sucre roux. Puis ajoutez le beurre ramolli.

4 Malaxez la préparation avec les mains puis émiettez-la du bout des doigts pour lui donner une consistance sableuse (comme une grosse semoule). Ajoutez la pâte sur les fruits en une couche régulière. Faites cuire au four 35 min environ, jusqu'à ce que le crumble soit bien doré. Servez tiède ou froid.

Les ingrédients pour 6 personnes

Pour les fruits
- 3 cuil. à soupe de rhum (facultatif)
- 1 poignée de raisins secs
- 1 bel ananas
- 2 cuil. à soupe de noix de coco râpée

Pour la pâte
- 100 g de beurre
- 120 g de farine
- 60 g de noix de coco râpée
- 80 g de sucre roux

Astuces_ • Si votre crumble dore trop vite lors de la cuisson, n'hésitez pas à le couvrir d'une feuille de papier d'aluminium et à baisser la température du four à 180 °C (th. 6).
• Si vous n'avez pas de rhum, faites tremper vos raisins secs dans un bol d'eau chaude.

le tuyau de laurence

Vous pouvez également faire tremper vos raisins secs dans du Malibu.

crumbles sucrés

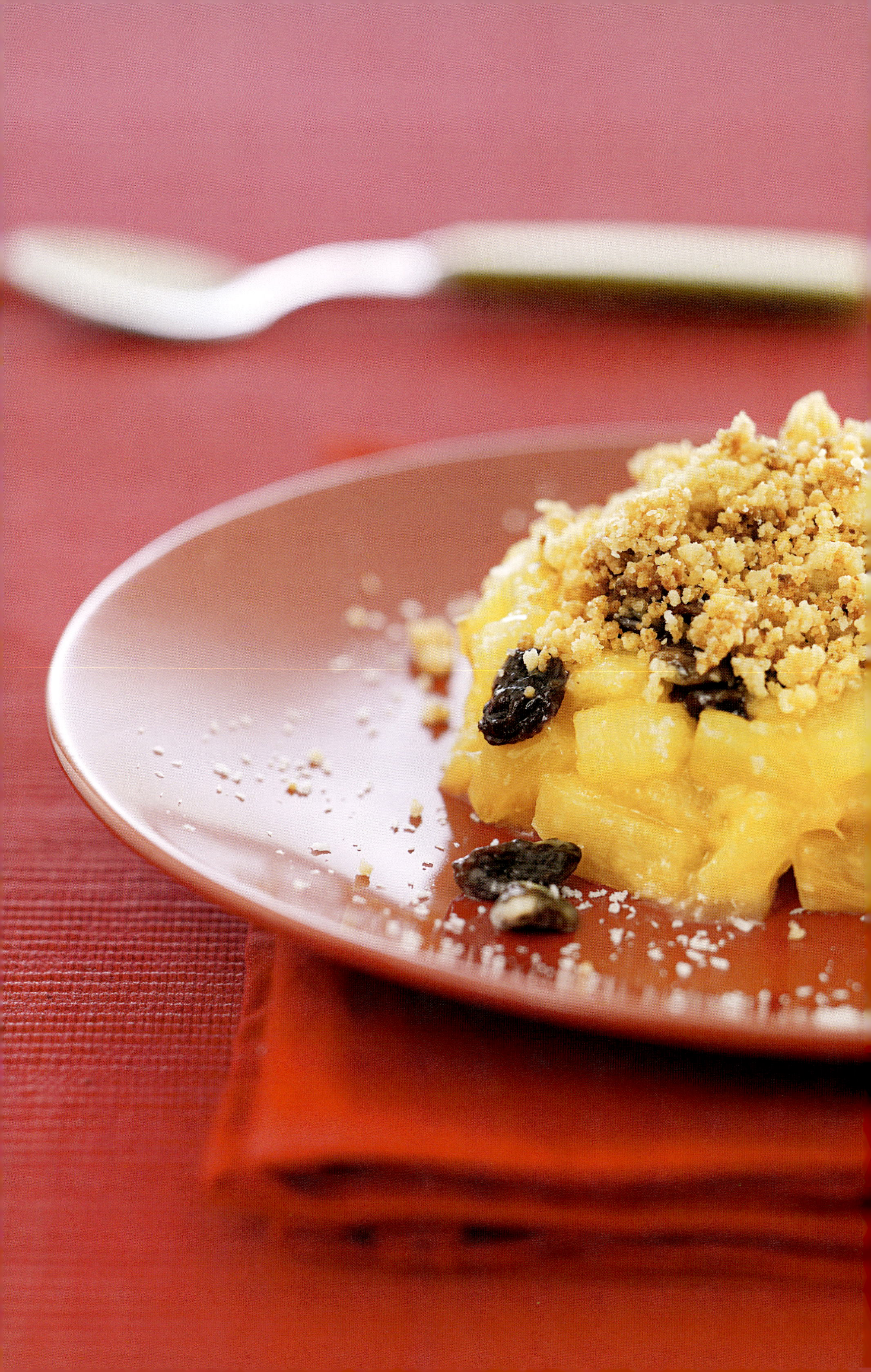

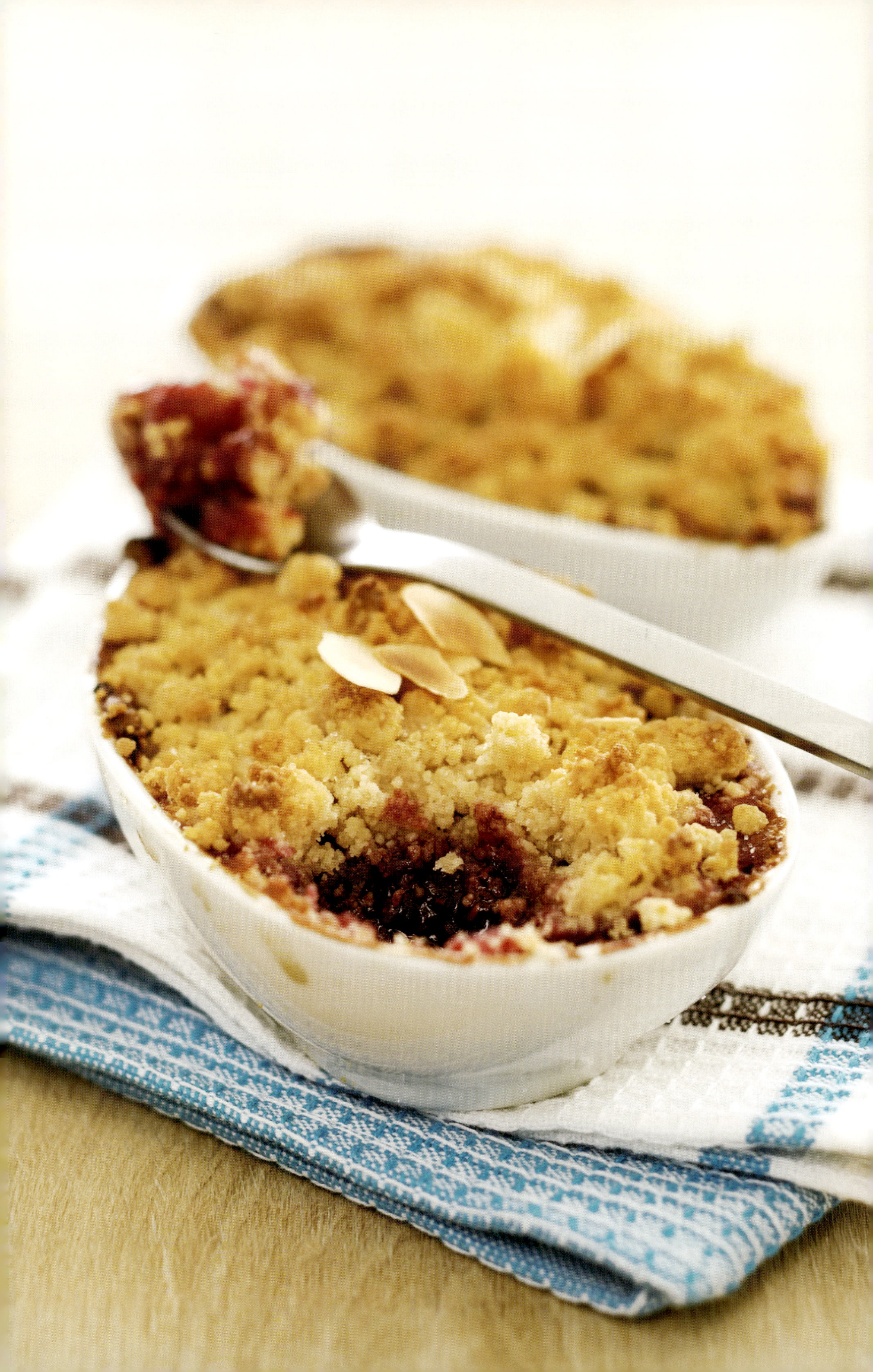

Crumble poires, framboises et amandes

PRÉPARATION 20 MIN I CUISSON 30 MIN I COÛT ★ I DIFFICULTÉ ★

1. Préchauffez le four à 200 °C (th. 6-7). Épluchez et coupez les poires en petits morceaux. Rincez les framboises à l'eau claire et séchez-les délicatement en les posant sur du papier absorbant.

2. Beurrez un moule puis saupoudrez-le avec les 2 cuil. à soupe de sucre en poudre. Répartissez les fruits dans le fond du moule et saupoudrez-les de sucre vanillé. Recouvrez le tout d'amandes effilées.

3. Pour la pâte à crumble, coupez le beurre en morceaux et faites-le ramollir au micro-ondes. Dans un saladier, mélangez bien la farine avec la poudre d'amandes et le sucre roux. Puis ajoutez le beurre ramolli.

4. Malaxez la préparation avec les mains puis émiettez-la du bout des doigts pour lui donner une consistance sableuse (comme une grosse semoule). Ajoutez la pâte sur les amandes effilées en une couche régulière. Faites cuire au four 25 à 30 min environ, jusqu'à ce que le crumble soit bien doré. Servez immédiatement.

Les ingrédients pour 6 personnes

Pour les fruits
4 poires mûres
250 g de framboises
1 noisette de beurre pour le moule
2 cuil. à soupe de sucre en poudre
1 sachet de sucre vanillé
100 g d'amandes effilées

Pour la pâte
125 g de beurre
90 g de farine
90 g de poudre d'amandes
100 g de sucre roux

Astuces_ • Pour varier les plaisirs, vous pouvez remplacer les poires par des pommes.
• Gardez quelques amandes effilées pour la décoration.

la botte secrète d'aude et leslie

Pour préparer ce crumble en toute saison, vous pouvez remplacer les framboises par 4 cuil. à soupe de gelée de framboises. Dans ce cas-là, prévoyez 5 à 6 poires.

le truc de stéphan

Faites varier la saveur de ce crumble en remplaçant la poudre d'amandes par la même quantité de cerneaux de noix finement hachés.

crumbles sucrés

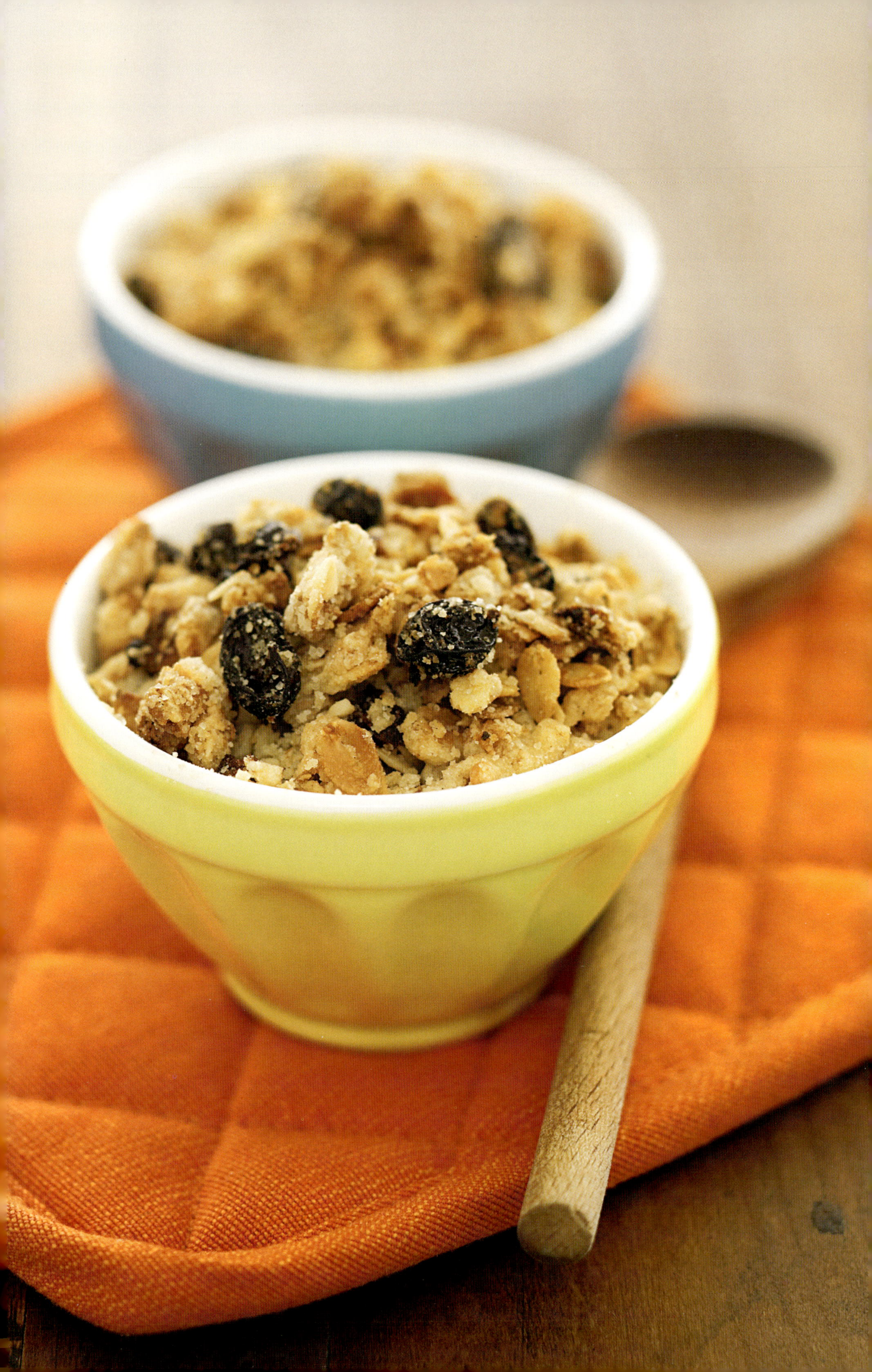

Crumble au muesli

PRÉPARATION 20 MIN | **CUISSON** 30 MIN | **COÛT** ★ | **DIFFICULTÉ** ★

→ UN CRUMBLE SURPRENANT QUI SE DÉGUSTERA SANS MODÉRATION À L'HEURE DU GOÛTER COMME AU PETIT DÉJEUNER. EN PLUS D'ÊTRE DÉLICIEUX, IL EST ÉQUILIBRÉ, IDÉAL POUR LES ENFANTS QUI BOUDENT LES TARTINES ET LES BOLS DE CÉRÉALES LE MATIN.

1 Préchauffez le four à 180 °C (th. 6). Épluchez et coupez les pommes et les poires en petits morceaux. Lavez les grains de raisin, coupez-les en deux et ôtez-en les pépins. Répartissez les fruits dans le fond d'un moule.

2 Concassez les noisettes dans un mortier (ou à l'aide d'un manche de couteau). Ajoutez-les sur les fruits. Puis saupoudrez le tout de cannelle.

3 Pour la pâte à crumble, coupez le beurre en morceaux et faites-le ramollir au micro-ondes. Dans un saladier, mélangez bien la farine avec le muesli et le sucre roux. Puis ajoutez le beurre ramolli.

4 Malaxez la préparation avec les mains puis émiettez-la du bout des doigts. Ajoutez-la sur les fruits en une couche régulière. Faites cuire au four 30 min environ, jusqu'à ce que le crumble soit bien doré. Servez tiède.

Les ingrédients pour 6 personnes

Pour les fruits
2 pommes
2 poires
15 grains de raisin muscat
1 poignée de noisettes non salées
3 pincées de cannelle en poudre

Pour la pâte
80 g de beurre
80 g de farine
80 g de muesli
80 g de sucre roux

Astuce_ Si la pâte au muesli dore trop rapidement en cours de cuisson, abaissez la température du four à 160 °C (th. 5-6) et couvrez votre crumble d'une feuille de papier d'aluminium.

la botte secrète d'aude et leslie

Pour varier les saveurs, pensez à utiliser des muesli nature ou aux fruits. Et pour un petit déjeuner gourmand, accompagnez-le d'un fjord ou d'un yaourt nature.

crumbles sucrés

crumbles sucrés

recette**pour**épater…

Crumble de fruits d'été et macarons aux amandes

PRÉPARATION 25 MIN | **CUISSON** 25 MIN | **COÛT** ★★ | **DIFFICULTÉ** ★★

→ UNE RECETTE ESTIVALE QUI ÉPATE À TOUS LES COUPS. LA SUBTILE ALLIANCE ENTRE LES PÊCHES, LES ABRICOTS ET LES MACARONS AUX AMANDES S'ACCOMPAGNE PARFAITEMENT D'UNE PETITE COUPE DE CHAMPAGNE.

1 Préchauffez le four à 180 °C (th. 6). Épluchez et coupez les pêches jaunes et blanches en petits morceaux. Arrosez-les de jus de citron. Lavez et coupez les abricots en petits morceaux. Répartissez les fruits dans le fond d'un moule et saupoudrez-les de sucre vanillé.

2 Pour la pâte à crumble, émiettez les macarons dans un mortier. Si vous n'avez pas de mortier, enveloppez-les d'un torchon et écrasez-les à l'aide d'un rouleau à pâtisserie ou d'un petit marteau. Coupez le beurre en morceaux et faites-le fondre au micro-ondes. Dans un saladier, à l'aide d'une spatule, mélangez les macarons en miettes avec le beurre fondu.

3 Émiettez la pâte au-dessus des fruits en une couche régulière. Faites cuire au four 25 min environ. Servez tiède ou froid.

Les ingrédients pour 4 à 6 personnes

Pour les fruits
3 pêches jaunes mûres
4 pêches blanches mûres
le jus de 1/2 citron
4 abricots mûrs
1 sachet de sucre vanillé

Pour la pâte
150 g de macarons italiens aux amandes (Amaretti)
80 g de beurre

Astuces_ • Pour réaliser cette recette en toute saison, vous pouvez utiliser des pêches et des abricots en conserve ou surgelés. • Vous pouvez trouver des macarons aux amandes (Amaretti) chez les traiteurs italiens ou dans les rayons spécialisés des supermarchés. • Pour rendre ce crumble encore plus appétissant, ajoutez quelques amandes effilées sur le dessus.

le truc de stéphan

Vous pouvez aussi réaliser cette succulente recette avec des brugnons, que vous trouverez plus longtemps sur les étals que les pêches. Choisissez-les bien mûrs.

crumbles sucrés

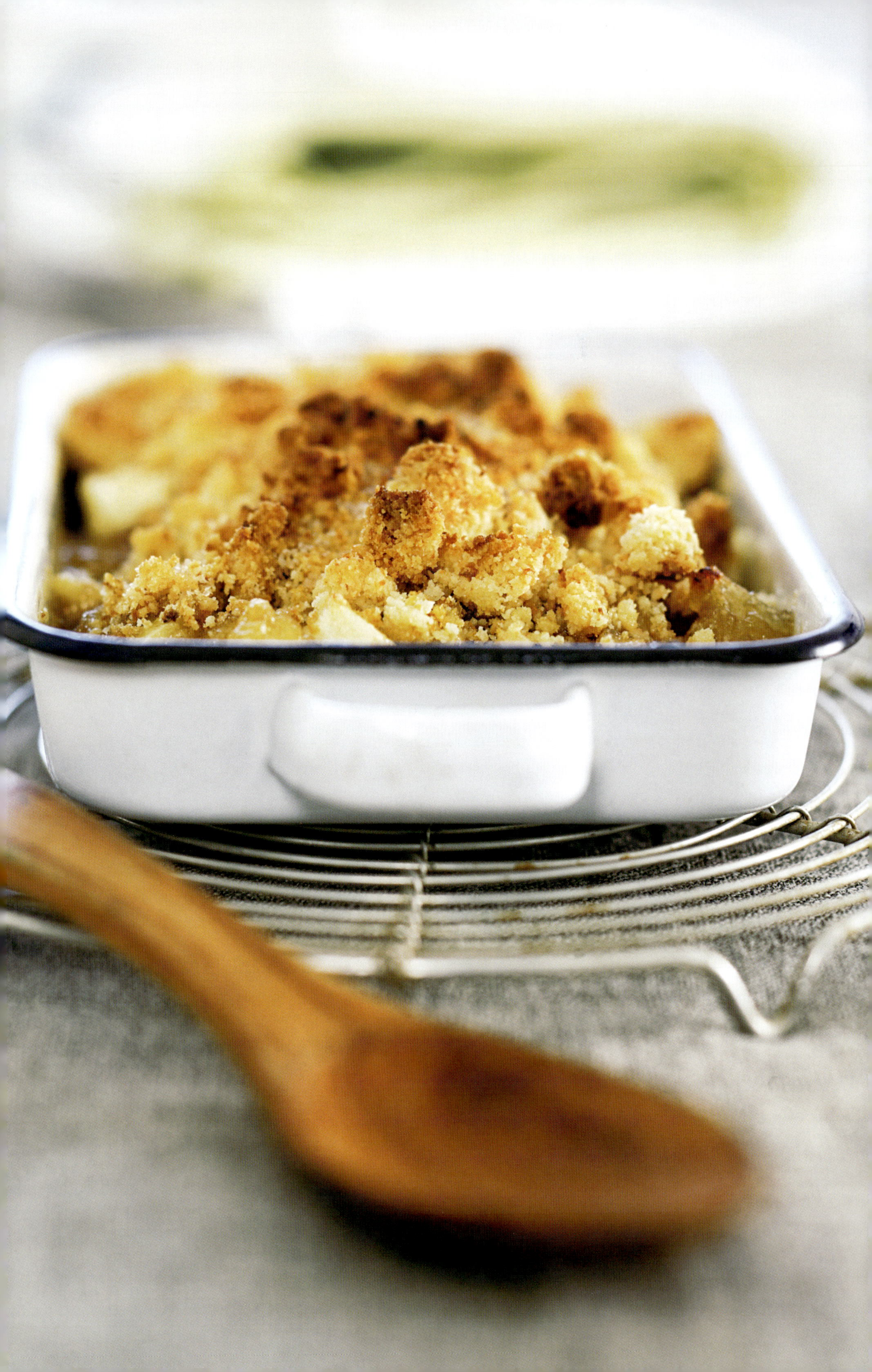

Crumble aux pommes et bananes flambées

PRÉPARATION 20 MIN | CUISSON 20 MIN | COÛT ★★ | DIFFICULTÉ ★★

1 Préchauffez le four à 180 °C (th. 6). Pelez les bananes et coupez-les en rondelles. Épluchez les pommes et coupez-les en petits morceaux. Dans une poêle, faites fondre les 30 g de beurre puis ajoutez les fruits. Faites-les revenir 3 à 4 min en les retournant régulièrement.

2 Ajoutez le sucre en poudre dans la poêle et laissez les fruits caraméliser légèrement. Flambez le tout au Cointreau : versez le Cointreau dans la poêle, craquez une allumette et approchez-la des fruits. Beurrez un moule. Répartissez les fruits flambés dans le fond du moule.

3 Pour la pâte à crumble, coupez le beurre en morceaux et faites-le ramollir au micro-ondes. Dans un saladier, mélangez la farine avec le sucre roux. Ajoutez le beurre ramolli.

4 Malaxez la préparation avec les mains puis émiettez-la du bout des doigts pour lui donner une consistance sableuse (comme une grosse semoule). Ajoutez la pâte sur les fruits flambés en une couche régulière. Faites cuire au four 15 min environ.
En fin de cuisson, faites dorer votre crumble 3 min sous le gril du four. Servez tiède ou froid.

Les ingrédients pour 4 personnes

Pour les fruits
3 bananes
2 pommes granny smith
30 g de beurre
30 g de sucre en poudre
2 cuil. à soupe de Cointreau
1 noisette de beurre pour le moule

Pour la pâte
100 g de beurre
100 g de farine
100 g de sucre roux

Astuce_ Soyez vigilant quand vous flambez vos fruits : ne le faites jamais sous une hotte en marche. L'appel d'air risquerait de provoquer une montée des flammes.

la botte secrète d'aude et leslie

Vous pouvez troquer le Cointreau contre d'autres alcools : calvados, rhum ou Grand Marnier…

crumbles sucrés

Crumble praliné aux abricots

PRÉPARATION 15 MIN **I CUISSON** 40 MIN **I COÛT** ★★ **I DIFFICULTÉ** ★

1 Préchauffez le four à 180 °C (th. 6). Lavez les abricots. Coupez-les en deux et dénoyautez-les. Dans un saladier, mélangez les demi-abricots avec le sucre en poudre et la liqueur d'abricot. Laissez reposer quelques instants.

2 Pendant ce temps, pour la pâte à crumble, coupez le beurre en morceaux et faites-le ramollir au micro-ondes. Dans un saladier, mélangez la farine avec le sucre roux. Ajoutez le beurre ramolli.

3 Malaxez la préparation avec les mains puis émiettez-la du bout des doigts pour lui donner une consistance sableuse (comme une grosse semoule).

4 Répartissez les demi-abricots dans le fond d'un moule. Saupoudrez-les de pralin avant d'ajouter la pâte sableuse en une couche régulière. Faites cuire au four 35 à 40 min environ, jusqu'à ce que la pâte soit bien dorée. Servez tiède.

Les ingrédients pour 6 personnes

Pour les fruits
1 kg d'abricots mûrs
2 cuil. à soupe de sucre en poudre
1 cuil. à soupe de liqueur d'abricot (facultatif)
3 cuil. à soupe de pralin

Pour la pâte
120 g de beurre
150 g de farine
120 g de sucre roux

Astuce_ Quand ce n'est plus la saison des abricots, pensez à utiliser des fruits en conserve ou surgelés.

la botte secrète d'aude et leslie

Pour un crumble encore plus gourmand, ajoutez 50 g de pistaches concassées non salées entre les fruits et la pâte. Accompagnez le tout d'une boule de glace à la pistache ou d'une grosse noisette de crème fraîche épaisse. Un régal !

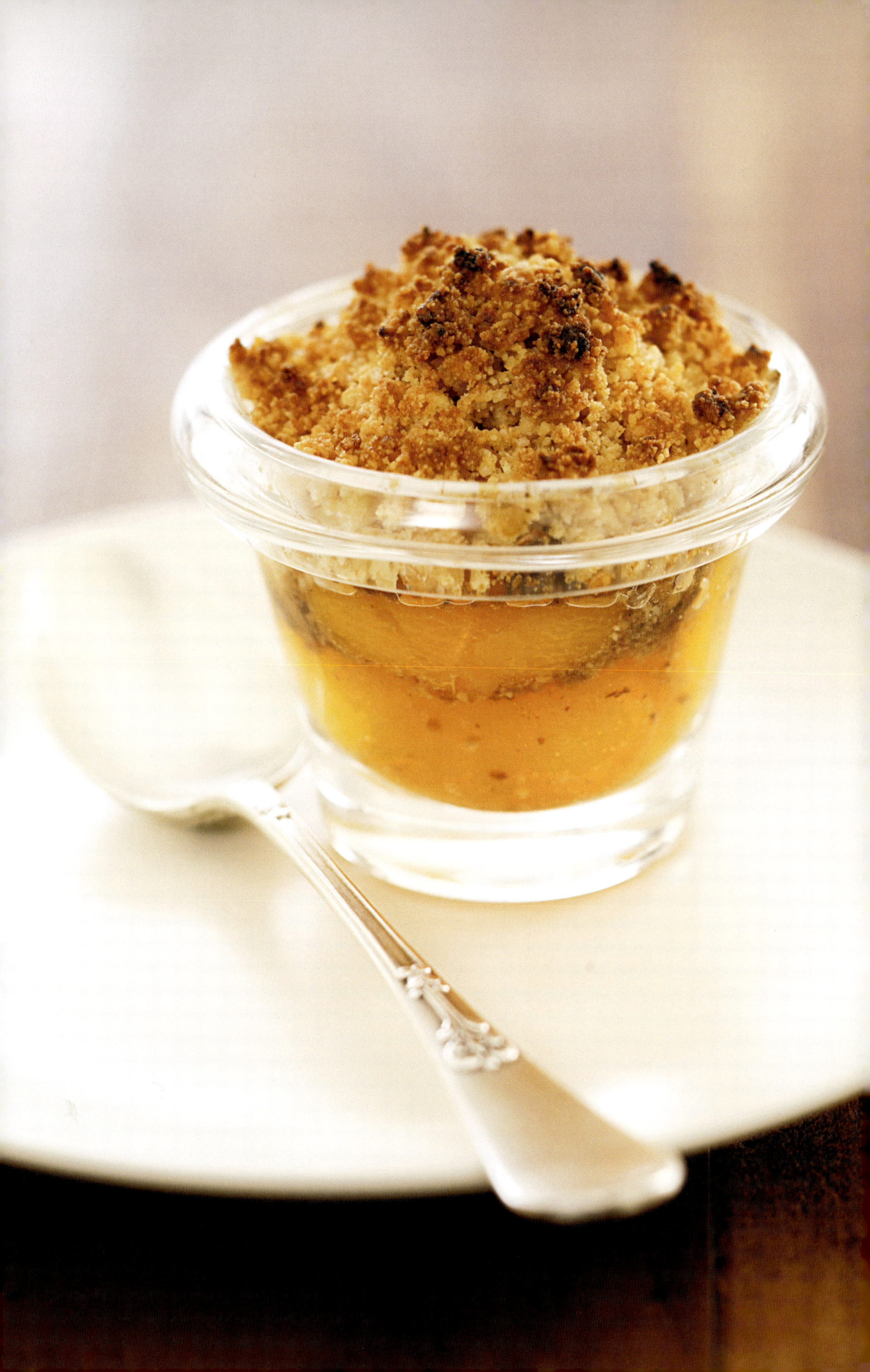

Crumble aux poires, fraises et spéculoos

PRÉPARATION 20 MIN **I CUISSON** 30 MIN **I COÛT** ★★ **I DIFFICULTÉ** ★★

→ UNE DÉLICIEUSE RECETTE QUI CASSE LES CODES DES CRUMBLES PUISQUE LA PÂTE EST RÉALISÉE AVEC DES SPÉCULOOS. CES PETITS BISCUITS À LA CANNELLE ET AU SUCRE ROUX QUI VIENNENT TOUT DROIT DE BELGIQUE SE MARIENT SUBTILEMENT AVEC LES POIRES ET LES FRAISES.

1 Préchauffez le four à 180 °C (th. 6). Rincez les fraises à l'eau claire, équeutez-les et séchez-les en les posant sur du papier absorbant. Épluchez les poires et coupez-les en morceaux. Passez au mixeur les fraises, les poires et la confiture de fraises, jusqu'à l'obtention d'une purée de fruits onctueuse. Beurrez un moule. Répartissez la purée de fruits dans le fond du moule.

2 Pour la pâte à crumble, déposez dans le bol d'un robot la farine, les spéculoos, le sucre et le beurre. Mixez par à-coups jusqu'à l'obtention d'une pâte sableuse.

3 Ajoutez la pâte aux spéculoos sur la purée de fruits en une couche régulière. Faites cuire au four 25 à 30 min environ. Servez immédiatement avec une boule de glace au spéculoos.

Les ingrédients pour 6 personnes

Pour les fruits

250 g de fraises

5 poires

2 cuil. à soupe de confiture de fraises

1 noisette de beurre pour le moule

6 boules de glace au spéculoos (facultatif)

Pour la pâte

50 g de farine

100 g de spéculoos

50 g de sucre roux

90 g de beurre

Astuce_ Si vous n'avez pas de robot, sachez que vous pouvez émietter les spéculoos dans un mortier ou avec le manche d'un couteau.

crumbles sucrés

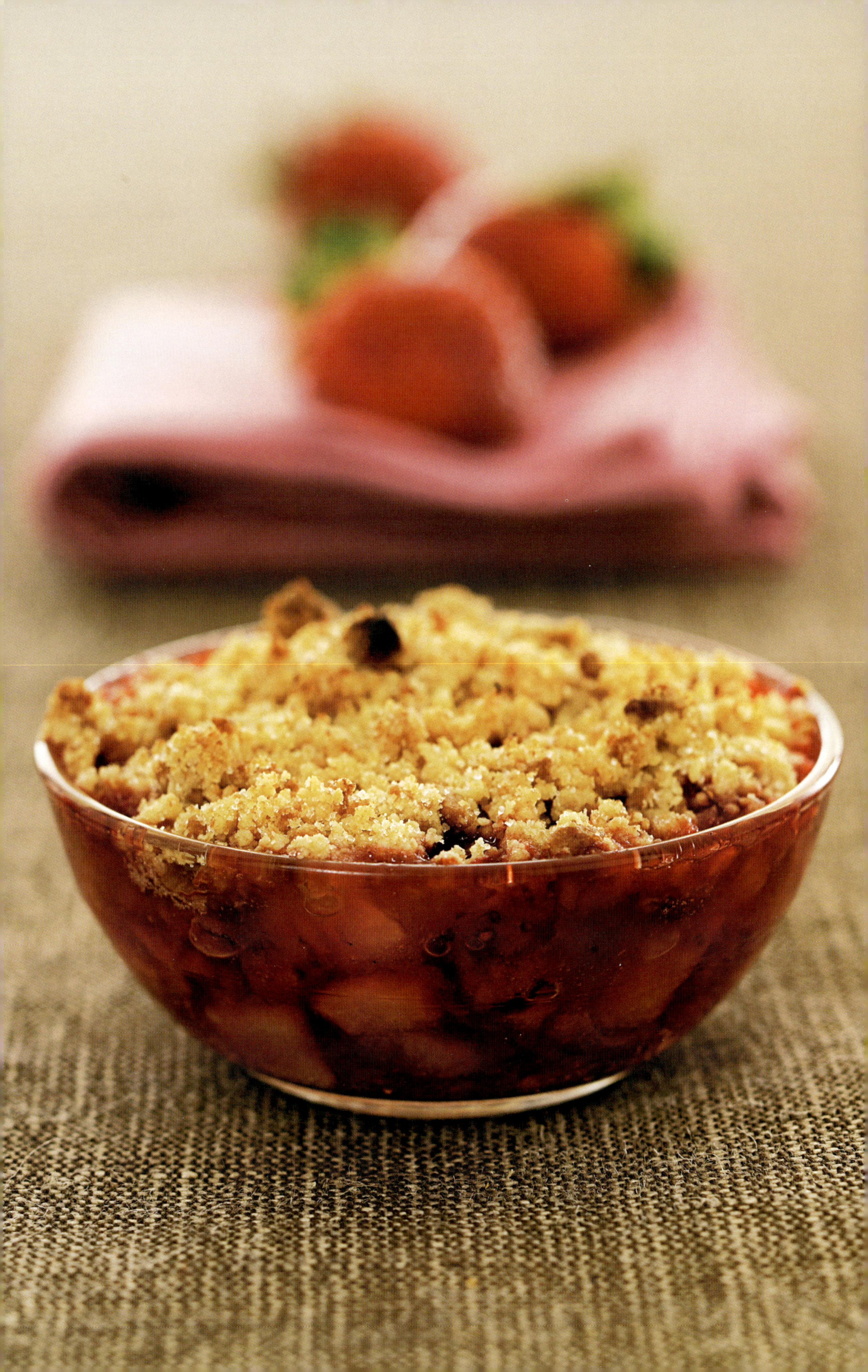

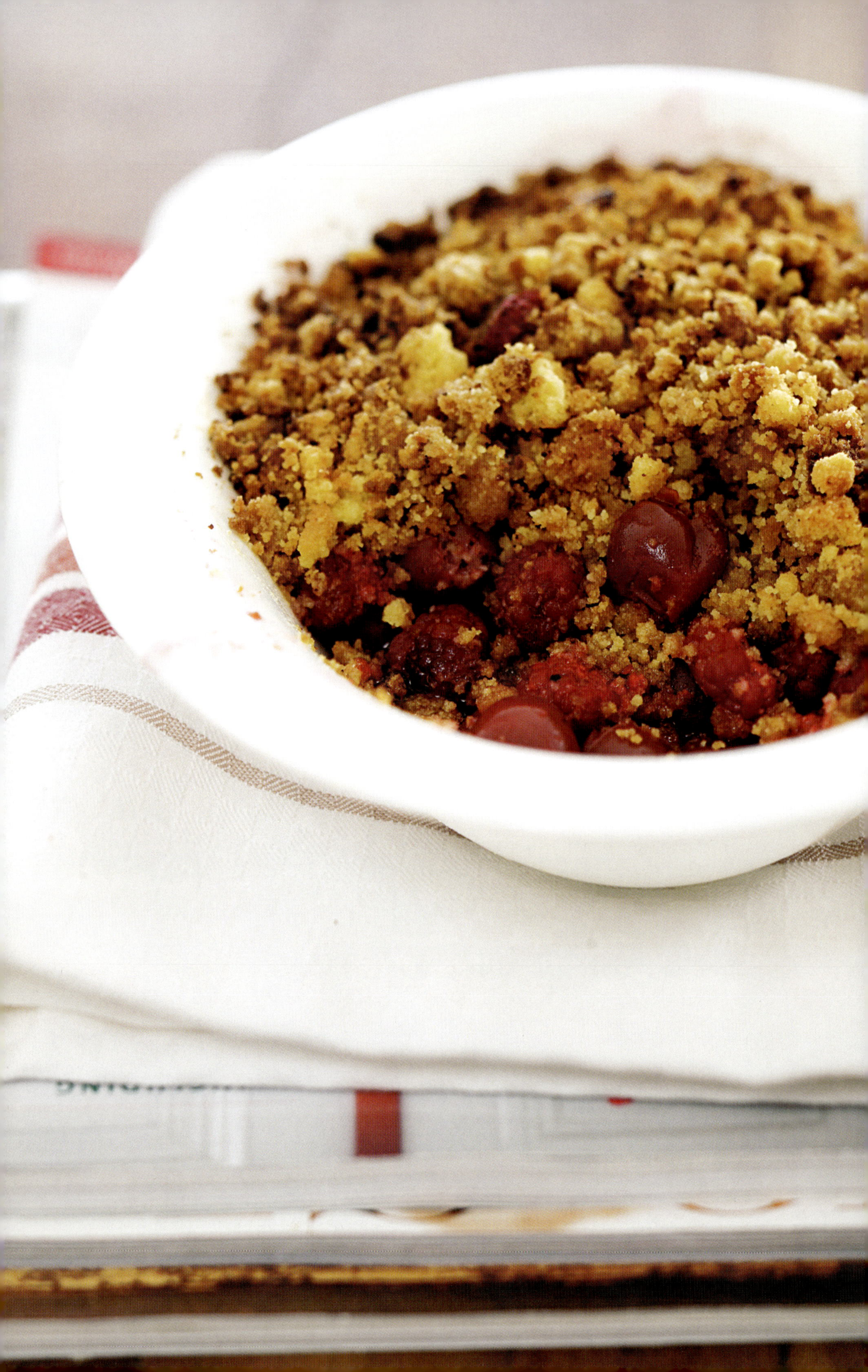

Crumble cerises, framboises et palets bretons

PRÉPARATION 20 MIN | **CUISSON** 15 MIN | **COÛT** ★★ | **DIFFICULTÉ** ★

→ VOICI UN CRUMBLE EXPRESS TRÈS SIMPLE À RÉALISER, OÙ LA PÂTE TRADITIONNELLE A ÉTÉ REMPLACÉE PAR DES PALETS BRETONS ÉMIETTÉS.

1 Préchauffez le four à 200 °C (th. 6-7). Lavez les cerises. Coupez-les en deux et dénoyautez-les. Rincez les framboises à l'eau claire et séchez-les en les déposant sur du papier absorbant. Répartissez les fruits dans le fond d'un moule puis saupoudrez-les de cannelle et de sucre en poudre.

2 Émiettez les palets bretons dans un mortier, avec le manche d'un couteau ou à la main. Puis, dans un saladier, mélangez les miettes de biscuits avec les 4 cuil. à soupe d'eau jusqu'à obtention d'une pâte sableuse.

3 Ajoutez la pâte aux palets bretons sur les fruits en une couche régulière. Faites cuire au four 15 min environ, jusqu'à ce que la pâte soit bien dorée.

Les ingrédients pour 4 à 6 personnes

Pour les fruits
800 g de cerises
125 g de framboises
3 pincées de cannelle en poudre
50 g de sucre en poudre

Pour la pâte
2 paquets de palets bretons
4 cuil. à soupe d'eau

Astuces_ • Pour avoir un maximum de saveur, vous pouvez rajouter 1 cuil. à soupe de kirsch dans les cerises. • Pour réaliser ce crumble en toute saison, vous pouvez remplacer les cerises et les framboises par des poires.

la botte secrète d'aude et leslie

Sachez que vous pouvez remplacer le sucre en poudre par un filet de miel, c'est un délice.

La tarte des Demoiselles Tatin

PRÉPARATION 25 MIN | **CUISSON** 35 MIN | **COÛT** ★ | **DIFFICULTÉ** ★★

→ CETTE DÉLICIEUSE TARTE EST NÉE DE L'ÉTOURDERIE DES DEUX SŒURS TATIN, QUI OUBLIÈRENT DE METTRE LA PÂTE SOUS LES POMMES. ELLES LA RAJOUTÈRENT AU DERNIER MOMENT SUR LE DESSUS ET… REMPORTÈRENT UN FRANC SUCCÈS !

1 Préchauffez le four à 240 °C (th. 8). Beurrez un moule à bord haut (moule à manqué) et réservez. Déroulez la pâte en la laissant sur le papier sulfurisé, et laissez-la reposer à température ambiante. Épluchez les pommes et coupez-les en 4 quartiers environ.

2 Pour le caramel, faites fondre, à feu doux, la moitié du sucre avec 3 cuil. à soupe d'eau, le jus de citron puis le beurre doux. Mélangez jusqu'à l'obtention d'un caramel blond et lisse, puis versez-le dans le moule.

3 Ajoutez les pommes, face bombée contre le caramel, en laissant un espace entre les fruits et le bord du moule. Ajoutez le beurre salé, l'autre moitié du sucre et le sucre vanillé.

4 Étalez la pâte sur les pommes et aplatissez-la pour qu'elle adhère bien. Puis recourbez les bords à l'intérieur. Faites cuire au four 30 à 35 min environ. À la sortie du four, attendez 30 secondes avant de retourner la tarte sur un plat pour la démouler. Servez votre tatin tiède accompagnée de crème fraîche épaisse.

Les ingrédients pour 4 à 6 personnes

- 1 noisette de beurre pour le moule
- 1 pâte brisée
- 8 pommes
- 100 g de sucre
- 1 cuil. à soupe de jus de citron
- 60 g de beurre doux
- 20 g de beurre salé
- 1 sachet de sucre vanillé
- 1 petit pot de crème fraîche épaisse

Astuces_ • Au moment du démoulage, n'attendez pas trop car le caramel colle au moule en refroidissant. Si c'est le cas, mettez à nouveau votre tatin au four 5 min, afin que le caramel se fluidifie. • Pour réussir à tous les coups, choisissez des pommes adaptées : reines des reinettes, canada gris ou boskoop. • Si votre tarte Tatin dore trop vite lors de la cuisson, n'hésitez pas à la couvrir d'une feuille de papier d'aluminium.

la botte secrète d'aude et leslie

Pour une version encore plus caramélisée, saupoudrez votre tatin (une fois démoulée) de sucre roux et repassez-la quelques minutes sous le gril du four avant de la servir.

le verre de vin qui va bien

Proposez un sauternes ou, plus modestement, un excellent monbazillac.

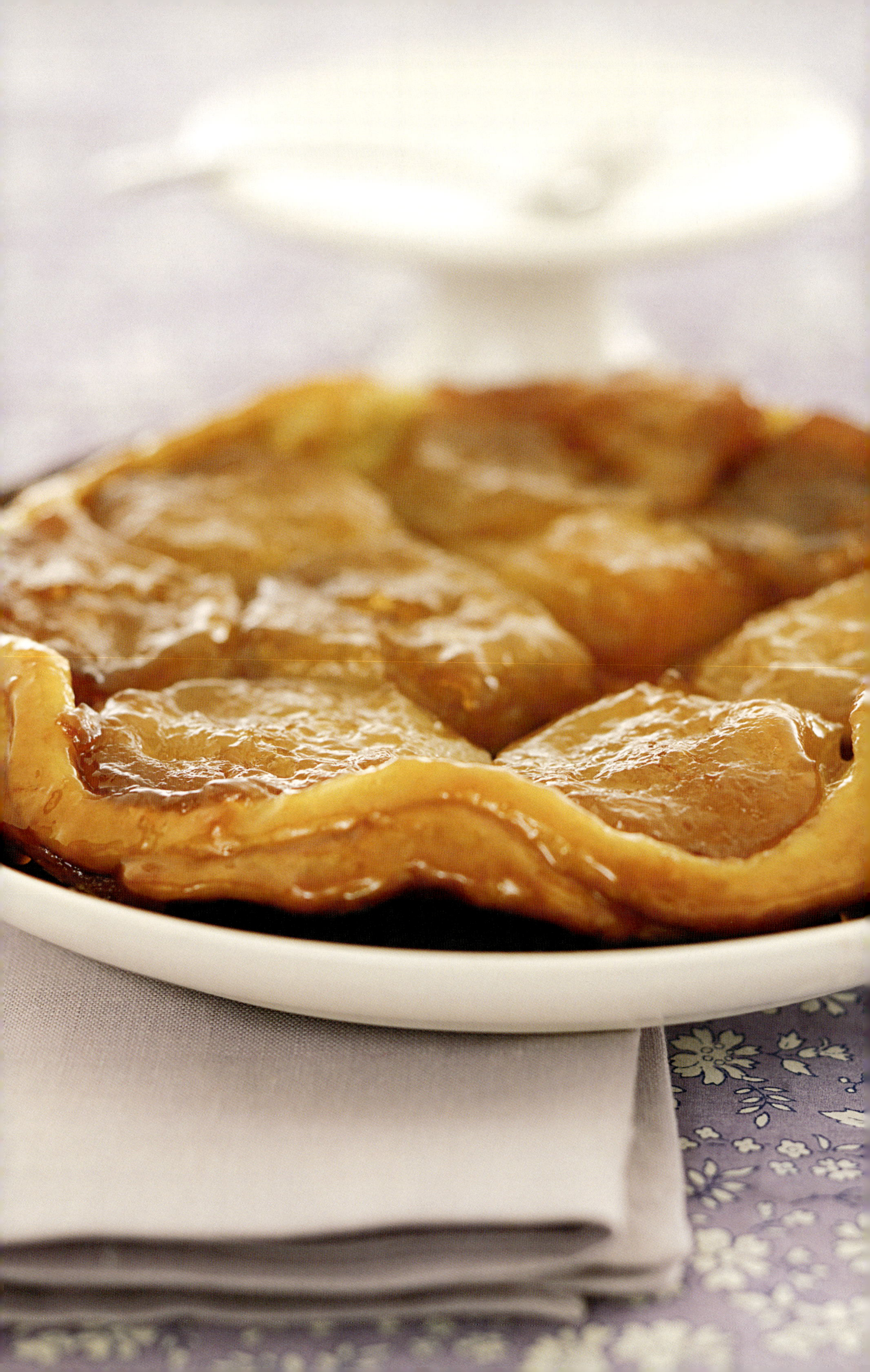

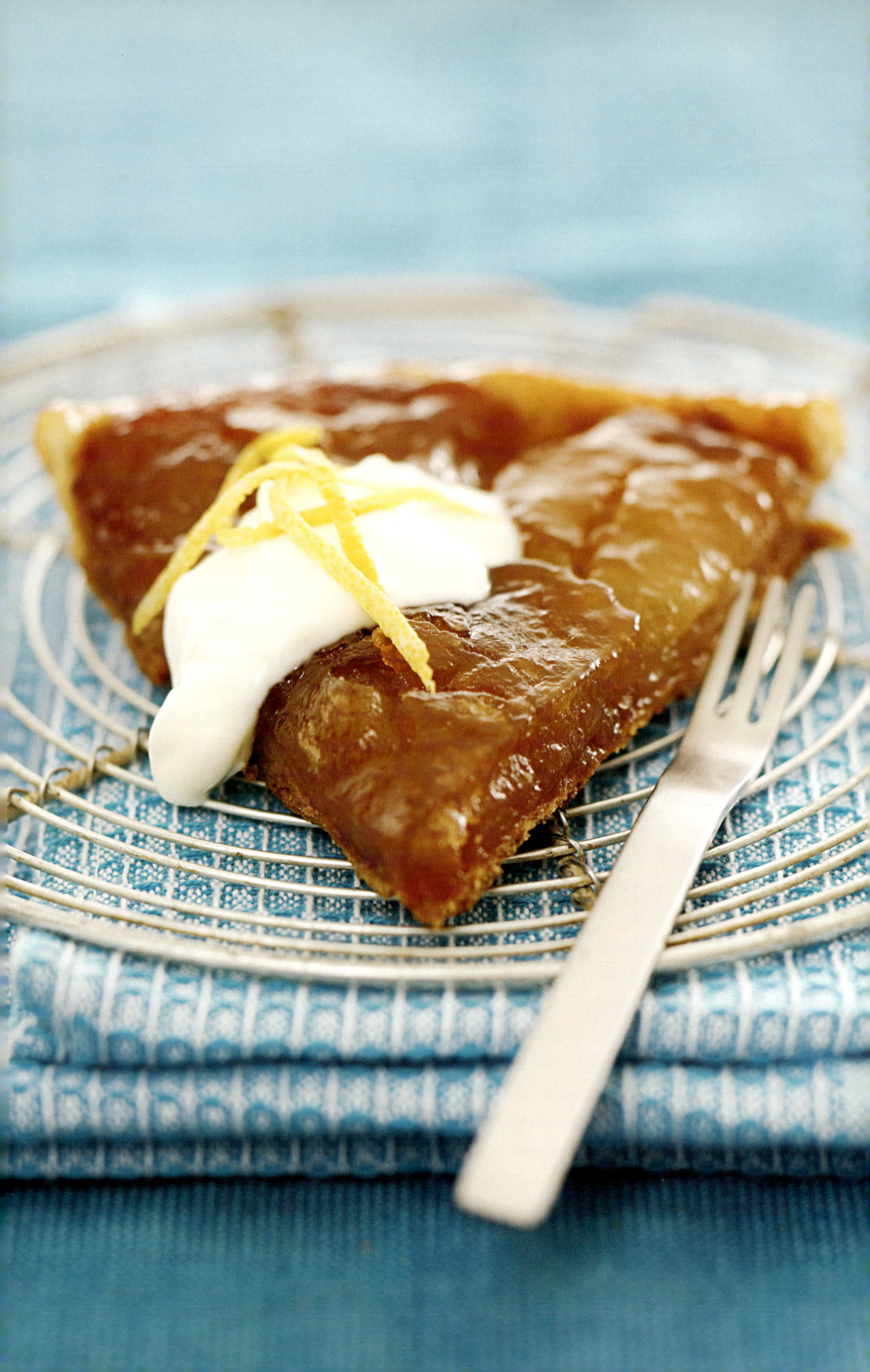

Tatin de pommes express

PRÉPARATION 15 MIN | **CUISSON** 25 MIN | **COÛT** ★ | **DIFFICULTÉ** ★

→ ON DOIT CE DESSERT ÉCLAIR À NOTRE COPINE LAURENCE QUI A TOUJOURS LE DON D'ADAPTER DES RECETTES VERSION « VITE FAIT, BIEN FAIT ».
TOUT SIMPLEMENT BLUFFANT !

1. Préchauffez le four à 210 °C (th. 7). Beurrez un moule à bord haut (moule à manqué). Versez le caramel liquide dans le fond du moule. Déroulez la pâte en la laissant sur le papier sulfurisé et laissez-la reposer à température ambiante.

2. Épluchez les pommes et coupez-les en quartiers. Ajoutez-les, face bombée contre le caramel, en laissant un espace entre les fruits et le bord du moule. Saupoudrez le tout de sucre vanillé.

3. Étalez la pâte sur les pommes et aplatissez-la pour qu'elle adhère bien. Puis recourbez les bords à l'intérieur. Faites cuire au four 25 min environ. À la sortie du four, attendez 30 secondes avant de retourner la tarte sur un plat pour la démouler.

Les ingrédients pour 4 à 6 personnes

- 1 noisette de beurre pour le moule
- 10 cuil. à soupe de caramel liquide tout prêt
- 1 pâte brisée pur beurre toute prête
- 6 pommes
- 1 sachet de sucre vanillé (facultatif)

Astuce_ La clé de la réussite : serrez bien vos quartiers de pommes les uns contre les autres avant d'aplatir la pâte.

la botte secrète d'aude et leslie

Vous pouvez rajouter quelques pincées de cannelle en même temps que le sucre vanillé. Un vrai régal.

tartes Tatin sucrées

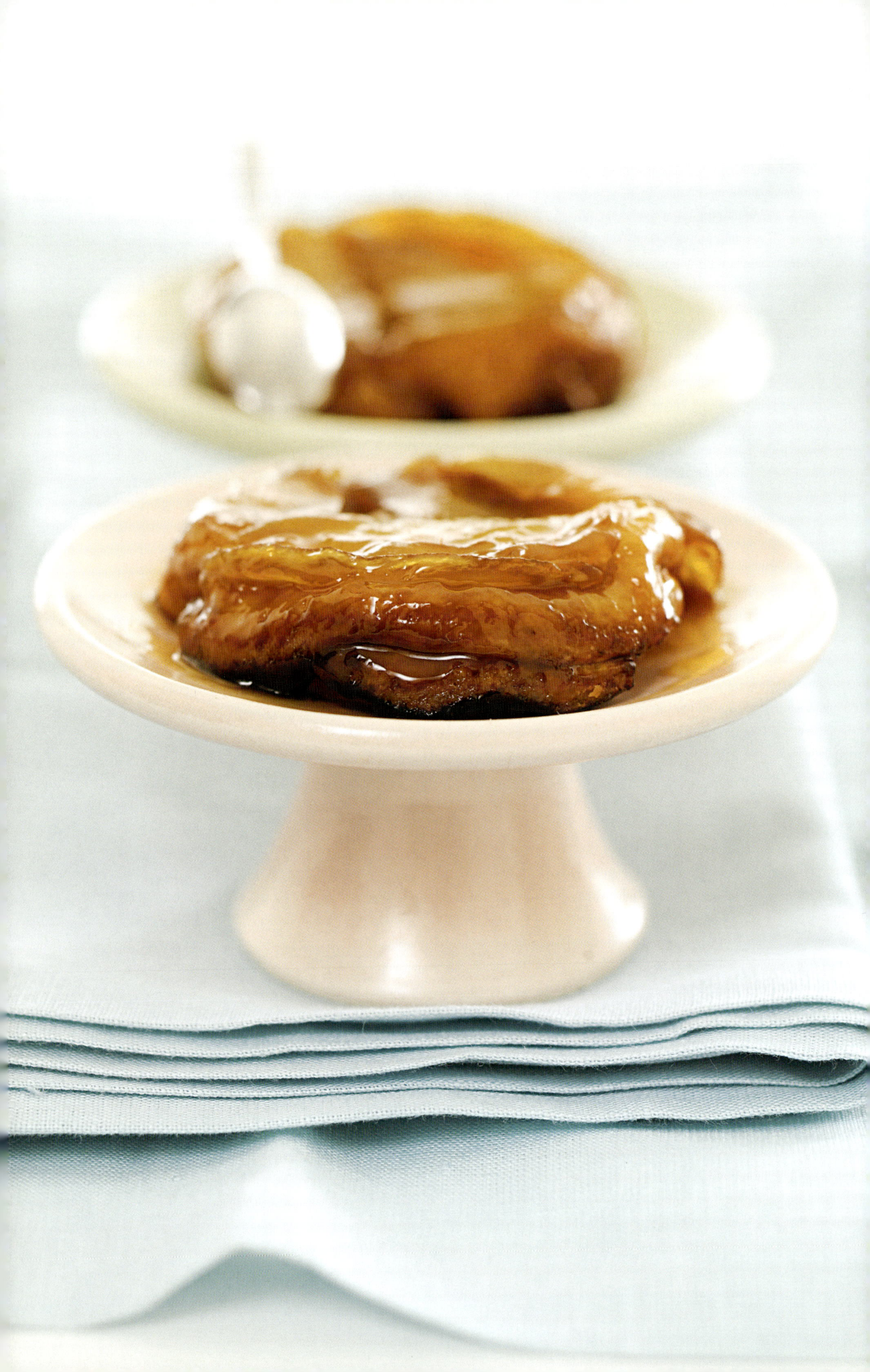

Tatin de mangues

PRÉPARATION 20 MIN | **CUISSON** 30 MIN | **COÛT** ★★ | **DIFFICULTÉ** ★★

1 Préchauffez le four à 210 °C (th. 7). Beurrez un moule à bord haut (moule à manqué). Épluchez les mangues et coupez-les en tranches autour du noyau.

2 Pour le caramel, faites fondre, dans une casserole à feu doux, le sucre roux avec 3 cuil. à soupe d'eau. Puis ajoutez le jus de citron, le beurre salé et le gingembre. Mélangez sans cesse jusqu'à l'obtention d'un caramel blond et lisse.

3 Plongez les tranches de mangue dans le caramel 2 min environ en les remuant délicatement pour bien les enrober. Puis disposez-les dans le fond du moule.

4 Étalez la pâte sur les mangues et aplatissez-la pour qu'elle adhère bien. Puis recourbez les bords à l'intérieur. Faites cuire au four 25 à 30 min environ.

Les ingrédients pour 4 à 6 personnes

1 noisette de beurre pour le moule
2 belles mangues mûres
50 g de sucre roux
1 cuil. à café de jus de citron
50 g de beurre salé
1 cuil. à café de gingembre en poudre (facultatif)
1 pâte brisée pur beurre

Astuces_ • Si vous voulez gagner du temps, sachez que cette recette fonctionne très bien avec des mangues surgelées. Pensez aussi aux fruits au sirop. • Pour varier les plaisirs, n'hésitez pas à troquer la pâte brisée contre une pâte sablée. • Vous pouvez aussi remplacer le gingembre en poudre par du gingembre frais râpé.

le tuyau de laurence

Ajoutez l'équivalent de 1 cuil. à café de zeste de citron vert finement coupé. Un côté acidulé à consommer sans modération.

le truc de stéphan

Pour bien réussir cette succulente recette, choisissez des mangues mûres mais encore légèrement fermes pour que la tarte, une fois cuite, garde sa forme.

Tatin de poires-chocolat

PRÉPARATION 20 MIN | **CUISSON** 30 MIN | **COÛT** ★★ | **DIFFICULTÉ** ★★

Les ingrédients pour 4 à 6 personnes

- 5 poires comices
- 80 g de beurre
- 75 g de sucre blanc
- 50 g de sucre roux
- 2 cuil. à café d'arôme naturel de vanille liquide
- 1 sachet de sucre vanillé
- 5 cuil. à soupe de pépites de chocolat
- 1 pâte feuilletée
- 3 cuil. à soupe d'amandes effilées

1 Préchauffez le four à 200 °C (th. 6-7). Épluchez les poires et coupez-les en tranches épaisses. Déposez le beurre en petits morceaux dans le fond d'un moule à bord haut (moule à manqué).

2 Pour le caramel, placez le moule sur la plaque électrique et faites fondre le beurre. Ajoutez le sucre blanc et le sucre roux et remuez sans cesse jusqu'à ce que le caramel blondisse (2 min environ).

3 Ajoutez la vanille liquide en mélangeant (1 min environ). Répartissez les tranches de poires en rosace dans le moule en laissant un espace entre les fruits et le bord du moule. Laissez-les caraméliser 2 min.

4 Hors du feu, saupoudrez les poires de sucre vanillé et ajoutez les pépites de chocolat. Étalez la pâte sur les poires et aplatissez-la pour qu'elle adhère bien. Puis recourbez les bords à l'intérieur. Faites cuire au four 25 à 30 min environ.

5 5 min avant la fin du temps de cuisson, faites poêler à sec les amandes effilées quelques instants, jusqu'à ce qu'elles soient bien dorées. À la sortie du four, attendez 30 secondes avant de démouler la tarte. Ajoutez les amandes effilées avant de servir.

Astuces_ • Nous vous proposons de réaliser votre caramel en posant directement le moule sur la plaque. Assurez-vous que votre moule s'y prête. Si vous avez un doute et pour tout savoir sur la préparation du caramel, reportez-vous p. 115. • Pour poêler à sec vos amandes effilées, il suffit de les verser dans une poêle antiadhésive sans matière grasse et de les laisser dorer quelques instants à feu moyen. • Cette recette fonctionne très bien avec des poires au sirop.

la botte secrète d'aude et leslie

Vous pouvez troquer les pépites de chocolat contre 1 poignée de raisins secs préalablement trempés dans 3 cuil. à soupe de rhum. À la place du sucre vanillé, saupoudrez vos poires de 3 cuil. à soupe de pralin. Un délice !

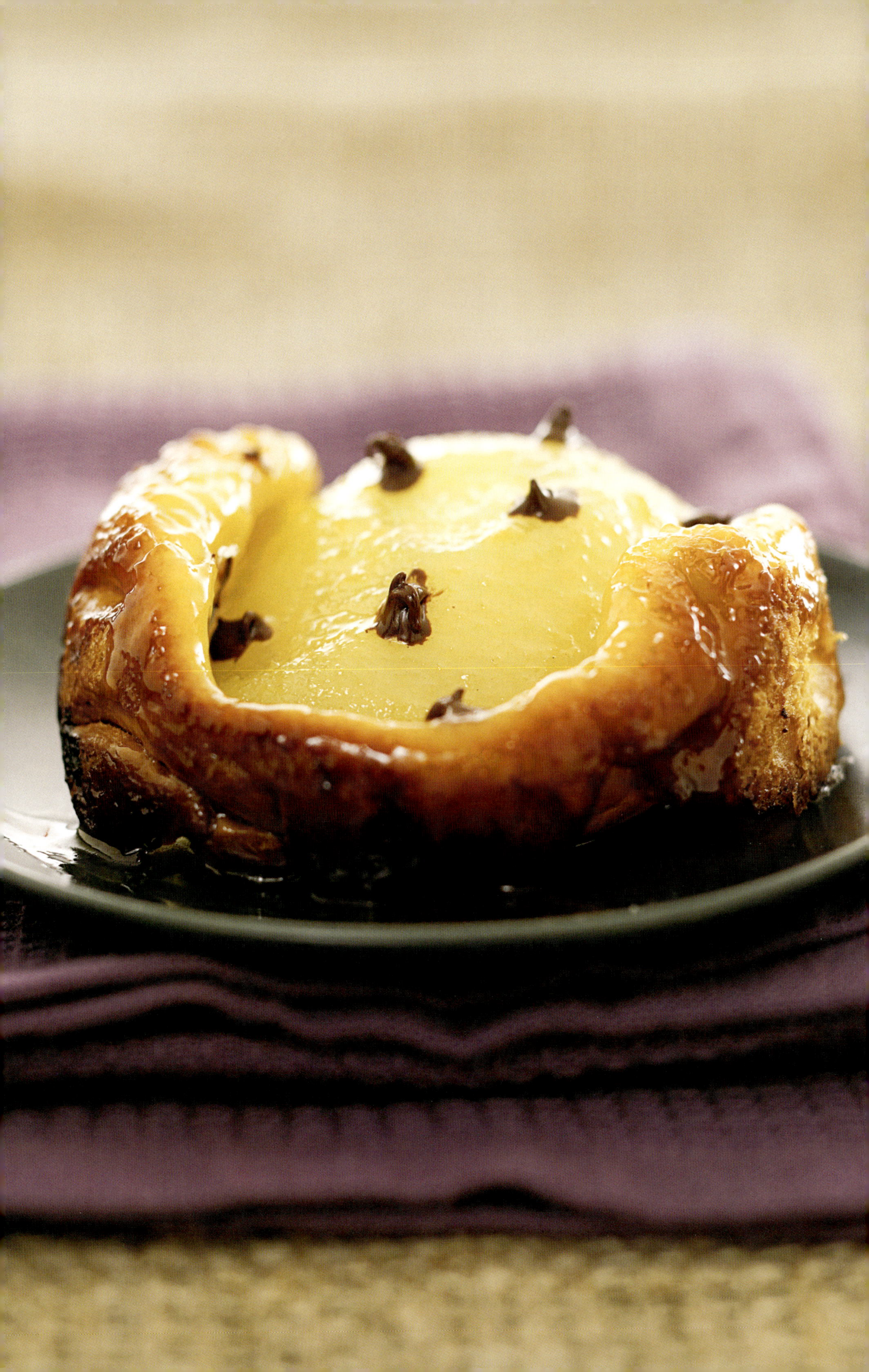

Tatin aphrodisiaque d'ananas au gingembre

PRÉPARATION 25 MIN | **CUISSON** 25 MIN | **COÛT** ★★ | **DIFFICULTÉ** ★ |
MATÉRIEL SPÉCIFIQUE 6 MOULES INDIVIDUELS

→ LE GINGEMBRE POSSÉDERAIT DES VERTUS STIMULANTES ET APHRODISIAQUES. DE QUOI DONNER UN COUP DE POUCE À VOTRE VIE AMOUREUSE !

1 Préchauffez le four à 200 °C (th. 6- 7). Beurrez 6 moules individuels. Dans une poêle, faites revenir les ananas avec le sucre et le beurre. Laissez-les décongeler et caraméliser 10 min environ.

2 Répartissez l'ananas caramélisé dans le fond des moules en laissant un petit espace entre les fruits et le bord des moules. Saupoudrez le tout de gingembre et de noix de coco râpée.

3 Étalez les pâtes brisées et découpez 6 disques au total, de diamètre légèrement supérieur aux moules. Déposez les disques de pâte sur les ananas et aplatissez-les pour qu'ils adhèrent bien. Puis recourbez les bords à l'intérieur. Faites cuire au four 25 min environ, jusqu'à ce que la pâte soit bien dorée. À la sortie du four, attendez 30 secondes avant de retourner les tartelettes sur un plat pour les démouler.

Les ingrédients pour 6 personnes

2 noisettes de beurre pour les moules
700 g d'ananas en morceaux surgelés
50 g de sucre roux
50 g de beurre
4 cuil. à café de gingembre frais râpé
6 cuil. à café de noix de coco râpée
2 pâtes brisées

Astuces_ • Cette tarte Tatin est également succulente avec de l'ananas frais. • Pour râper le gingembre, ôtez la peau beige et utilisez les trous les plus larges de la râpe.

le truc de stéphan

Le gingembre frais possède une saveur délicieuse et inimitable mais fragile : utilisez-le aussitôt après l'avoir râpé.

le tuyau de laurence

Ajoutez du gingembre confit coupé finement, cela rehaussera le goût de votre tarte et l'effet visuel est très sympa.

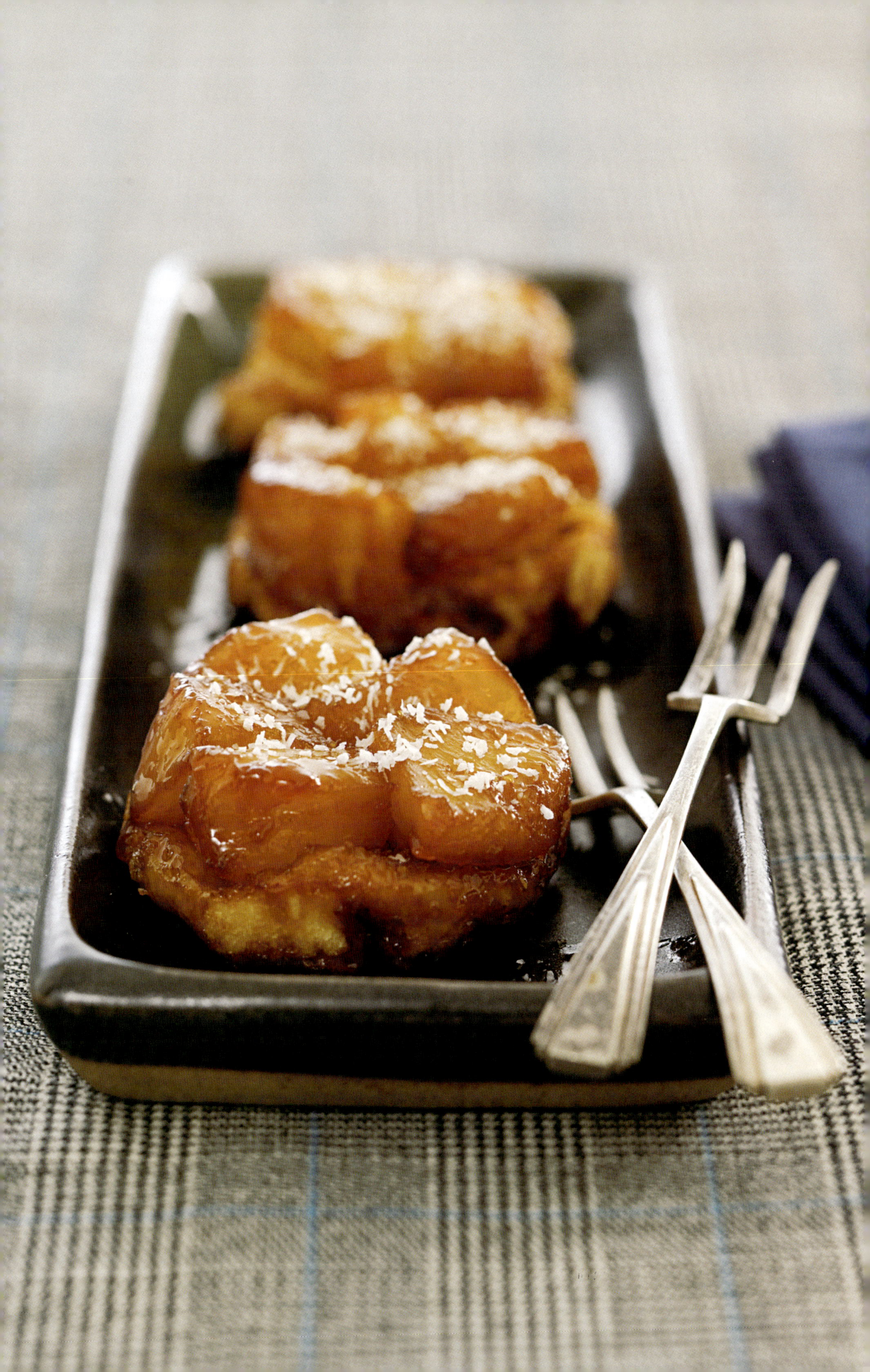

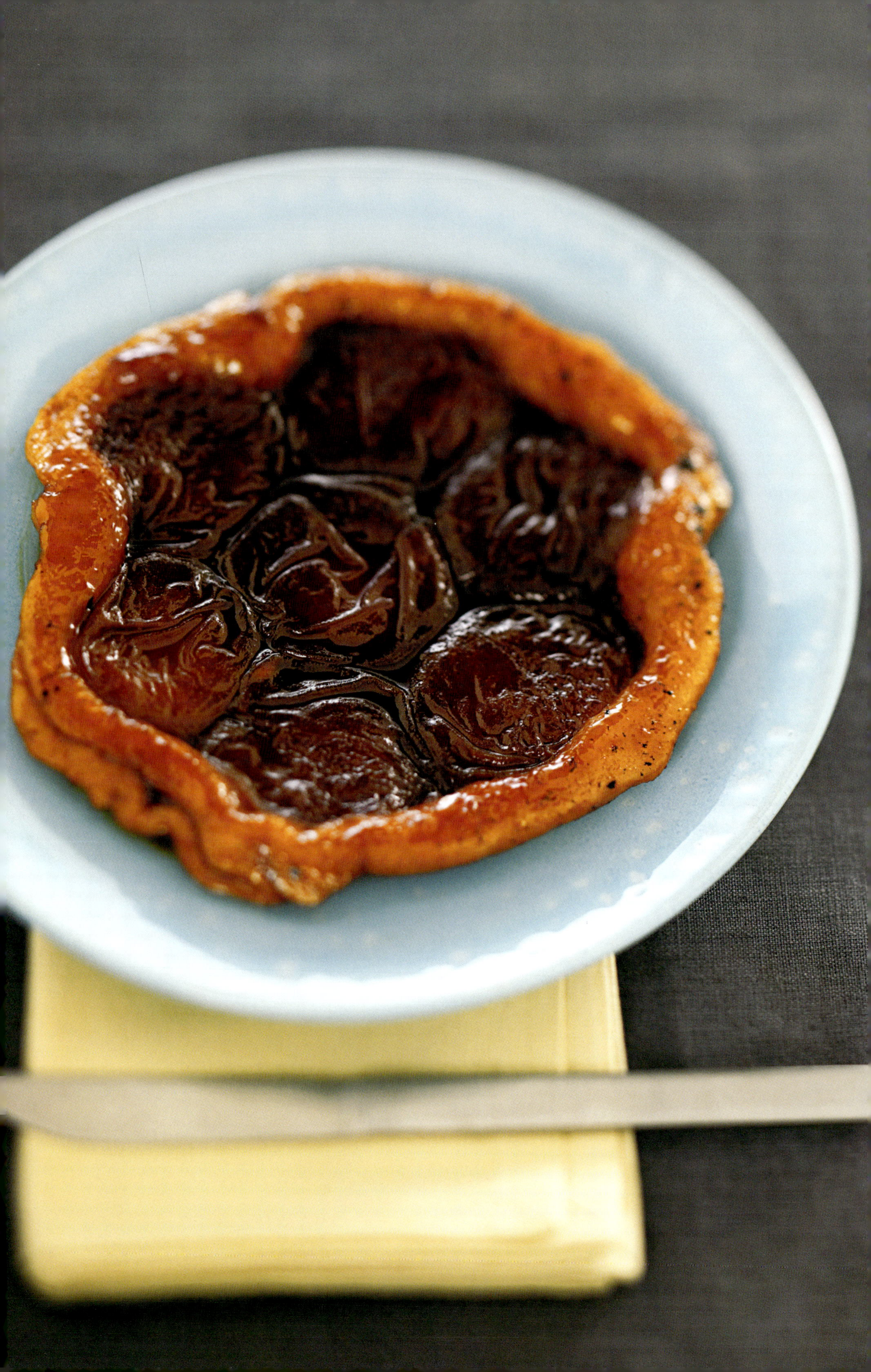

Tatin pralinée aux abricots

PRÉPARATION 15 MIN | **CUISSON** 30 MIN | **COÛT** ★ | **DIFFICULTÉ** ★★

1. Préchauffez le four à 210 °C (th. 7). Lavez les abricots, coupez-les en deux et ôtez les noyaux. Déposez le beurre en petits morceaux dans le fond d'un moule à bord haut (moule à manqué).

2. Pour le caramel, placez le moule sur la plaque électrique et faites fondre le beurre. Ajoutez le sucre et remuez sans cesse à l'aide d'une spatule en bois jusqu'à ce que le caramel commence à blondir (2 min environ).

3. Déposez les demi-abricots, face bombée dans le caramel, en laissant un espace entre les fruits et le bord du moule. Laissez-les caraméliser 3 min environ.

4. Hors du feu, saupoudrez les abricots de pralin. Étalez la pâte sur les abricots et aplatissez-la pour qu'elle adhère bien. Puis recourbez les bords à l'intérieur. Faites cuire au four 30 min environ. À la sortie du four, attendez 30 secondes avant de retourner la tarte sur un plat pour la démouler.

Les ingrédients pour 4 à 6 personnes
- 10 à 12 abricots (selon leur grosseur)
- 50 g de beurre
- 50 g de sucre
- 5 cuil. à soupe de pralin
- 1 pâte brisée

Astuces_ • Dans cette recette, nous vous proposons de réaliser votre caramel en posant directement le moule sur la plaque. Avant de vous lancer, assurez-vous que votre moule se prête à cette manipulation. Si vous avez un doute et pour tout savoir sur la préparation du caramel, reportez-vous p. 115. • Si vos abricots ne sont pas très sucrés, doublez les proportions de caramel.

la botte secrète d'aude et leslie

À la place du pralin, vous pouvez saupoudrer vos abricots de pain d'épice émietté ou de galettes Saint-Michel écrasées. Pour un contraste chaud-froid, accompagnez chaque part d'une boule de glace à la noisette, au pain d'épice ou à la vanille.

le tuyau de laurence

À déguster sans plus attendre avec une glace à la pistache !

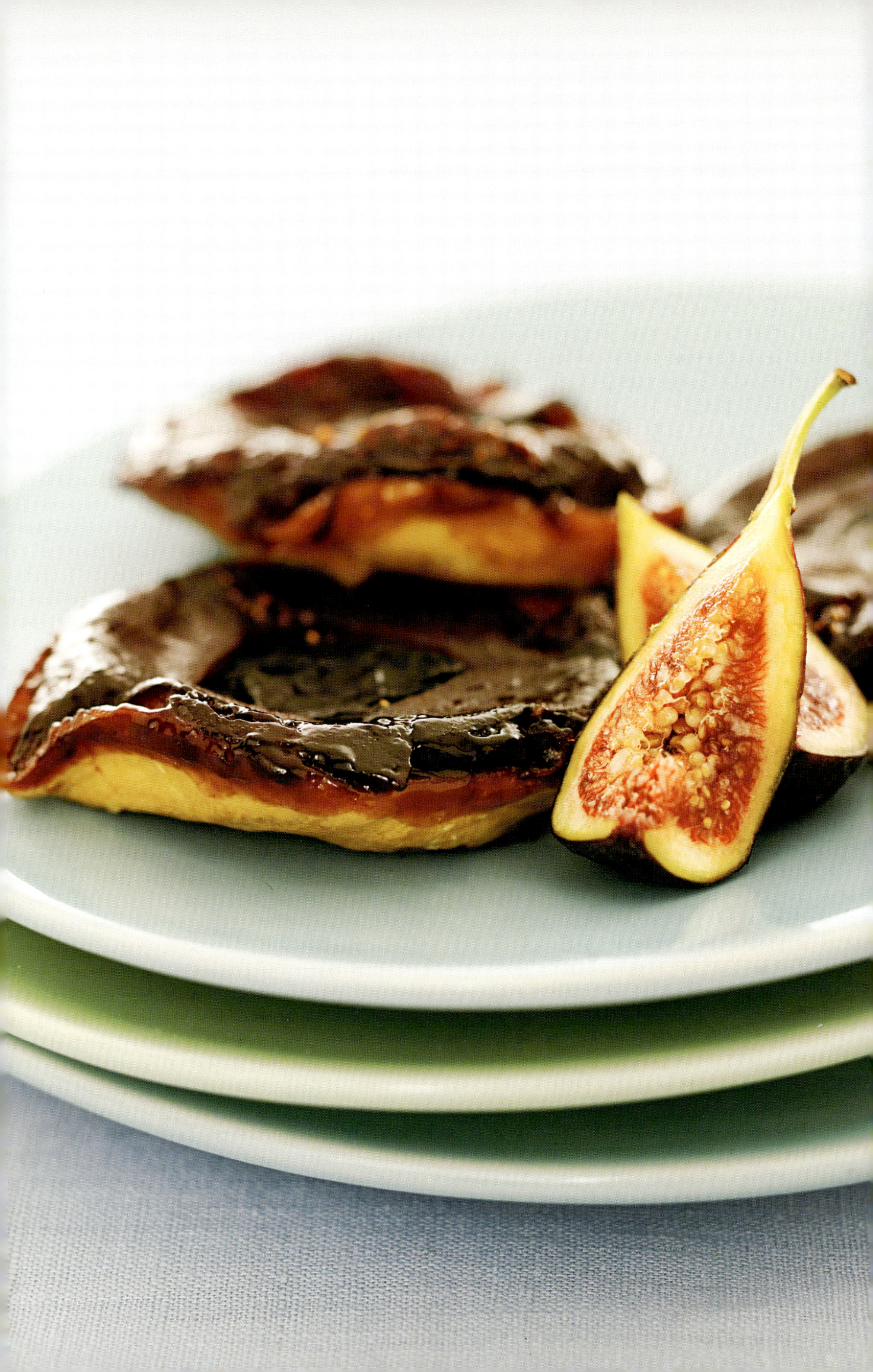

Tatin pommes-figues

PRÉPARATION 25 MIN | **CUISSON** 30 MIN | **COÛT** ★★ | **DIFFICULTÉ** ★★

1 Préchauffez le four à 210 °C (th. 7). Beurrez un moule à bord haut (moule à manqué) et réservez. Épluchez les pommes et coupez-les en 4 quartiers. Lavez les figues, séchez-les et coupez-les en deux. Coupez les fruits secs (figues et dattes) en tout petits morceaux.

2 Pour le caramel, faites fondre, dans une casserole à feu doux, le sucre avec 3 cuil. à soupe d'eau, le jus de citron puis le beurre. Mélangez sans cesse jusqu'à l'obtention d'un caramel blond et lisse, puis versez-le rapidement dans le moule pour éviter qu'il ne se fige.

3 Ajoutez les fruits, face bombée contre le caramel, en alternant pommes et figues et en laissant un espace entre les fruits et le bord du moule. Ajoutez le sucre vanillé et les fruits secs.

4 Étalez la pâte sur les fruits et aplatissez-la pour qu'elle adhère bien. Puis recourbez les bords à l'intérieur. Faites cuire au four 30 min environ. À la sortie du four, attendez 30 secondes avant de retourner la tarte sur un plat pour la démouler.

Les ingrédients pour 4 à 6 personnes

- 1 noisette de beurre pour le moule
- 3 pommes
- 5 figues fraîches mûres
- 3 figues sèches
- 3 dattes
- 10 morceaux de sucre
- 1 cuil. à soupe de jus de citron
- 50 g de beurre
- 1 sachet de sucre vanillé
- 1 pâte brisée pur beurre

Astuces_ • Si vos figues ne sont pas suffisamment mûres, épluchez-les avant de les déposer dans le moule. • Pour réussir à tous les coups, choisissez des pommes adaptées : reines des reinettes, canada gris ou boskoop. • Au moment du démoulage, n'attendez pas trop car le caramel colle au moule en refroidissant. Si c'est le cas, mettez à nouveau votre tatin au four 5 min, afin que le caramel se fluidifie.

Tatin de mirabelles

PRÉPARATION 25 MIN | **CUISSON** 30 MIN | **COÛT** ★★ | **DIFFICULTÉ** ★★

1. Préchauffez le four à 210 °C (th. 7). Lavez les mirabelles, coupez-les en deux et dénoyautez-les. Déposez le beurre en petits morceaux dans le fond d'un moule à bord haut (moule à manqué).

2. Pour le caramel, placez le moule sur la plaque électrique et faites fondre le beurre. Ajoutez le sucre et remuez sans cesse jusqu'à ce que le caramel commence à blondir (2 min environ).

3. Déposez les mirabelles dans le caramel en laissant un espace entre les fruits et le bord du moule. Laissez-les caraméliser 3 min.

4. Hors du feu, saupoudrez les mirabelles de sucre vanillé. Étalez la pâte sur les fruits et aplatissez-la pour qu'elle adhère bien. Puis recourbez les bords à l'intérieur. Faites cuire au four 25 à 30 min environ. À la sortie du four, attendez 30 secondes avant de démouler la tarte. Saupoudrez le tout de graines de sésame juste avant de servir.

Les ingrédients pour 4 à 6 personnes
- 1 kg de mirabelles
- 50 g de beurre
- 50 g de sucre
- 1 sachet de sucre vanillé
- 1 pâte feuilletée
- 3 cuil. à soupe de graines de sésame (facultatif)

Astuce_ Nous vous proposons de réaliser votre caramel en posant directement le moule sur la plaque. Assurez-vous que votre moule s'y prête. Si vous avez un doute et pour tout savoir sur la préparation du caramel, reportez-vous p. 115.

la botte secrète d'aude et leslie
Ajoutez un petit filet de miel liquide sur cette tatin encore tiède... Croyez-nous, c'est à se damner !

le tuyau de laurence
Mariez les mirabelles avec quelques rondelles de banane, un vrai délice.

le truc de stéphan
Si vous partagez cette tarte entre amis, faites bouillir un peu d'eau-de-vie de prune, versez-la sur le gâteau puis grattez une allumette et faites flamber !

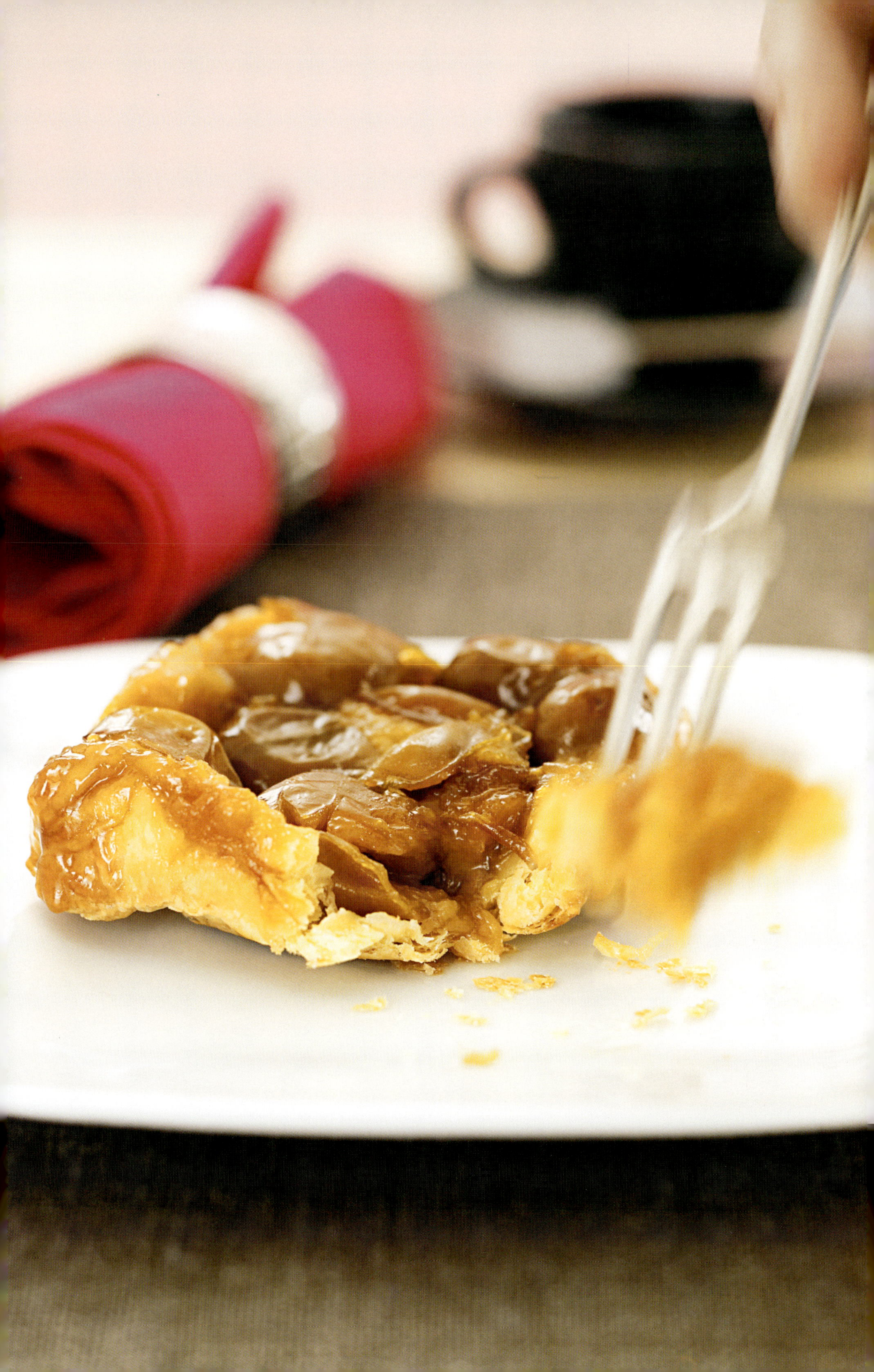

Clafoutis Tatin

PRÉPARATION 15 MIN **I CUISSON** 40 MIN **I COÛT** ★ **I DIFFICULTÉ** ★

→ VOICI UN MIX ORIGINAL ENTRE DEUX RECETTES MYTHIQUES. ENTRE LE MOELLEUX DE LA PÂTE À CLAFOUTIS ET LA SAVEUR CARAMÉLISÉE DES FRUITS, ON OBTIENT UN DESSERT SUCCULENT. ET DIRE QU'EN PLUS, CETTE RECETTE EST INRATABLE !

1 Préchauffez le four à 200 °C (th. 6-7). Beurrez un grand moule à bord haut (moule à manqué), et versez-y le caramel liquide. Épluchez les poires et coupez-les en quartiers. Déposez-les en rosace sur le caramel.

2 Dans un saladier, battez à l'aide d'un fouet les œufs avec le sucre, la crème liquide et le lait. Ajoutez la poudre d'amandes et la farine en pluie en continuant de fouetter pour éviter les grumeaux. Versez cette pâte sur les fruits. Faites cuire au four 40 min environ. Servez tiède ou froid.

Les ingrédients pour 6 personnes

1 noisette de beurre pour le moule
8 cuil. à soupe de caramel liquide tout prêt
5 poires
3 œufs
100 g de sucre
20 cl de crème liquide
20 cl de lait
2 cuil. à soupe de poudre d'amandes
70 g de farine

Astuce_ Si votre tatin dore trop vite lors de la cuisson, n'hésitez pas à la couvrir d'une feuille de papier d'aluminium.

la botte secrète d'aude et leslie

Accompagnez cette recette d'un coulis de chocolat chaud.
On ne vous en dit pas plus, c'est juste le paradis !

108 tartes Tatin sucrées

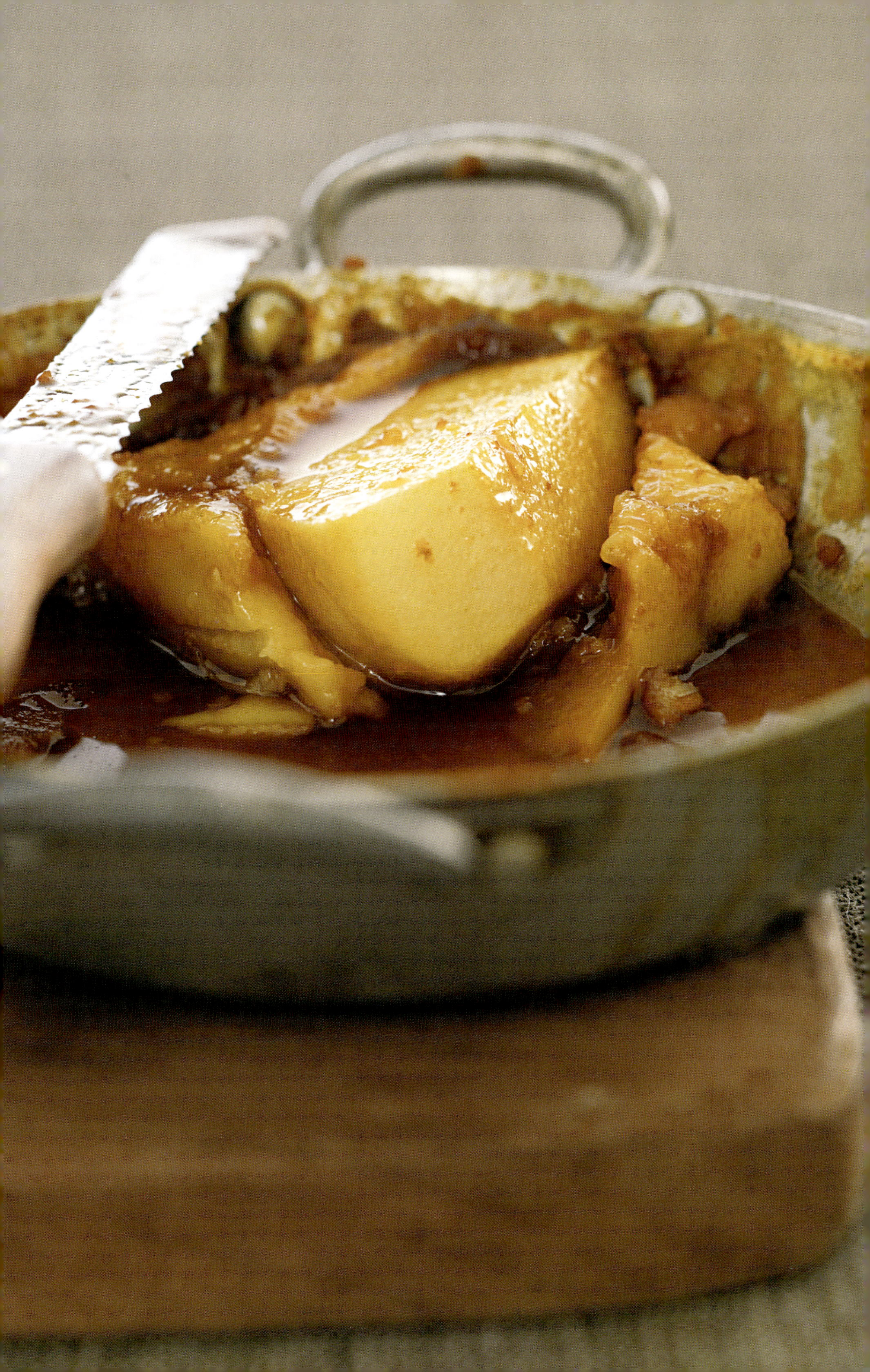

je veux en savoir plus !

Coupez le beurre en morceaux / UNE CONSISTANCE HOMOGÈNE ET LISSE / Ajoutez les quartiers de fruits / **Retournez délicatement** / **d'un coulis de tomates** / Pâte feuilletée / RÉCHAUFFER UN CRUMBLE / **Farine 3 g** / aplatissez-la pour qu'elle adhère bien / mélangez à la main la farine avec le sucre et le beurre / POUR LAVER FACILEMENT LA CASSEROLE / **Éviter que la pâte ne gonfle lors de la cuisson** / Crème épaisse / À ARROSER VOTRE CRUMBLE D'UN FILET DE MIEL / Fruits secs / **des petits bocaux de conserve** / LE RECOUVRIR D'UNE FEUILLE DE PAPIER D'ALUMINIUM / pour cuisiner à l'improviste / **une consistance sableuse** / POUDRE D'AMANDES / **Ajoutez au choix dans la pâte** / AU ROBOT-MIXEUR / les saupoudrer de 2 cuil. à soupe de sucre en poudre / EN UNE COUCHE RÉGULIÈRE SANS LA TASSER. / Quel moule utiliser ? / **jusqu'à ce que le caramel commence à blondir** / vous ferez le plein de vitamines / L'ACCOMPAGNANT D'UNE BOULE DE GLACE, D'UNE NOISETTE DE CRÈME FRAÎCHE / **À la sortie du four** / **La clé de la réussite** / un four préchauffé à 210°C / **DE LES COUPER EN MORCEAUX**

Je veux la technique !
Savoir faire la pâte à crumble

À la main

1 Coupez le beurre en morceaux et faites-le ramollir au micro-ondes.

3 Malaxez la préparation puis émiettez-la du bout des doigts pour lui donner une consistance sableuse (comme une grosse semoule).

4 Ajoutez la pâte sur les fruits en une couche régulière sans la tasser.

2 Dans un saladier, mélangez à la main la farine avec le sucre et le beurre ramolli.

La clé de la réussite
La pâte ne doit jamais avoir une consistance homogène et lisse.
Si c'est le cas, rajoutez de la farine et du sucre pour qu'elle redevienne sableuse.

Au robot-mixeur

1. Coupez le beurre en cubes et mettez-le directement dans le bol de votre robot.
2. Ajoutez le sucre et la farine. Mixez par à-coups pour réduire tous les ingrédients en une pâte sableuse (comme une grosse semoule).
3. Ajoutez la pâte sur les fruits en une couche régulière sans la tasser.

Tout connaître sur les crumbles

Accompagner...

... les crumbles sucrés
Lorsque vous servez votre crumble chaud ou tiède, jouez sur le contraste chaud-froid en l'accompagnant d'une boule de glace, d'une noisette de crème fraîche épaisse ou de crème Chantilly.
Pour une version light, misez sur du fromage blanc à 20 % de matière grasse.
Pensez aussi à arroser votre crumble d'un filet de miel, de caramel ou de chocolat fondu, ou d'un coulis de fruits rouges.

... les crumbles salés
Ils s'accompagnent idéalement d'un coulis de tomates, de poivron, d'un filet de citron ou d'huile d'olive.
Quelques gouttes de tabasco viendront apporter un peu de piquant.
Pour une version plus light, prévoyez une sauce au yaourt allégé aromatisée aux fines herbes.

Réchauffer un crumble
Il suffit de le recouvrir d'une feuille de papier d'aluminium et de le passer une dizaine de minutes dans un four préchauffé à 200 °C (th. 6-7).

Présenter un crumble

Pour le plaisir des yeux, vous pouvez servir vos crumbles dans des verres transparents ou dans des petits bocaux de conserve. Vous pouvez les faire cuire dans des ramequins individuels. Jouez aussi sur la forme des moules : étoile, carré, cœur...

Rehausser le goût des pâtes à crumble

Pour les crumbles sucrés
Ajoutez au choix dans la pâte : cannelle, gingembre en poudre ou râpé, poudre de noisettes, poudre d'amandes, noix de coco râpée, muesli, corn-flakes, gâteaux émiettés (spéculoos, palets bretons, petits-beurre...).

Pour les crumbles salés
Ajoutez au choix dans la pâte : piment de Cayenne ou d'Espelette en poudre, gingembre, cumin, curry, noix de muscade...

Quels fruits pour vos crumbles ?

Les fruits frais pour un maximum de saveurs
Il suffit de les éplucher et de les couper en morceaux avant de les déposer dans le fond d'un moule. Ajoutez ensuite la pâte à crumble. Non seulement vous vous régalerez, mais en plus vous ferez le plein de vitamines.

Les fruits surgelés pour gagner du temps
Quand vous utilisez des fruits surgelés, il suffit de les déposer dans le fond d'un moule beurré, de les saupoudrer de 2 cuil. à soupe de sucre en poudre et de les faire cuire 10 min environ dans un four préchauffé à 210 °C (th. 7). Il ne vous restera plus qu'à ajouter la pâte à crumble et à mettre au four selon le temps de cuisson indiqué dans la recette.

Les fruits en conserve pour cuisiner à l'improviste
Si vous avez recours aux conserves, égouttez bien les fruits avant de les couper en petits morceaux. Un moyen idéal de réaliser des recettes à la dernière minute.

Savoir faire une tarte Tatin sucrée

La méthode classique

1 Versez le caramel (cf. méthode ci-après) dans le fond d'un moule à manqué beurré.

2 Ajoutez les quartiers de fruits, face bombée contre le caramel, en les serrant bien et en laissant un espace entre les fruits et le bord du moule.

3 Étalez la pâte sur les fruits et aplatissez-la pour qu'elle adhère bien.

4 Recourbez les bords à l'intérieur avant de mettre au four.

5 À la sortie du four, attendez 30 secondes avant de passer la lame d'un couteau autour de la tarte pour décoller les bords.

je veux la technique !

6 Retournez délicatement la tarte sur un plat pour la démouler.

La méthode pratique

Sachez que la plupart de nos recettes de tartes Tatin sucrées suivent les grandes lignes de la méthode classique. Toutefois, il est aussi possible de préparer votre caramel directement dans le moule à manqué.

1 Placez le moule directement sur la plaque électrique.

2 Faites-y fondre le beurre. Ajoutez le sucre et remuez sans cesse à l'aide d'une spatule en bois jusqu'à ce que le caramel commence à blondir.

3 Déposez les fruits dans le caramel en laissant un espace entre les fruits et le bord du moule. Laissez-les caraméliser à nouveau 3 min.

4 Hors du feu, aplatissez la pâte et mettez au four.

Mise en garde : avant de vous lancer dans une recette où l'on doit poser le moule directement sur la plaque électrique pour réaliser le caramel, assurez-vous que le moule se prête à cette manipulation. Si vous avez un doute, préparez votre caramel soit à la casserole, soit au micro-ondes (comme indiqué ci-après).

je veux la technique !

Tout connaître sur les tartes Tatin

Éviter que la pâte ne gonfle lors de la cuisson

Réalisez un petit trou au centre de la pâte à l'aide de la pointe d'un couteau. La vapeur pourra ainsi s'échapper lors de la cuisson. Vous pouvez aussi piquer la pâte à l'aide d'une fourchette avant de la mettre au four.

Quel moule utiliser ?

Choisissez un moule à bord haut (un moule à manqué). Évitez les moules à tarte dont les bords sont trop bas. Préférez les moules antiadhésifs : ils faciliteront le démoulage et éviteront que le caramel ne colle dans le fond du moule.

Savoir faire le caramel

Version traditionnelle : à la casserole

1. Dans une casserole à feu doux, faites fondre 50 g sucre avec 3 cuil. à soupe d'eau.

2. Mélangez sans cesse jusqu'à ce que le caramel commence à blondir.

3. Ajoutez 1 cuil. à café de jus de citron, pour éviter la cristallisation du caramel, puis 60 g de beurre coupé en morceaux. Mélangez bien jusqu'à l'obtention d'un caramel blond et lisse.

4. Versez-le rapidement dans le moule pour éviter qu'il ne se fige.

Version express : au micro-ondes

1. Humectez 200 g de sucre en morceaux avec 4 cuil. à soupe d'eau.

2. Faites chauffer dans votre micro-ondes 2 min à la puissance maximale.

3. À la sortie du four, mélangez bien puis repassez au micro-ondes par tranches de 15 secondes jusqu'à ce que le caramel soit blond et lisse.

4. Ajoutez 1 cuil. à café de jus de citron, pour éviter la cristallisation du caramel, puis versez-le rapidement dans le moule pour éviter qu'il ne se fige.

Comment se débarrasser du caramel ?

Pour laver facilement la casserole qui a servi à réaliser votre caramel, remplissez-la d'eau chaude et faites-la bouillir 5 bonnes minutes en grattant le fond à l'aide d'une cuillère en bois.

je veux la technique !

À garder sous le coude

s'en sortir sans balance

→ Ce tableau vous donne les principales équivalences poids et volumes pour les ingrédients les plus courants.

Ingrédients	1 cuil. à café	1 cuil. à soupe	1 verre à moutarde
Beurre	7 g	20 g	–
Cacao en poudre	5 g	10 g	90 g
Crème épaisse	1,5 cl	4 cl	20 cl
Crème liquide	0,7 cl	2 cl	20 cl
Farine	3 g	10 g	100 g
Gruyère râpé	4 g	12 g	65 g
Liquides divers (eau, huile, vinaigre, alcools)	0,7 cl	2 cl	20 cl
Maïzena	3 g	10 g	100 g
Poudre d'amandes	6 g	15 g	75 g
Raisins secs	8 g	30 g	110 g
Riz	7 g	20 g	150 g
Sel	5 g	15 g	–
Semoule, couscous	5 g	15 g	150 g
Sucre en poudre	5 g	15 g	150 g
Sucre glace	3 g	10 g	110 g

Mesurer vos liquides

1 verre à liqueur = 3 cl
1 tasse à café = 8 à 10 cl
1 verre à moutarde = 20 cl
1 bol = 35 cl

Pour info

1 œuf = 50 g
1 noisette de beurre = 5 g
1 noix de beurre = 15 à 20 g

bien régler son four

→ Pas facile de connaître la température dans un four ! Voici une table très simple à utiliser et valable pour la plupart des appareils vendus dans le commerce.

Température (°C)	30	60	90	120	150	180	210	240	270
Thermostat	1	2	3	4	5	6	7	8	9

→ Les temps de cuisson donnés dans les recettes peuvent varier légèrement selon les types d'appareils. En effet, dans un four à chaleur tournante, les plats cuisent de manière plus homogène et plus vite que dans les fours qui chauffent à partir d'une source (four à gaz, four électrique).

Rappelez-vous aussi que pour réaliser une bonne cuisson, un préchauffage est toujours nécessaire.

les indispensables en cuisine

→ Pour cuisiner entre potes ou pour des potes sans souci, il faut avoir sous la main quelques produits tout simples, faciles à trouver.
Voici une petite liste de « basiques », grâce auxquels vous pourrez faire la grande majorité des recettes de cette collection.

Dans le placard

Épices
- Cannelle
- Coriandre
- Cumin
- Curry
- Gingembre
- Herbes de Provence
- Mélange aux 4 épices
- Noix de muscade
- Paprika
- Poivre du moulin et concassé
- Thym
- Vanille en gousse

Liquides
- Huiles de tournesol, d'olive, de sésame et de noix
- Rhum (pour la pâtisserie)
- Vinaigres de vin, blanc, balsamique et de Xérès
- Vin rouge et blanc sec

à garder sous le coude

Condiments
- Moutarde forte et à l'ancienne
- Moutardes parfumées (à l'estragon, au poivre vert)
- Sauce pesto
- Sauce soja
- Sel fin et gros sel
- Tabasco
- Tapenade d'olives noires

Et aussi
- Amandes effilées
- Anchois, thon et sardines à l'huile d'olive
- Bouillon cube
- Câpres
- Chocolat à cuire et chocolat en poudre
- Cornichons
- Farine
- Fruits secs (amandes, raisins, pignons, noisettes, abricots, figues)
- Lait de coco
- Levure chimique
- Maïzena
- Miel
- Olives en boîte
- Pâtes de toutes formes
- Poudre de noisettes et poudre d'amandes
- Riz rond et riz parfumé
- Semoule
- Sucre en poudre, sucre glace et sucre vanillé
- Tomates en boîte, concentrées et séchées en bocal

Dans le réfrigérateur

Légumes
- Ail
- Carottes
- Citrons
- Échalotes
- Oignons
- Pommes de terre
- Tomates

Laitages et œufs
- Beurre
- Crème liquide
- Fromage frais
- Lait
- Œufs
- Parmesan

Et aussi
- Feuilles de brick
- Pâtes à tarte (brisée, sablée, feuilletée)

Dans le congélateur

Herbes et épices hachées
- Aneth
- Basilic
- Ciboulette
- Coriandre
- Gingembre haché
- Persil

Légumes
- Champignons de Paris
- Épinards
- Petits pois
- Tiges de citronnelles

Et aussi
- Pâtes à tarte (brisée, sablée, feuilletée)

avoir le bon matériel

→ Pas besoin de grand-chose pour faire de grandes recettes !
Voici une petite liste d'ustensiles à avoir dans la cuisine.

Cuire
- Casseroles (une grande et une petite)
- Moules à tartes et à pâtisserie
- Marmite en fonte
- Plaque à rôtir
- Poêles à fond antiadhésif (une grande et une petite)
- Wok (éventuellement)

Couper
- Aiguiseur à couteaux
- Couteau économe
- Gros couteau dit « éminceur »
- Petit couteau
- Petite planche à découper en plastique

Mélanger
- Saladiers
- Cuillères en bois
- Fouet
- Spatules

Divers
- Batteur électrique
- Essoreuse à salade
- Ficelle de cuisine
- Mixeur
- Passoires, ou chinois (une fine, une plus grosse)
- Rouleau à pâtisserie
- Verre mesureur

Table des recettes

Retrouvez en couleur les « recettes pour épater ».

CLAFOUTIS TATIN	**108**
CRUMBLE À LA RHUBARBE	**61**
CRUMBLE ANANAS ET COCO	**76**
CRUMBLE AU MUESLI	**81**
CRUMBLE AU SAUMON ET À L'ANETH	**10**
CRUMBLE AUX FRUITS ROUGES	**57**
CRUMBLE AUX KIWIS	**58**
CRUMBLE AUX MÛRES SIMPLISSIME	**72**
CRUMBLE AUX POIRES, FRAISES ET SPÉCULOOS	**88**
CRUMBLE AUX POMMES ET BANANES FLAMBÉES	**85**
CRUMBLE AUX QUETSCHES, NOISETTES ET PAIN D'ÉPICE	**70**
CRUMBLE CERISES, FRAMBOISES ET PALETS BRETONS	**91**
CRUMBLE COURGETTES ET BOURSIN	**20**
CRUMBLE D'AGNEAU, ORIGAN ET PARMESAN	***23***
CRUMBLE D'AUBERGINES, MOZZARELLA ET PIGNONS	**15**
CRUMBLE DE FRUITS D'ÉTÉ ET MACARONS AUX AMANDES	***83***
CRUMBLE DE LÉGUMES AU CURRY	**19**
CRUMBLE DE POULET À L'ESTRAGON	**28**
CRUMBLE DE TOMATES AU CHÈVRE FRAIS	**12**
CRUMBLE ÉPINARDS, FETA ET RAISINS SECS	**17**
CRUMBLE EXPRESS GLACÉ	**75**
CRUMBLE FIGUES ET CANNELLE	**67**
CRUMBLE POIRES, FRAMBOISES ET AMANDES	**79**
CRUMBLE POIRES, ROQUEFORT ET NOIX	**24**
CRUMBLE POIRES, PRUNES ET NOISETTES	**52**
CRUMBLE POMMES, COINGS ET ABRICOTS SECS	**68**
CRUMBLE PRALINÉ AUX ABRICOTS	**86**
LA TARTE DES DEMOISELLES TATIN	**92**
LE VRAI CRUMBLE AUX POMMES	**62**
MINI-CRUMBLES DE POIRES AUX DEUX CHOCOLATS	**55**
MINI-CRUMBLES DE SAINT-JACQUES AUX POIREAUX	**27**
MINI-CRUMBLES MANGUES, FRUITS DE LA PASSION ET COCO	**64**

TARTELETTES TATIN AU MAGRET DE CANARD	**40**
TARTELETTES TATIN DE FOIE GRAS AUX POMMES VERTES	**35**
TATIN APHRODISIAQUE D'ANANAS AU GINGEMBRE	**100**
TATIN D'AUBERGINES AUX POIVRONS	**45**
TATIN D'ENDIVES AU CURRY	**36**
TATIN DE BOUDIN NOIR	**48**
TATIN DE BROCOLI, MOZZARELLA ET PETITS LARDONS	**51**
TATIN DE COURGETTES AU BOURSIN	**39**
TATIN DE MANGUES	**97**
TATIN DE MIRABELLES	**106**
TATIN DE POIRES-CHOCOLAT	**98**
TATIN DE POMMES DE TERRE AU BRIE	**30**
TATIN DE POMMES EXPRESS	**95**
TATIN DE SAUMON AUX ÉPINARDS	**42**
TATIN DE TOMATES AU CHÈVRE ET AU BASILIC	**32**
TATIN FAÇON TARTIFLETTE	**47**
TATIN POMMES-FIGUES	**105**
TATIN PRALINÉE AUX ABRICOTS	**103**

Table des matières

CRUMBLES SALÉS

CRUMBLE AU SAUMON ET À L'ANETH	10
CRUMBLE DE TOMATES AU CHÈVRE FRAIS	12
CRUMBLE D'AUBERGINES, MOZZARELLA ET PIGNONS	15
CRUMBLE ÉPINARDS, FETA ET RAISINS SECS	17
CRUMBLE DE LÉGUMES AU CURRY	19
CRUMBLE COURGETTES ET BOURSIN	20
CRUMBLE D'AGNEAU, ORIGAN ET PARMESAN	23
CRUMBLE POIRES, ROQUEFORT ET NOIX	24
MINI-CRUMBLES DE SAINT-JACQUES AUX POIREAUX	27
CRUMBLE DE POULET À L'ESTRAGON	28

TATIN SALÉES

TATIN DE POMMES DE TERRE AU BRIE	30
TATIN DE TOMATES AU CHÈVRE ET AU BASILIC	32
TARTELETTES TATIN DE FOIE GRAS AUX POMMES VERTES	35
TATIN D'ENDIVES AU CURRY	36
TATIN DE COURGETTES AU BOURSIN	39
TARTELETTES TATIN AU MAGRET DE CANARD	40
TATIN DE SAUMON AUX ÉPINARDS	42
TATIN D'AUBERGINES AUX POIVRONS	45
TATIN FAÇON TARTIFLETTE	47
TATIN DE BOUDIN NOIR	48
TATIN DE BROCOLI, MOZZARELLA ET PETITS LARDONS	51

CRUMBLES SUCRÉS

CRUMBLE POIRES, PRUNES ET NOISETTES	52
MINI-CRUMBLES DE POIRES AUX DEUX CHOCOLATS	55
CRUMBLE AUX FRUITS ROUGES	57
CRUMBLE AUX KIWIS	58
CRUMBLE À LA RHUBARBE	61
LE VRAI CRUMBLE AUX POMMES	62
MINI-CRUMBLES MANGUES, FRUITS DE LA PASSION ET COCO	64
CRUMBLE FIGUES ET CANNELLE	67
CRUMBLE POMMES, COINGS ET ABRICOTS SECS	68
CRUMBLE AUX QUETSCHES, NOISETTES ET PAIN D'ÉPICE	70
CRUMBLE AUX MÛRES SIMPLISSIME	72
CRUMBLE EXPRESS GLACÉ	75

CRUMBLE ANANAS ET COCO	**76**
CRUMBLE POIRES, FRAMBOISES ET AMANDES	**79**
CRUMBLE AU MUESLI	**81**
CRUMBLE DE FRUITS D'ÉTÉ ET MACARONS AUX AMANDES	**83**
CRUMBLE AUX POMMES ET BANANES FLAMBÉES	**85**
CRUMBLE PRALINÉ AUX ABRICOTS	**86**
CRUMBLE AUX POIRES, FRAISES ET SPÉCULOOS	**88**
CRUMBLE CERISES, FRAMBOISES ET PALETS BRETONS	**91**

TATIN SUCRÉES

LA TARTE DES DEMOISELLES TATIN	**92**
TATIN DE POMMES EXPRESS	**95**
TATIN DE MANGUES	**97**
TATIN DE POIRES-CHOCOLAT	**98**
TATIN APHRODISIAQUE D'ANANAS AU GINGEMBRE	**100**
TATIN PRALINÉE AUX ABRICOTS	**103**
TATIN POMMES-FIGUES	**105**
TATIN DE MIRABELLES	**106**
CLAFOUTIS TATIN	**108**

JE VEUX LA TECHNIQUE !

SAVOIR FAIRE LA PÂTE À CRUMBLE	**112**
TOUT CONNAÎTRE SUR LES CRUMBLES	**113**
SAVOIR FAIRE UNE TARTE TATIN SUCRÉE	**115**
TOUT CONNAÎTRE SUR LES TARTES TATIN	**117**
SAVOIR FAIRE LE CARAMEL	**117**

À GARDER SOUS LE COUDE

S'EN SORTIR SANS BALANCE	**118**
BIEN RÉGLER SON FOUR	**119**
LES INDISPENSABLES EN CUISINE	**119**
AVOIR LE BON MATÉRIEL	**121**

TABLE DES RECETTES ... **122**

Ma recette qui dépote...

PUBLI-COMMUNIQUÉ

La cuisson saveur
avec le gaz naturel

Profiter de la douceur d'instants partagés, de sourires et de fous rires autour d'un plat mitonné ensemble… C'est aussi goûter au confort de vie DolceVita qui, grâce au gaz naturel, nous offre une cuisine toute en saveurs.

Cuisiner avec le gaz naturel est une évidence. Précise et sûre, l'intensité de la flamme peut varier à loisir. Souple et modulable, elle saisit en toute puissance ou fait doucement mijoter, instantanément, d'un seul geste, comme par magie ! La cuisson au gaz naturel s'adapte à toutes les envies, pour des recettes toujours gagnantes. C'est un atout de plus pour réussir du plus simple au plus élaboré des repas !

UNE CUISSON SAVOUREUSE ET MOELLEUSE

En brûlant, le gaz naturel produit de l'humidité. Inutile donc de rajouter de l'eau en cours de cuisson aux plats qui cuisent au four. De plus, la cuisson dans un four alimenté au gaz naturel préserve les sels minéraux contenus dans les aliments. Viandes, poissons, volailles, tartes et gratins dorent lentement, tendrement et délicieusement…

UNE CUISSON SUR MESURE

La cuisson au gaz naturel, c'est aussi, aujourd'hui, avoir accès à de nombreuses innovations technologiques. Les brûleurs se sophistiquent en se dotant de fonctions sur mesure :
- le brûleur « wok » à double anneau de flammes permet de mitonner à l'orientale ou à l'asiatique, mais également de concocter d'inimitables confitures ;
- le brûleur « mijotop » transmet la chaleur, sans contact avec la flamme. Il est approprié aux cuissons délicates ;
- le brûleur « poissonnière » permet de cuire uniformément les poissons et viandes de grande taille.
Ces brûleurs nouvelle génération sont également pensés pour nous faciliter la vie. Plus efficaces en termes de puissance, ils sont aussi plus faciles à entretenir. Fini les grilles difficiles à nettoyer, les nouveaux brûleurs 3 branches se mettent directement au lave-vaisselle !

LA PRÉCISION EN PLUS

Pour un confort d'utilisation maximal, les cuisinières au gaz naturel sont pourvues de systèmes de réglage de haute précision.
L'allumage est instantané grâce au système électronique ; une seule main suffit pour allumer sous les casseroles ! Par ailleurs, sur les appareils les plus récents, un minuteur associé à chaque brûleur coupe automatiquement l'arrivée de gaz naturel quand le temps programmé est écoulé.

LE GAZ NATUREL, UNE ÉNERGIE ÉCONOMIQUE

Faire la cuisine au gaz naturel, c'est aussi choisir l'une des énergies les moins chères du marché qui, assortie à des équipements performants et à des tarifs ajustés à votre consommation annuelle, vous permet de cuisiner en toute liberté.

POUR EN SAVOIR PLUS SUR LES OFFRES DOLCEVITA
Vous pouvez joindre un Conseiller Gaz de France au :
0 810 140 150 (prix d'un appel local)
ou vous connecter sur l'espace DolceVita du site
www.gazdefrance.fr

Le conseil DolceVita de Gaz de France

- **Pour une bonne cuisson** et un meilleur entretien de vos ustensiles, utilisez toujours des casseroles aux diamètres adaptés à la taille des brûleurs de votre cuisinière. Réglez l'intensité de la flamme de sorte qu'elle ne dépasse pas les bords des récipients.

Gaz de France, SA au capital de 903 000 000 € - 542 107 651 RCS Paris - Photos : Médiathèque Gaz de France/Nathalie de Moussac - Conception/Réalisation : UNÉDITE

Gaz de France
DolceVita

Remerciements

Mille mercis à Laurence et Stéphan, les deux autres piliers de la popote des potes, Brigitte une éditrice hors pair, Raphaële, Mélanie, Johanna et Camille, le quatuor de choc d'Hachette.
Mais aussi Malo et Laetie, Adrien et Christophe, Sophie pour ses précieux conseils en orthographe, Léon pour ses tests, tous nos copains pour avoir joué les cobayes, nos sœurettes et évidemment nos parents qui ont su faire de nous de bonnes vivantes.
Sans oublier Flocon et Routoutou, toujours partants pour finir les restes !

Aude et Leslie

Merci à Hélène Fullanas pour son aide précieuse et appréciée de tous.

John

Toutes les photos de reportage de Philippe Vaurès-Santamaria ont été réalisées à L'atelier des Chefs.

Direction, Stephen Bateman et Pierre-Jean Furet
Responsable éditoriale, Brigitte Éveno
Conception graphique, Dune Lunel
Réalisation, Les PAOistes
Coordination et suivi éditorial, Raphaële Huard
Corrections, Anne Vallet
Fabrication, Claire Leleu
Partenariats, Sophie Augereau (01.43.92.36.80)

L'éditeur remercie Mélanie Le Neillon pour son aide précieuse et ses relectures attentives.

© 2005, HACHETTE LIVRE (Hachette Pratique)

Imprimé en Espagne par Graficas Estella - dépôt légal : novembre 2005
23.01.5809.02.1 • 2012358098

Découvrez L'atelier des Chefs, la nouvelle génération de cours de cuisine accessibles à tous

Du lundi au samedi avec des cours d'1/2 heure à 2 heures, initiez-vous à la cuisine dans une ambiance conviviale et dégustez sur place ce que vous avez préparé.

À L'atelier des Chefs, vous trouverez également tout ce qui peut vous servir pour faire la cuisine : ustensiles, livres, épicerie fine...

Renseignements et réservations sur www.atelierdeschefs.com

L'atelier des chefs
10, rue de Penthièvre, 75008 Paris, tél. 01 53 30 05 82